Christianity:

Basis - Past - Present - Future

Christianity:

Basis - Past- Present - Future

Manfred Davidmann

Social Organisation Limited

Published by Social Organisation Limited
Euro House, 1394 High Road, London, N20 9YZ, United Kingdom
Contact: books@socialorganisation.eu
www.socialorganisation.eu

Manfred Davidmann proves by methods of biblical archaeology what Jesus really taught, how Paul changed what Jesus had taught, how Paul's ideology became Christianity's official doctrine. Outstanding are the sections on Paul and the Gospels. The author reviews the Russian Orthodox Church's social and church-state policies. He analyses the Social Policies (Doctrine) of the Roman Catholic Church, the consequences for Catholics, and he states that challenging decisions are needed. Manfred Davidmann concludes that Christianity (Liberation Theology) is struggling forward towards its roots in response to the social and economic problems of global humanity at the present time. Towards what Jesus taught. Following the publication of Manfred Davidmann's works about the Meaning of Genesis, and of the publicity it generated, the 'Creationism' hypothesis was abandoned as untenable. The author exposes and proves the basic underlying causes of what seems to be progressive breaking down of family life and of social strength, and he states new insights.

Published by Social Organisation Limited in 2019

ISBN 978-0-85192-062-7

Printed and bound by Witley Press Ltd
24-26 Greevegate, Hunstanton, Norfolk, PE36 6AD, United Kingdom

Cover design by Dr. Angelika Schaumberg

CONTENTS

"It appears that the teachings of the religious hierarchy condemn their Christian believers to sufferings and hardships while the hierarchy seems to tell the believers to blame themselves and not the religious hierarchy!

To me it seems unreasonable for the Church to guide its believers into following the word of man (Paul) instead of following the word of God, apparently telling believers to blame themselves for the inevitable harsh and bitter consequences of following the Church's teachings, of following the words of Paul instead of following the teachings of Jesus."

Manfred Davidmann

In accordance with Manfred Davidmann's will and wishes his works are published in form of books.

Manfred Davidmann is the author of this book's content (Chapter 2 to Chapter 16).

These chapters were selected from Manfred Davidmann's publications on the https://www.solhaam.org website and in books, considering as well the author's notes about this book's content and title.

Following the author's wording and style, the description on page 4, 'Contents', 'Overview' (Chapter 1) and the text for the cover's back page have been added in order to complete the book for publication. Additions to the author's original text are stated and marked *.

In loving memory of Manfred Davidmann who taught people worldwide to live by the social laws and social system of the Pentateuch which underlie Judaism, Christianity, Islam and Democracy.

Dr. Angelika Schaumberg, Social Organisation Limited, 2019

Chapter 1

Overview

2   Liberation Theology: Basis - Past - Present - Future

Here Manfred Davidmann combines information from both Christian and Jewish sources and discusses the origin of Christianity. He shows that it is possible to analyse effectively how the Christian Canon developed, the order in which the material was written, the arguments for and against basic tenets of the faith.

Liberation theologians maintain that Christian belief and practice ranges along a continuous scale between two forms, one at each end. At one end of this scale is the kind which in effect serves the establishment, that is those in authority such as a government, and this kind teaches that reward will be a better life in a life to come. Liberation theologians advocate the second kind of Christianity, at the other end of the scale. They emphasise compassion and leadership in the struggle against oppressors, in the struggle for a better life here and now in this life.

Manfred Davidmann concludes that Christianity is struggling forward towards its roots in response to the social and economic problems of global humanity at the present time. Towards what Jesus taught, towards the social laws and social system of the Torah which were being argued about and discussed by Paul and the writers of the Gospels (see the later 'Origin of Christianity').

**3   Origin of Christianity and Judaism:
What Actually Happened, What Jesus Actually Taught and Later Changes**

In 'Origin of Christianity and Judaism', Manfred Davidmann proves what Jesus really taught: The social laws of the Torah have to be followed. These social laws guarantee equality, social justice and security, and a good life for all members of the community. These laws protect people from exploitation, oppression and enslavement through need. Early Christians, being mostly Jews, followed these laws.

Manfred Davidmann then proves how these essential social laws of the Torah were bypassed and ceased to be observed, in Judaism and in Christianity at the same time.

He describes and proves how Paul changed what Jesus had taught, how Paul's ideology serves the establishment instead of the people, and how this became Christianity's official doctrine. On the other hand Manfred Davidmann shows that the Talmud (especially the Mishnah) tells how Hillel changed Judaism in the same way, to what it is today.

The Dead Sea Scrolls, within the context of the findings reported here, become much more meaningful. In turn, the knowledge gained from them is part of the pattern of events recorded here for the first time.

What you find here is scientific analysis of facts established by the methods of biblical archaeology.

Outstanding are the sections on Paul and the Gospels: Manfred Davidmann shows that Paul's ideology was first opposed and that successive gospel writers then changed the record in Paul's favour, and how they did it.

4   The God-given Human Rights, Social Laws and Social System

This chapter is a comprehensive statement of the God-given human rights and obligations which underlie freedom, liberty, independence and well-being. They underlie and determine a good life of high quality. People at all stages of development are struggling to achieve these rights and benefits, all over the planet.

Directly relevant to today's social and economic problems, these rights and obligations determine the quality of life in areas such as social and economic security, social responsibility and accountability, ownership and decision-making, government and management, humane behaviour, teamwork and trustful cooperation.

These human rights, these social rules and this social system, are the very foundation of the three main religions of Judaism, Christianity and Islam.

What these religions have in common is that in each case a ruling elite succeeded in bypassing or overturning the religion's essential God-given benevolent social provisions and human rights, in this way exposing their communities and whole populations to oppression and exploitation.

What Manfred Davidmann has done with his works on the Pentateuch and the Bible, on religion and church-state relations, is to expose and correct the misinterpretations and mistranslations of the past. His works are major breakthroughs, constituting essential information for understanding the meaning and significance of the Pentateuch and the Bible.

5 Family, Community, Sex and the Individual

This work examines root causes of what are now major social problems and shows how to resolve the problems by dealing with their basic causes.

Human beings work primarily for their family and members of a family stand by, support and help each other in times of need. The family is the basic unit of society and it looks after the interests of all its members, as individuals as well as collectively. This gives great strength to each member of the family in the struggle for daily bread, security and happiness.

Manfred Davidmann exposes the causes of what seems to be progressive breaking down of family life and of social strength. This report is an unprecedented and comprehensive overview, states new insights, proves basic underlying causes.

For example, in a comprehensive review, Manfred Davidmann defines the role of the family as being:

To struggle as a family to survive.

To protect and support mother and children until children become mature and independent adults capable of providing for themselves.

To provide a good standard of living and a life of high quality. Which includes struggling against oppression and exploitation - and sometimes one has to fight to preserve a good way of life.

To serve the interests of, and to support, each member of the family. In turn, each member of the family supports the family.

Here he also covers and reports on the impact of casual sexual relations and its effects on individuals, family and community, on the social strength of individuals and communities.

Manfred Davidmann was the first to clearly describe and show, the effects of increasing life spans on the family, on its members and on their responsibilities. He also illustrated the underlying basis of teamwork within the family, stating the various roles and responsibilities and functional relationships of its members for effective teamwork within the family.

5.1 Men and Women, Family and Children; Dominance, Oppression and Exploitation

5.2 Family's Role and Life in the Real World; Protecting, And Caring for, the Next Generation; Causes of Social Break-up

5.3 Family's Role in the Real World: Teamwork in an Age of Specialisation and Accelerating Change and Gaining Strength in the Struggle for a Better Life

6 Using Words to Communicate Effectively

Shows how to communicate more effectively, covering aspects of thinking, writing, speaking and listening as well as formal and informal communications.

Consists of guidelines found useful by university students and practising middle and senior managers.

7 CHURCH AND STATE, GOVERNMENT AND RELIGION

7.1 Church and State, Government and Religion: Judaism, Christianity and Islam

Shows that underlying Judaism, Christianity and Islam are the Pentateuch's benevolent and egalitarian social laws and social system. Reveals for each religion the controversies and conflicts between church and state, between beliefs and practice.

7.2 Church and State, Government and Religion: Religion, Government and Education

Illustrates conflicting aims and interests of state and church with reference to teaching evolution (creationism) and teaching immorality (state-condoned promiscuity). Relative authority of Bible, common law, case law, religious leaderships, judges.

7.3 Social Concept (Policies) of the Russian Orthodox Church: Letter to the Russians

Reviews the Russian Orthodox Church's social and church-state policies. The church is shown to be quoting out of context from Paul's letter to the Romans, in relation to what seems to be a central core teaching on Christian church-state relationships.

7.4 Social Policies (Doctrine) of the Roman Catholic Church: An Evaluation

The essential and fundamental social doctrines are evaluated in plain and meaningful language. About important principles of faith in relation to globalisation and benevolent church-state-people policies. Aims of the Church's doctrines and the consequences for Catholics. Challenging decisions are needed.

7.5 The Global (Worldwide) Struggle for a Better Life
and
The Root of all Evil, the Source of All Good, and the Messianic Struggle

Combines major advances in human knowledge and key findings, from Manfred Davidmann's published works and teachings, into a comprehensive but detailed overview of the life we lead, of life's problems and struggles, of the (worldwide) struggle for a better life, and of the Messianic struggle of good against evil.

In this report, Manfred Davidmann exposes humanity's innermost secrets to the light of day.

As you read the report, you are brought ever closer to humanity's hidden core confrontations and the reality of the struggle for a better life. That is, you will see what humankind is struggling against; you will see the fundamental cause. You will see the core and source of evil, corruption, brutality, perversion, oppression and enslavement.

This report is about past and present struggles, achievements and defeats, about whole communities betrayed and misled, about religious teachings distorted and even turned upside down. And it is about how to achieve our own well-being, about our ensuring that we as individuals have good and satisfying lives.

And you will see how that which is good arises from the selfless and unstinting efforts of human beings cooperating for the common good.

'And if the facts are unexpected or if you do not like the facts then don't blame me. I am merely recording them', says Manfred Davidmann.

7.6 Creationism and Intelligent Design, Evolution, Education or Indoctrination

Conflicts have arisen because parts of Genesis have been mistranslated or misinterpreted.

The 'Creationism' hypothesis apparently assumes that the resulting erroneous text correctly states God's deeds. And the 'Intelligent Design' hypothesis apparently assumes that the same erroneous text correctly states the deeds of some other supernatural being.

Manfred Davidmann's research and discoveries showed and proved that the source text of Genesis corresponds in the major steps to the order in which the earth and life are known to have been formed and developed. Described is the formation of the earth and early plant life, and evolution by the 'survival of the fittest'. The evolution from reptilian to mammalian instincts, feelings and behaviour is clearly stated, as is the evolution and corresponding behaviour, feeling and thinking of human beings from humanoids (animals resembling humans) through Homo erectus (early man) to Homo sapiens (human beings, ourselves).

There is no conflict or contradiction between what is recorded in the source Genesis text and our scientific knowledge about evolution of human beings and of our planet.

8   Press Notices about Genesis and Evolution

Following the publication of Manfred Davidmann's report ('The Meaning of Genesis: Creation, Evolution and the Origin of Evil'), and of the publicity it generated, the 'Creationism' hypothesis was abandoned as untenable. But a similar hypothesis was then put forward called 'Intelligent Design'.

However, later publicity over a period of about seven months, resulted in increased interest in the original and scientific discoveries of Manfred Davidmann.

9   Creationism and Intelligent Design, Evolution, Education or Indoctrination.
And
Reading, Interpreting, Translating of Ancient Consonantal Texts like the Bible or the Koran.

10   Faith and Trust in God, No Matter by What Name called

A statement of belief and request for support and aid, to God no matter by what name called, in the worldwide struggle for a better and more secure life. Combined with a description of mutual responsibilities and care, of corresponding guidance and protection.

11   Christianity at the Crossroads, at the Final Parting of the Ways

12   The choice is yours:
Unemployment, Charitable Social Security and Today's Religious Teachings
or
High Standard of Living, Satisfying Work and a Good Life, as God-given rights.

About social and economic security, government and management, equality and ownership, the role of biblical prophets and their warnings, and now.

This theme brings together in one place relevant material on core problems of our times, drawn from Manfred Davidmann's published works. Essential reading for quickly absorbing the substance of his teachings, for those aiming to make this a better world.

Chapter 2

Liberation Theology: Basis - Past - Present - Future

Summary

Here Manfred Davidmann combines information from both Christian and
Jewish sources and discusses the origin of Christianity. He shows that it
is possible to analyse effectively how the Christian Canon developed,

the order in which the material was written, the arguments for and against basic tenets of the faith.

Liberation theologians maintain that Christian belief and practice ranges along a continuous scale between two forms, one at each end. At one end of this scale is the kind which in effect serves the establishment, that is those in authority such as a government, and this kind teaches that reward will be a better life in a life to come. Liberation theologians advocate the second kind of Christianity, at the other end of the scale. They emphasise compassion and leadership in the struggle against oppressors, in the struggle for a better life here and now in this life.

Manfred Davidmann concludes that Christianity is struggling forward towards its roots in response to the social and economic problems of global humanity at the present time. Towards what Jesus taught, towards the social laws and social system of the Torah which were being argued about and discussed by Paul and the writers of the Gospels (see the later 'Origin of Christianity').

Life is a Struggle – Why?

Let me begin by telling you what is probably humanity's most closely guarded secret of our time.

After all, you will want to know why life is a struggle, why life is so tough for so many human beings on this planet.

You will want to know why thousands of years of struggle, why the enormous technological powers we command, why the vast human manpower, abilities and skills which are now at our disposal, have failed to provide us with secure lives of high quality.

And you will want to know that we have reached a major parting of the ways. We now have to either improve matters once and for all or else suffer consequences which threaten our survival on this planet as human beings.

And you will also want to know what can be done to improve matters.

So let us start by asking some basic questions:
> Why do we have to struggle?
> What are we struggling against?
> What are we struggling for?
> Why do we not have good lives of high quality?

Opposition

Where there is struggle there must be resistance, there is opposition. We have to struggle because our attempts to achieve good lives for ourselves and our children are being resisted, are opposed.

You know as well as I do that we have to struggle to protect earlier gains as well as to improve our lives. Hence we are struggling to defend our present standard of living and we are struggling to better it.

And this means that the opposition is attacking us to lower our standard of living and to prevent us from improving it.

You have known or suspected this already. Perhaps not in such clear simple language. Hardly anyone I have met has not at some time in their lives wondered why life was so tough and thought that we as thinking feeling human beings ought to be able to do very much better.

So now more questions present themselves:

> Who or what is doing all this to us, is attacking us? Who or what is attempting to reduce the quality of our lives, is attempting to prevent us from improving it? Who or what is attempting to increase the toughness of life itself, is attempting to increase our need?

> Why this intense, brutal and hidden struggle when there is enough for all of us, when all can have good secure lives of high quality.

> Why is it done in such a hidden way, why the secrecy?

Good and Evil

Two sides are struggling with each other. This is, indeed, common knowledge.

We talk about 'good', and we talk about 'evil'. Opposites, struggling with each other. 'Good' and 'evil' struggle with each other and 'evil' is powerful and operates in furtive ways. Those who are good, who are on the side of good, sometimes have to endure and suffer much as a result.

The words 'good' and 'evil' are but labels for real and active basic forces or groups of people who are struggling with each other. It follows that many people who are good and yet lead hard lives and suffer, are casualties of conflict.

We are on the side of good while evil can be powerful. Surely evil can remain powerful only for as long as it remains hidden. It can manipulate and harm human beings only while hiding behind secular and religious masks of innocence and benevolence. Hence the masks.

In secular terms, what is it that would wish to prevent us from increasing our standard of living, that would wish to reduce our standard of living and our social security?

The answer is simple.

Struggle Against Those who Wish to Oppress so as to Exploit

We are struggling against those who wish to exploit others, who wish to oppress so as to exploit, who see their wealth and power increasing whenever they lower our pay relative to their own so as to increase their own profits and wealth and power over us.

It is they who wish to reduce, and so struggle to reduce, our social security since higher unemployment, greater personal need, and physical as well as emotional weakness, reduce our bargaining strength and make us more dependent on them for survival. They are enabled in this way to exploit us through our need and to push down our pay even further when compared with their own much greater gains. And this is why they are operating so furtively behind their masks.

Views of Reality

If you now feel like putting this down and doing something else, then you are being manipulated through your emotions. You can counter this by following some simple rules of communication, namely 'Listen to the full story before you make up your mind' and 'Do not jump to conclusions (such as good or bad, valid or invalid) before you have evaluated the evidence'.

And if the facts are unexpected or if you do not like the facts then don't blame me. I am merely recording them.

A key feature of reality, that is of what is actually happening, is that our attention is side-tracked into dead-end alleys and into self-defeating directions, away from real and towards fictitious foes. In this way the oppressor divides us against each other, a process known as 'divide and conquer'.

Oppressors can do such things because they operate and manipulate in furtive secretive ways within our communities, forming and manipulating our view of reality to make us serve willingly regardless of the cost to us, to our families and to our children.

Judaism

When Facts are Difficult to Find

When facts are difficult to find then let history speak. Let us look at the events which preceded Christianity and took place at its birth.

To do this we need first to look at Jewish belief and practice as it was at that time.

Recorded in the Pentateuch (Torah; Five books of Moses; Part of Old Testament) is the fascinating story of the struggle of the enslaved people for their freedom, of freedom gained by acts of God against the oppressor, of the consequent writing down of rules of behaviour and of a social system which, as is clearly stated, underlie all freedom and independence of mind and person.

The Social System and Laws of the Pentateuch

At this point let me give you some idea of the social system of the Pentateuch.

This, the small print of the Covenant, simply states that all are equal, that no person may oppress or exploit another, that all have the right to be free and independent masters of their own fate.

The country's wealth, and this applies particularly to productive capital, belongs to all equally and needs to be shared out.

Every person has the right to social security. This means that people are entitled to be supported by the community not only when they fall on hard times but also to maintain their independence as independent breadwinners for their families.

For example, the community has to provide backup funds to those who need them and they have to be provided as and when required. To prevent people being exploited through their need these funds have to be provided without charging interest and such 'loans' are cancelled every seventh year if the borrower has been unable to repay them. {2, 6}

Judaism is the only religion which states that God's will is that all people are equal and that they are entitled to an equal and fair share of the common wealth, that people serve the community which in turn serves them and that people need to behave in ways which guarantee their strength and independence as individuals and as a community.

Wherever there is freedom and independence and good life of high quality on this planet it exists to the extent to which the local communities approach and follow and live according to these social laws and according to this social system, as written down over three thousand years ago and recorded in the Pentateuch (Torah). {1}

The role of those who are rich is seen to be that of administering money on behalf of the community and not that of enriching themselves at the expense of the community. People are entitled to support from the community, not just when they are hungry or starving but to maintain their independence and improve their security {2, 6} at the common level.

It was laws such as these which the rich simply did not want to apply and instead of the community finding ways of disciplining them to make sure that they obeyed and followed the laws, they (the rich and powerful) had the laws changed on their own behalf to suit themselves. {3-6}

So about two thousand years ago, just before and during the formative years of Christianity, the Jewish establishment argued against the social laws and social system of the Pentateuch and succeeded in having the core laws of the Pentateuch bypassed and the whole social system abrogated, in effect annulled.

They then proceeded to cover the whole subject with written verbal smokescreens until even the memory of what they had done faded away and was forgotten.

What had taken place became what must surely be one of the most closely guarded secrets of the ages, only unearthed and published about ten years ago in 'The Truth about Hillel and his Times'. {4, 6}

What Determined the Outcome

What determined the outcome as before was that the people did not hold their establishment accountable for what the establishment was doing.

It was because the people could not ensure observance of the laws by their establishment that the country was lost on each occasion in the past. {2-3, 5-6}

The Law and How it was Being Changed were Written Down at the Time

Those Jews who objected bitterly to what their own establishment was doing decided to write down what the law was and how it was being changed and by whom. {1}

This process of writing and compiling what came to be known as the 'Talmud', took about as long to complete as that of finalising the Christian Canon, and both took place at the same time. The Talmud was then frozen, canonified, remained unaltered. Later comments or discussions were added by printing them beside or around the unchanged original text.

The unchanged original text of the Talmud provides us with unique and deep insight into the events preceding the destruction of Jerusalem and into the beginnings of Christianity. {4}

What we see recorded so uniquely, so faithfully and at such cost in the Talmud is a clear description of what happened to Jewish belief and practice in the days preceding Christianity and during Christianity's formative years. {4, 5}

It was because the writers felt so strongly about the brutal events which had taken place that they described, and so exposed for the first time, the basic core forces or groups of people who are struggling with each other.

In the Pentateuch we see described for the first time the history of the conflict between these two elemental and hidden forces or people, as well as a clear statement of how people need to behave if they wish to be free and independent and have lives of high quality. In the Talmud there is another clear statement of the existence of these forces, of how they operate and of the steps which need to be taken to ensure that good triumphs over evil, that freedom and independence take the place of oppression and exploitation. {4, 5}

The Jewish religion is the only one which lays down a system of social organisation and of individual behaviour which enables individuals to gain strength as individuals and as communities, which will ensure a good life of high quality here and now in this life. It states that this is the right of every individual and the Pentateuch gives rules of behaviour to ensure this among those who follow its laws.

However, the Judaism people practice today is far removed from that of the Pentateuch, because the Jewish establishment illegally edited out from belief and practice the social laws which ensured equality of wealth and guaranteed independence from oppression and exploitation.

What they left was an empty but warm shell of ritual and the laws of behaviour which give people strength.

Christianity

Compiling of the Christian Canon and of the Jewish Talmud

It does seem more than coincidence that it took about four hundred years to complete the Talmud and that contemporaneously it took roughly the same time for Christianity to finalise what it believes in, namely for the Church hierarchy to select and approve the Bible books which were included in the Canon and thus became accepted as official doctrine.

The way in which the Talmud developed was that it was written in two distinct parts. {4}

First was written the Mishnah ('Repetition') which describes the reality of the conflict, the participants, the sides they represent, what happened.

Then, much later, was written the Gemara ('Tradition') which contains arguments and stories intended to make points about the Mishnah and most of the Talmud consists of Gemara.

At the end of the writing of the Gemara the actual message in the Mishnah had been buried in a mass of stories and arguments. From that time onwards the essential core legislation of the Pentateuch had been negated and bypassed and buried under arguments about many subjects.

It seems that a very similar process took place within Christianity as took place within Judaism. It took about four hundred years for written material and for people's memories to be changed, edited and modified, to conform to the establishment point of view.

If it had just been a matter of recording facts, of recording the truth, the whole truth and nothing but the truth (the truth, nothing left out and nothing added), it would not have taken so long.

After ten or so generations people would be regarding as factual that which they were being told was factual. It may well have taken that long before the hierarchy's teachings had argued away evidence contrary to the establishment's viewpoint or buried it out of sight or declared it to be against established doctrine, in such ways discrediting opposing viewpoints which called for social justice according to the word of God.

The processes by which the establishment changed belief and practice at the time are clearly described in the contemporaneously written Talmud, as are the arguments used by both sides and how the people felt about what the scholars were doing on behalf of the rulers and their establishment. {5}

It follows that Christianity arose from the activities of Jews who, arguing against what their own establishment was doing, were however unable to prevent their establishment from editing out the essential social core laws from Jewish belief and practice. These Jews somehow got together to follow the word of God and then appear to have found that the only way to do this was to form separate communities outside the control of the Jewish establishment.

One of these seems to have been the Essenes whose Qumran scrolls appear to date back to the period just before and during the birth of Christianity and who lived together in co-operative communities. {5}

We see that Jewish attempts to argue against their establishment were by themselves unable to change the course of events. Their record of what the establishment had done and was doing was being buried under a mass of abstract arguments and stories.

The Christian Canon (New Testament) was being compiled during roughly the same period. What became the Christian Canon, meaning by this the 'agreed' version of events and teachings, also took hundreds of years before it was 'agreed'.

It simply took that long before a version was compiled which was acceptable to Christian establishments, which in this way was biased towards the point of view of the establishments, towards what the establishment wanted included or excluded, wanted said or unsaid. It continued to be compiled till it was approved by the establishments and here also the relevant social laws were side-tracked and bypassed. {10}

Struggle in All Institutions

When might is right then those who rule oppress so as to exploit. They somehow gained control and thus power over others. Those who are subservient to them (to their 'establishment') are all around us in all institutions.

Those who wish to oppress so as to exploit, who wish to get personal advantage for themselves at the expense of others, without regard to the cost to individuals or the community, are all around us at all levels.

So struggle between authoritarian ownership and rule on the one hand and people power on the other is taking place all around us in all institutions and groups and at all levels. The struggle is between on the one hand those who wish to use and misuse other people, who wish to order them about and domineer, who are greedy and, on the other hand, those to whom people are important and matter.

The oppressors operate in hidden ways, attempting to change our perception of reality, doing so bit by bit, then as today. So they distort, and maintain past distortions, to make us behave in ways which harm ourselves, which weaken us, which rob us of our individual and community independence and freedom, which enslave us.

But, having gained power and control, they then keep in place those laws of behaviour which give spiritual and character strength to individuals because they wanted their people to have the spiritual strength and character to serve, work and fight for them.

It appears that 'fundamentalist' religions, sects and organisations generally condition their adherents into blind obedience to the dictates of their figurehead(s) (head office establishment) combined with subservience towards authoritarian rulers and their establishments.

Subservience of 'fundamentalists' to the dictates of the rulers becomes evident when one considers what they stand for, that is whether they serve either the rulers or else God and people, in this life. Here one should consider particularly the social content of their teachings and their actions towards people.

They are trying to persuade us to accept the hardships and suffering we suffer so unnecessarily, misusing 'religion' for making us subservient to the exploiter.

We Struggle

Within democracy we can struggle openly towards real freedom but when we make progress towards merely power-sharing, the rulers' establishment attempts to persuade people to behave in ways which weaken people so that they lose their gains and can again be pushed into hardship and exploited further.

Hence the increasing promiscuity, viciousness, crime, unemployment, social insecurity, hardship and family breakup in democracies. These weaken the population and are aimed at preventing moves towards greater and real independence and freedom. {7}

To free ourselves from mental conditioning and brainwashing we have to follow the rules of behaviour such as the Ten Commandments and apply the social system of the Pentateuch. {2, 7}

Wherever there is any spiritual and material freedom today it exists because people followed these laws (rules) of behaviour and it exists to the extent to which they do so.

In other words, such freedom as we have exists because people followed and follow the teachings of Judaism and Christianity since the same rules are common to both Judaism and Christianity - the Pentateuch is part of both religions.

They Recorded

What Actually Happened and Why

One of the important aspects of the recent discoveries {1} about the material in the Talmud is that many, if not most, of the stories cannot be taken at their face value. The real meaning of the story, namely the message it contains and was written to convey, is below the surface but is consistent and clear. The stories hang together once you penetrate the smokescreen and become aware of the reality they are dealing with. {3-5}

The study of the meaning of the stories we have been told in the New Testament about Jesus and his sayings should now become a fairly straightforward matter, after studying the conventions used in the Talmud by writers who were compiling and writing the Talmud while the Christian Canon was being written and compiled. {1}

It then also becomes possible to analyse and show how the Canon developed, the order in which the material was written, the arguments for and against basic tenets of the faith.

All the indications are that the same sequence of events which was recorded with such clarity and certainty in the Talmud {1} is also told in the New Testament. It appears that the same and similar conventions and methods were used {10} to ensure that the story, the arguments both ways and the messages would be understood by those who had eyes to see (who had ears to hear).

The same techniques were used by the one side to ensure there could be no possibility of misunderstanding or intentional misinterpretation, by the other to distract attention from key matters and arguments, to bury essential core matters under and within much less important material.

The methods and techniques used by the writers of the Talmud are clearly illustrated by examples of their use in 'Freedom Now, Freedom for Ever'. {1}

What the Central Arguments and Confrontations are About

However, we are told that the matter at issue between Jews and their own establishment, and later between Christians and those Jews who blindly followed their own establishment, and then between Christians and their own establishment, was the keeping as a matter of belief and practice of the social laws and system of the Pentateuch.

What we are now seeing are dissenting voices being raised among deprived Christian communities such as disadvantaged South African negroes, South American indians, Indian indians, Filipinos. We see them arguing for a Christian belief which puts equality and independence among their most important goals, if not as the most important goal.

These 'liberation theologians' maintain that there are two kinds of Christianity.

One kind serves a ruling establishment, such as a home government, colonising empire or multinational, to convert conquered or dependent subject people into obedient oppressed and exploited subjects, brainwashing them into believing that their miserable lives are the will of god, that there is hope and that they will be rewarded by a better life in a life to come.

But liberation theologians advocate the second kind of Christianity which is one of compassion and leadership in the struggle against oppressors, in the struggle for a better life here and now in this life.

Life Here and Now

There is no way in which 'religion' can be separated from life here and now, from the events of the day, from life as it is and from life as it ought to be.

The questions one must ask about any religion are 'who benefits', who gains, who or what is favoured or supported by its teachings or beliefs, who or what is being preached against. To see what they are for, to see what they are against. Primarily one must ask 'who gains', because it is the person who gains who is the originator, who is controlling, who is being served by the 'religion'.

After all, a good life of high quality is now available to all individuals on this planet, it being entirely up to us whether we now organise to achieve this or whether we continue to let so many millions suffer and starve, whether we continue to let so many millions be oppressed and exploited by the few.

Yet most of us are still living in some kind of hell on earth instead of leading good and satisfying lives of high quality at a high standard of living.

But wherever there is extreme poverty and suffering and pain you are likely to find Christians and Jews who are struggling on the side of the oppressed. Christians, for example, such as priests who provide encouragement and guidance to oppressed and suffering people in their struggle for a better life against the ruling establishment, against the established ruling oppressors, doing so at much risk and without thought of personal gain.

Christianity Struggling Forward towards its Roots

So we see Christianity struggling forwards towards its roots.

It is doing so in accordance with the Cause-and-effect Relationship of the Pentateuch. This clearly states that inhumanity, suffering and oppression will increase until people return and follow the laws of the Pentateuch. These laws include its laws of behaviour and its social laws and its social system and these provide fairness and equality, independence and freedom, for all.

It is only when people struggle for a better life, struggle for these laws to be applied and followed, that a better quality of life can be achieved on this planet for all human beings, instead of just for a few at the expense of extreme poverty for the rest. {2}

New Branches of Christianity

So we now have new branches of Christianity forming themselves in different parts of the world. Consisting of Christians who are guiding and supporting deprived and suffering groups of people in their struggle for a better life: Liberation theologians in South America, the writers of the Kairos document in South Africa.

They are arguing that there are two kinds of Christianity. They say that there is the kind of Christianity that serves the rulers and their establishment and thus those who oppress and exploit. They say that there is also another kind of Christianity which bases its belief and practice on compassion for the poor and according to Christian texts which side with the poor against the rich, with the poor against the oppressor.

Their arguments are intuitive, abstract and based on emotions. Their arguments and beliefs are based on feelings and emotions no matter how good and right and proper, are based on biblical texts quoted out of context. They are based on a Canon which was compiled and edited by men at a time when the ruling establishment had absolute power and was thus able to ensure that its point of view carried greater weight {10}.

As long as this remains the basis of the beliefs of liberation theologians, then their beliefs can at some time in the future once again be negated and countered and turned into impotent dead-end or self-destructive directions by abstract arguments and statements about feelings and emotions, by quoting out of context.

Basic Beliefs

Christianity is struggling towards its roots.

This is similar to the situation the Jewish people found themselves in, in the days preceding Christianity.

Christianity was an attempt to return to the basic and core social laws and system of the Pentateuch after these had been subverted by the Jewish establishment. Now we see Christians intuitively moving in the direction of the social laws of the Pentateuch stating that Christianity itself had been subverted in the past by the establishment and that it is now necessary to reinstate the basic social laws of justice and human fairness.

Such attempts to return to a social system of fairness and equality and independence can be turned and defeated by the establishment just as was done in the early days of Christianity.

The way to prevent this happening again is to base the belief clearly on the God-given written social laws and social system and laws of behaviour of the Pentateuch (Torah). Belief would then be based on a deep understanding of the hidden reality of life, of the hidden manipulations of brutal inhuman oppressors against human beings who have to defend themselves and struggle against these inhuman mentalities in human form.

The Torah clearly shows how independence, freedom and the right to the land we live in, can be gained now and can be gained for ever. (1, 8}

The Right to the Land We Live In

In the language of religion, the land does not belong to anyone other than God.

Those who live in it may use and so benefit from the land but only as long as they follow God's laws.

If they do not, then in due course the land is repossessed and transferred to someone else.

Ignorance is no excuse. Those who stop following the law lose their entitlement to use it and are in due course driven out and persecuted.

History of the Jewish people in Israel proved this matter again and again.

In everyday language and in the language of science we know that people are affected and changed by their own behaviour and that communities stand or fall according to their actions, as a result of the behaviour of the community as a whole.

Oppress and exploit and your community will get weaker and weaker and fail in the end.

Follow a pattern of social behaviour and establish a social system which are based on social fairness and justice and you will gain strength and prosper and continue to do so while you are doing it.

Hence the right to the land and the future prosperity of its inhabitants depends on following these social laws and the social system of the Pentateuch.

Ignorance is no excuse. Ignorance cannot alter the effects of one's own actions.

Independence and Social Security; Material and Spiritual Freedom.

Our rapidly advancing knowledge and technology give the establishment new human and technological knowledge in fields such as biology, genetics, computer applications and manipulation by world-wide media. They are apparently already thinking of using knowledge such as this to change our way of life to oppress, exploit and enslave people in new ways.

Part of the struggle is that each one of us is subjected to establishment propaganda, conditioning and brainwashing attempts, to their use of the media for moulding our behaviour and thus our lives, to their present-day 'fundamentalist' conditioning {9}, to their 'social engineering' attempts.

It is important to counter this day by day and at all levels.

But we must advance towards real independence of mind and towards material independence and social security, towards freedom, by following the rules of behaviour and the social system of the Pentateuch.

This is the step ahead from democracy towards real material and spiritual freedom and this is the nature of the struggle. Like it or not, we are all part of it.

If the establishment were successful against us, then Genesis states that the planet would need to be, and would be, rendered uninhabitable for human beings.

References

{ 1} In 'Judaism: Basis - Past - Present - Future, Part 1'
Manfred Davidmann
ISBN 978-0-85192-060-3
see chapter 2.1: 'Struggle for Freedom:
The Social Cause-and-Effect Relationship'

see chapter 2.2: 'History Speaks: Monarchy,
Exile and Maccabees'

see chapter 2.3: 'At the Time of Jesus,
This is What Actually Happened in Israel:
The Truth about Hillel and his Times'

see chapter 2.4: 'One Law for All: Freedom Now,
Freedom for Ever'

{ 2} In 'Judaism: Basis - Past - Present - Future, Part 1'
Manfred Davidmann
ISBN 978-0-85192-060-3
see chapter 2.1: 'Struggle for Freedom:
The Social Cause-and-Effect Relationship'

{ 3} In 'Judaism: Basis - Past - Present - Future, Part 1'
Manfred Davidmann
ISBN 978-0-85192-060-3
see chapter 2.2: 'History Speaks: Monarchy,
Exile and Maccabees'

{ 4}   In 'Judaism: Basis - Past - Present - Future, Part 1'
       Manfred Davidmann
       ISBN 978-0-85192-060-3
       see chapter 2.3: 'At the Time of Jesus,
       This is What Actually Happened in Israel:
       The Truth about Hillel and his Times'

{ 5}   In 'Judaism: Basis - Past - Present - Future, Part 1'
       Manfred Davidmann
       ISBN 978-0-85192-060-3
       see chapter 2.4: 'One Law for All: Freedom Now,
       Freedom for Ever'

{ 6}   In 'Judaism: Basis - Past - Present - Future, Part 1'
       Manfred Davidmann
       ISBN 978-0-85192-060-3
       see chapter 5: 'The Right to the Land of Israel'

{ 7}   If You Want a Future, Read On ...
       David Baram*; 1978
       ISBN 0 85192 008 X

{ 8}   The Way Ahead for Israel:
       Policies for a Better Future
       Manfred Davidmann
       ISBN 0 85192 041 1

{ 9}   Compare with writings of the Essenes' Qumran
       scrolls: Children of Light, Children of Darkness;
       Prophet of Light, Prophet of Darkness.
       See {5}, p23.

{10}   See chapter 3:
       'Origin of Christianity and Judaism:
       What Actually Happened,
       What Jesus Actually Taught and Later Changes'
       Manfred Davidmann

Additions by the Editor:

David Baram*: Manfred Davidmann is the author of this work.

Chapter 3

Origin of Christianity and Judaism: What Actually Happened, What Jesus Actually Taught and Later Changes

Notes <..>
References {..}
Press Notice

Summary

In 'Origin of Christianity and Judaism', Manfred Davidmann proves what Jesus really taught: The social laws of the Torah have to be followed. These social laws guarantee equality, social justice and security, and a good life for all members of the community. These laws protect people from exploitation, oppression and enslavement through need. Early Christians, being mostly Jews, followed these laws.

Manfred Davidmann then proves how these essential social laws of the Torah were bypassed and ceased to be observed, in Judaism and in Christianity at the same time.

He describes and proves how Paul changed what Jesus had taught, how Paul's ideology serves the establishment instead of the people, and how this became Christianity's official doctrine. On the other hand Manfred Davidmann shows that the Talmud (especially the Mishnah) tells how Hillel changed Judaism in the same way, to what it is today.

The Dead Sea Scrolls, within the context of the findings reported here, become much more meaningful. In turn, the knowledge gained from them is part of the pattern of events recorded here for the first time.

What you find here is scientific analysis of facts established by the methods of biblical archaeology.

Outstanding are the sections on Paul and the Gospels: Manfred Davidmann shows that Paul's ideology was first opposed and that successive gospel writers then changed the record in Paul's favour, and how they did it.

Early Christians

The first Christians were Jewish Christians. The Pentateuch <1> was of great importance to them and they kept its laws, keeping the sabbath and performing circumcision.

Christian beliefs were spreading largely among Jews, and Christianity was a group within Judaism.

They were called Jewish Christians because their membership consisted largely of Jews who had joined them and followed their beliefs and teachings.

They believed Jesus was a prophet who had tried to make people more aware of the intent of the Pentateuch and had tried to intensify the application of its laws.

As Jews had in any case to follow and live according to the Pentateuch's laws, so what were Jews and Jewish Christians arguing about?

At issue are the laws of behaviour and the social system which are laid down in the Pentateuch {13}:

> The Pentateuch states that all are equal, that no person may oppress or exploit another, that all have the right to be free and be independent masters of their own fate.

> Every person is entitled as a matter of right to social security. This means that people are entitled to be supported by the community not only when they fall on hard times but also to maintain their independence as independent breadwinners for their families.

> For example, the community has to provide backup funds to those who need them and they have to be provided as and when required. To prevent people being exploited through their need these funds have to be provided without charging interest and such 'loans' are cancelled every seventh year if the borrower has been unable to repay them.

> The country's wealth, and this applies particularly to productive capital, belongs to all equally and has to be shared out. This equal and fair distribution of the community's wealth has to be updated at regular intervals.

> The role of those who are rich is seen to be that of administering their wealth and money on behalf of and for the community and not that of enriching themselves at the expense of the community.

The laws of the Pentateuch have to be followed and applied by Jews as a matter of law in their daily lives.

However, it was such laws of behaviour and such social system laws which the rich simply did not want to apply and they, the rich and powerful, had the application of the laws changed to suit themselves. {13-16}

Jesus tried to reverse this situation and to have such laws applied by people in their everyday lives.

Paul

Paul was Jewish and persecuted the Christians who were renewing their knowledge of the laws and the application of the laws in their daily lives. So he was acting on the side of, that is for, the oppressive establishment.

He was unsuccessful in this as Jewish Christianity spread and continued to spread.

He then said that he had had a 'vision' and called himself a Christian but he preached not for but against the social laws and against the social system of the Pentateuch. He preached against material independence, against social security, against freedom from oppression and exploitation.

What he preached was the political ideology of an oppressive establishment which wanted to be able to oppress so as to exploit without hindrance.

This brought him into conflict with Jewish Christians and with the mostly Jewish Christian communities. He then concentrated on gaining converts from gentiles (people who are not Jewish) who presumably knew nothing or little about the laws of the Pentateuch and who would thus be more likely to follow his teachings without arguing about its content.

Paul's letters (epistles) are the oldest part of the New Testament. The Gospels followed - as far as we know Matthew's was written first, then Mark's, then Luke's. Luke also wrote The Acts. It seems that Paul's letters were written about 50 AD and the gospels about 70-100 AD.

What stands out is that no one before Paul wrote such letters and that no one did so afterwards. They give his own point of view and personal ideology and he gives them an authority which they would not otherwise have had by means of a self-proclaimed vision.

The gospels as a whole relate to the life and death of Jesus but Paul's letters seem to be more a vehicle for pronouncements directed against observance of laws ensuring freedom, independence and equality.

Paul's teachings were accepted to a considerable extent and the Gentile Christians' stories about the beginning of Christianity do differ from those of the Jewish Christians. It is the versions of the Gentile Christians which were included in the Christian Canon and became official doctrine.

I suppose that what I am saying is that changes which were made as time progressed were at times 'politically' motivated towards putting across Paul's 'message', towards indoctrinating people with the political ideology of an oppressive establishment which wanted to be able to oppress so as to exploit without hindrance.

Romans

For no apparent reason, without justification and without stating a source, Paul says in his letter to the 'Romans' {5} <4> that:

1. All authority comes from God,
   so that rulers (those who are in a position of authority) have
   been appointed by God.
   Hence let every person
   submit to those who rule.

2. It follows that whoever resists the rulers
   resists whom God has appointed
   and those who resist rulers will be punished,

3. for rulers do not terrorise those whose conduct is "good", but
   those whose conduct is "evil".

   If you want to live without fearing the person who is in
   authority, then do what is "good" and you will be praised,

4. for he rules over you in God's place for your own good.

   But if you do that which is "evil", be afraid,
   for his is not an empty threat;
   he will in God's place punish the doer of "evil".

5. Therefore one must be obedient,
   to avoid their anger (if you do not obey)
   and because to obey is the right thing to do.

6. For the same reason you also pay taxes,
   for those in authority collecting taxes
   are acting on God's behalf.

7. Pay all those in authority what they demand,
   taxes, revenues, respect, honour.

8. Your only obligation to others is to love one another;
   Because he who loves another has fulfilled "the law".

9. For this
   You shall not commit adultery,
   You shall not murder,
   You shall not steal,

You shall not bear false witness,
You shall not covet;
and if there be any other commandment,
it is summed up in this saying:
You shall love your neighbour as yourself.

10. Love does not do harm to a neighbour;
therefore love (is) the fulfilling of the law.

Romans 13, 1-7

Astonishingly and without good reason he states that those in authority rule by 'divine right', that whatever they do is justified because in his opinion they act on God's behalf. Whatever those in authority do or want is called 'good' by Paul and those who resist or oppose them do 'evil' and will be punished. Paul wants all to obey those in authority and to be obedient, to pay taxes and revenues, to respect and honour those in authority.

He is arguing that one must fear and obey those in authority and do for them and give them all they ask, without regard to how selfish, rotten, corrupt, inhuman, vicious, murdering or evil they may be.

What Paul is saying and putting forward in this letter is neither God's word nor is it what Jesus taught. Under the disguise of a religious sermon Paul is spreading political propaganda, trying to brainwash people into willingly serving and loving those who exploit and oppress so as to exploit.

Look again at the social laws and system of the Pentateuch <2> and you will see how the laws of the Pentateuch ensure freedom and material independence and provide a good life of high quality here and now, backed by effective social security. No one may oppress or exploit another and all are equal, as a matter of law.

It is these laws of behaviour, it is these social laws and this social system which Paul opposes and he next attempts to stop people from keeping these laws.

Romans 13, 8-10

Paul lists only the last five of the Ten Commandments <3>. These five commandments protect people against anti-social behaviour of others by prohibiting the doing of that which would harm or injure other people, prohibiting adultery, murder, theft, false witness and coveting.

He continues by saying
      (1) "Love does not do harm to a neighbour", and
      (2) "all 'other' commandments are contained in
         'You shall love your neighbour as yourself'".

He also says
      (3) "Love is the fulfilling of the law" and
      (4) "He who loves another has fulfilled the law"

and concludes
      (5) Therefore your only obligation to others is to love one
         another.

The word 'love' is a label for something which is vague and abstract and quite meaningless until it is clearly, precisely and unambiguously defined in detail. 'Love does not do harm to a neighbour' and 'You shall love your neighbour as yourself' are vague and do not stand up to examination.

It would be illogical to argue that step (2) follows from step (1).

One person's idea of 'love' could be another person's 'insult' or 'hurt'.

To say that 'You shall love your neighbour as yourself' contains all the other laws, is in effect abrogating, bypassing, annulling these laws by replacing them with a person's likes and dislikes, even by a pervert's feelings.

There is simply no basis for saying that "Love is the fulfilling of the law" and that "He who loves another has fulfilled the law".

Paul himself leaves us in no doubt about his intentions when he says that "Your only obligation to others is to love one another". His intentions are to stop people from observing other laws.

The laws he does not wish people to observe include the first five commandments (of the Ten Commandments) which he pointedly left out from his list and thus include the social laws and the social system laws which together ensure freedom and material independence and social security.

When Moses brought the tables of the law he brought 'freedom upon the tables'. It is the Ten Commandments as a whole which underlie freedom, independence and strength to oppose and resist oppression.

And the first five commandments which Paul is attempting to stop people from observing are those which directly relate to freedom and independence, which give the working population strength in their struggle for a better life for themselves and their children against those who oppress and exploit.

These laws state <3> that:

> The only way to gain and keep freedom and independence and a good life free from oppression and exploitation is to follow all these laws.
>
> One must not respect or serve oppressing, exploiting or enslaving beliefs or ideologies.
>
> One must not use God's name to lend authority to a statement which it would not otherwise have or to a false or misleading statement.
>
> One must observe the sabbath day, the seventh day which is a day of rest from work for all, on which all are equal and rest, on which our servants rest just as we do, remembering that it was God who by a mighty hand and by an outstretched arm freed us from most brutal service.
>
> One must honour one's father and one's mother and willingly accept God's commands and the tradition, knowledge and life experience of one's parents so that one will progress and advance in understanding and in life and so that one will have long and secure lives of high quality in the land God gives one.

Among the social laws of the Pentateuch, for example, are the kingship laws {3} which state that those in authority must not oppress people so as to increase their own possessions and power, that they must not put themselves above the people and so enrich themselves. They are warned against oppressing people and against forming enforcing squads or organisations so as to multiply their own power, must not be promiscuous and must not amass wealth. They must know and observe the law and its intent and aim to see the law applied.

The Pentateuch states the Ten Commandments, the social laws and the social system laws and states in religious language the effects when people either follow or else reject these laws. But it also states that this is a scientific Cause-and-effect relationship, lists causes and effects and states that the effects are reversible dependent on how people behave {17}.

Paul is apparently unaware of the inevitable inescapable consequences of breaking the law, of not living according to the social laws, and so makes changes which would have and have had disastrous consequences for those who attempted to put into effect what he proposes.

We will see how Matthew struggled to put the record straight, struggled to record what Jesus actually taught. Throughout the ages, Christians of goodwill chose intuitively to interpret Paul's statements about those in authority as meaning that 'the authority of those in authority only comes from God to the extent to which they themselves live according to and apply the Ten Commandments, the social laws and the social system laws' and that only those can 'love one another' who comply with all these laws.

Gospels

Matthew's gospel was the first to be written. It is closest to the events and so perhaps it is not surprising that it has always been the most popular and revered of the gospels.

It was later followed by Mark's and this in turn was followed by Luke's gospel. It seems the later authors were aware of and knew the earlier gospels and this appears confirmed by the successive changes which were made which changed the record of what Jesus taught and of the meaning of the stories and of the arguments.

Changes are still being made today but even when made with the best of intentions are slowly changing and distorting what was there before. An example of how editing changes both content and meaning of a statement can be found in note <4>.

What Jesus taught, and the kind of changes which were made later, becomes clear when one compares the versions recorded in the three gospels in the order in which they were written.

Jesus Taught: About The Rich Young Man

This story, of course, makes a particular point, presents an important statement.

It is also labelled by a key phrase as one of a group of connected statements or as an argument in a series of connected arguments. Here the key phrase is 'But many that are first will be last, and the last first'.

Outstanding is how the later subsequent changes made to the text fundamentally changed the intended meaning of the story.

Matthew records {8} that

Jesus said that 'good deeds' by themselves are not enough to gain eternal life. Whoever keeps the commandments enters eternal life. To be a 'good person' and enter eternal life one has to keep the commandments.

Asked to state which of the commandments should be kept, Jesus lists the laws which have to be observed. It is immediately obvious that Jesus is here recorded as listing those commandments referred to by Paul in his letter to the Romans {7} <5> which included Paul's 'You shall love your neighbour as yourself', this being where Paul said that it is these laws, and only these, which need to be kept.

Matthew's gospel was written after Paul wrote his letters and Paul wrote his letters some considerable time after the death of Jesus. Hence we suddenly find ourselves understanding this story as an important statement about whether all or only some of the laws should be kept, about whether or not some laws should be discarded, about removing from observance those laws which restrain the rich and powerful from oppressing and exploiting people.

Important is that Matthew is recording what Jesus taught and that this outweighs and overrules whatever Paul may have said to the contrary.

> Matthew states that Jesus' list includes the fifth commandment (Honour your father and your mother ...) and leaves out the tenth (You shall not covet ...). As 'You shall not covet' applies equally well to the rich as to the poor, this makes the clear point, and emphasises it, that the laws which are left out are those which protect people against oppression and exploitation, which restrain and restrict the behaviour of the rich and powerful.
>
> The rich young man then tells Jesus that he has kept all the laws Jesus listed and asks what else he must do, which other commandments need to be kept.
>
> If nothing else were required Jesus would have said so. But Jesus makes the point that there are other requirements, summing them up by saying "Sell what you possess and give to the poor ... and follow me.", referring in this way to the other laws from the Ten Commandments and to the social laws and social system of the Pentateuch <2>.
>
> Those who are rich are commanded to, and must, provide funds to those whose independence is threatened or who are in need. These funds must be provided free of interest so that the needy cannot be exploited through their need. Those who are supported are under obligation to repay the capital but every seventh year all outstanding amounts have to be cancelled, again to prevent the rich from exploiting the needy through their need. These are examples of what Jesus is referring to.
>
> The rich and powerful ignored laws such as these and wanted the system of social organisation and social security annulled and deleted from observance. This had been happening and the

53

people were suffering. But here Jesus is telling the rich that to be rewarded by God, that is to fulfil the law, they would need to keep the social laws.

And when Jesus adds '... and follow me' he is asking the rich young man (that is, the rich and powerful) to follow what Jesus teaches.

But the man would not do so 'because he had great possessions' and went away.

We are told that the rich and powerful would not follow Jesus when he asked them to return to God by keeping the social laws, when he asked them to stop oppressing and exploiting those in need.

And so Jesus says to his disciples that 'it will be hard for a rich man to enter the kingdom of heaven'. The rich and powerful are not observing the social laws and as a result suffer and will suffer the inevitable consequences.

So Jesus taught that all the laws had to be kept, that belief and practice included and had to include the Ten Commandments, the social laws and the social system of the Pentateuch. Paul, however, acted on behalf of the rich and powerful when he tried to convince people that those in authority were God's representatives on earth and that the social laws did not have to be kept.

Paul's letter to the Romans was written before the gospels. Matthew's later gospel records what Jesus actually taught and clearly makes the point that Paul was trying to subvert and turn upside down that which Jesus taught. As Matthew records what Jesus taught, this outweighs and overrides what Paul said.

It would seem that those who later favoured Paul's pro-establishment ideology could not challenge Matthew's earlier record. Hence, as we shall now see, Matthew's record was subtly changed in later gospels, in an attempt to distort and hide that which Jesus had taught so as to weaken arguments against Paul's ideology.

Jesus Taught: Censored!

We can now compare how later gospel writers recorded the same story. We will see how successive changes, one by one, subtly change meaning and intent further and further away from what was there initially, namely away from the clear record and statement about what Jesus taught and towards obscure abstract matters.

54

The story begins:

Matt. 19, 16-30	Mark 10, 17-31	Luke 18, 18-30
Jesus is asked	Jesus is asked	Repeats Mark's version
"Teacher, what good deed must I do to have eternal life?"	"Good teacher, what must I do to inherit eternal life?"	
and replies	and replies	
"Why do you ask me about what is good?	"Why do you call me good?	
One there is who is good. If you would enter life, keep the commandments."	No one is good but God alone	

Jesus said that 'good deeds' by themselves are not enough to gain eternal life. Whoever keeps the commandments enters eternal life. To be a 'good person' and enter eternal life one has to keep the commandments.

Mark subtly changes this to have a completely different meaning. He records Jesus as saying that only God is 'good'.

Luke repeats Mark's version.

The story continues as follows:

Matt.	Mark	Luke
Jesus is then asked which commandments should be kept and says:	Jesus continues, saying: "You know the commandments:	Repeats Mark's version
"You shall not kill; You shall not commit adultery; You shall not steal; You shall not bear false witness;	Repeats Matthew's list	
Honour your father and mother, and	Repeats Matthew's version	
You shall love your neighbour as yourself."	Leaves this out	
The young man continues his questioning by asking Jesus:	The man then says to Jesus:	
"All these I have observed; what do I still lack?"	"All these I have observed from my youth."	

Those who are rich and powerful want to have removed the restraints which prevent them from exploiting the people and from oppressing so as to exploit. They want to have deleted from observance those laws which Jesus did not list. This is what Paul is advocating and it seems that what Jesus has said is what Paul wants.

The rich young man then tells Jesus that he has kept all the laws Jesus listed and asks what else he must do, which other commandments need to be kept. This makes the point that there are other requirements, that is other laws, which have to be observed and which Jesus is asked to list.

Mark again changes the text subtly so as to obscure and so delete the statement that all the laws have to be observed.

Matthew's 'Which commandments should be kept?' becomes Mark's 'You know the commandments'. So Mark's Jesus implies that the listed commandments are the only ones, that those which are not listed and which protect people from oppression and exploitation simply do not exist, do not need to be observed.

Paul has said {6} that 'You shall love your neighbour as yourself' contains and thus replaces the laws which are not listed here. Indeed this is the only argument being put forward against laws which protect people.

So Mark simply leaves out 'love your neighbour as yourself'. By doing so he deletes what is a clear pointer to the core argument of the story, to the intent and meaning of what Jesus is saying.

Mark's modified version simply states that these are the laws and that the man has observed the laws all his life.

Luke repeats Mark's version.

The story continues as follows:

Matt.	Mark	Luke
Jesus replies:	Repeats Matthew's version	Repeats Mark's version
... sell what you possess and give to the poor		
... and follow me.		

The commandments clearly state that independence and freedom from oppression are God-given rights and that one may not 'have other gods'. In other words, the laws of the Pentateuch may not be annulled or replaced.

There are strict laws regulating the behaviour of rulers, of the rich, of the powerful, of the establishment. Their role is to serve the people and they must not make the people serve them, and the role of the rich is that of administering their wealth on behalf of the community.

Here Jesus is telling the rich that if they wish to be rewarded by God they will need to follow that which Jesus teaches by keeping all the commandments and the social laws of the Pentateuch.

The story then continues as follows:

Matt.	Mark	Luke
Then the man	... his countenance fell and he	... he became sad
went away	went away	
sorrowful	sorrowful	
for he had great possessions	for he had great possessions	for he was very rich

We are here told that those who were rich and powerful would not follow Jesus' teachings and deserted him.

Mark repeats Matthew's record.

Luke, however, leaves out the statement about what action the rich person (a 'ruler' in Luke's version) took following Jesus' call to duty.

We see that at this point Luke takes further what Mark did earlier on, making changes which weaken, hide and cover up the intended meaning of the story. He does so by relating the story to 'rulers' instead of to those who were rich and powerful, and by deleting from the story that they would not follow Jesus' teachings and that they deserted him.

The story then continues as follows:

Matt.	Mark	Luke
And Jesus said to his disciples	And Jesus looked around and said to his disciples	Jesus looking at him said
"... it will be hard for a rich man to enter the kingdom of heaven.	"How hard it will be for those who have riches to enter the kingdom of God!"	"How hard it is for those who have riches to enter the kingdom of God!
...it is easier for a camel to go through the eye of a needle than for a rich man to enter the kingdom of God."	Repeats Matthew's version	Repeats Mark's version

In Matthew's gospel Jesus is making a specific point which applies in general. Those who are rich and powerful and who are not observing the important social laws, suffer and will suffer the unavoidable consequences as a result.

Mark again weakens the connection between the different interconnected parts of Jesus' statement by giving the impression that what Jesus says is somehow connected with those present instead of being generally applicable. He does so by saying that Jesus 'looked around' before making his point.

Luke here also further weakens the general applicability of what he records Jesus as saying. In his version Jesus specifically looks at one person when making the point.

The story The Rich Young Man continues but there is one sentence at the end which is the label, tag or key phrase. A key phrase links the statement or argument in one section to other related statements or arguments elsewhere. Here the key phrase is 'But many that are first will be last, and the last first.'

Immediately following the story about The Rich Young Man is that about The Labourers in the Vineyard {9}.

Here the owner of the vineyard (rich, ruler, powerful, ruling or controlling establishment) decides to pay the same amount to his labourers regardless of the time worked by them, regardless of some having worked many hours while some worked only a few.

He decided whom to pay and how much and for what, without regard to considerations of performance, equality, fairness or social justice.

The way his labourers are paid is unequal, unfair and unjust and this story constitutes a severe criticism of how servants and labourers were being treated at that time.

This story about the Labourers not only immediately follows that of The Rich Young Man, but it is the only one in Matthew's gospel which has the same key phrase. And indeed it is making the same point about the rich and powerful not keeping the commandments and social laws and in this way we are told that we have correctly understood the lesson in 'The Rich Young Man'.

The key phrase itself is a vivid statement of an unfair system and society.

Both Mark and Luke excluded this story from their gospels, presumably because it confirmed the real meaning of what Jesus taught in a direct and powerful way and which could not easily be modified to change its obvious meaning.

But Luke attempts to muddle up the significance of the key phrase and to confuse us by leaving it out from his version of 'The Rich Young Man' and inserting it into another story, in a story of his own. Significantly, the words in Luke's key phrase {11} are transposed and given superficial meaning:

Matt.	Mark	Luke
But many that are first will be last, and the last first.	Repeats Matthew's version	Leaves out this key phrase from his version.
		Inserts the key phrase into another story

At the Time of Jesus

Outstanding is that the contemporaneously written, agreed and finalised Christian Canon and Jewish Talmud were shaped by and independently record the same confrontations and struggle and sequence of events we have here seen unfold.

The agreement between Christian and Jewish writings is so complete that we are now reasonably certain about the main course of events.

Christian Canon

We have already seen <6> that Paul's letters (epistles) are the oldest part of the New Testament, probably written about 50 AD, some considerable time after the death of Jesus. What stands out is that no one before Paul wrote such letters and that no one did so afterwards.

The gospels followed. Matthew's was apparently written first, then Mark's, then Luke's. Luke also wrote The Acts. It seems the gospels were written about 70-100 AD.

Matthew's record was subtly changed in later gospels. We saw how successive changes, one by one, changed meaning and intent further and further away from what is recorded in Matthew's gospel.

Further and further away from Matthew's clear record and statement about what Jesus taught, obscuring and confusing that which Jesus taught so as to weaken arguments against Paul's ideology.

What became the Christian Canon, meaning by this the 'agreed' version of events and teachings, took about four hundred years before it was 'agreed' {25}. It apparently took about four hundred years for written material and for people's memories to be changed, edited and modified, to conform to the establishment point of view.

If it had just been a matter of recording facts, of recording the truth, the whole truth and nothing but the truth (the truth, nothing left out and nothing added), it would not have taken so long. After ten or so generations people would be regarding as factual that which they were being told was factual.

So it continued to be compiled till it was approved by the Christian establishments and so presumably biased towards the point of view of the establishment, towards what the establishment wanted included or excluded, wanted said or unsaid.

It may well have taken such a long period of time before the hierarchy had argued away evidence contrary to the establishment's viewpoint or buried it out of sight or declared it to be against established doctrine, in such ways discrediting opposing viewpoints which called for social justice according to the word of God.

A similar if not identical process took place within Judaism during roughly the same period of time and here also the relevant social laws were side-tracked and bypassed.

Jewish Talmud

The Talmud was written contemporaneously with the gospels. Both the Talmud and the Christian Canon were completed and agreed, canonified and frozen, at about the same time. From then on the Talmud's text remained unchanged.

The Talmud was compiled separately in Jerusalem and in Babylon, starting in the first century AD. It took about four hundred years for the Talmud to be compiled in Jerusalem and about five hundred years in Babylon {19}. The Babylonian Talmud is considerably longer than the Jerusalem Talmud and the Babylonian Talmud is regarded as far more authoritative than that produced in Jerusalem.

The Jewish establishment (secular and religious) had been and was changing the application of the laws of the Pentateuch so that 'the law was becoming like two laws'. The Talmud was then written to record what was happening so that future generations would become aware of the course of events and of who had been doing what to whom. They also wanted future generations to learn from the lessons of the past so as to be able to reverse the tragedy of the destruction of the country, of Jerusalem, of the people.

The Talmud records events, legal decisions, traditions, discussions, arguments and stories. It was written in two distinct parts {19}. First was written the Mishnah ('Repetition') which includes information about the reality of the conflict, the participants, the sides they represent, what actually happened. Then, much later, was written the Gemara ('Tradition') which contains arguments and stories intended to make points about the Mishnah and most of the Talmud consists of Gemara.

By the time the writing of the Gemara was finished the actual message in the Mishnah had been buried in a mass of stories and arguments. From that time onwards the essential core legislation of the Pentateuch had been negated and bypassed and buried under arguments about many subjects.

What we see is that Jewish attempts to argue against their establishment were by themselves unable to change the course of events {25} and that their record of what the establishment had done and was doing was being buried under a mass of abstract arguments and stories.

The Talmud is part of Jewish religious teachings and so Jews did not on the whole openly write about Christian activists, Christian beliefs and Christians. Since they were writing about the same events and issues Christians were writing about, they tended to conceal what they were doing.

Events and Struggle

It does seem more than a coincidence that it took roughly the same period of time for Christianity and Judaism to contemporaneously finalise the Christian Canon and the Jewish Talmud, respectively.

The Talmud, however, is far longer than the New Testament and, as said already, was in part written to record what was happening so that future generations would become aware of the course of events and of who had been doing what to whom. So that future generations could learn from the lessons of the past so as to be able to reverse the tragedy of the destruction of the country, of Jerusalem, of the people.

The processes by which the establishment changed belief and practice at the time were much the same in both religions and are still used and applied today. The Talmud clearly describes what actually happened, describes these processes of change as well as the arguments used by both sides and how the people felt about what the scholars were doing on behalf of the rulers and their establishment. {15-16}

The Jewish establishment was not following the laws of the Pentateuch, was oppressing and exploiting the people. We then see Jewish communities arguing against what the Jewish establishment was doing, see them trying to live according to the laws of the Pentateuch, being or including the Jewish Christian communities.

Both the Talmud and the Canon tell of an outsider, of an outside establishment orientated ideology, corrupting what was being taught and undermining what people believed, corrupting and undermining what Jesus had taught.

The inevitable result of the establishment's activities was that Jerusalem and the country were laid waste and the terrible suffering of the people {13}.

In both religions the establishment versions became accepted as official doctrine. But the Talmud also records what needs to be done to correct matters and describes the basic confrontation between on the one side God and people and on the other side those who wish to oppress so as to exploit. In this way it describes in clear and unambiguous terms the source of conflict and strife, defining in clear terms both good and evil. The Christian Canon succeeded in doing much the same, doing so in religious language, in religious terms.

The adherents of both religions were and are taught to follow that which is good and to struggle against that which is evil. However, the definitions of good and evil and the knowledge of the source of evil are intuitive and uncertain. They need to be clearly stated in terms of the Ten Commandments and of the social laws and system of the Pentateuch, if this planet is to remain inhabitable for human beings.

We now know {13} that the consequences of not doing so cannot be avoided, that they are inevitable, that ignorance is no excuse.

Same Struggle, Same Political Ideology

We saw already {15; 16} that Jews did not openly write about Christian activists, Christian beliefs and Christians, that they wrote about them in a roundabout way. For example, a positive statement would be expressed using negatives or else turned upside down by stating its opposite. An additional label or phrase is used to confirm that one's understanding of the real meaning of the statement is correct and not merely a figment of one's imagination.

Here is an example of how in the Talmud a negative version records the beliefs of early Christians {23}:

In the Talmud, a 'student' says that	Same statement, expressed positively
An evil eye,	Adopting the right belief,
the evil inclination	a corresponding right way of life
and hatred for creatures	and love of people
put a man out of this world.	fit a man for the kingdom of heaven.

I understand that in early Christian writings people who have evil eyes, who have eyes which offend, are people who have the wrong belief from a Christian point of view. So the negative statement on the left, when expressed positively, becomes a summary of early Christian belief.

The name of the student confirms that this is a statement of early Christian beliefs. His name is given as Joshua ben Hananiah, which is Joshua the son of Hananiah. The common Greek form of the Hebrew name Joshua is Jesus, his father's name Hananiah means 'Graciously given of the Lord' and of Joshua it was said that 'Happy is she that bare him'. The talmudic text of which this is a part also confirms that it is Christians as such which are being referred to in this way.

Here is another example from the Talmud which illustrates rather beautifully how opposites are used forcefully and convincingly to make a specific point which would have been unacceptable to the religious establishment if it had been openly stated {22}. We are told that

- "Naaman was a resident alien.
- Nebuzaradan was a righteous proselyte,
- the descendants of Sisera studied Torah (the Pentateuch) in Jerusalem;
- the descendants of Sennacherib taught Torah to the multitude; who were these? - Shemaiah and Avtalyon.
- The descendants of Haman studied Torah at Bene Berak."

Here we are told of great and famous people serving God, studying and teaching the Pentateuch and its laws, serving God and people. Or so it may appear at first glance.

We know next to nothing about Shemaiah and Avtalyon, but all the other people mentioned here are among the worst enemies of the Jewish people. Nebuzaradan, for example, was captain of the guard of Nebuchadnezzar, king of Babylon, and commanded the forces which burned down Jerusalem and destroyed the first Temple.

In this way the Talmud records what would have been unacceptable to the religious establishment at that time, namely that Shemaiah and Avtalyon are among the worst and most destructive enemies of the Jewish people.

Paul and Hillel

The earliest of the Christian writings to be accepted as part of the Christian Canon and thus playing an important part in moulding early Christian beliefs, were Paul's letters. In the Talmud, we read about

Hillel as a key and central figure who played a key part in moulding Jewish beliefs. This is what they are recorded as saying:

Paul {6}:

> Your only obligation to others is to love one another; Because he who loves another has fulfilled the law. ... and if there be any other commandment, it is summed up in this saying: You shall love your neighbour as yourself.

Hillel {20}:

> What is hateful to you, do not to your neighbour; that is the whole Torah (Pentateuch), while the rest is commentary thereon; go and learn it.

'What is hateful to you, do not to your neighbour' is the negative form of 'You shall love your neighbour as yourself'.

Taken with the other parts of these statements, as well as with the context in which they are made, it can be seen that the statements are in effect identical. When the Talmud contains information about and quotes Hillel, then it seems to be writing about and quoting Paul.

Paul, Hillel and Christianity

We saw <6> that Jewish Christians believed in the laws of the Pentateuch and struggled for the application of these laws in daily life, struggling against an oppressive establishment which argued against and did not keep the social laws.

Paul preached against material independence, against social security, against freedom from oppression and exploitation. What he preached was the political ideology of an oppressive establishment.

This brought him into conflict with Jewish Christians and with the mostly Jewish Christian communities and he was unsuccessful in changing their beliefs and practices. He then concentrated on gaining converts from gentiles (people who are not Jewish) who presumably knew nothing or little about the laws of the Pentateuch and who would thus be more likely to follow his teachings without arguing about its content.

Paul's teachings were accepted to a considerable extent and it is the versions of the Gentile Christians which were included in the Christian Canon and became official doctrine.

So let us see what else the Talmud tells us about Hillel, let us see what the Talmud tells us about these events.

Hillel, Paul and Judaism

We are told {20} that there were two men, each with his own followers, who in effect founded two schools of conflicting religious thought. These men were called Shammai and Hillel. Shammai was strict in the application of the laws while Hillel was lenient. A gentile asked to be converted on condition that he would be taught the whole of the Torah (Pentateuch) while he stood on one foot. Shammai, when asked, refused to do so. Hillel, on the other hand, replied saying

> What is hateful to you, do not to your neighbour; that is the whole Torah (Pentateuch), while the rest is commentary thereon; go and learn it.

We saw that in this way the Talmud states what Paul stated. Jewish Christians kept the laws and expected converts to keep the laws. But when Paul converted gentiles to Christianity he told them that only some of the laws needed to be kept, that they did not need to keep the social laws.

The Talmud tells {21} how Hillel gained a following and took control. We are told that he did so

1. because he was taught by Shemaiah and Avtalyon, and
2. that he took over from the Bene Bathyra, having
3. persuaded them to hand over by using abstract rules of logic and association for interpreting the law.

We saw already that the Talmud counts Shemaiah and Avtalyon among the worst and most destructive enemies of the Jewish people, representing those who wish to oppress and exploit. And Hillel told the Bene Bathyra that he ruled over them because he had served Shemaiah and Avtalyon, while they (the Bene Bathyra) had dared not to serve them.

The Bene Bathyra, the sons or children of Bathyra, of those who are doing the cutting (circumcision), who are carrying out the Brit, the sons or children of the Covenant. It would seem that this again could refer equally well to Paul and his ideology taking over from, gaining ascendancy over, the Jewish Christians as these practised circumcision.

Before these rules of logic and association were introduced, the law seems to have been decided according to the Pentateuch and in line with its intent. The use of such rules resulted in laws which were unrelated, or perhaps even outside or opposed to the meaning of the original text of the Pentateuch, and in this way controversy increased in Israel. As the pupils of Hillel increased in number, so controversy increased in Israel.

An example of such an illogical argument (including in this logical arguments based on false presuppositions or assumptions, being equally misleading) is Paul's statement {5} <5> in Romans about rulers representing God and acting for God.

One of the core social laws in the Pentateuch is that those whose independence or material security was threatened had to be provided by the community, that is by those who are rich, with the funds required to meet their needs. The money had to be provided free of interest and if those who had been given such funds had not been able to repay them then such debts were cancelled after a period of time which could not exceed seven years. Every seventh year was a Year of Release in which such debts were cancelled. This is part of a system of social security which also protects those in need from exploitation and oppression by those who control the community's wealth, by those who are rich and powerful.

It is recorded {18} in what is apparently the oldest, that is earliest, part of the Talmud that Hillel saw that those who were rich did not provide the needed funds and so broke the laws. He is then recorded as having laid down that all the rich had to do was to declare in writing before a judge that they would collect any outstanding funds whenever they desired and that they could then collect at will.

The rich and powerful break the laws and Hillel in effect cancels the application of the laws they do not want to keep! In this way Hillel by bypassing the application of a basic Pentateuch law withdrew an essential protection from the people which protected those who are in need from economic and later more direct oppression and enslavement by those who control money or who have money.

In the whole of the vast Talmud there are only two rulings recorded in the Mishnah, the oldest part of the Talmud, as having been made by Hillel. What they have in common is that in each case he ruled in favour of the rich. He favoured the rich at the expense of the poor. He exposed the people to exploitation through need.

Hillel and Paul are again saying and applying the same ideology.

Paul wrote {4} that 'For the law brings wrath, but where there is no law there is no transgression'. Paul held that the God-given laws of Moses (the Pentateuch) resulted in punishment for those who broke the law and that people would be freed from this when the laws were abolished, when they stopped following them.

This is what Hillel gave as his reason for saying that funds provided for the needy would have to be repaid by the needy to the rich.

Origin of Christianity

Now let us combine what we know with other available information. For the first time we can now see the whole pattern of events.

On the one hand we have the Jewish people who are protected by Jewish law from need and from being exploited because of need. On the other we have the rulers and their establishment who wish to oppress their people so as to exploit them.

Two sides do not engage in such bitter controversy without very real cause. What is at stake is on the one hand power and wealth for a few at the expense of the many; and on the other hand freedom, independence and a good life as against oppression and exploitation.

There are movements and so-called religions which condition and brainwash their members into working so as to enrich the founders or the establishment, or which brainwash members into obediently working for and serving the leadership in unquestioning obedience.

Also one has to realise that when it suits their purpose those who run countries will encourage and use religion. Such a 'religion' may be used as a tranquilliser to prevent the population from complaining about being downtrodden and exploited. The message the religion then spells out is 'never mind a hard life now, reward will come in the next life'.

The Jewish religion, however, is quite different and does not readily lend itself to such misuses.

So what happened was that those who wished to rule over, and exploit, the Jewish people, took over the religion and from within changed its pattern of observance. So that it served the rulers and establishment instead of serving God and people.

What we see is the struggle of the two sides within the Jewish establishment. Corrupting them, setting them against each, misusing religion to gain adherents and servile followers. Changing religious beliefs and practices to make religious teachings serve the rulers and their establishment.

And we see the struggle against these changes, see how people struggled in very cruel and tough and difficult times to return to the social teachings of the Torah, to regain spiritual freedom and material independence and a good life for all.

So now let us take up the course of events from the time of the Maccabean uprising.

Maccabean Rule

Historical Events   <7>

Mattathias, his sons and his grandson John Hyrcanus battled together and supported one another and John Hyrcanus was able to build the country and complete the work the others had started.

To begin with all were united and struggled against the brutal oppression. They struggled for Torah <8>, freedom and the people. Against them were foreign invaders who believed in slavery and who were trying to impose their way of life through imposing their beliefs.

The uprising gained ground, the country was built and enlarged until it became strong and independent through one central unifying purpose: to build a country in which Jewish people could live as Jews and practise their faith. Single minded, the members of the Maccabean family were loyal to the brother who was in command at the time. As soon as the commanding brother died, the next one was ready to take over and was in turn supported by the rest of the family.

With Aristobulus I it seems that power had corrupted but he did not rule for long but Alexander Yannai concentrated secular and religious power in his hands and conflict deepened as a result.

Following the popular uprising for Judaism, for Jewish law and thus for freedom, the rulers formed a dynasty and a supporting establishment, had tasted power and meant to cling to it.

Two generations later the situation had changed and we see increasing internal confrontation, a struggle between people and Torah on the one hand against oppressive rulers and their oppressing establishment on the other.

Instead of serving God and people, the rulers battled for power with each other, allied themselves with foreign powers against each other. In so doing they divided the people and weakened all.

It was the military commander (younger brother) who started the civil war against his elder brother (High Priest and heir to the throne), for the succession, for personal power. In the end he lost.

His son tried the same: This resulted in the handing over of the country and its people to Herod and the subsequent introduction by Herod of 'hellenisation'. This meant the introduction and popularisation of a foreign ideology, based on, and supporting, slavery. It was indeed this which the Maccabees had struggled against.

The Jewish leadership, the Jewish establishment, disregarded the welfare of the people, disregarded Jewish law, disregarded the intent and purpose of Jewish law.

The religious hierarchy became subservient to the secular rulers, with the rulers presumably using the religious hierarchy to motivate and tranquillise their people.

Talmudic Account

This is also how these events are portrayed in the Talmud, but the Talmud identifies the two sides, more precisely, much clearer.

The events are portrayed as a struggle between on one side the social laws and the social system of the Torah, and on the other side oppressing exploiting authoritarian rulers and masters. The struggle takes place during the five generations which follow Simeon (that is, the Maccabean dynasty), the last of these five generations being that of Hillel and Shammai.

This is how the two sides, the two opponents, are identified and described:

On the one side Simeon the Just <9> says that the world is based on the Torah, divine service and the practice of kindness. He believes that the freedom and protection the law provides is essential, that the world is based on it. The world depends on the law, on it being observed and thus applied, and on the practice of kindness. This is a statement of the Jewish position.

The other side, that of 'Antigonus of Socoh', is that which opposes and struggles against Jewish beliefs of freedom, justice and good life for all, stands for an ideology based on oppression and slavery, stands for central authoritarian rule and establishment.

So us to leave us in no doubt about this, the Talmud clearly announces what this side stands for by quoting its main teaching:
> Do not serve for pay, serve without expecting pay. Expect only to receive an unconditional gift to which you have no claim and fear 'heaven'.

'Be afraid and serve for the crumbs you may be thrown' is clearly the opposite of Jewish law.

Freedom, independence and justice are from then on under attack by an internal opposition which wishes to weaken or reverse the intent of the law, so as to be able to oppress so as to exploit. The struggle between the two opponents is then shown taking place pair by pair, generation by generation.

The story is told in two separate places in the Talmud. Both tell the same story, make the same point, namely that as the generations passed so religious power and control passed from Torah observance to observance which in key matters served an oppressive establishment. The Talmud not only tells us that it happened but in which generation control of the religious hierarchy moved from the Beth Din (religious authority) to the Nasi (prince; ruler and his establishment). {15}

The authority rested with the Beth Din and thus with the Av Beth Din (Head of religious authority) for three generations (pairs). In the last two generations it is the Nasi (Head of secular authority) who has the authority, who has the power, who decides, who controls the religious hierarchy and thus what it teaches.

Early Church

Information from Dead Sea Scrolls

Early Christians

What follows under this subheading is based on books by Michael Baigent and Richard Leigh {27}, and Hugh Schonfield {28}. The authors take into account much work published by others, including particularly that of Robert Eisenman. <10>

The 'Damascus Document' speaks of a remnant of Jews who remained true to the Law. Their 'Teacher of Righteousness' took them to a place called 'Damascus' in a wilderness, where they entered into a renewed 'Covenant' with God. They obeyed the Law of Moses and referred to themselves as 'the Keepers of the Covenant'.

Eisenman considers that the word 'Essene' originated from the Hebrew 'Osei ha-Torah' ('Doers of the Law'; 'Osreem'). The Qumran community also referred to themselves as the 'Keepers of the Covenant', (Hebrew: 'Nozrey ha-Brit'). The Jewish sect which later became known as Christians were called 'Nozrim' (early Hebrew name). The 'early Christians' referred to themselves as 'Nazorean' or 'Nazarene' <11>. These all derive from the same source, refer to the keeping of the Covenant.

The Qumran community's ruling body, the Council of the Community, was actually located in Jerusalem at the time of the Early Church. The Early Church in Jerusalem, like the Qumran community, were 'zealous for the Law'. Hence it does seem that "the Early Church and the Qumran community were one and the same".

The authors also note that "The defenders of Masada used precisely the same calendar as that used by the Qumran material: a unique solar calendar, in contrast to the lunar calendar of the official 'Sadducee' establishment and of later rabbinical Judaism."

'The Liar' and Paul

The authors {27} say that the Dead Sea Scrolls tell that 'The Teacher of Righteousness' had two separate and distinct adversaries.

One of these is called the 'Liar' and apparently came from within the community.

The Habakkuk Commentary shows that he is persuading members of the community to break the New Covenant and to stop following the law.

The Damascus Document speaks of those 'who enter the New Covenant in the land of Damascus, and who again betray it and depart', speaks of those 'who deserted to the Liar'.

He 'led many astray', raised 'a congregation on deceit' and is 'pregnant with [works] of deceit'.

The authors say that 'These, of course, are precisely the transgressions of which Paul is accused in The Acts of the Apostles'. They also say that 'If 'Damascus' is understood to be Qumran, ... Saul's (of Tarsus, Paul) expedition suddenly makes perfect historical sense.'

Paul opposed the requirement that Gentile converts had to become full Jews and busied himself founding a new religion. During the next three centuries, say the authors, the movement coalesced around Paul's teachings. Thus "an entirely new religion was indeed born - a religion which came to have less and less to do with its supposed founder."

The 'The Wicked Priest'

The 'Teacher's' second adversary was from outside. This was the 'Wicked Priest', a representative of the establishment who had betrayed his function and his faith by conspiring against 'Poor', against those 'zealous for the Law'.

What the Dead Sea Scrolls Tell Us

We see that the Dead Sea Scrolls tell the same story.

A remnant of Jews remained true to the Law, would not accept establishment-orientated religious teachings.

The Qumran community and early Christians (Early Church) and probably also the defenders of Masada, obeyed the law of Moses, referred to themselves as 'Keepers of the Covenant'. The Early Church and the Qumran community were apparently parts of the same movement.

The Jewish priestly hierarchy which was in control of mainstream Judaism was establishment-orientated and this was reflected in its teachings.

But Jews were rallying around the 'Teacher of Righteousness', around Jesus, who was preaching a return to the social laws and social system of the Torah, to the keeping of the Covenant.

No wonder the followers of the Teacher of Righteousness met with opposition and enmity from the establishment's priestly hierarchy, were opposed by 'The Wicked Priest'.

So at Qumran (apparently referred to as 'Damascus') was established a communal settlement. Property was owned communally, in keeping with the social laws of the Torah as they understood them.

A convert of three years' standing left them. He is called 'The Liar' and persuades members to break their renewed Covenant and to stop following the law. He deceives and leads many astray, raising a congregation of his own by deceit.

We are also told that this is what Paul did. 'Paul opposed the requirement that Gentile converts had to become full Jews and busied himself founding a new religion' {27}.

So 'The Liar' and Paul are apparently the same person.

'During the next three centuries ... the movement coalesced around Paul's teachings.' Thus "an entirely new religion was indeed born - a religion which came to have less and less to do with its supposed founder." {27}

The establishment-orientated religious hierarchy was in control. A remnant of Jews kept alive the knowledge of the law of Moses. They gained motivation, numbers and strength by rallying round and following the teachings of Jesus (Teacher of Righteousness), in spite of opposition from the religious establishment.

So Paul (The Liar) infiltrates the movement and changes its beliefs into a new establishment-orientated religion.

Talmudic Account

The same events are recorded in the Talmud {15; 16}. The names are changed, of course. Jesus is referred to as 'Shammai', Paul is referred to by the name 'Hillel'. The names themselves confirm the identification, are based on what happened to them, on what happened to their teachings. 'Hillel' means 'Made bright by God' while 'Shammai' means 'Laid waste by God'.

The last Maccabean generation was the fifth after Simeon (not counting Simeon). That places Hillel and Shammai, listed as of the fifth generation, into the Herodian period and this would be right.

So the Talmud records the confrontation between Paul's and Jesus' teachings as a confrontation between the teachings of Hillel and Shammai, records that disputes multiplied from the time of Hillel, records disputes between their respective followers.

The Talmud describes clearly and precisely the confrontation between them, what they stand for, what happened and what could be done about it.

For example the Talmud shows that the law never did follow Hillel, that the law was not as taught by the establishment. The establishment, however, misrepresented what was there, subtly changing its meaning much as was done by successive gospel writers.

The Talmud leaves no doubt about how ordinary people felt about what the establishment scholars had been and were doing to Jewish Law, to the Torah of Moses.

The confrontation between Hillel and Shammai and the subsequent confrontation between their followers (Beth Hillel and Beth Shammai), and their fascinating and relevant political arguments (voting, majority, mud-slinging, censorship, discrediting the opposition, etc) are described in detail by Davidmann {15; 16}.

This is What Actually Happened

1.   The Jewish people are taught to observe, and observe, the laws of the Torah (Pentateuch, the five books of Moses).

     The Torah's social laws and its social system provide the only known basis for a fair and equitable society: for the existence of communities in which people trust one another, co-operate with each other for the common good, have freedom from oppression, have spiritual and material independence, have a good life.

2.   Subjection of the people by foreign (Hellenistic, Seleucid) dictatorship which believes in and supports slavery, oppression through need, exploitation of the working population by their masters (rulers).

It aims to wipe out belief in and application of the social laws of the Torah. Brutal persecution of the people.

The Maccabean uprising frees the people and re-establishes observance of the social laws of the Torah.

One of the Maccabean brothers leads the uprising. On his death the next brother assumes command. Simeon, the third brother to command, is appointed Ethnarch (Ruler), High Priest, Commander. All power thus centred in one person.

3. During the five generations after that of Simeon, that is during the Maccabean dynasty, the secular rulers gained control of the religious hierarchy and of what was being taught. There was discontent and opposition, but what was taught became increasingly establishment-orientated, serving an oppressing and exploiting establishment. The social laws ceased to be applied as a comprehensive system, as a way of life.

4. A remnant of Jews kept alive the knowledge of the law of Moses. They gained motivation, numbers and strength by rallying round and following the teachings of Jesus (Teacher of Righteousness) - Qumran community, Early Church - in spite of opposition from the religious establishment.

5. Paul (The Liar) infiltrates the movement and changes its teachings into a new religion, into a new establishment-orientated religion "which came to have less and less to do with its supposed founder (Jesus)." {27}

6. The Talmud records the confrontation between Paul's and Jesus' teachings as a confrontation between the teachings of Hillel (Paul) and Shammai (Jesus).

7. The establishment later misrepresented what is there, subtly changing its meaning much as was done by subsequent Gospel writers.

For example the Talmud shows that the law never did follow Hillel, that the law was not as taught by the establishment. Yet the establishment today still presents Hillel as one of the wisest of the sages and maintains that the law follows his teachings.

Appendix 1

TEN COMMANDMENTS

RELIGIOUS LANGUAGE	PLAIN ENGLISH
1	
I am the Lord your God, who brought you ... out of the house of bondage.	This is the voice of freedom. I proved this by freeing you from enslavement.
And the tables were the work of God, and the writing was the writing of God, freedom upon the tables {1}.	What is being given to you is the pattern of behaviour which underlies all freedom.
You shall have no other gods before Me.	If you want freedom and a good life then there is no other way.
2	
You shall not make for yourself a graven image, even any manner of likeness, of anything that is in heaven above, or that is in the earth beneath, or that is in the waters under the earth.	You shall not bow down to or serve any other kind of god or image or likeness of anything whatsoever.
You shall not bow down to them, nor serve them.	
For I the Lord your God am a jealous God, visiting the iniquity of the fathers upon the children, and upon the third and upon the fourth generation of them that hate Me, but showing mercy to the thousandth generation of those who love Me and keep My commandments.	Those who respect and serve other gods, respect or serve oppressing, exploiting or enslaving beliefs or ideologies, they hate me and they and their children will suffer the consequences even on the fourth generations.
	But those who love Me and keep My commandments are shown mercy to the thousandth generation.

3

You shall not take the name of the Lord your God in vain; for the Lord will not hold him guiltless who takes his name in vain.

You shall not use God's name to lend authority to a statement which it would not otherwise have or to a false or misleading statement.

4

Observe the sabbath day, to keep it holy, as the Lord your God commanded you. Six days shall you labour, and do all your work;

Observe the sabbath day, the seventh day which is a day of rest from work for all,

but the seventh day is a sabbath to the Lord your God: in it you shall not do any manner of work - you, nor your son, nor your daughter, nor your man-servant, nor your maid-servant, nor your ox, nor your ass, nor any of your cattle, nor the stranger who is within your gates;

on which all are equal and rest,

that your man-servant and your maid-servant may rest as well as you.

on which your servants rest just as you do.

And you shall remember that you were a servant in the land of Egypt, and the Lord your God brought you out from there by a mighty hand and by an outstretched arm; therefore the Lord your God commanded you to keep the sabbath day.

You shall remember that it was God who freed you from most brutal service by a mighty hand and by an outstretched arm.

Therefore God commanded you to keep the sabbath day.

5

Honour your father and your mother, as the Lord your God commanded you; that your days may be long, and that it may go well with you, on the land which the Lord your God gives you.

Honour your father and your mother and willingly accept God's commands and the tradition, knowledge and life experience of your parents so that you will progress and advance in understanding and in life and so that you will have long and secure lives of high quality in the land God will give you.

6

You shall not murder.

7

You shall not commit adultery.

8

You shall not steal.

9

You shall not bear false witness against your neighbour.

10

You shall not covet your neighbour's wife; neither shall you desire your neighbour's house, his field, or his man-servant, or his maid-servant, his ox, or his ass, or any thing that is your neighbour's.

Appendix 2

Maccabean Dynasty (The Hasmoneans) {14}

Oppression and Uprising

We know little about life in Israel during the period of about 300 years between the time of the return from Babylon and the time of the taking over of the country by the Seleucids. We do know that religious observance was so important that people would not even defend themselves when attacked on the Sabbath (the weekly day of rest) so as not to desecrate it.

Following the conquest of the country by Alexander the Great, the Greek (Macedonian, Seleucid) rulers started a process of hellenisation.

Among the Jewish leadership were those who served the rulers by offering greater annual taxes for the sake of obtaining personal power. They collected them from the people.

The country was ruled by Hellenistic dynasties. At the same time the rulers opposed and weakened the influence of the Jewish religion. The people suffered and became more and more discontented.

Mattathias Maccabeus (a country priest) rebelled against pagan worship. The people could stand no more and led first by Mattathias and then by his son Judah Maccabee they rebelled against the imposed vicious rule of the Seleucids.

Liberating the Country, Centralising Power
(The Hasmonean brothers)

Mattathias had five sons. The first to lead the uprising was Judah Maccabee.

When Judah Maccabee fell in battle, his brother Jonathan took over the leadership. Jonathan was appointed high priest about eight years later.

Jonathan in turn was followed by another brother, Simeon. A few years after he had assumed the leadership, Simeon was confirmed by the 'Great Assembly' as high priest, ethnarch (ruler) and commander of the Jewish people. Simeon's positions were to be hereditary.

Appointing Jonathan as high priest transferred religious authority and power to a secular leader. When the Great Assembly confirmed Simeon's position, they confirmed that religious and secular as well as military authority and power had been vested in one person and were to be hereditary.

What had happened was that able military and secular leadership absorbed religious authority and power. That this concentration of all authority and power in the hands of one person was to be permanent and later to be transferred to his descendants is an indication that the establishment of the day was already consolidating its own position.

Combining all power in the hands of a single ruler is against the spirit and intent of Jewish law. Religious authority should serve God and people.

What is at stake are the social laws and social system of the Torah <8>, which protect people from oppression and exploitation. The Torah's laws and system provide and ensure a fair division of the country's wealth as well as spiritual and material freedom and independence. All backed by full social security, all implemented by benevolent administration which in this way serves God and people. {13}

If religious authority is combined with secular rule, then religious authority will be misused to serve its own hierarchy, to serve the ruler and the establishment of the day, instead of serving God and the people. {14}

Power Centred on Ruler, Start of Discontent
(First generation after Simeon)

Simeon was succeeded by John Hyrcanus I who ruled 30 years. He successfully in consolidated gains which had been made and expanded the area under his control.

But the struggle was not just between the Jewish people and the Seleucid rule but also between the Jewish people and their own ruler. What we know is that during his reign opposition against the combination of religious and secular power, against the dominating role of the hereditary ruler and his establishment in all aspects of life, began to be felt.

It was a struggle against those rich and 'high born' who were in sympathy with and actively supported Hellenistic ideas of authoritarian exploitation, it being the mass of the population who would not readily relinquish their beliefs, their rights under the Torah.

Conflict Between Royal Brothers, Increased Conflict Between Opposing Factions
(Second generation after Simeon)

John Hyrcanus I was succeeded for about a year by his eldest son Judah Aristobulus I. When Judah Aristobulus died his brother Alexander Yannai ruled Judea for just under thirty years.

During Alexander Yannai's reign the conflict between opposing factions deepened. It seems that he was ruthless and that secular and religious power were concentrated in his hands to a previously unknown extent.

When Alexander Yannai died the leadership passed to his wife, Salome Alexandra.

Queen Salome Alexandra ruled for about nine years. She had two sons. The older son was Hyrcanus II, the younger son was Aristobulus II.

The elder son, namely Hyrcanus II, was high priest and considered the heir to the throne. The younger brother, namely Aristobulus II, was the military commander.

Queen Salome Alexandra seems to have attempted to emphasise the role of religion in government, perhaps hoping to reverse the trend which had been away from the social laws and social system of the Torah and towards centralised power and exploitation of the people.

Civil War by Aristobulus Against Hyrcanus
(Third generation after Simeon)

It seems that civil war broke out while the Queen was still alive and that the younger brother who was the military commander (Aristobulus II) was able to defeat his elder brother who was high priest and heir to the throne (Hyrcanus II).

When Queen Salome Alexandra died the younger brother (Aristobulus II) proclaimed himself king and high priest. The elder brother (Hyrcanus II) surrendered his power to the younger brother as he had been defeated in battle. The younger brother (Aristobulus II) ruled for about four years.

Hyrcanus then obtained the support of the Nabateans by promising to hand over to them some parts of Judea. He defeated Aristobulus and besieged him in Jerusalem.

But by this time the Romans had arrived in Syria which had become a Roman province. The Roman commander (Scaurus), apparently favouring Aristobulus in return for a large sum of money, told the Nabateans to withdraw from Jerusalem and this they did.

Shortly afterwards a new Roman commander, namely Pompey, took over the command. The dispute between the brothers was taken to him and it seems that he favoured Hyrcanus. Aristobulus surrendered to Pompey but managed to get away. The Roman army advanced on Jerusalem and while Hyrcanus' followers opened the gate of the city to the Romans, it took the Romans three months to take the Temple Mount. It seems that thousands of its defenders were killed.

This was virtually the end of independence for the country as they were now subservient to the Roman governor of Syria. Judea was very much reduced in size and its rulers were not allowed to call themselves kings. Once again the Jews were obliged to pay taxes to a foreign government.

What had happened was that the two brothers, struggling against each other for the sake of personal power, had involved foreign powers. The brothers were seemingly more concerned with struggling against each other than with the future existence, welfare and strength of the people and the country as a whole.

Civil War by Aristobulus' Son Antigonus Against Hyrcanus.
(Fourth generation after Simeon)

It was Aristobulus II who started the civil war which in the end resulted in the country being overrun, the country and its people losing their independence to the Romans. His youngest son was called Antigonus.

When the Parthians invaded Rome's eastern provinces, Antigonus allied himself with them so as to replace his uncle Hyrcanus, so as to rule himself.

Aided by the Parthians, Antigonus was thus able to make himself king of Judea. But Herod was given the title 'king' by the Romans. This was in 40 BCE. Herod returned to Israel with some Roman legions and started to take the country from Antigonus. After the Romans defeated the Parthian armies they were able to considerably reinforce the Roman legions which were fighting Antigonus.

Jerusalem was taken by Herod and the Romans after a siege lasting five months and Antigonus was defeated. Antigonus was put to death by Herod and so Herod ruled Judea for Rome, an Edomite king over the Jewish people.

End of Dynasty: Herod
(Fifth generation after Simeon)

During the course of his campaign against Antigonus, Herod had also married Mariamne (Fifth generation after Simeon), a granddaughter of Hyrcanus II.

Once again the Jewish people had been divided against each other by behaviour contrary to basic Jewish law. In this case the result was the ending of the rule of the Maccabean dynasty, of the revolt for the application of Jewish law in everyday life.

The people were ruled by an Edomite king who may have been regarded as Jewish by some but whose whole actions showed that Judaism and behaviour according to Jewish law were very far from his thoughts.

By this time the social laws and social system of the Torah were apparently not being applied and kept as a comprehensive whole. What remained was a shell of warm religious observance of ceremonial procedures which establishment orientated scholars argued about and concentrated attention on to while sidestepping the core of the belief.

Notes

<1> Pentateuch. The five books of Moses, namely Genesis, Exodus, Leviticus, Numbers and Deuteronomy. Also called Torah. Part of Old Testament.

<2> See section on 'Early Christians'.

<3> See Appendix 1, 'Ten Commandments'.

<4> The text used is both that of the Revised Standard Version (RSV) of 1952 and of 1971, as well as King James' Version (KJV). There are important differences between different texts and editions. For example (Romans 13, 9):

RSV 1971	KJV
The commandments,	For this,
"You shall not commit adultery,	Thou shalt not commit adultery,

kill,	kill,
steal,	steal,
	bear false
	witness,
covet,"	covet;
and any other	and if (there be) any
commandment,	other commandment
are summed up in	it is briefly
this sentence,	comprehended in
	this saying, namely
"You shall love your	Thou shalt love thy
neighbour as	neighbour as
yourself"	thyself.

<5>   See section on 'Romans'

<6>   See section on 'Paul'

<7>   For a more detailed, generation by generation, account of events see Appendix 2 'Maccabean Dynasty (The Hasmoneans)'.

<8>   When I refer to the 'Torah', then I am always referring to the five books of Moses, that is, to the Pentateuch.

<9>   Simeon was the third of the Maccabean brothers to head the uprising against the Seleucids and was appointed both high priest, ethnarch (ruler) and commander of the Jewish people by the 'Great Assembly'. These were hereditary appointments.

<10> Much more information is given by the authors, with detailed references to the work of others which is quoted or taken into account.

<11> 'Contrary to the assumptions of later tradition, it ('Nazorean' or 'Nazarene') has nothing whatever to do with Jesus' alleged upbringing in Nazareth, which, the evidence (or lack of it) suggests, did not even exist at the time.' {27}

References

Pentateuch

{ 1}   Exod **32**, 16

{ 2}   Deut **5**, 6-18; Exod **20**, 2-14

{ 3}   Deut **17**, 14-20

New Testament

{ 4}   Romans **4**, 15

{ 5}   Romans **13**, 1-10

{ 6}   Romans **13**, 8-9

{ 7}   Romans **13**, 9

{ 8}   Matt **19**, 16-30

{ 9}   Matt **20**, 1-16

{10}   Mark **10**, 17-31

{11}   Luke **13**, 30

{12}   Luke **18**, 18-30

Freedom Now, Freedom for Ever

{13}   In 'Judaism: Basis - Past - Present - Future, Part 1'
        Manfred Davidmann
        ISBN 978-0-85192-060-3
        see chapter 2.1: 'Struggle for Freedom:
        The Social Cause-and-Effect Relationship'

{14}   In 'Judaism: Basis - Past - Present - Future, Part 1'
        Manfred Davidmann
        ISBN 978-0-85192-060-3
        see chapter 2.2: 'History Speaks: Monarchy,
        Exile and Maccabees'

{15}   In 'Judaism: Basis - Past - Present - Future, Part 1'
         Manfred Davidmann
         ISBN 978-0-85192-060-3
         see chapter 2.3: 'At the Time of Jesus,
         This is What Actually Happened in Israel:
         The Truth about Hillel and his Times'

{16}   In 'Judaism: Basis - Past - Present - Future, Part 1'
         Manfred Davidmann
         ISBN 978-0-85192-060-3
         see chapter 2.4: 'One Law for All: Freedom Now,
         Freedom for Ever'

{17}   See {13}, Appendix 4, p34

{18}   See {15}, pp 6, 13, 25

{19}   See {15}, p16

{20}   See {15}, p32 (Talmud, Shab 31a)

{21}   See {15}, p34

{22}   See {15}, p35 (Talmud, San 96b)

{23}   See {16}, p32 (Talmud, Aboth 2, 8-14)

Liberation Theology

{24}   See chapter 2:
         'Liberation Theology: Basis – Past – Present – Future'
         Manfred Davidmann

{25}   See {24}, p7

{26}   See {24}, p9

Dead Sea Scrolls

{27}   The Dead Sea Scrolls Deception <10>
         Michael Baigent and Richard Leigh
         Jonathan Cape, London, 1991
         ISBN 0-224-02761-1

{28}   The Essene Odyssey
         Hugh Schonfield
         Element Books, 1984

Press Notice

Jesus Taught ... (Censored!).
A Report by Manfred Davidmann Explores What Jesus Actually Taught.   (Dallas News)

In his report 'Origin of Christianity and Judaism', Manfred Davidmann proves that the Christian Canon and the Jewish Talmud, which were contemporaneously written, agreed and finalised, independently record the same confrontations and struggle and sequence of events.

The agreement between Christian and Jewish writings is so complete that, as a result of Manfred Davidmann's work, we are now reasonably certain about the main course of events. For the first time we can now see the whole pattern.

The social laws of the Pentateuch have to be followed. These laws ensure equality, social justice and security, and a good life for all members of the community. They protect people from exploitation, oppression and enslavement through need.

The Jewish people had undertaken to live accordingly, to apply these laws in their daily lives. But their own rulers had negated the application of these rules of behaviour and oppression and exploitation of the people followed.

Manfred Davidmann proves what Jesus really taught. Jesus taught that all the God-given Pentateuch's laws had to be kept, that belief and practice had to include them. Early Christians, being mostly Jews, followed his teachings.

And we see how the Christian establishment of that time then in effect negated the application of these benevolent rules of behaviour. The Christian establishment's version became accepted and the people were once again exposed to oppression and exploitation.

Manfred Davidmann shows, from Christian and Jewish texts of that time, how the essential social laws of the Pentateuch (Torah) were bypassed and ceased to be observed, in Christianity and in Judaism.

He describes and proves how Paul changed what Jesus had taught, how Paul's ideology serves the establishment instead of the people, and how this became Christianity's official doctrine.

Outstanding are the sections on Paul and the Gospels: Manfred Davidmann shows that Paul's ideology was first opposed and that successive gospel writers then changed the record in Paul's favour, and how they did it.

The Jewish Talmud (especially its oldest part, the Mishnah) records how Judaism was changed in the same way, to what it is today.

In the Talmud, Jews did not openly write about Christian activists, Christian beliefs and Christians.

Where Pentateuch and Talmud contain hidden information, then this is pointed to, stated and confirmed, in a number of different independent ways. This was done to ensure the message would be understood as it was intended to be understood.

The report details two fascinating examples of such coded statements, about the beliefs of the early Christians, and about Judaism's 'Paul', convincingly making specific points which would have been unacceptable to the religious establishment at that time, if they had been openly stated.

> See chapter 3:
> 'Origin of Christianity and Judaism:
> What Actually Happened,
> What Jesus Actually Taught and Later Changes'
> Manfred Davidmann

Chapter 4

The God-given Human Rights, Social Laws and Social System

Introduction

This report is a comprehensive statement of the God-given human rights which underlie all human freedom, liberty and independence, and which underlie and determine a good life of high quality. People at all stages of development are struggling to achieve these rights and benefits, all over the planet.

Directly relevant to today's social and economic problems, these rights and obligations determine the quality of life in areas such as social and economic security, social responsibility and accountability, ownership and decision-making, government and management, humane behaviour, teamwork and trustful cooperation.

These human rights, these social rules and this social system, are the very foundation of the three main religions of Judaism, Christianity and Islam.

When the Pentateuch <1> was written, people had but little knowledge about science or evolution compared with what is known today. So concepts for which we now have precise terms were described rather than stated. Instead of the term 'scientific law' being used, for example, we see described that 'what is written applies to all people, present or absent, past or future, will happen regardless of how one feels about it, that the results of certain actions are reversed if the actions are reversed'. <2>

And concepts and descriptions were expressed in religious terms so that they could be understood and followed by the population.

What these religions have in common is that in each case a ruling elite succeeded in bypassing or overturning the religion's essential God-given benevolent social provisions and human rights {1, 2, 14-15, 6-9}, in this way exposing their communities and whole populations to oppression and exploitation.

Now that our technological progress so vastly exceeds our social organisation and behaviour, the survival of our species is in doubt. Hence the urgency of the need to apply these rules of behaviour in our daily lives. Here the aim is to show what needs to be done and how it can be achieved.

What Manfred Davidmann has done with his works on the Pentateuch and the Bible, on religion and church-state relations, is to expose and correct the misinterpretations and mistranslations of the past. His works are major breakthroughs, constituting essential information for understanding the meaning and significance of the Pentateuch and the Bible.

In his "Meaning and Significance of the Names of God in Genesis" {1}*, Manfred Davidmann proved the meaning and significance of the different names of God which had been lost. In "Meaning and Intent of

91

Genesis: Essential Notes on Hebrew Grammar" {2}*, he stated the fundamental rules which were ignored at time of translation because required background knowledge was not available, with consequent mistranslations. And in "Bible Translations, Versions, Codes and Hidden Information in Bible and Talmud" {3}*, he showed how changes made in the past obscured the intended meaning.

Further, the Pentateuch records and details the Social Cause-and-Effect Relationship, a fundamental scientific law which is stated as such and which was discovered there by Manfred Davidmann. This states that the consequences of keeping or not keeping the social laws are inescapable, that what happens to one is in the end the inevitable result of one's own behavior. It is stated to enable people to benefit from knowing the effects of their behavior.

Ignorance of these rules of behavior is no excuse and the relationship applies to all. History and social science confirm it, the prophets knew and understood it and predicted accordingly. Jesus confirmed it; the Koran records Prophet Mohammed repeatedly confirming the Pentateuch, referring to it both as a guide and as a warning.

Whole communities prosper or suffer as a consequence of their collective behavior. Manfred Davidmann says, "The consequences of our behavior cannot be avoided but we can change the course of events by changing our behavior."

Good and Evil and the Difference between Them   {3}

The first volume of the Pentateuch (Genesis) describes how plants and animals were formed, evolved and populated the planet. It describes how the behaviour of successive life forms changed as they evolved into human beings. {3}

Evolution had turned into a bitter struggle for the survival of the fittest, where the most fittest was the most vicious and violent. The most 'advanced' species was the species which was the most vicious. Life was brutal and dominated by evil. This is how reptiles came to dominate the earth.

Then mammals evolve from reptiles, and develop feelings of care and affection towards others. Genesis describes {3} that from them evolved a mammalian human-like life form (homo erectus) whose behaviour was more beast-like than human, without knowledge of good and evil and unable to distinguish between them.

Genesis states {3} that if there is to be further development towards good then there has to be knowledge of and understanding of good and evil and of the difference between them so that people can choose between them. And that consequently the human brain evolved from the mammalian brain.

The increased brain capacity and the evolution of the neocortex {10} enable humans (Homo sapiens) to know the difference between good and evil and human beings with their larger brains spread across the planet and replaced Homo erectus.

In this way the Pentateuch, in religious language, records {3} the evolution (creation) and behaviour of human beings who know of, can distinguish between and can choose between, good and evil.

The human brain underlies free will, enabling us to decide independently whether to do good or evil, that is what to do or not to do.

But this needs to be supplemented with the ability to think clearly, to assess and evaluate on the basis of knowledge of good and evil and of the essential need for behaving humanely, for following (doing) good instead of evil.

It is here that the relevance and importance of the Pentateuch's social laws and teachings <3> become apparent. The Pentateuch adds to mere mechanistic and chance processes the knowledge that human beings need to, and have to, behave humanely if they wish to prosper and succeed. Stating clearly what is, and is not, humane behaviour, clearly defining the difference between good (including human rights and justice) and evil, adding that human beings stand or fall by the way they behave. {12}

And it is the God-given social laws and social system of the Pentateuch which define and state human rights and behaviour which people need to follow if they wish to prosper and succeed, if they wish to have a high standard of living and a life of high quality.

Unavoidable Consequences of One's Behaviour (Social Cause-and-Effect Relationship <2> {12})

A covenant is an agreement in which each of the parties undertakes duties and obligations towards the other. And the Pentateuch records God's promise that human beings will have a good life of high quality as long as human beings fulfil their obligations under the covenant, as long as human beings follow God's laws, as long as they behave like human beings. <4>

This is also recorded in the Pentateuch as a fundamental scientific law, the Social Cause-and-Effect Relationship {12} <2>, in the language of religion. This states that the consequences of keeping or not keeping the Pentateuch's laws are inescapable, that what happens to one is in the end the inevitable result of one's own behaviour. Also clearly stated is that this is a scientific law which was defined and stated using the language of religion so that people would benefit from knowing the effects (consequences) of their behaviour. The relationship is stated in precise terms. History {2} and social science {21} confirm it.

We are told that the relationship applies to all without exception and at all times, wherever one may be, regardless of type of government, form of religion or social system or country. It applies whether you like it or not, agree or disagree.

The consequences of one's behaviour are detailed both ways, clearly and powerfully illustrating intermediate stages between the two ends of the scale, and we are told that the process is reversible: Increasingly disregarding the laws (rules of behaviour) results in greater suffering and oppression, increasingly behaving according to the laws results in greater freedom, liberty, independence and a better life.

The relationship applies to all. Ignorance is no excuse, not knowing the law does not prevent consequences of one's behaviour, and the relationship is stated in a way which enables people to benefit from knowing the effects of their behaviour, even if they do not understand the underlying relationship.

The relationship is clearly stated in the Pentateuch {12}, confirmed by Jesus {1} and then by Mohammed. The Koran records Mohammed repeatedly confirming the Pentateuch, referring to it both as a guide and as a warning {9}, and Arab and Muslim history illustrates the working of the cause-and-effect relationship.

Freedom and independence of mind and person and the quality of life depend on one's behaviour. The consequences of one's behaviour are inevitable, inescapable. Keeping or disregarding the Pentateuch laws has consequences which cannot be avoided. Whole communities prosper or suffer (are 'persecuted') as a consequence of their individual and thus collective behaviour.

Those who behave according to the law have good and satisfying lives, gain social and military strength. Behaviour which is contrary to the law lowers the quality of life, increases internal stress and conflict to the point of social disruption and military weakness.

If we want freedom, independence, good life of high quality, then we have to follow these laws. If we do not, then we lose freedom, independence, good life and the country in which we live. The consequences of our behaviour cannot be avoided but we can change the course of events by changing our behaviour.

Planet-wide Danger

By the end of the twentieth century a new factor had entered the equation. {21}

Up to now when some people suffered, when a village was wiped out in a war fought for the benefit of another establishment, when a whole country and its people were devastated, it did not mean the end of humanity. The point is that as a result of the impact of technology and increasing speed of transport and communication it is possible for the first time in the history of human beings on this planet for just one or only a very few socially irresponsible persons to do something or to introduce changes which could destroy us all as human beings or else make this planet uninhabitable for human beings.

I showed twenty years ago in 'Social Responsibility, Profits and Social Accountability' {21} that we were experiencing a sequence of accidents and catastrophes which were occurring more and more frequently and were affecting more and more people.

Since then most people have become aware of this. But I also showed what could and should be done about this trend of events.

So now we do not have a choice. If we do not now observe and put into effect the social laws (rules) and social system of the Pentateuch and its code of behaviour then the planet will become uninhabitable for human beings.

Humane Behaviour

Trustful Co-operation (Ten Commandments)

The Ten Commandments <5> are so important and are so well known because it is behaviour in accordance with these rules of behaviour which is the basis for people trusting each other and so for people co-operating and working well with each other. They underlie freedom, independence and strength to oppose and resist oppression. Wherever there is any independence of the mind and material freedom today it exists because people followed these rules of behaviour and it exists to the extent to which they do so. To free ourselves from mental manipulation, conditioning and brainwashing we need to follow them. {12}

In other words, following the provisions of the law results in freedom and ensures it, ensures strength and security. {17}

Take these two commandments (principles of behaviour):
>You must not steal.
>You must not desire anything which belongs to your neighbour.

Much trust and community friendliness is gained when people follow these principles.

But look around you. These principles are at times applied ruthlessly to protect the possessions of the rich from the starving poor who see no other way to survive apart from stealing some scraps of food.

I may be overstating the case so as to make a point. But consider that these laws apply equally to the rich and powerful. It is also the rich and powerful who must not steal from the poor even the little which the poor have. It is the rich and powerful who must not cast longing glances at what little the rest of us possess, it is the rich and powerful who must not aim to gain at our expense.

And now consider this {24}:

>Shareholders would not even consider handing their moneys over to a corporation without in return becoming an owner of a corresponding part of the corporation, without getting a corresponding number of shares in return.

>But customers are not given a choice. Corporations (their owners) simply take their customers' moneys
>>(a) for getting back money already spent on the business and
>>(b) for expanding the business
>without in return giving customers (or the community) corresponding ownership rights.

>To 'rob' is to take unlawfully. But we are here looking at moneys being taken legally and largely without the owners' (customers') knowledge or agreement.

>What is taking place is perhaps best described as 'legalised robbery'.

>What we see is a people divided against each other, conflict and struggle.

We are resisting oppression and exploitation and building a better world for ourselves and our children. Our strength depends on co-operation between men and women, on the family, on developing our human potential by controlling the sexual urge, on being able to trust each other and rely on each other. Consider these commandments {12}:

> You must not commit murder.
> You must not bear false witness against your neighbour.
> You must not commit adultery.

People who behave promiscuously (permissively) have sexual relations before marriage, or after marriage with a person other than their spouse. Promiscuity turns men against women, and women against men, and robs both of the support of their family {13, 16}. Hence this prohibition of promiscuous behaviour. <6>

Another commandment <5> is

> Honour your father and your mother and willingly accept the stated principles of behaviour, and the tradition, knowledge and life experience of your parents so that you will progress and advance in understanding and in life and so that you will have long and secure lives of high quality in the land in which you live.

In other words, when your parents believe in the principles stated here, and apply them in their daily lives, then one must learn and respect these teachings. One must not be led astray, no matter how plausible the persuading voices or images in one's social environment seem to be. In one's impressionable years one must not be led astray from the principles of behaviour stated here as these principles underlie freedom and independence and a good and secure life of high quality.

Morality (Men and Women, Family and Family Purity) {16}

Genesis <7> shows human beings becoming aware of the existence of good and evil and of the difference between them, shows human beings learning to choose that which is good and gaining social strength and good lives of high quality as a result. It is about human beings struggling to stop behaving like our beastlike primitive ancestors and instead doing what is good, learning to behave like human beings, to behave humanely.

And underlying humane behaviour is the need, the necessity, to control and overcome the brutalising influences we are struggling against, to control the sex impulse, so as to achieve good lives of high quality.

And what we have in the Pentateuch are rules of behaviour which point to the essence of humane behaviour. We know that ignoring them results in social corruption, oppression and exploitation of the many by the few. And we know that following these rules ensures social strength and a good life for all. {12}

97

Normal for human beings is an exclusive sexual relationship between husband and wife within a monogamous single life-long relationship (family) which ensures the young are protected for the many years before they reach maturity, and which protects and supports husband and wife as they grow old. On marriage the male accepts responsibility for the resulting family for life. {3, 13}

> For a comprehensive review of the role of the family and of a family's members, of the impact of casual sexual relations on individuals, family and community, on the effect of increasing lifespans, on dominance, oppression and exploitation within and without the family, on teamwork within the family, on the effects of promiscuous behaviour on social strength of individuals and communities, see {13}.

Those who behave humanely, morally, can trust each other, cooperate with each other, grow, gain strength together, prosper.

All other sexual relations are abnormal and we are told {16} the effects (consequences) of inhuman beastlike (unrestrained, uncontrolled) sexual behaviour.

Those who behave immorally weaken their family and social strength. Those who initiate moral behaviour, who behave morally and humanely, gain strength and standing, and those who support them in this are supported in return. Confirmed by history {12, 2}, we see it taking place all around us.

And sexual relations outside marriage are prohibited before and during marriage.

A clear way of stating
> the importance of chastity,
> that human beings can and do control their sexual urges,
> the importance and necessity for the human male to control the beastlike sexual urge lurking at the border of the conscious.

Sodomy, having sexual relations between persons of the same sex, is unnatural and abnormal, corrupting and destructive of human society and humane behaviour, is punished with utmost severity.

And incest, having sexual relations between members of a close or extended family, is abnormal, corrupting and destructive of family trust, family life and family strength. Incest is primitive beastlike behaviour and perpetrators are punished with utmost severity.

The Pentateuch contains detailed statements about what constitutes abnormal, promiscuous, adulterous sexual relations and prostitution, with associated comments and severe penalties. <8>

Morality and family, individual and social strength, are interrelated. Morality more than any other factor determines the strength and well-being of individuals, families and communities. So morality is of determining importance and these laws of behaviour need to be protected, applied and enforced.

Social and Moral Problems of Our Times

The consequences of immorality cannot be avoided. {12} <2>

The Pentateuch's warnings, punishments and penalties concerning morality are in most cases to the male. It is males who are behind the corrupting of family morality and who are attempting to brutalise women so as to make women more readily available for sex. Even brainwashing and manipulating women into making themselves available. With consequent weakening and breaking up of family, society and quality of life. {13}

Conditioning, persuading, inducing or compelling a person to have sex before marriage, person to person or through the media, is in my opinion an act of rape. The younger the person, the worse is the offence.

Morality has to be protected by punishing immorality, by protecting women and punishing men and women who behave immorally. By punishing those who spread immorality and seduce others into immoral behaviour.

In democracies or when people are struggling for their liberty, authoritarians condone and promote promiscuity so as to weaken the family and weaken the population. People are subjected to conditioning towards immorality to weaken the working population to make them easier to exploit, to weaken the society and democracy. <9>

But when in control, dictatorships of left or right or religious absolutist hierarchies then pedal back to gain strength for their people, so that they will fight for and protect, and slave for, their manipulating rulers. <10>

Hence the importance of morality, of Pentateuch morality and laws of behaviour, of protecting communities and people by restraining immoral behaviour, conditioning and propaganda, by appropriately punishing the perpetrators.

Social Strength

The Pentateuch states what has to be done and what is prohibited, by positive and negative rules of behaviour. {2}

Positive rules state what has to be done so as to create a just and strong society. And point the way ahead towards greater strength, freedom, liberty and a good way of life.

Negative rules (prohibitions) state what must not be done and such rules protect the people from oppression and exploitation, from the antisocial behaviour of others, safeguard the people's strength and freedom.

But support and co-operation have to be two-way flows. The community supports the individual but only if the individual supports the community. Those supported by the community are under obligation to support others in need of support, when able to do so, to share with others who are in need. Where 'need' includes the need for capital to secure their operation, to achieve the general standard of living and quality of life.

Which means that benefits and support from the community are given only to those who believe in its benevolent principles and live accordingly. 'Supporting the community' includes helping to spread knowledge and understanding of its principles. <11>

Throughout, it is only those who themselves keep and apply the benevolent social laws given in this report in their daily lives who are entitled to these rights. Otherwise, to give but one example, funds provided by the community free-of-interest to a non-member (stranger) might be used by the stranger to exploit people by lending funds to others and charging interest so as to enrich himself.

Social and Economic Security

All persons have the right to be free and independent masters of their own fate and no person may oppress or exploit another. Because people can be exploited through their needs there has to be a system of social and economic security which guarantees freedom from needs and so protects people from becoming dependent on others for essential income, protects against loss of material independence and which protects them from losing their spiritual independence.

Every community member is entitled as a matter of right to social security <12>. This means that community members are entitled to be supported by the community not only when they fall on hard times but also to maintain their independence as independent breadwinners for their families. For example, the community has to provide backup funds to those who need them and they have to be provided as and when required.

To prevent people being exploited through their need these funds have to be provided without charging interest. They are called 'loans' because the recipient is under moral obligation to repay them to the community if he can do so. However, such 'loans' are cancelled every seventh calendar year if the borrower has been unable to repay them. <11>

These essential social provisions of the Pentateuch are clear and to the point. This is what is laid down as a matter of law {12}:

1. The community has to provide ('lend') money to those who need it, free of interest.
2. All such loans, if outstanding, are to be cancelled every seventh year.

Work and Leisure

Weekly Day of Rest

Every seventh day is a day of rest for all, for those who are employed as well as for those who employ. Work stops on the weekly day of rest, the Sabbath, to let those who labour have a regular day of rest. On this day the servant is as free as the master, the worker is as free as the employer. The weekly day of rest has spread and benefits almost all the civilised world. {12} <11>

Sabbatical Year

Community members are entitled to a sabbatical year every seventh year. During this year they are entitled to be freed from work at the expense of the community. <13> {12}

Academics already enjoy regular sabbatical years. During this period they are paid their salaries. {19}

Free to travel, train for more skilled or better work, update knowledge, study, gain greater understanding, qualify. Those on a sabbatical must not work for pay, or produce to sell, during that year but receive the average rate earned by community members during the previous calendar year. <11>

Consider what sabbatical years would mean. For you and for others who would during such a year be free to do as they pleased. We could have much more satisfying lives, we could do much for our own communities, could do much for those in need, for those who are underdeveloped and unable to afford our own expert skills. {19} <14>

Freedom, Liberty and Independence

The words freedom, liberty and independence are usually given subtly different meanings, as follows:

Freedom	The right and power to act, speak, or think freely.
Liberty	The state of being free from oppression or imprisonment.
Independence	Self governing and not depending on another for livelihood or subsistence.

Freedom, liberty and independence go hand-in-hand, support and complement each other. Liberty includes being free from slavery or despotic control by others, means being free from social, economic, political, mental or physical control by others, means being free from antisocial control or manipulation by others. And independence includes not being dependent on, and not being controlled by, another person, group, organisation, or thing.

But it is the social rules and social system of the Pentateuch which in effect state that all are equal, that no person may exploit another or oppress so as to exploit. All have the right to be free and independent masters of their own fate and there has to be a system of social security which guarantees not just freedom from need but also protection against loss of material and spiritual independence.

Government and Management

Here we are looking at the laws of the Pentateuch which control the behaviour and limit the power {12, 2} of government, of top executives and of the establishment, of those in positions of trust, responsibility or authority. The Pentateuch {11} leaves little doubt about what they must not do.

We saw already that

> Positive laws state what has to be done so as to create a just and strong society. And point the way ahead towards greater strength, freedom, liberty and a good way of life.

> Negative laws (prohibitions) state what must not be done and such laws protect the people from oppression and exploitation, from the antisocial behaviour of others, safeguard the people's strength and freedom.

And so the laws quoted here protect people, safeguard their strength and freedom, and need to be applied.

These laws of government relate to 'rulers', apply to all in positions of trust, responsibility or authority, no matter whether secular, religious or military, no matter what the hierarchy or organisation.

Such people may not amass servants and may not oppress the people for their own benefit. They may not amass possessions and wealth, may not grasp power or behave promiscuously.

In other words, they may not put themselves above others by grasping power, may not satisfy personal desires at the expense of others.

And a ruler (person in position of trust, responsibility or authority) has to follow these laws and abide by them every day if he wishes 'to prolong his days in his kingdom, he and his children'. For 'kingdom' read 'position' and include 'influence'.

So the Pentateuch laws quoted here protect people and safeguard their strength and freedom by laying down that those in positions of trust, responsibility or authority may not grasp power, may not oppress the people, may not behave promiscuously, may not enrich themselves. Those in authority must not oppress people so as to increase their own possessions and power, must not form enforcing squads or organisations so as to multiply their own power, must not behave promiscuously, must not gain wives or wealth. {12}

Equality and Ownership

Ownership {24} is the right to possess something and to decide what is to be done with it. If I own something it belongs to me and I decide what is to be done with it. An example would be owning a house.

Possession is having something in one's custody as distinct from owning it. If I possess something it belongs to another but I can decide how to use it. An example would be renting a house.

Another example would be deciding what to do with my money (ownership) or deciding and controlling the use of money belonging to someone else (possession).

And considering the right to ownership, two questions need to be considered. Namely where does the right come from and how is it exercised.

The right to own property varies among societies. Ownership laws which assign ownership 'rights' to owners have been devised by the owners themselves or by those who serve them. {20}

Ownership of land and means of production, of funds and wealth, has always been accumulated at someone else's expense. All belonged to the community, belonged to all alike. And this is what Chapter 5 of Genesis appears to be saying {18}.

A human right is a something one may legally or morally claim, is the state of being entitled to a privilege or immunity or authority to act. Human rights are those held to be claimable by any living person, apply to all living people. Every living person is entitled to them.

So ownership of land and means of production, of funds and wealth, rightfully belongs to the community, belongs to all alike, is a human right. Those who have accumulated them have only possession, which means they can use and apply them but may do so only on behalf of, and for the benefit of, the community and that they are accountable to the community for the way in which they do so. {19}

Hence we have the use of possessions as long as we use them to provide a good living for our family, and beyond that for the benefit of the community. For the benefit of others less able or fortunate, for the benefit of the community around us and then for the benefit of communities abroad.

But we may only support those who themselves genuinely support our benevolent ideals and principles and their application and who themselves live and act accordingly, who behave humanely. {12} <15>

A maximum differential of two, the maximum gross earnings being twice the minimum earnings, within a country and also between countries, would seem a reasonable target to achieve under present more extreme circumstances. {19}

Bearing this in mind, the country's wealth, and this includes productive assets and capital, including land, enterprise and corporation ownership, property, bank deposits and reserves, belongs equally to all community members and needs to be shared out <16>.

To be shared out family by family {12}, where 'family' is a life-long single union {13} between husband and wife. With shares updated at regular intervals of between three and not more than five calendar years <17>. Each receives a share of the community's total net assets <18>, their 'Asset Share'. An Asset Share cannot be sold but the owner has the right to determine its use and to the resulting benefits.

The Worldwide Struggle for God-given Human Rights {17, 13}

Freedom, Liberty and Independence {17}

Humane behaviour is aimed at survival of the young and of the family, and then is for the good of one's family, other people and the community. It is based on feelings of care and affection for others. From this emerges a sense of social responsibility: people matter and are important, need to be treated well and looked after, are entitled to share equally. Backed up by knowledge, understanding and reason. {10}

We know that dominating others is conditioned, that is unnatural, behaviour which is destructive of humane behaviour. A throw-back to the level of the unthinking unfeeling primitive animal. {10}

Genesis says much in chapters 5 and 6. About inhuman behaviour, about possessions, ownership and riches, about domineering, oppression and misusing people by force.

And knowledge of good and evil enables us to choose that which is good (humane) and to overcome that which is inhumane (beast-like, evil).

These themes are continued in Genesis and in the other four volumes (books) of the Pentateuch. We are told about the obligatory social laws and social system which have to be kept if evil is to be overcome, are told about consequent reward and punishment, justice and retribution, so that human beings can have good lives of high quality.

Those who follow and keep the benevolent social laws of the Pentateuch have in the past been opposed by dictatorships of both right and left, by those who wish to establish and support such dictatorships, by those who wish to oppress so as to exploit people. Openly under dictatorship and in more hidden ways under other forms of government.

Dictatorships both of the left and of the right, or those who approve or condone such systems, have also attempted to discredit and wipe out from human memory that which God's prophets teach us, namely the social laws and social system of the Pentateuch. {1, 2, 4, 5}

What we see in the working environment is a worldwide struggle to achieve a humane way of life, each person, family or community struggling to advance at their own level of development, struggling against those who wish to dominate, exploit, oppress. A struggle whose successful outcome depends on trustful cooperation, companionship and teamwork. {13, 23, 22}

The struggle is against those who wish to dominate other people. Against those who want primitive power over others, against those who wish to exploit, against those who may brutally and without feeling oppress human beings so as to exploit them. And 'to exploit' includes the whole range of antisocial decisions and activities of those who put profit before people and community. {21}

Human rights are based on controlling primitive dominant behaviour, on concern, care and affection for our young, for our families, people and communities, and express themselves in cooperation and teamwork between men and women to achieve a good life of high quality.

Defence {13}

Sometimes one has to fight to preserve a good way of life, to prevent others from taking what has been achieved. Or one may be expected to fight on behalf of those who dominate and exploit.

Our primitive animal ancestors behaved instinctively. Hunt for food, kill or be killed, fight or flee. Self before others, regardless of needs of others, marking out and defending territory, might being right.

Later mammals tend to have feelings, care and affection for their young. Human beings think as well as feel, and care for and look after their young for many years.

Having to fight, maim and kill amounts to a throwback to primitive animal behaviour, to behaviour which puts self before others. A throwback to beast-like behaviour for those who attack, to beast-like behaviour to counter beast-like behaviour for those who defend.

But one way of countering viciousness is by greater strength. If attacked, we have to defend ourselves.

Authoritarian organisations are much less effective than participative ones. In authoritarian organisations morale is low, people cease to care and tend to work against each other instead of cooperating with each other for the benefit of the organisation. {25-26}

Human beings cooperate well and achieve effective teamwork. Reason and evaluation can temper (add to, or change) emotional and instinct-motivated behaviour and combine with cooperation and teamwork so as to counter, and overcome, threats.

One has to be stronger than the enemy, socially as well as militarily. Essential is greater social as well as military strength. But the authoritarian mind (which includes the military) has to be balanced to prevent it from taking over, has to be motivated towards 'good'.

So we must not allow ourselves to be corrupted by what has to be done when fighting to preserve and secure that which is good, our way of life. Those who fight on our communities' behalf need to know, believe in, and practice, the word of God every day of their lives.

Responsibility and Accountability

Human beings found an effective defence against antisocial manipulations, namely the basic principle that we are responsible and accountable for what we do and how we do it. Obeying an order is no excuse. It does not matter whether the order comes from a secular or religious source or whether it pops up in one's mind. The person taking the decision, the person giving the order, the person carrying out the order, are each responsible for what they do or omit to do, and for the consequences.

Conclusion

So what one aims to achieve is

> to apply in our lives, and in the communities in which we live, the God-given benevolent social laws and social system of the Pentateuch,
>
> so as to achieve a good and secure life of high quality,
>
> by working for the benefit of the community, and
>
> by taking part in the struggle for a better life.

And we need to co-operate with each other as individuals, families and communities, supporting each other in this common struggle for a better life.

It appears that hurt and pain, oppression and exploitation, suffering and hardship, can and should be transformed and countered by an applied sense of social responsibility, by a sense of common purpose and cooperation between people working together in teams. That is by a sense of, and by the satisfaction of, achievement in locating, countering and overcoming the source of the suffering.

Colloquially speaking, there is enough food here for everyone. Pick your ground, pick whichever you think is most important and then use your knowledge, abilities and skills to achieve the good way of life portrayed in this report.

Your life is likely to be a much more rewarding life of higher quality.

Notes <..>

< 1> Also known as the 'Five Books of Moses' and as 'Torah'.

< 2> In {12} see section on 'The Social Cause-and-Effect Relationship'.

The Social Cause-and-Effect Relationship is also listed (in biblical language and in plain English) in Appendix 4 of {12}, with references to the Pentateuch text.

< 3> The Pentateuch (Five Books of Moses, at times called 'Torah') consists only of the five books of Moses.

Those wishing to give other writings an appearance of greater authority refer to these other writings as if they were part of 'Torah'. Those doing so appear to be spreading a kind of misleading political propaganda.

< 4> In {18} see 'Behaviour and Consequences (Genesis Chapter 9)'

< 5> For a full listing of the Ten Commandments, in biblical and plain English, see Appendix 5 of {12}. For a good discussion of its provisions see {12}.

< 6>   Normal for human beings is an exclusive sexual relationship between a husband and a wife who joined together to form a life-long family so as to ensure that their children are protected for the many years before they reach maturity. And the family protects and supports husband and wife as they grow old. {3, 13}

People who behave humanely, morally, can trust each other, co-operate with each other, grow, gain strength together, prosper.

All other sexual relations are abnormal, immoral. Those who behave immorally weaken their family and social strength. Those who initiate moral behaviour, who behave morally and humanely, gain strength and standing. {16}

Hence the
          importance of chastity,
          of human beings controlling their sexual urges,
          and for the human male to control the sexual urge lurking at
          the border of the conscious.

And on marriage the male accepts responsibility for the resulting family for life. {13}

< 7>   First volume of the Pentateuch (Five Books of Moses).

< 8>   Largely in Leviticus.

< 9>   See {13}

<10>   See {17}

<11>   For more information about, and other listings of, the Pentateuch's social rules of behaviour and about its social system, see {12, 17, 16, 4}

<12>   Social security also includes provision covering unemployment, ill health and old age, provided cooperatively {19}. <19>

<13>   At present people would take their sabbatical
        year in turn, one-seventh of the community in
        any one year, including one-seventh from each of
        the different occupations.

<14>   It must be up to the individual to select and
        choose what he wants to do. Sabbaticals are not
        an opportunity for the government, the state, a
        political party, a religious hierarchy or the
        management of an organisation to direct or train
        its employees, to condition through some kind of
        educational scheme, to pressurise one way or
        another. {19}

<15>   In {18} see 'Social Laws, Social System'

<16>   Companies and corporations present annual
        accounts to their shareholders including Funds
        Flow statements. Community accounts should be
        made available also in form of a 'Funds Flow'
        statement, as these can show clearly in
        meaningful terms where the funds have come
        from and what has been done with them. In terms
        such as 'Received from Income Tax', 'Received
        from Corporation Tax', 'Spent on Unemployment
        Benefit', 'Spent on Payments to Corporations', and
        so on.

<17>   At the time the Pentateuch was written, the
        sharing out of assets was to be updated after
        every 49 years. At present, updating at regular
        intervals of between three and not more than
        five calendar years is more appropriate.

<18>   'Net assets' is the amount of money which would
        be left for distributing among the owners if
        everything belonging to an enterprise were sold
        and all its debts paid.

<19>   The level of support (such as what proportion of
        the community's income is to be spent on health
        care) needs to be decided by the population, for
        example by referendum on basis of valid clearly-
        stated information compiled by concerned
        community groups.

References {..}

{ 1} See chapter 3:
'Origin of Christianity and Judaism:
What Actually Happened,
What Jesus Actually Taught and Later Changes'
Manfred Davidmann

{ 2} In 'Judaism: Basis – Past – Present – Future, Part 1'
Manfred Davidmann
ISBN 978-0-85192-060-3
see chapter 2.2: 'History Speaks:
Monarchy, Exile and Maccabees'

{ 3} In 'God and People:
The Social Laws and Social System Underlying
Judaism, Christianity, Islam and Democracy'
Manfred Davidmann
ISBN 978-0-85192-054-2
see chapter 6.1: 'The Meaning of Genesis:
Creation, Evolution and the Origin of Evil'

{ 4} In 'Judaism: Basis – Past – Present – Future, Part 1'
Manfred Davidmann
ISBN 978-0-85192-060-3
see chapter 4: 'Causes of Antisemitism'

{ 5} In 'Islam: Basis – Past – Present – Future'
Manfred Davidmann
ISBN 978-0-85192-053-5
see chapter 2: 'Prophet Mohammed's
Struggle for a Better Life for All'

{ 6} In 'Islam: Basis – Past – Present – Future'
Manfred Davidmann
ISBN 978-0-85192-053-5
see chapter 4: 'The Divine Right to Rule'

{ 7} In 'Islam: Basis – Past – Present – Future'
Manfred Davidmann
ISBN 978-0-85192-053-5
see chapter 5: 'Compiling the Koran: Hadiths
(Traditions) State the Underlying Reality'

{ 8}   In 'Islam: Basis – Past – Present – Future'
Manfred Davidmann
ISBN 978-0-85192-053-5
see chapter 6: 'Uthman's Rearrangement of the
Chronological (as revealed) Koran's Chapters'

{ 9}   In 'Islam: Basis – Past – Present – Future'
Manfred Davidmann
ISBN 978-0-85192-053-5
see chapter 7: 'Prophet Mohammed's Word of
Allah and the Voice of the Ruling Elite'

{10}   In 'The Human Mind and How it Works:
Group Minds in Action:
How the Human Group Mind Shapes
the Quality of Our Life and Living'
Manfred Davidmann
ISBN 978-0-85192-055-9
see chapter 2: 'How the Human Brain
Developed and How the Human Mind Works'

{11}   Pentateuch, Deuteronomy 17: 14-20

{12}   In 'Judaism: Basis – Past – Present – Future, Part 1'
Manfred Davidmann
ISBN 978-0-85192-060-3
see chapter 2.1 : 'Struggle for Freedom:
The Social Cause-and-Effect Relationship'

{13}   See chapter 5:
'Family, Community, Sex and the Individual'
Manfred Davidmann

{14}   In 'Judaism: Basis – Past – Present – Future, Part 1'
Manfred Davidmann
ISBN 978-0-85192-060-3
see chapter 2.3: 'At the Time of Jesus,
This is What Actually Happened in Israel:
The Truth about Hillel and his Times'

{15}   In 'Judaism: Basis – Past – Present – Future, Part 1'
Manfred Davidmann
ISBN 978-0-85192-060-3
see chapter 2.4: 'One Law for All: Freedom Now,
Freedom for Ever'

{16}   In 'God and People:
        The Social Laws and Social System Underlying
        Judaism, Christianity, Islam and Democracy'
        Manfred Davidmann
        ISBN 978-0-85192-054-2
        see chapter 6.3: 'The Meaning of Genesis:
        Morality, Sexual Behaviour and Depravity'

{17}   In 'God and People:
        The Social Laws and Social System Underlying
        Judaism, Christianity, Islam and Democracy'
        Manfred Davidmann
        ISBN 978-0-85192-054-2
        see chapter 6.4: 'The Meaning of Genesis:
        Nephilim, Dominance and Liberty'

{18}   In 'God and People:
        The Social Laws and Social System Underlying
        Judaism, Christianity, Islam and Democracy'
        Manfred Davidmann
        ISBN 978-0-85192-054-2
        see chapter 6.2: 'The Meaning of Genesis:
        Pre-flood Evils and the Social Problems of
        Our Time'

{19}   In 'Cooperatives and Cooperation:
        Causes of Failure, Guidelines for Success'
        Manfred Davidmann
        ISBN 978-0-85192-056-6
        see chapter 3: 'Causes of Failure, Guidelines for
        Success'

{20}   In 'The Real World in Which We Live:
        The Social Rules and Social System under
        Which We Suffer, Struggle, Survive and Prosper'
        Manfred Davidmann
        ISBN 978-0-85192-058-0
        see chapter 10: 'What People are Struggling
        Against: How Society is Organised for Controlling
        and Exploiting People'

{21} In 'Messianic Struggle:
      The Worldwide Struggle for a Good
      and Secure Life for All, Here and Now'
      Manfred Davidmann
      ISBN 978-0-85192-059-7
      see chapter 2: 'Social Responsibility, Profits and
      Social Accountability'

{22} In 'The Human Mind and How it Works:
      Group Minds in Action:
      How the Human Group Mind Shapes
      the Quality of Our Life and Living'
      Manfred Davidmann
      ISBN 978-0-85192-055-9
      see chapter 7: 'Motivation Summary'

{23} In 'The Real World in Which We Live:
      The Social Rules and Social System under
      Which We Suffer, Struggle, Survive and Prosper'
      Manfred Davidmann
      ISBN 978-0-85192-058-0
      see chapter 16: 'The Will to Work:
      What People Struggle to Achieve'

{24} In 'The Real World in Which We Live:
      The Social Rules and Social System under
      Which We Suffer, Struggle, Survive and Prosper'
      Manfred Davidmann
      ISBN 978-0-85192-058-0
      see chapter 12: 'Understanding How Society is
      Organised for Controlling and Exploiting People'

{25} In 'Management and Leadership:
      Local, National, Multinational (Global),
      Principles and Practice'
      Manfred Davidmann
      ISBN 978-0-85192-057-3
      see chapter 2: 'Style of Management and
      Leadership'

{26}   In 'Management and Leadership:
Local, National, Multinational (Global),
Principles and Practice'
Manfred Davidmann
ISBN 978-0-85192-057-3
see chapter 3: 'Role of Managers under
Different Styles of Management'

Additions by the Editor:

{1}*   In 'God and People:
The Social Laws and Social System Underlying
Judaism, Christianity, Islam and Democracy'
Manfred Davidmann
ISBN 978-0-85192-054-2
see chapter 6.6: 'The Meaning of Genesis:
Meaning and Significance of the Names of
God in Genesis'

{2}*   In 'God and People:
The Social Laws and Social System Underlying
Judaism, Christianity, Islam and Democracy'
Manfred Davidmann
ISBN 978-0-85192-054-2
see chapter 6.7: 'Meaning and Intent of Genesis:
Essential Notes on Hebrew Grammar'

{3}*   In 'God and People:
The Social Laws and Social System Underlying
Judaism, Christianity, Islam and Democracy'
Manfred Davidmann
ISBN 978-0-85192-054-2
see chapter 6.8: 'The Meaning of Genesis:
Bible Translations, Versions, Codes and
Hidden Information in Bible and Talmud'

Press Notice

'The God-given Human Rights, Social Laws and Social System': A Report by Manfred Davidmann.   (Los Angeles Times)

What Manfred Davidmann has done with his works on the Pentateuch and the Bible, on religion and church-state relations, is to expose and correct the misinterpretations and mistranslations of the past. His works are major breakthroughs, constituting essential information for understanding the meaning and significance of the Pentateuch and the Bible.

In his report "Meaning and Significance of the Names of God in Genesis" {1}*, Manfred Davidmann proved the meaning and significance of the different names of God which had been lost. In "Meaning and Intent of Genesis: Essential Notes on Hebrew Grammar" {2}*, he stated the fundamental rules which were ignored at time of translation because required background knowledge was not available, with consequent mistranslations. And in "Bible Translations, Versions, Codes and Hidden Information in Bible and Talmud" {3}*, he showed how changes made in the past obscured the intended meaning.

And so Manfred Davidmann's report "The God-given Human Rights, Social Laws and Social System" is a comprehensive statement of the human rights and obligations which underlie freedom, liberty, independence and well-being, and which are largely unknown or ignored.

Directly relevant to today's social and economic problems, these rights and obligations determine the quality of life in areas such as social and economic security, social responsibility and accountability, ownership and decision-making, government and management, humane behaviour, teamwork and trustful cooperation.

Further, the Pentateuch records and details the Social Cause-and-Effect Relationship, a fundamental scientific law which is stated as such and which was discovered there by Manfred Davidmann. This states that the consequences of keeping or not keeping the social laws are inescapable, that what happens to one is in the end the inevitable result of one's own behavior. It is stated to enable people to benefit from knowing the effects of their behavior.

Ignorance of these rules of behavior is no excuse and the relationship applies to all. History and social science confirm it, the prophets knew and understood it and predicted accordingly. Jesus confirmed it; the Koran records Prophet Mohammed repeatedly confirming the Pentateuch, referring to it both as a guide and as a warning.

Whole communities prosper or suffer as a consequence of their collective behavior. Manfred Davidmann says, "The consequences of our behavior cannot be avoided but we can change the course of events by changing our behavior."

He states "A new factor has entered the equation. It is now possible for the first time in the history of human beings on this planet for just one or only a few socially irresponsible persons to do something or to introduce changes which could destroy us all or else make this planet uninhabitable for human beings ..."

... and that "if we do not now observe and put into effect the social rules and social system first described in the Pentateuch, then the planet is likely to become uninhabitable for human beings."

When a scientist of Manfred Davidmann's proven track record (of achievement and objectivity) and international standing makes such a statement, this needs to be taken seriously.

> See chapter 4:
> 'The God-given Human Rights, Social Laws and Social System'
> Manfred Davidmann

Additions by the Editor:

{1}* In 'God and People:
The Social Laws and Social System Underlying
Judaism, Christianity, Islam and Democracy'
Manfred Davidmann
ISBN 978-0-85192-054-2
see chapter 6.6: 'The Meaning of Genesis:
Meaning and Significance of the Names of
God in Genesis'

{2}* In 'God and People:
The Social Laws and Social System Underlying
Judaism, Christianity, Islam and Democracy'
Manfred Davidmann
ISBN 978-0-85192-054-2
see chapter 6.7: 'Meaning and Intent of Genesis:
Essential Notes on Hebrew Grammar'

{3}*   In 'God and People:
The Social Laws and Social System Underlying
Judaism, Christianity, Islam and Democracy'
Manfred Davidmann
ISBN 978-0-85192-054-2
see chapter 6.8: 'The Meaning of Genesis:
Bible Translations, Versions, Codes and
Hidden Information in Bible and Talmud'

Chapter 5

Family, Community, Sex and the Individual

Introduction

The work, analysis and findings reported here investigate casual sex and its effects on individuals, family and community. Also investigated is dominance and confrontation within the family and in the working environment, how men and women relate to each other, and the role of the family in bringing up children.

This report examines root causes of major social problems and shows how to resolve the problems by dealing with their basic causes. The report pulls together information from earlier reports and adds some important sections. The new material deals with how sex affects the individual, with sexual restraint and control, and with the evolution and current role of the family and of its members.

In this report are statements about effects on people, or how people respond, on how people behave, and so on. In all such cases it is understood that in every case there is a range of effects or behaviour from one end of a spectrum to the other, that what applies to one does not apply to another. So while the statements made in the report apply to a whole group or population, they cannot be said to apply to all individuals or to specific individuals.

But the effects I listed in the earlier publications now appear obvious and in the USA steps are being taken to halt and reverse the increasing corruption of their communities.

Role of the Family

How Human Beings Evolved

As far as we know the human brain evolved in three main stages {12}. Its ancient and primitive part is the innermost reptilian brain. Next evolved the mammalian brain by adding new functions and new ways of controlling the body. Then evolved the third part of the brain, the neocortex, the grey matter, the bulk of the brain in two symmetrical hemispheres, separate but communicating. To a considerable extent it is our neocortex which enables us to behave like human beings. {11}

Human emotional responses depend on neuronal pathways which link the right hemisphere to the mammalian brain which in turn is linked to the even older reptilian brain.

For human beings, primitive (reptilian) instinctive urges and behaviour are overlaid by mammalian care and affection for one's young and human care and affection for one's family and community. {11}

So the human brain includes a wide range of emotions, of feelings, of care and affection, and the capability for objective and logical thinking and evaluation.

Compared with most, if not all, other animals we also have much longer lifespans and it takes a long time before a human baby becomes an adult. Born after nine months in the mother's womb, followed by 4 to 5 years as infant, then 8 to 10 years as child being educated, and say 6 to 9 years as adolescent, about 18 to 25 years old when becoming an adult and independent member of the community.

There is a whole scale of behaviour from human to the beast-like, from behaviour based on affection for the other person to, at the other end, uncontrolled behaviour such as rape, and the seduction of the young which I see as another form of rape.

Mammalian and human parts of our brain control our reptilian ancestor's instinctive copulation urges {11}. It seems as if rapists and paedophiles do not restrain and control their bottom-level beast-like instincts, and it seems to be these which urge them on.

The instinctive sex urge aims to ensure the survival of the species. We have been able to adapt and advance by a process of natural selection and a key characteristic which distinguishes human beings from animals is that we can control the sex urge.

Role of the Family

Something like 200 million years of evolution are behind us, from reptilian beast through mammalian animal to human being. Human beings are mammals and are unique in that our children need protecting and bringing up in a humane, emotionally and mentally stimulating environment for between 18 and 21 years, to enable them to mature into socially responsible adults {11}. Men and women co-operate with each other and look after each other and their children, within the family, to do just that.

So the role of the family is

> To struggle as a family to survive.
>
> To protect and support mother and children until children become mature and independent adults capable of providing for themselves.
>
> To provide a good standard of living and a life of high quality. Which includes struggling against oppression and exploitation. And sometimes one has to fight to preserve a good way of life.
>
> To serve the interests of, and to support, each member of the family. In turn, each member of the family supports the family.

Hence human beings work primarily for their family and members of a family stand by, support and help each other in times of need. The family is the basic unit of society and it looks after the interests of all its members, as individuals as well as collectively. This gives great strength to each member of the family in the struggle for daily bread, security and happiness.

Protecting and Caring for the Next Generation

There is a genetic difference between men and women. It is women who bear the child and who need protecting and looking after while bearing the child and after childbirth. There clearly are close emotional bonds between mother and child.

It is women who generally look after people, after the welfare and well-being of the members of the family. Care, concern, affection and love, feelings and emotions, are important and matter, and women developed, and have, much skill and expertise in such matters. It is generally men who struggle outside the family to secure survival and good living for the family. A struggle for survival in a seemingly hostile environment engineered by other humans.

Primarily the family exists to protect and support its young, and this means supporting and looking after the female bearing the child within her body, through birth and while she is protecting and teaching the young how to behave. It is usually the woman whose role it is to ensure the family provides the young with the humane, emotionally and mentally stimulating environment they need to enable them to mature into socially responsible adults. She is assisted in this by her spouse, depending on her needs and depending on his own work. But it is usually the woman who copes with the personal and emotional problems of the family's members and this is challenging, demanding and difficult work demanding social ability and skills as well as care, affection, understanding and concern for people.

In the kibbutzim, that is in Israel's co-operative settlements, children were brought up communally in age groups, away from their parents. One age group would progress together from creche to nursery and then to school, living together during the week and seeing their parents, or living with their parents, only at weekends.

This may have freed both parents for work and defence in the initial struggle for survival. But the practice was continued when successful, possibly to free women for work and so increase production. But it was done at the expense of the family.

Of any group in the country, the kibbutz children consequently showed the highest incidence of mental problems. The kibbutzim have had to backtrack and now give their children a more normal and strengthening family-life experience with their parents. {13}

When women are persuaded to regard work outside of the family as more important than caring for the young or the family's members, they are in effect handing over the family's key role to outsiders such as day-care businesses and television programme makers. With disastrous

122

results on the way the young perceive home life and adult behaviour, tending to condition the young into behaving like fictional and unreal role models, for example concerning sexual behaviour. Instead of gaining an adult understanding of the reality of living, of family values and relationships, instead of understanding and experiencing socially-responsible behaviour caring for and living with other people, instead of seeing adults (parents) behave in socially responsible way struggling in a hostile environment to do the best they can for the young and for each other.

The number of young people who run away from home and family, often becoming homeless, placing themselves at a big disadvantage right at the beginning of their lives, speaks for itself.

The family needs food and shelter and while the female looks after its young and its people, it is usually the male who struggles outside the immediate family to provide it with an income, with a standard of living, to the best of his ability {4, 5}. He is assisted in this when required by his spouse to an extent which depends on her own work within the family. He struggles outside the family to provide it with a good life against those who wish to profit from the family's needs, against those who wish to exploit, who may even wish to oppress so as to exploit.

Sexual Relations

Sex and the Individual

Sex is habit-forming and addictive but can be controlled when the will is there, when the individual is motivated to control it.

Young people are persuaded to have sex for the first time, are seduced, by those who crave for sex regardless of the cost to the young person being misused by being seduced. The cost to the young can be great. The earlier the age of seduction, the more ingrained is the habit, the greater the difficulties of later controlling it.

Having sex for the first time, first intercourse between adults, is a deeply emotional experience which binds people together in a strong bond of care and affection for each other. That is why 'men wish to sleep around but wish to marry virgins', or a succession of virgins if they are rich enough to afford the divorces.

Should the lovers separate, the emotional cost for the seduced is high indeed. Desperate feelings of isolation, loneliness, betrayal. Shock. Almost unbearable. Reluctance to commit oneself again.

With the next relationship there is still commitment, care and affection but more reserved, there is reluctance to commit oneself completely, to commit one's emotions completely, so as to avoid the pain of separation if this should occur again.

After repeated separations, there is little or no emotional commitment or care for the other person. Sex is casual, the individual sleeps around, attempting to gain the pleasure sex can bring. Looking for sex regardless of thought or feelings or care for the other person, regardless of the cost to the other person.

It appears to be well known that those who engage in sexual relations outside marriage find themselves looking in vain for the affection which is missing to an ever-greater extent from their relationships, become less and less able to commit themselves to the other person, mean ever less to each other.

So people who are aware of the likely consequences tend consciously to refrain from promiscuous relationships. When unaware of the consequences, people tend intuitively to put on the brake when tempted to behave promiscuously.

Effect on Behaviour and Community

Some men are persuaded into sleeping around, in turn attempting to persuade women to make themselves available for casual sex. When women were persuaded to make themselves sexually available they relaxed the control which had kept in check the primitive instinctive urge to copulate. Women had protected society by their chastity, had by their chastity compelled men to support and look after the mother (his wife) and their children while support was needed while the young were developing into adults, had protected and maintained the family and the community in this way.

Casual sex weakens and deadens feelings of care and affection for the other person, for partner or spouse, changing feelings of care and affection into a desire to use others for selfish pleasure regardless of the cost to the other person. So people who sleep around, who are addicted to casual sex, use other people to obtain sex, do so without concern or affection for their partners. They may then begin to behave in ways which harm other people, and may begin to pursue their own selfish interests. Apathy and neglect towards others can result.

124

Society corrupts itself when human care, affection and concern for one's own family, and for other people, is weakened, is bypassed by self-interest at expense of others.

There is increasing wanton antisocial behaviour such as vandalism and mugging. There is a loss of internal security, by loss of property and by attack against the person. The quality of life is lowered even further by those who pursue personal gain regardless of its cost to other people.

All this was clear in the seventies:

> In all countries where sex education has been introduced the same corruptive pattern of social change has been observed {3}: sexual experimentation starts and promiscuity increases. Promiscuity leads to increasing sexual dissatisfaction, to the weakening of family life and marriage bonds and to sexual excesses. The substitute satisfactions of smoking, drinking, and drug-taking increase and there is a lowering of the age of those involved. There is an upsurge in wanton destructive aggression in the community and a rise in aggressive juvenile delinquency. There is increasing concern over the harm done on young children by the practices and by the lack of concern and commitment of their parents, and concern has already been expressed over increasing male impotence. These effects are now obvious to any intelligent reader of the informed press.

> ... Increasing divorce rates, the resultant delinquency of children, the casual and inhuman ways some parents treat each other and their children, are almost the direct outcome of pre-marital and adulterous, that is promiscuous, sexual relations.

Destructive aggression, viciousness and brutality of people towards each other, disregard of the value of the individual and of life itself, are not normal behaviour. People who behave in such ways become isolated and divided against each other.

Women and men may then use sex as a way of getting what they want from their partner, as a way of dominating the partner. While unlikely to be stated in such simple terms between them, their actions convey the message 'do what I want and you can have sex as a reward. Obstruct me or refuse to do what I want and I will not have sex with you' which is a kind of punishment. We see assertiveness and conflict instead of affection and co-operation.

Partnerships and marriages break up when difficulties arise. People leave without regard or concern for the interests of the other members, of partner, spouse or children. They leave when they would be better off alone, when there is illness, when their present partner becomes unemployed, when a younger or wealthier 'partner' becomes available.

People who behave promiscuously (permissively) have sexual relations before marriage, or after marriage with a person other than their spouse. Promiscuity turns men against women, and women against men, and robs both of the support of their family.

> Let me put it to you in another way {2}. It is only a few years ago that you went out for the evening without bothering to lock the door. Nowadays you make sure you fasten the windows as well and in some areas keep a light on and the radio going. Just think of what has been happening to crime, delinquency, drug addiction, the younger age of those involved and the increasingly brutal way people treat each other, leaving aside dishonest business dealings. Look at the increasing number of divorces and thus of one-parent families, look at the even larger number of children being brought up in this way. ... it is happening in other democratic countries. And it is nothing new. It has happened again and again. Whenever democracy raised its head, the same knife was used to chop it off.

> History shows that free societies which allow themselves to become 'permissive' (promiscuous) weaken themselves to the point where their civilisation destroys itself, or is destroyed by outsiders. Those who wish to weaken democracy condone or encourage 'permissiveness'. On the other hand, those who restrict sex to within marriage gain creativity and increase their strength.

Sexual Restraint and Control

It is control of the sexual urge which distinguishes human beings from animals. Promiscuous unrestrained sexual behaviour indicates cold inhuman, often harsh, behaviour towards others, is characteristic of the cold unemotional behaviour of those who exploit others. Sexual self-control and restraint indicates human caring behaviour.

As permissiveness has increased so we have seen increasing the number of people using others for their own gratification and pleasure without care or concern for them, and also the number of parents behaving brutally towards each other and their children. A process driven by those who want sexual gratification, knowingly or unknowingly without regard to the costs their 'partners' have to pay.

Basic is that people behave in a way which enables them to trust and assist each other, that men and women co-operate with each other in a way which will protect and strengthen both, behaving in a way which ensures that all benefit from gains made.

So within a family, between husband and wife, it is the other person who comes first. When each spouse tries to make the other spouse happy, when each will go without something so as to make the other happy, then both can be happy.

Consider Jewish family law and traditions. When the wife has her period she is considered to be emotionally fragile. So the husband refrains from having sex from a few days before her period starts until a few days after it stops. He refrains out of care, consideration and affection for her, for his wife. She is different, has different needs, his self-denial for her sake continually renews the bonds of affection between them. As does their mutual practice of supporting each other, of putting the other person first when it comes to satisfying each other's needs. Whether or not you agree with the reasoning, sexual control is practised regularly for the sake of the other person and this strengthens the individual and cements the marriage.

Sexual restraint is an exercise in self-control, in controlling and so modifying what in the reptilian-animal part of our brain is a primitive and powerful urge aimed at the survival of the species. Sexual restraint changes it from an animal's instinctive behaviour into human behaviour based on concern and affection for the welfare of others. Not easy to do but it can be done as bereaved spouses or discarded partners can testify. Addiction to casual sex, to sleeping around, to promiscuity, is difficult to control but it can be done and the gains to the person doing so are enormous.

The United States government in 1997 set aside USD 250 million to teach children sexual abstinence, "teaching the social, psychological, and health gains to be realised by abstaining from sexual activity", teaching "abstinence from sexual activity outside marriage as the expected standard for all school-age children". {10}

Restraining and controlling sexual urges by restricting sex to within marriage gives strength to the family, to the individual and to the community, and underlies success in the struggle for a higher standard of living and higher quality of life for each and all.

Dominance

Dominance Within the Family

Within the family we should see co-operation and teamwork between equals who divide up the work which has to be done between them in a functional way so that each becomes expert and effective in his or her part of what has to be done.

But on the whole a family's income is usually earned by the male and income and money pass through his hands to the family. He then may, if he so wishes, use this controlling position to dominate the female. This applies equally well to the female who is a breadwinner, who may then use her controlling position to dominate. And applies also when the income of one is much larger than that of the other.

And both are in the position to use sex as a means of dominating the other, if they so wish. Rewarding compliance with sex, punishing disagreement by withholding sex.

Women have at times been persuaded by traditions or beliefs into accepting domination and sometimes exploitation as the norm. And women have in the past been denied education and full equality with men within the family and in the community in which they live.

The words 'assertiveness' and 'asserting' are used at times to indicate that one person is attempting to dominate the other. Dominating and 'asserting' put one person's personal gain, likes, dislikes against the other person's interests, introduces conflict and competition into what should be co-operation and teamwork.

Considering only women and children, the family protects women and children while children grow to maturity, till children become independent adults. It also protects women from disadvantages resulting from caring for and looking after the family during this period.

What keeps the family in place and gives it strength is restricting sex to within marriage. Men are then motivated to marry, to provide and care for wife and children, and themselves gain much strength from doing so.

When women are persuaded to make themselves available for sex outside marriage they help to dismantle not only their own protection and security but also that of their children.

In such circumstances the selfish instinctive behaviour of the non-feeling primitive animal is asserting itself, is attempting to dominate, overcome and control human feeling of care, affection, concern for members of one's own family and for other people in human societies.

Living in a Hostile Environment

We have seen that when one member of a family dominates others, that competition, conflict and struggle replace co-operation and teamwork. All the family's members suffer as a result.

We know that dominating does not work in normal circumstances. Authoritarian organisations are much less effective than participative ones. In authoritarian organisations morale is low, people cease to care and tend to work against each other instead of co-operating with each other for the benefit of the organisation. Which applies equally well to a family. {7, 8}

In the working environment women are just as oppressed and exploited as men are. When women receive lower wages for work of equal value then this is bad for men and women alike. When some people in a group are being underpaid, the pay of the others is being pushed down.

Outside the family a struggle is taking place. The breadwinner is competing for work and income on behalf of the family. He is also struggling against those who wish to exploit him (and thus his family) and who oppress so as to exploit.

So outside the family we see a widespread struggle against those who wish to dominate other people. Against those who want primitive power over others, against those who wish to exploit, against those who may brutally and without feeling oppress human beings so as to exploit them. And 'to exploit' includes the whole range of antisocial decisions and activities of those who put profit before people and community. {6}

We also saw that on the whole it is men who earn the family's income which then often passes through their hands to the family. And that as a result of the work men do outside the family, it is largely men who gain controlling positions in the working environment.

So on the surface it may seem as if it is men who try to dominate women within the family, that it is men who oppress and exploit women in the working environment.

Anyone who sees men and women co-operating with each other within a family, struggling side by side, back to back, and sees them co-operating with each other and helping each other in the outside working environment, for a more secure and better life for their families, knows how strong and effective they are together.

Blaming men as such, within the family and outside it, when women are oppressed and exploited, amounts to putting women against men, to separating them from each other. A 'divide so as to conquer' process which weakens both in their joint struggle for a better life. It robs men of the support of their families when they are struggling outside the family against being exploited, it robs women of the support of their families while bringing up children to adulthood, when improving their skills or knowledge when returning to work or to improve the quality of their lives.

Dominance and oppression take place within and outside the family, against men and women alike. Both men and women are exploited and oppressed in the working environment to a very considerable degree.

What we see in the working environment is a world-wide struggle to achieve a humane way of life, each person, family or community struggling to advance at their own level of development, struggling against those who wish to dominate, exploit, oppress. A struggle whose successful outcome depends on trustful co-operation, companionship and teamwork. {4, 5}

Sometimes one has to fight to preserve a good way of life, to prevent others from taking what has been achieved, or one is expected to fight on behalf of those who dominate and exploit.

The fighting is usually done by men who are conditioned to fight, maim and kill. Their training weakens and bypasses humane emotions of care, concern and affection for other people, in effect tends to brutalise them.

And we now see in some countries women joining the armed forces, police and security organisations and being trained in somewhat similar ways.

Our primitive animal ancestors behaved instinctively. Hunt for food, kill or be killed, fight or flee, copulate, care for own young for a very short and limited period. Self before others, regardless of needs of others, marking out and defending territory. Later mammals tend to have feelings, care and affection for their young. Human beings think as well as feel, and care for and look after their young for many years.

So conditioning to fight, maim and kill amounts to a throwback to primitive animal behaviour, to behaviour which puts self before others. A throwback to beast-like behaviour for those who attack, to beast-like behaviour to counter beast-like behaviour for those who defend.

But only some people behave in such corrupted ways. There are those many who put people first, who know the difference between human and inhuman behaviour, who believe in participative behaviour and in democratic government.

We saw that casual sex dehumanises, that it blocks affection and increases cold and selfish behaviour against others, that society corrupts itself when promiscuity (casual sex) spreads.

Promiscuity attacks human beings in their struggle for a better life as it:

1. Conditions people into primitive selfish uncaring behaviour which uses other people for personal gain (pleasure), creating a non-caring society, putting people against each other, at times brutalising them.

2. Weakens the family and all its members and so adversely affects the young and the way people treat each other. It weakens all the family's members by robbing them of emotional and economic support, and so makes it easier to exploit them through their needs.

Those who behave promiscuously pay a heavy price, namely lose the ability to form a satisfying emotionally deeply binding lasting and shared relationship with one other person. They also lose the emotional strength and economic backup such a shared relationship brings.

The media seem to be concentrating on portraying superstition, violence and casual-sex behaviour as acceptable, so strengthening primitive uncaring and antisocial behaviour towards others. And images penetrate deeply into the human mind.

Sexually explicit and pornographic material would seem to be taking this process even further.

So media are at present persuading and conditioning people into thinking that antisocial behaviour will not have unpleasant consequences. However, the cost to the community of the kind of negative and antisocial behaviour outlined in the sections above, of the lowering of the quality of life, is enormous. {6}

What we see is an almost intentional-seeming conditioning towards antisocial behaviour which breaks up families and so weakens individuals, and which divides people against each other and so weakens them even further.

It looks as if men are being conditioned into opting out of their responsibilities for family, wife and children. Women, on the other hand, are apparently being conditioned into giving away the real support and security they and their children could expect from husband and family, for no real gain.

To answer the question: "Who encourages antisocial behaviour?" we need to ask: "Who benefits from antisocial behaviour?" {6}

So who profits from promiscuity? At first glance it would seem that manufacturers of contraceptives and contraceptive devices have a vested interest as have organisations or associations whose income is derived from selling contraceptives and contraceptive devices. And possibly those whose income depends on advising on the use and application of contraceptives, depending on the extent to which their income depends on this.

And it is those who wish to weaken democracy and freedom who could be expected to condone and thus permit and encourage promiscuous behaviour as promiscuous behaviour separates people and turns them against each other, as it turns men against women and women against men. Indeed, they will condone and encourage any movement which turns men and women against each other so as to rob both of the strength to resist oppression and exploitation, to rob both of the strength which comes from men and women co-operating with each other.

Human rights are based on controlling primitive dominant behaviour, on concern, care and affection for our young, our families, for people, for our communities, and express themselves in co-operation and teamwork between men and women to achieve a good life of high quality.

Men and women are struggling together to achieve a better life, a humane way of living and government, and social security.

And there are ways of teaching social responsibility, of teaching the young how to take responsibility for others, how to care for, work with and look after other people. Social responsibility, the caring, giving and sharing with others, the taking on of responsibility for others including conflict management, can be and is being taught. {14}

It is in democracies that high standards of living have been achieved. In democracies people can struggle openly for a better life but we see that what has been gained has to be defended and extended.

Family's Role and Life in the Real World

The Family

The family is the basic unit of society. Its strength depends on the ability of the partners to commit themselves to each other, that is its strength depends on those who restrict sexual relations to within marriage. Men and women who do so practice a form of self-control which enables them to form a deep and lasting relationship, which in turn lays the basis for happy and contented family life for themselves and their children. The relationship between them is based on mutual trust and respect arising from the sure knowledge that they are in a vital exclusive relationship to each other, that they are working and co-operating with each other for the common good of themselves and their children.

Human beings work primarily for their family and members of a family stand by, support and help each other in times of need.

Smash the family and you undermine the strength of the people. I understand the resulting disruption was so marked in Russia that they had to back-pedal. One of the first things the Khmer Rouge did in Cambodia was to smash the family to make the people dependent on the state.

It is tough when you have to go to work to earn the money, do the shopping, look after the kids and do everything yourself. The one thing you cannot afford to be is to be ill. And you have no time for the kids either. And in a one-parent family, what the children miss is the parent's caring co-operative behaviour, is the example of responsible people looking after each other. The boy being brought up by the mother knows that both of them were left to look after themselves by the father and that is not a good example to model himself on. If you are struggling on your own so as to survive you don't have time or energy to think of freedom or to work for the community or for the betterment of humankind. {2}

Each member of the family gets strength from the others. Two heads are better than one, and work divided between two people in such a way that each can become expert in his or her own area is done much better than one person trying to do it all. The family gives people enormous emotional and economic strength to overcome life's problems. Husband and wife battle on together back-to-back and they do so successfully regardless of how tough the struggle may be. You cannot win all the battles but what cements the relationship is not just battles won but battles fought together. The depth of such a relationship between husband and wife and the wealth of strength it gives regardless of the opposition, this you know as well as I do. The children follow the example of their parents, gain the same strength and pass it on. It all depends on deep and secure emotional involvement between two people, between husband and wife. {2}

Those who understand its effects know that when sex is restrained and controlled, it performs the enormously important function of creating a special single deep emotional relationship between two people which gives them the strength to overcome life's problems, to form a strong family unit which serves and protects all its members. To be strong the relationship has to be unique and secure. It depends on the ability of the partners to commit themselves to each other. The depth of such a relationship between husband and wife can be appreciated as one sees them both battling on together successfully regardless of how tough the struggle may be.

Increasing Lifespans

Tabulating the figures already mentioned and extending the time period to the end of life, key events <1> look something like this:

Length of Period (Years)	Age (Years of Age)	Period	Event
4 - 5		Infant	
8 - 10		Child	
6 - 9		Adolescent	
	18 - 21		Becoming an adult member of family and community.
	25		Adult and independent member of family and community.
	18 - 24		Single
	20 - 26		Marriage (Children born over period of 6 years)
	41 - 47		Children become adults
	75 - 80		Death

Simplifying this a little, we have:

Age (Years of age)	Event or Period
0 - 21	Childhood and adolescence
21 - 23	Adult and single
23	Marriage
23 - 33	Children's childhood
33 - 44	Children's adolescence
44	Children now adult and largely independent
78	Life ends

Only about 100 years ago in the developed countries a person's lifespan was about 45 years, just long enough to bring up the next generation and help them to find their feet in the community. We now live another 35 years or so which enables us to do much more with our lives after our children have become independent. And our lives now look something like this:

Age **Event or Period**
(Years of
age)

Working outside the family (largely men)
21 - 65 At work
65 - 78 Receiving pension, freed from
         having to work

Within family (largely women)
21 - 23 At work
   23   Marriage
23 - 33 Bringing up the children during
         their childhood
33 - 44 Looking after children during
         their adolescence
44 - 65 At home or at work, as needed or
         as the individual wishes
65 - 78 Receiving pension, free from
         having to work

We saw earlier that the needs of children to be provided with caring and affectionate family life is of overriding importance <2>.

But outstanding is that those looking after people within the family, now have about 20 years of active life which can be spent as they wish, either working outside the family in paid employment, as independent professionals, or serving the community in other ways.

It is not easy to return to paid work as a professional after years of absence looking after one's family. After such a time lapse much has been forgotten and knowledge, equipment and techniques will have changed. And what is missing on returning to professional work is the years of experience which would have been gained had one stayed at work. It is then more than likely that positions of greater responsibility, and promotion to higher levels, will not be gained by those who return to work after such a long absence.

So on returning to work, women are at a disadvantage because of the time spent bringing up the children, and this disadvantage is likely to lower the level at which they can find work or work for the rest of their active life.

The family compensates women for this life-long contribution towards the upbringing of the children. It is the role of the spouse, of the husband, to continue to provide for the family. A life-long contribution from him which means she does not lose out for the rest of her life because she stayed at home to look after the children, the husband's input into the family balancing her input of bringing up the children and looking after the family's members.

As the children grow older, say 14 years old, women can usually spend increasing amounts of time updating or learning and developing skills and abilities for their future or continuing work after the children have grown up. Which is not easy to do and needs the support of her spouse.

Women, after children have grown up and backed by the family, can choose work outside the family to fulfil themselves as pay is less important for a second income.

Much professional work can now be home based. Home working may be less rewarding but is more convenient. Much can be gained by husband supporting his wife as far as he is able.

Looking at life from point of view of one's career, that is from the point of view of those who believe in profiting by compelling people through need to work for less than a fair share of the added value they produce, amounts to sacrificing the interests of one's family, and thus of oneself. The employer profits at the expense of the social and human welfare of the family's members.

What we see outside the family is a pattern of differentials which rewards service to the owners and their establishment rather than ability or service to the community. The nurse, the fire-fighter, the police officer and the teacher are at present paid comparatively little for the work they do. {1}

The community's basic needs are often not met by an uncaring social environment and the community's well-being depends on people, generally women, who use whatever time they have available, for caring for people both within and outside of family life. An employer's profit-orientated work can be well paid, community service-orientated work is not. And it is largely women who, caring for the welfare of the community, are generally the prime movers in self-help, support, protest and pressure groups, pushing forward also with other social and welfare issues.

Such work and public demonstrations and protests on such issues, are now an essential survival mechanism under beginning-of-twentyfirst-century conditions. {6}

Women's work in family and society determines individual emotional strength and well-being, the quality of life and the welfare of people as a community, and needs to be recognised and acknowledged.

Teamwork Within the Family

Teamwork implies sharing work and responsibilities in a way which ensures that all that has to be done is done well.

Success is measured by social and mental well-being as well as by standard of living and quality of life, of the family as a whole and of each member.

Key feature of the whole system is that both spouses work for the benefit of their family, of its individual members, and beyond that for the larger community of which the family is a part.

All are equal as people. What has to be done is shared out between them according to individual skill, ability, knowledge and experience. And in the end all share equally in the family's gains and losses. In other words, all are equal, contribute to the best of their ability, and stand or fall together.

The relationship between the two spouses is a functional relationship {9} and functional relationships are often misunderstood and misrepresented.

The spouses share out between themselves what needs to be done, each specialising, concentrating on, areas of work in accordance with their abilities, knowledge, understanding, likes and dislikes of each.

Equal as people, each takes the decisions falling within their own area of competence and responsibility. The husband may decide which car is to be bought or about getting a new job, the wife about which school the children should go to or where the family should live. But each discusses matters with the other family members before deciding from the point of view of what is best for the family as a whole.

They do not waste their time competing with each other but add their knowledge and experience to the decision-taking process of the other. In general, the person who decides would be the one most competent to take such decisions.

Such a functional division of work and responsibilities, of co-operation and teamwork between experts, enables us to survive and do well in the dangerous environment in which we find ourselves.

Consider shopping for food. The shopping expert takes into account the likes and dislikes of the other members of the family. And the expertise involved in shopping can be appreciated by considering what has to be thought about while shopping. How fresh is the food, how long will it have to be stored at home, how much does it cost here compared with elsewhere, has it been genetically modified and what does this mean for us. And what about nitrates in water, heavy metals, herbicides, pesticides, irradiated foods, chemical additives, more expensive organic foods, fat and sugar contents and other health risks.

It would be a waste of time for each to become expert in this field. It would be useless for each of the two people to do so and to argue continually about what is to be done. They would in this way be competing with each other by attempting to show that one is better than the other.

Conclusions

This report deals with the root causes of the major social problems. It shows how to resolve the problems by dealing with their basic causes.

Family and Children

200 million years of evolution are behind us, from reptilian beast through mammalian animal to human being. Human beings are mammals and we are unique in that our children need protecting and bringing up in a humane, emotionally and mentally stimulating environment for between 18 and 25 years, to enable them to mature into socially responsible adults. Men and women co-operate with each other and look after each other and their children, within the family, to achieve this.

Hence human beings work primarily for their family and members of a family stand by, support and help each other in times of need. The family is the basic unit of society and it looks after the interests of all its members, as individuals as well as collectively. This gives great strength to each member of the family in the struggle for daily bread, security and happiness.

Men and Women

Co-operation between men and women, within the family and as equals, would seem to be essential when bringing up their children under modern conditions of rapid change at an accelerating rate of change.

It is women who generally look after the young and other family members as people. This is the key role within the family and it occupies women full-time for some years if it is to be done well, and for more years on an at least part-time basis.

But we live much longer and the time spent full-time at home looking after the family places women at a disadvantage when returning to work outside the family after the children have been brought up. So women need to be supported when returning to work.

The family compensates women for this life-long contribution towards the upbringing of the children. It is the role of the spouse, of the husband, to continue to provide for the family. A life-long contribution from him which means she does not lose out for the rest of her life because she stayed at home to look after the children, the husband's input into the family balancing her input of bringing up the children and looking after the family's members.

Women, after children have grown up and with the family's backing, can choose work outside the family to fulfil themselves as pay is less important for a second income.

It is largely women who, caring for the welfare of the community, are generally the prime movers in self-help, support, protest and pressure groups, pushing forward also with other social and welfare issues.

Such work and public demonstrations and protests on such issues, are now an essential survival mechanism under beginning-of-twentyfirst-century conditions.

The work women do in family and society determines individual emotional strength and well-being, the quality of life and the welfare of people as a community and needs to be recognised and acknowledged.

The report discusses in some detail what is required if husband and wife are to work together as an effective team within the family.

Casual Sex

Casual sex is addictive, weakens and deadens feelings of care and affection for the other person, for partner or spouse, changing feelings of care and affection into a desire to use others for selfish pleasure regardless of the cost to the other person.

So people who sleep around, who are addicted to casual sex, use other people to obtain sex, do so without concern or affection for their partners. Apathy and neglect towards others can result.

Society corrupts itself when human care, affection and concern for one's own family, and for other people, is weakened, is bypassed by self-interest at the expense of others.

Those who sleep around pay a heavy price, namely lose the ability to form a satisfying emotionally deeply binding lasting and shared relationship with one other person. They also lose the emotional strength and economic backup such a shared relationship brings. Promiscuity turns men against women, and women against men, and robs both of the support of their family.

In such ways promiscuity breaks up families, weakens the strength of individuals and thus of the community to resist exploitation and oppression. So it would seem to be those who wish to weaken democracy and freedom who condone and thus permit and encourage promiscuous behaviour.

What keeps the family in place and gives it strength is restricting sex to within marriage. Men are then motivated to marry, to provide and care for wife and children, and themselves gain much strength from doing so. When women are persuaded to make themselves available for sex outside marriage they help to dismantle not only their own protection and security but also that of their children.

A key characteristic which distinguishes human beings from animals is that we can control the sex urge. Sex is habit-forming and addictive but can be controlled when the will is there, when the individual is motivated to control it.

In the USA steps are being taken to halt and reverse the increasing corruption of their communities by teaching the young the gains to be achieved by abstaining from sexual activity outside marriage.

There are ways of teaching social responsibility, of teaching the young how to take responsibility for others, how to care for, work with and look after other people. Social responsibility, the caring, giving and sharing with others, the taking on of responsibility for others including conflict management, can be and is being taught.

Dominance, Oppression and Exploitation

When one member of a family dominates others, then competition, conflict and struggle replace co-operation and teamwork. Dominance weakens all the family's members, robbing them of emotional and economic support, and so makes it easier to exploit them through their needs. All the family's members suffer as a result.

In the working environment we see a world-wide struggle to achieve a humane way of life, each family, person or community struggling to advance at their own level of development, struggling against those who wish to dominate, exploit, oppress. A struggle whose successful outcome depends on trustful co-operation, companionship and teamwork.

We know that dominating does not work in normal circumstances. Authoritarian organisations are much less effective than participative ones. In authoritarian organisations morale is low, people cease to care and tend to work against each other instead of co-operating with each other for the benefit of the organisation. Which applies equally well to a family.

Promiscuous behaviour and casual sexual relationships separate people and turn them against each other, turn men against women and women against men. Promiscuous behaviour and casual sexual relationships break up families, isolate people and rob people of the strength to resist exploitation and oppression.

So it appears that it is those who wish to weaken democracy and freedom who could be expected to condone and thus permit and encourage promiscuous behaviour and casual relationships.

Strength to resist oppression and exploitation comes from men and women co-operating with each other and so men and women struggle together to achieve a better life, a humane way of living and of government, and social security.

Human rights are based on controlling primitive dominating behaviour, on concern, care and affection for our young and our families, for people and for our communities. Human rights express themselves in co-operation and teamwork between men and women to achieve a good life of high quality.

It is in democracies that a high standard of living has been achieved. In democracies people can struggle openly for a better life but we see that what has been gained has to be defended and extended.

Notes and References

Notes

<1> See section on 'How Human Beings Evolved'.

For more background, see section on 'Development of Brain Functions in Humans' in reference {11}.

<2> See section 'Protecting and Caring for the Next Generation'.

The kibbutzim in Israel brought up children communally, away from their parents, and had to backtrack when they became aware of the consequences {13}.

References

{ 1} In 'Messianic Struggle:
The Worldwide Struggle for a Good and
Secure Life for All, Here and Now'
Manfred Davidmann
ISBN 978-0-85192-059-7
see chapter 3: 'Work and Pay, Incomes and
Differentials: Employer, Employee and Community'

{ 2} If You Want a Future, Read On ...
David Baram*
Social Organisation Limited

{ 3} Sex:
Louise W. Eickoff
Consultant Psychiatrist
Guardian, 1970 Sep 12

{ 4} In 'The Human Mind and How it Works:
Group Minds in Action:
How the Human Group Mind Shapes
the Quality of Our Life and Living'
Manfred Davidmann
ISBN 978-0-85192-055-9
see chapter 9: 'The Will to Work:
What People Struggle to Achieve'

{ 5} In 'The Human Mind and How it Works:
      Group Minds in Action:
      How the Human Group Mind Shapes
      the Quality of Our Life and Living'
      Manfred Davidmann
      ISBN 978-0-85192-055-9
      see chapter 7: 'Motivation Summary'

{ 6} In 'Messianic Struggle:
      The Worldwide Struggle for a Good and
      Secure Life for All, Here and Now'
      Manfred Davidmann
      ISBN 978-0-85192-059-7
      see chapter 2: 'Social Responsibility, Profits and
      Social Accountability'

{ 7} In 'Management and Leadership:
      Local, National, Multinational (Global),
      Principles and Practice'
      Manfred Davidmann
      ISBN 978-0-85192-057-3
      see chapter 3: 'Role of Managers under
      Different Styles of Management'

{ 8} In 'Management and Leadership:
      Local, National, Multinational (Global),
      Principles and Practice'
      Manfred Davidmann
      ISBN 978-0-85192-057-3
      see chapter 2: 'Style of Management and
      Leadership'

{ 9} In 'Management and Leadership:
      Local, National, Multinational (Global),
      Principles and Practice'
      Manfred Davidmann
      ISBN 978-0-85192-057-3
      see chapter 6: 'Organising'

{10} Abstinence conundrum
      Tamar Lewin
      Guardian, 13/05/97

{11}   In 'The Human Mind and How it Works:
Group Minds in Action:
How the Human Group Mind Shapes
the Quality of Our Life and Living'
Manfred Davidmann
ISBN 978-0-85192-055-9
see chapter 2: 'How the Human Brain
Developed and How the Human Mind Works'

{12}   A Triune Concept of the Brain and Behaviour
P D MacLean
University of Toronto Press

{13}   In 'Judaism: Basis - Past - Present - Future, Part 2'
Manfred Davidmann
ISBN 978-0-85192-061-0
see chapter 4: 'Kibbutzim'

{14}   To Give or Not To Give
'Everyman' TV documentary
Editor: Jane Drabble; Producer: Angela Kaye
Broadcast on 5/1/92 by BBC 1
Based on book 'The Altruistic Person' by
Professor Sam Oliner

Additions by the Editor:

David Baram*:   Manfred Davidmann is the author of this work.

Press Notice

'Family, Sex and the Individual; Women's Liberation, Feminism and Community'*: a Report by Manfred Davidmann. (KGW NewsChannel 8)

This report examines root causes of what are now major social problems and shows how to resolve the problems by dealing with their basic causes.

Human beings work primarily for their family and members of a family stand by, support and help each other in times of need. The family is the basic unit of society and it looks after the interests of all its members, as individuals as well as collectively. This gives great strength to each member of the family in the struggle for daily bread, security and happiness.

And in the report "Family, Sex and the Individual", Manfred Davidmann exposes the causes of what seems to be progressive breaking down of family life and of social strength.

This report is an unprecedented and comprehensive overview, states new insights, proves basic underlying causes.

For example, in a comprehensive review, Manfred Davidmann defines the role of the family as being:

> To struggle as a family to survive.

> To protect and support mother and children until children become mature and independent adults capable of providing for themselves.

> To provide a good standard of living and a life of high quality. Which includes struggling against oppression and exploitation - and sometimes one has to fight to preserve a good way of life.

> To serve the interests of, and to support, each member of the family. In turn, each member of the family supports the family.

The report also investigates the impact of casual sexual relations and its effects on individuals, family and community, on the social strength of individuals and communities.

Further, the report examines and relates dominance and confrontation within the family to that in the working environment and considers oppression and exploitation within and outside the family.

Manfred Davidmann was the first to clearly describe and show, eight years ago, the effects of increasing life spans on the family, on its members and on their responsibilities. He also illustrated the underlying basis of teamwork within the family, stating the various roles and responsibilities and functional relationships of its members for effective teamwork within the family.

In this report are also sections about
     Protecting and caring for the next generation;
     Sexual relations;
     Dominance within the family;
     Living in a hostile environment;
     Increasing life spans;
     Teamwork within the family.

See chapter 5:
     'Family, Community, Sex and the Individual'
     Manfred Davidmann

Additions by the Editor:

* This title was used by Manfred Davidmann on his website (https://www.solhaam.org). Later the author used the title 'Family, Community, Sex and the Individual' for this work.

Men and Women, Family and Children; Dominance, Oppression and Exploitation

Family and Children
Men and Women
Dominance, Oppression and Exploitation
Sources

We are here dealing with the root causes of our major social problems, showing how to resolve the problems by dealing with their basic causes.

Family and Children

200 million years of evolution are behind us, from reptilian beast through mammalian animal to human being. Human beings are mammals and we are unique in that our children need protecting and bringing up in a humane, emotionally and mentally stimulating environment for between 18 and 25 years, to enable them to mature into socially responsible adults. Men and women co-operate with each other and look after each other and their children, within the family, to achieve this.

The family looks after the interests of all its members, as individuals as well as collectively. Members of a family stand by, support and help each other in times of need.

This gives great strength to each member of the family in the struggle for daily bread, security and happiness. Hence human beings work primarily for their family and the family is the basic unit of society.

Men and Women

Co-operation between men and women, within the family and as equals, would seem to be essential when bringing up their children under modern conditions of rapid change at an accelerating rate of change.

It is women who generally look after the young and other family members as people. This is the key role within the family and it occupies women full-time for some years if it is to be done well, and for more years on an at least part-time basis.

But we live much longer and the time spent full-time at home looking after the family places women at a disadvantage when returning to work outside the family after the children have been brought up. So women need to be supported when returning to work.

The family compensates women for the life-long effects of their contribution towards the upbringing of the children. It is the role of the spouse, of the husband, to continue to provide for the family. A life-long contribution from him which means she does not lose out for the rest of her life because she stayed at home to look after the children, the husband's input into the family balancing her input of bringing up the children and looking after the family's members.

Women, after children have grown up and with the family's backing, can choose work outside the family to fulfil themselves as pay is less important for a second income.

It is largely women who, caring for the welfare of the community, are generally the prime movers in self-help, support, protest and pressure groups, pushing forward also with other social and welfare issues.

Such work and public demonstrations and protests on such issues, are now an essential survival mechanism under beginning-of-twentyfirst-century conditions.

A key characteristic which distinguishes human beings from animals is that we can control the sex urge. Sex is habit-forming and addictive but can be controlled when the will is there, when the individual is motivated to control it.

In the USA steps are being taken to halt and reverse the increasing corruption of their communities by teaching the young the gains to be achieved by abstaining from sexual activity outside marriage.

There are ways of teaching social responsibility, of teaching the young how to take responsibility for others, how to care for, work with and look after other people. Social responsibility, the caring, giving and sharing with others, the taking on of responsibility for others including conflict management, can be and is being taught.

Dominance, Oppression and Exploitation

When one member of a family dominates others, then competition, conflict and struggle replace co-operation and teamwork. Dominance weakens all the family's members, robbing them of emotional and economic support, and so makes it easier to exploit them through their needs. All the family's members suffer as a result.

In the working environment we see a world-wide struggle to achieve a humane way of life, each family, person or community struggling to advance at their own level of development, struggling against those who wish to dominate, exploit, oppress. A struggle whose successful outcome depends on trustful co-operation, companionship and teamwork.

We know that dominating does not work in normal circumstances. Authoritarian organisations are much less effective than participative ones. In authoritarian organisations morale is low, people cease to care and tend to work against each other instead of co-operating with each other for the benefit of the organisation. Which applies equally well to a family.

Strength to resist oppression and exploitation comes from men and women co-operating with each other and so men and women struggle together to achieve a better life, a humane way of living and of government, and social security.

Human rights are based on controlling primitive dominating behaviour, on concern, care and affection for our young and our families, for people and for our communities. Human rights express themselves in co-operation and teamwork between men and women to achieve a good life of high quality.

It is in democracies that a high standard of living has been achieved. In democracies people can struggle openly for a better life but we see that what has been gained has to be defended and extended.

Sources

See chapter 5:

> 'Family, Community, Sex and the Individual'
> Manfred Davidmann

from which this theme's information was extracted.

Also see

> In 'The Human Mind and How it Works:
> Group Minds in Action:
> How the Human Group Mind Shapes
> the Quality of Our Life and Living'
> Manfred Davidmann
> ISBN 978-0-85192-055-9
> see chapter 10: 'Democracy, Socialism
> and Communism: The Worldwide Struggle
> for a Better Life'

and

> In 'Management and Leadership:
> Local, National, Multinational (Global),
> Principles and Practice'
> Manfred Davidmann
> ISBN 978-0-85192-057-3
> see chapter 2: 'Style of Management and
> Leadership'

and

> In 'The Human Mind and How it Works:
> Group Minds in Action:
> How the Human Group Mind Shapes
> the Quality of Our Life and Living'
> Manfred Davidmann
> ISBN 978-0-85192-055-9
> see chapter 2: 'How the Human Brain
> Developed and How Human Mind Works'

Family's Role and Life in the Real World; Protecting, and Caring for, the Next Generation; Causes of Social Break-up

The Family

For human beings, primitive (reptilian) instinctive urges and behaviour are overlaid by mammalian care and affection for one's young and human care and affection for one's family and community.

> See 'How the Human Brain Developed and How the Human Mind Works' {1}*,

Compared with most, if not all, animals we also have much longer lifespans and it takes a long time before a human baby becomes an adult. Born after nine months in the mother's womb, followed by 4 to 5 years as infant, then 8 to 10 years as child being educated, and say 6 to 9 years as adolescent, about 18 to 25 years old when becoming an adult and independent member of the community.

So the role of the family is

> To struggle as a family to survive.

> To protect and support mother and children until children become mature and independent adults capable of providing for themselves.

> To provide a good standard of living and a life of high quality. Which includes struggling against oppression and exploitation. And sometimes one has to fight to preserve a good way of life.

> To serve the interests of, and to support, each member of the family. In turn, each member of the family supports the family.

Hence human beings work primarily for their family and members of a family stand by, support and help each other in times of need. The family is the basic unit of society and it looks after the interests of all its members, as individuals as well as collectively. This gives great strength to each member of the family in the struggle for daily bread, security and happiness.

Protecting and Caring for the Next Generation

It is women who generally look after people, after the welfare and well-being of the members of the family. Care, concern, affection and love, feelings and emotions, are important and matter, and women developed, and have, much skill and expertise in such matters. It is generally men who struggle outside the family to secure survival and good living for the family. A struggle for survival in a seemingly hostile environment engineered by other humans.

> See 'The Will to Work: What People Struggle to Achieve' {2}*,
>
> and 'Motivation Summary' {3}*.

Primarily the family exists to protect and support its young, and this means supporting and looking after the female bearing the child within her body, through birth and while she is protecting and teaching the young how to behave. It is usually the woman whose role it is to ensure the family provides the young with the humane, emotionally and mentally stimulating environment they need to enable them to mature into socially responsible adults. She is assisted in this by her spouse, depending on her needs and depending on his own work. But it is usually the woman who copes with the personal and emotional problems of the family's members and this is challenging, demanding and difficult work demanding social ability and skills as well as care, affection, understanding and concern for people.

When women are persuaded to regard work outside of the family as more important than caring for the young or the family's members, they are in effect handing over the family's key role to outsiders such as day-care businesses and television programme makers, with disastrous results on the way in which the young perceive home life and adult behaviour.

Such outsiders tend to condition the young into behaving like fictional and unreal role models, for example concerning sexual behaviour. Instead of gaining an adult understanding of the reality of living, of family values and relationships, instead of understanding and experiencing socially-responsible behaviour caring for and living with

152

other people, instead of seeing adults (parents) behave in socially responsible way struggling together in a hostile environment to do the best they can for the young and for each other.

Behaviour and Community

Society corrupts itself when human care, affection and concern for one's own family, and for other people, is weakened, is bypassed by self-interest at expense of others.

There is increasing wanton antisocial behaviour such as vandalism and mugging. There is a loss of internal security, by loss of property and by attack against the person. The quality of life is lowered even further by those who pursue personal gain regardless of its cost to other people.

Destructive aggression, viciousness and brutality of people towards each other, disregard of the value of the individual and of life itself, are not normal behaviour. People who behave in such ways become isolated and divided against each other.

Partnerships and marriages break up when difficulties arise. People leave without regard or concern for the interests of the other members, of partner, spouse or children. They leave when they would be better off alone, when there is illness, when their present partner becomes unemployed, when a younger or wealthier 'partner' becomes available.

Basic is that people behave in a way which enables them to trust and assist each other, that men and women co-operate with each other in a way which will protect and strengthen both, behaving in a way which ensures that all benefit from gains made.

So within a family, between husband and wife, it is the other person who comes first. When each spouse tries to make the other spouse happy, when each will go without something so as to make the other happy, then both can be happy.

Family's Role and Life in the Real World

Human beings work primarily for their family and members of a family stand by, support and help each other in times of need.

Smash the family and you undermine the strength of the people. I understand the resulting disruption was so marked in Russia that they had to back-pedal. One of the first things the Khmer Rouge did in

Cambodia was to smash the family to make the people dependent on the state.

It is tough when you have to go to work to earn the money, do the shopping, look after the kids and do everything yourself. The one thing you cannot afford to be is to be ill. And you have no time for the kids either. And in a one-parent family, what the children miss is the parent's caring co-operative behaviour, is the example of responsible people looking after each other. The boy being brought up by the mother knows that both of them were left to look after themselves by the father and that is not a good example to model himself on. If you are struggling on your own so as to survive you don't have time or energy to think of freedom or to work for the community or for the betterment of humankind.

In the kibbutzim, that is in Israel's co-operative settlements, children were brought up communally in age groups, away from their parents. One age group would progress together from creche to nursery and then to school, living together during the week and seeing their parents, or living with their parents, only at weekends.

This may have freed both parents for work and defence in the initial struggle for survival. But the practice was continued when successful, possibly to free women for work and so increase production. But it was done at the expense of the family.

Of any group in the country, the kibbutz children consequently showed the highest incidence of mental problems. The kibbutzim have had to backtrack and now give their children a more normal and strengthening family-life experience with their parents.

See 'Kibbutzim' {4}*.

Each member of the family gets strength from the others. Two heads are better than one, and work divided between two people in such a way that each can become expert in his or her own area is done much better than one person trying to do it all. The family gives people enormous emotional and economic strength to overcome life's problems. Husband and wife battle on together back-to-back and they do so successfully regardless of how tough the struggle may be. You cannot win all the battles but what cements the relationship is not just battles won but battles fought together. The depth of such a relationship between husband and wife and the wealth of strength it gives regardless of the opposition, this you know as well as I do. The children follow the example of their parents, gain the same strength and pass it on. It all depends on deep and secure emotional involvement between two people, between husband and wife.

Sources

See chapter 5:
> 'Family, Community, Sex and the Individual'*
> Manfred Davidmann

from which this theme's information was reproduced here.

{1}* In 'The Human Mind and How it Works:
Group Minds in Action:
How the Human Group Mind Shapes
the Quality of Our Life and Living'
Manfred Davidmann
ISBN 978-0-85192-055-9
see chapter 2: 'How the Human Brain
Developed and How Human Mind Works'

{2}* In 'The Human Mind and How it Works:
Group Minds in Action:
How the Human Group Mind Shapes
the Quality of Our Life and Living'
Manfred Davidmann
ISBN 978-0-85192-055-9
see chapter 9: 'The Will to Work:
What People Struggle to Achieve'

{3}* In 'The Human Mind and How it Works:
Group Minds in Action:
How the Human Group Mind Shapes
the Quality of Our Life and Living'
Manfred Davidmann
ISBN 978-0-85192-055-9
see chapter 7: 'Motivation Summary'

{4}* In 'Judaism: Basis - Past - Present - Future, Part 2'
Manfred Davidmann
ISBN 978-0-85192-061-0
see chapter 4: 'Kibbutzim'

Additions by the Editor:

In the original text of this chapter on the https://www.solhaam.org website Manfred Davidmann referred to other reports in form of links.

Here these reports are marked * and the sources are stated.

Family's Role in the Real World:
Teamwork in an Age of Specialisation and Accelerating Change
and
Gaining Strength in the Struggle for a Better Life

The family needs food and shelter and while the female looks after its young and its people, it is usually the male who struggles outside the immediate family to provide it with an income, with a standard of living, to the best of his ability. He is assisted in this when required by his spouse to an extent which depends on her own work within the family. He struggles outside the family to provide it with a good life, against those who wish to profit from the family's needs, against those who wish to exploit, who may even wish to oppress so as to exploit.

Each member of the family gets strength from the others. Two heads are better than one, and work divided between two people in such a way that each can become expert in his or her own area is done much better than one person trying to do it all. The family gives people enormous emotional and economic strength to overcome life's problems. Husband and wife battle on together back-to-back and they do so successfully regardless of how tough the struggle may be. You cannot win all the battles but what cements the relationship is not just battles won but battles fought together. The depth of such a relationship between husband and wife, and the wealth of strength it gives regardless of the opposition, this you know as well as I do. The children follow the example of their parents, gain the same strength and pass it on. It all depends on deep and secure emotional involvement between two people, between husband and wife.

Outside the family a struggle is taking place. The breadwinner is competing for work and income on behalf of the family. He is also struggling against those who wish to exploit him (and thus his family) and who oppress so as to exploit.

In the working environment women are just as oppressed and exploited as men are. When women receive lower wages for work of equal value then this is bad for men and women alike. When some people in a group are being underpaid, the pay of the others is being pushed down.

Anyone who sees men and women co-operating with each other within a family, struggling side by side, back to back, and sees them co-operating with each other and helping each other in the outside working environment, for a more secure and better life for their families, knows how strong and effective they are together.

All are equal as people. What has to be done is shared out between them according to individual skill, ability, knowledge and experience. And in the end all share equally in the family's gains and losses. In other words, all are equal, contribute to the best of their ability, and stand or fall together.

Teamwork implies sharing work and responsibilities in a way which ensures that all that has to be done is done well. Success is measured by social and mental well-being as well as by standard of living and quality of life, of the family as a whole and of each member.

Within the family we should see co-operation and teamwork between equals who divide up the work which has to be done between them in a functional way so that each becomes expert and effective in his or her part of what has to be done.

The spouses share out between themselves what needs to be done, each concentrating on areas of work in accordance with their abilities, knowledge, understanding, likes and dislikes.

Equal as people, each takes the decisions falling within their own area of competence and responsibility. The husband may decide which car is to be bought or about getting a new job, the wife about which school the children should go to or where the family should live. But each discusses matters with the other family members before agreement is reached about what is best for the family as a whole.

Such a functional division of work and responsibilities, such co-operation and teamwork, enable us to survive and do well in the dangerous environment in which we find ourselves.

Consider shopping for food. The shopping expert takes into account the likes and dislikes of the other members of the family. And the expertise involved in shopping can be appreciated by considering what has to be thought about while shopping. How fresh is the food, how long will it have to be stored at home, how much does it cost here compared with elsewhere, has it been genetically modified and what does this mean for us. And what about nitrates in water, heavy metals, herbicides, pesticides, irradiated foods, chemical additives, fat and sugar contents and other health risks, and more expensive organic foods.

It would be a waste of time for each to become expert in this field. It would be useless for each of the two people to do so and to argue continually about what is to be done. They would in this way be competing with each other by attempting to show that one is better than the other.

Family members do not waste their time competing with each other but add their knowledge and experience to the decision-taking process of the other. In general, the person who decides would be the one most competent to take such decisions.

Co-operation between men and women, within the family and as equals, would seem to be essential when bringing up their children under modern conditions of rapid change at an accelerating rate of change.

Strength to resist oppression and exploitation comes from men and women co-operating with each other and so men and women struggle together to achieve a better life, a humane way of living and of government, and social security.

It is in democracies that a high standard of living has been achieved. In democracies people can struggle openly for a better life but we see that what has been gained has to be defended and extended.

Human rights are based on controlling primitive dominating behaviour, on concern, care and affection for our young and our families, for people and for our communities. Human rights express themselves in co-operation and teamwork between men and women to achieve a good life of high quality.

The relationship between the two spouses is a functional relationship and functional relationships are often misunderstood and misrepresented. Women, for example, have at times been persuaded by traditions or beliefs into accepting domination and sometimes exploitation as the norm. And women have in the past been denied education and full equality with men within the family and in the community in which they live.

Source:

See chapter 5:
'Family, Community, Sex and the Individual'
Manfred Davidmann

Chapter 6

Using Words to Communicate Effectively

Summary

Shows how to communicate more effectively, covering aspects of thinking, writing, speaking and listening as well as formal and informal communications.

Consists of guidelines found useful by university students and practising middle and senior managers.

Communicating with Words

Communication is the transmission of meaning to others.

Important is that 'meaning' is transferred. In other words, it is important the other persons understand what we want them to understand, that they understand the intended meaning.

More precisely, purposeful communication is the transmission of intended meaning to others.

Implied is

1. that the sender of the communication has clear knowledge and understanding of the meaning he wishes to convey, and

2. that the receiver interprets the message in such a manner that he receives the intended meaning.

Hence for effective communication the sender must determine the purpose of the communication and use words which have the same meaning for sender and receiver.

Meaning of Words

The scientific study of meaning is called Semantics.

Words and Labels

Words are labels. Labels are arbitrary.

Most common cause of misunderstanding arises from assuming that the word (a label) is the object. Two people can then be arguing about a concept, referring to it by using the same word, arguing because this word means something different to each of them.

So to be meaningful, words must establish the same thought (reference) in both the sender and receiver of a communication.

Words vary considerably as regards their value for communication. They differ in their level of abstraction. The greater the level of abstraction, the less meaning do they have.

Levels of Abstraction

1   Objects

Objects represent a relatively low level of abstraction as they can be seen and touched and their characteristics detailed accurately.

Here words are labels for objects such as table or chair.

2   Events

In addition to objects, both action and time are implied, and so these are more complex.

Examples are: Accident, sale, party.

3 Generalisations

Words are also used as labels for groups and collections of objects or events. These generalisations are more abstract and less precise.

Examples of such labels are: Furniture, machine tools, employees, parents.

Employees, for example, can be full-time, part-time, shift working, office working, home working, male, female, young, old, single, married, unskilled, skilled, professional, and more.

4 Value Judgements or Ideology

Value judgements and ideology are at the highest level of abstraction and words used as labels for them are quite useless for effective communication until the meaning of the word used is clearly defined in detail.

Examples of such labels are: Beautiful, valuable, necessary, luxury, lazy, free enterprise, truth.

Such words can be strung together and mixed with generalisations to provide good-sounding speeches and statements of the kind politicians like to use, to provide speeches and statements with no real meaning attached to the words used. Listeners or readers use their own idea of what the words mean and so their understanding of what is being said differs widely from person to person.

I listed the word 'truth' as an example of a label for a meaningless abstraction. Surely 'truth' ought to be more than a meaningless value judgement, so let us look at this in more detail.

Consider two media reports of a current event. Each reports the same event, each apparently telling the truth, each report giving its viewers different impressions of what actually happened.

How come? Can there be more than one truth?

Such reports may tell only part of what happened, may report only what seems relevant to the reporter, may then be selecting what seems to support the particular viewpoint of those who prepared the report.

Compare these 'truths' with that demanded from a witness in a court of law: 'The truth, the whole truth and nothing but the truth.'

Which means that what is required in a court of law is the truth with nothing taken away and nothing added.

If we agree on this as a definition, then the word 'truth' has become more meaningful.

Formal and Informal Communications

A distinction needs to be made between formal and informal communications. Formal communication implies that a record is kept, that what has been said or written can be attributed to its originator.

On the whole, written communications are formal. But statements may be qualified by phrases such as 'preliminary thoughts are ...'.

Oral (spoken) communication consists of direct or transmitted speech between two or more people. Oral communications are more likely to be misinterpreted than written ones, were regarded as informal but are now often recorded and treated as formal. Missing from such recordings is the body language consisting of facial expressions and gestures.

Consider an informal chat by telephone getting comments on matters of joint concern before producing a final report. Important is the possibility of a two-way flow of information, of immediate feedback, of a frank unreserved exchange of information, opinions and ideas.

The informal nature of such exploratory conversations is often ignored. People's preliminary thoughts can then be quoted against them as if they had been fully considered.

Although an answering (recording) machine ought to bleep at regular intervals while recording, conversations can be recorded in different ways by one person without the other being aware of this.

Hence one needs to make sure the other person is aware of the informal nature of the conversation. In other words, that the other person knows the conversation is not to be recorded and that the information is to be regarded as confidential until the matter has been fully considered.

There are, however, many formal oral communications, such as selection, grievance or appraisal interviews, or when negotiating. Characteristic is that a record is kept by those participating.

Rumours are hearsay. One person tells the next who tells another, and so on. But there are personal barriers as people tend to keep back, elaborate or enhance information in accordance with their likes and dislikes. Hence information tends to change in emphasis and content as it is passed from person to person. This makes rumours so unreliable a source of information.

Improving Communication

1. Clarify your own ideas before attempting to communicate them.
2. Be clear about the purpose of the communication. For example, its purpose could be to inform others, to obtain information or to initiate action.
3. See if the other person can repeat what you have said, in his or her own words.

Effective communication, however, depends also on attentive listening.

Effective Listening

Do not jump to conclusions before hearing what the other person has to say, and do not interrupt.

Interrupting prevents effective and meaningful communication, can prevent the speaker from making a valid point. Think how you would feel if you were interrupted just before making your key point.

It is up to the sender (originator) of the communication to use words which have the same meaning also for the receiver, for the listener. To ensure that you have understood the communication (message) correctly, you can repeat it in your own words to the other person.

For example, after being told how to get to a particular street one can ask "You mean, take the second street on the left?". Answers like "Yes, it is" or "Take the third on the left" confirm or improve our understanding of what we had been told.

And so, for effective listening:

1. Avoid jumping to conclusions, avoid making value judgements such as good or bad, desirable or undesirable, true or false, while the speaker is talking.
2. Listen to the full story.
3. Restate the other person's position in your own words.

Letters and Reports

1. Avoid slogans, catchwords (buzz-words), jargon.

   Use words or phrases which you could use naturally in conversation. Exception are technical terms and abbreviations which your reader will understand.

2. Use simple words and few of them.

3. Keep paragraphs and sentences short.

4. In-house e-mail is fast. Copies are readily distributed to all those interested and reach their destination almost immediately.

   Fast method for causing chaos as mistakes spread rapidly. Effects snowball as others act quickly using the mistaken information.

   Better to prepare draft replies but only post the replies after some hours, which allows considering, validating, completing and improving the draft.

Traps to Avoid

1. Avoid being blinded by words or phrases which sound good, expert, impressive, plausible or likely. Ask for a definition or explanation to be given in clear, simple, meaningful language.

2. Avoid being misled by illogical arguments, misleading publicity or propaganda.

   When propaganda is logical, and seen to be logical, it is difficult to argue against, to counter. Such propaganda is usually misleading because it is the premise, the first argument or underlying assumption, which misleads.

   In other words, a logical argument can be based on false assumptions or misleading information.

Chapter 7

CHURCH AND STATE, GOVERNMENT AND RELIGION

This series of works together lays bare the controversies between church and state, between religious belief and practice on the one hand, and the government on the other. Each work is self-standing but together they provide the knowledge needed for understanding the causes of conflicts and point to solving them.

The works in this series bring together findings and conclusions from Manfred Davidmann's published reports and provide new knowledge and insights, exploring their subject in depth, generally in advance of current knowledge.

Chapter 7.1:

**Church and State, Government and Religion:
Judaism, Christianity and Islam**

Chapter 7.2:

**Church and State, Government and Religion:
Religion, Government and Education**

Chapter 7.3:

**Social Concept (Policies) of the Russian Orthodox Church:
Letter to the Russians**

Chapter 7.4:

**Social Policies (Doctrine) of the Roman Catholic Church:
An Evaluation**

Chapter 7.5:

**The Global (Worldwide) Struggle for a Better Life and
The Root of all Evil, the Source of All Good,
and the Messianic Struggle**

Chapter 7.6:

**Creationism and Intelligent Design, Evolution,
Education or Indoctrination**

Church and State, Government and Religion: Judaism, Christianity and Islam

Introduction

The world in which we live at present is in turmoil, in a mess. So we want to know why and what can be done about it.

We begin by looking at church and state, government and religion, at their aims and purpose, at the conflicts and confrontations between them. And start by describing what words such as state and religion mean and imply, as follows:

Government

The group or organisation ruling a country or conducting its affairs. It can also refer to the government's style of management (authoritarian or participative, dictatorship or democracy).

Religion

A system of faith and worship, based on belief in the existence of a benevolent God, usually expressed by believers living according to its doctrine (principles, rules of behaviour, customs).

State

Somewhat vague term which refers to the combination of government and the community (country, population) being governed. Its use ignores important distinctions between people, government and the government's style of management, and their often conflicting interests. For example it does not distinguish between a government which serves its people and one which serves a country's rulers.

Church

Refers to the religion's clergy, or to its hierarchy. It can also refer to the religion's organisation, its decision-taking processes, the doctrine it follows and the policies it applies.

But then there are different kinds of states and different kinds of churches {10}:

Some states consist of governments which serve the rulers by oppressing the people so that they can be exploited and such states stifle opposition and protest. Here those at the top and their experts tell people what they should do and have to do.

Other states consist of governments where those who govern serve the people and are accountable to them, where decisions are made at the lowest possible level by referendum with experts explaining the consequences both ways when a decision has to be made.

Similarly some churches serve rulers and in effect condition their people into gladly serving the rulers, into gladly allowing themselves to be exploited, the general approach then being 'gladly accept the tough life you are leading, the reward will come in a next life'.

And other churches preach that it is the will of God that all people are equal, that no person may exploit another, that it is the role of the establishment to serve the people.

The history of the religions of Judaism, Christianity and Islam illustrates the underlying conflict and the present-day confrontations between church and state, government and religion, and points to ways of solving (healing) them.

Pentateuch {3}

What stands out is that human beings, guided by God, learned the difference between the brutal behaviour of their beastly ancestors, and the humane socially-responsible behaviour of human beings.

Following a fundamental revelation, their struggles and achievements were recorded in the Pentateuch <1>, as were the social system and social rules of behaviour which underlie a good life of high quality combining freedom, independence and liberty <2>. Positive and constructive, rewarding what is good, punishing that which is inhuman, providing social security and a good life of high quality.

The whole history of the people and the essential social laws of behaviour and social system, were then recorded in the Pentateuch which has been handed down unaltered to this day. <1>

The beliefs of Judaism, Christianity and Islam include the social laws and social system of the Pentateuch and each of these religions experienced major conflicts and strife between church and state, religion and government. The struggle between them is about the application in our everyday lives of the social provisions of the Pentateuch.

So first we look at some key social laws of the Pentateuch, and describe its social system, to illustrate what the confrontation between 'church' and 'state' is about. <3>

Social and Economic Security

All persons have the right to be free and independent masters of their own fate and no person may oppress or exploit another. Because people can be exploited through their needs there has to be a system of social and economic security which guarantees freedom from needs and so protects people from becoming dependent on others for essential income, protects against loss of material and spiritual independence.

This is what is laid down as a matter of law {6}:

1. The community has to provide ('lend') money to those who need it, free of interest.
2. All such loans, if outstanding, are to be cancelled every seventh year.

Trustful Co-operation (Ten Commandments)

The Ten Commandments <4> are so important and are so well known because behaviour in accordance with these rules is the basis for people trusting each other and so for people co-operating and working well with each other. The Ten Commandments underlie freedom, independence and strength to oppose and resist oppression. Wherever there is any independence of the mind and material freedom today it exists because people followed these rules of behaviour and it exists to the extent to which they do so. {6}

Take these two commandments (principles of behaviour):

You must not steal.

You must not desire anything which belongs to your neighbour.

Much trust and community friendliness is gained when people follow these principles.

But consider that these laws apply equally to the rich and powerful. It is also the rich and powerful who must not steal from the poor even the little which the poor have. It is the rich and powerful who must not cast longing glances at what little the rest of us possess, it is the rich and powerful who must not aim to gain at our expense.

Government and Management

The laws of the Pentateuch control the behaviour and limit the power of 'rulers', that is of government, of top executives and of the establishment, of those in positions of trust, responsibility or authority, no matter whether secular, religious or military, no matter what the hierarchy or organisation. {6-7}. The Pentateuch {11} states clearly what they must not do.

They may not amass servants and may not oppress the people. They may not amass possessions and wealth, may not grasp power or behave promiscuously. In other words, they may not put themselves above others by grasping power, may not satisfy personal desires at the expense of others.

And a ruler (person in position of trust, responsibility or authority) has to follow these laws and abide by them every day if he wishes 'to prolong his days in his kingdom, he and his children'. For 'kingdom' read 'position' and include 'influence'.

These Pentateuch laws lay down that those in positions of trust, responsibility or authority must not oppress people so as to increase their own possessions and power. These laws forbid personal gain from the misuse of authority, wealth or position. Those in positions of trust, responsibility or authority may not grasp power, may not oppress the people, may not behave promiscuously, may not gain wives or wealth. {6}

Equality and Ownership

The country's wealth <5> belongs equally to all community members and needs to be shared out family by family {6}, where 'family' is a life-long single union {4} between husband and wife. With shares updated at regular intervals of between three and not more than five calendar years <6>. Each receives a share of the community's total net assets <7>, their 'Asset Share'. An Asset Share cannot be sold but the owner has the right to determine its use and to the resulting benefits.

But only those are supported who themselves genuinely support the Pentateuch's benevolent ideals and principles and their application and who themselves live and act accordingly, who behave humanely. {6}

Liberation Theology {5}

According to Liberation theologians, Christian belief and practice ranges along a continuous scale between two kinds, one at each end of the scale.

At one end is the kind which in effect serves the rulers and their establishment, those in authority such as a government or multinational, those who oppress and exploit. It teaches that the reward for this life's hardships will be a better life in a life to come.

At the other end is another kind of Christianity which bases its belief and practice on compassion for the poor and according to Christian texts which side with the poor against the rich, with the poor against the oppressor.

171

Liberation theologians advocate the second kind of Christianity which is one of compassion and leadership in the struggle against oppressors, in the struggle for a better life here and now in this life.

How come there are such widely differing kinds of belief and practice?

Among deprived Christian communities such as disadvantaged African negroes, South American indians, Indian indians and Filipinos, we now hear voices which distance themselves from ruler-serving Christian beliefs. We see them arguing for a Christian belief which puts equality and independence among their most important goals. And wherever there is extreme poverty and suffering and pain you are likely to find Christians who are struggling on the side of the oppressed. Such as priests who provide encouragement and guidance to oppressed and suffering people in their struggle for a better life against the ruling establishment, against established ruling oppressors, doing so at much risk and without thought of personal gain.

The underlying teachings of the Jewish and Christian religions are based on God's teachings as recorded in the Pentateuch. All people are considered equal and entitled to share in the wealth of their community. No wonder that 'it is in countries following the social teachings of Christianity and Judaism ('Christian' countries, democracies) that people have the highest standard of living, have lives of high quality', gained as the result of past and present struggle against those who wish to exploit, against those who wish to oppress so as to exploit.

However, what happened in the past was that those who ruled, and those who wished to rule and exploit, changed patterns of belief and observance, doing so from within, being opposed by the people with varying degrees of success. This explains why there appear to be different kinds of Christian belief and practice.

And next we look at what happened to Judaism, Christianity and Islam in the past, at the conflicts and confrontations between their teachings and the ruling establishment of the day, at these interactions between church and state, religion and government.

We now look at how the Pentateuch's rules and their application were changed in the past, why they were changed and by whom, who gained and who lost, at the extent to which present belief and practice differs fundamentally from the revealed word of God. A fascinating journey which will take us through Judaism to Christianity and Islam, and then to life and living in our times.

Judaism {7}

The Monarchy (David and Solomon)

At the beginning of this period the Hebrew tribes are scattered and on their own, each more or less fighting its own battles and looking after its own interests. We see people enjoying freedom and following the Pentateuch's laws.

Then we see the tribes coming together under a single central rule with combined forces. The opposing foreign tribes were defeated. The result was a country and a people which were united and powerful. Military success went hand in hand with bringing the tribes together in one united country.

The successful military leader, King David, ruled the country. Secular and religious authority were apparently concentrated in his hands.

Then we see those who rule using their power for their own benefit and to impose their rule. We see the emergence of those who grasp power and rule and then weaken Pentateuch law so as to rule more forcefully, so as to oppress, so as to exploit the people. This led inevitably to internal confrontation and conflict which divided the country.

During the period of the monarchy, that is during the period of Saul, David and Solomon, we see central military authority being more effective in an emergency and see the military leader subsequently taking over the administration, taking over the government. This is followed by increasing centralisation of power and the formation of an establishment (secular and religious) which serves the source of power and is used to oppress the people.

What we see is increasing centralisation of power, increasing corruption and oppression, increasing enslavement of the people with consequent social stress and subsequent destruction.

The popular leader, initially supported by those who were oppressed and in need, became powerful. He started to use the people for personal gain. But David ruled for 40 years and became rich and powerful. He had properties throughout the land and took concubines and wives. He instituted a 'levy', a form of conscription.

King Solomon, greatly praised, of such wonderful wisdom, of great power, wealth and horses, having many wives. But his reign was immediately followed by the kingdom splitting into two kingdoms which fought each other, which largely disregarded Pentateuch law until both kingdoms were destroyed and the people exiled to Babylon. Much has been written about Solomon and his glorious reign, his wisdom and his riches. But Jewish scripture and other ancient sources look at his reign from the point of view of the people over whom he ruled and tell another and completely different story. {7}

Solomon continued the process David had started. Under his reign the king's power over the people increased. It is plainly told, consistent and to the point.

He ignored basic Pentateuch law and weakened its application so as to weaken resistance to oppression, so as to oppress the people.

He started to oppress the people just as soon as he was unopposed and had undisputed authority.

We are being told that he obtained his wealth by taxing the people, that this was paid as an annual tax and that this was a heavy burden on the people.

He instituted both tax collecting and a compulsory labour service.

King Solomon built the first Temple and he also built a palace for himself.

It took seven years to build the Temple and after that it took thirteen years to build Solomon's palace. Solomon's palace occupied over four times the groundspace which the Temple occupied. {7}

The king soon ignored the laws of the Pentateuch which clearly states that he should not oppress the people so as to increase his own possessions and power, that he should not put himself above the people and so enrich himself. The Pentateuch warns against him oppressing people so as to multiply his power (horses), it prohibits his taking a large number of wives and the amassing of silver and gold.

We are told that he broke the 'kingship' laws, the laws of government which protect the people.

The whole record of Solomon's reign shows a ruler who is more concerned with personal wealth and power than with leading the people towards a better life.

Solomon died after he had reigned for forty years and Rehoboam his son took over.

And Rehoboam answered the people roughly and said 'My father made your yoke heavy, I will add to your yoke; my father punished you with whips, but I will punish you with scorpions'. So he told the people he would oppress them even more than his father Solomon had done. {7}

Oppression increased during Solomon's reign and once again it was the internal conflicts which broke up the country and so destroyed it.

Israel then rebelled against the descendants of David, and installed Jeroboam king over all Israel. However, the tribe of Judah followed the descendants of David. In this way Solomon's kingdom split up into two separate kingdoms, namely Judah and Israel (Samaria).

Rehoboam (Solomon's son) ruled over Judah, and Jeroboam ruled over Israel (Samaria). Jeroboam in effect abrogated the application of the Pentateuch laws.

The application of the Pentateuch, the basic constitution which protects the people, had been abrogated and the people were worse off than before, had even less protection against the ruler and his establishment, against the misuse of his power.

It seems to me that during the period of the monarchy and of the two kingdoms there was a continuous struggle between the forces which supported God, Judaism and the people, and those forces which supported central rule, the establishment and oppression of the people. It was the rulers who generally acted contrary to Jewish law and the Jewish religion seems to have been belittled, opposed and in some ways negated by them.

It would seem that religious and secular authority were in effect centred on the king (ruler) who soon ignored the God-given benevolent social provisions of the Pentateuch. Authority for belief and practice were combined in the person of the ruler who used his authority (power) for his own personal selfish gain and disregarded the very social laws and system for the application of which the Hebrew people had been fighting for and which underlay his success.

Maccabean Dynasty (The Hasmoneans)   <8> {7}

We know little about life in Israel during the period of about 300 years between the time of the return from Babylon and the time of the taking over of the country by the Seleucids in 198 BCE. We do know that religious observance was so important that they would not even defend themselves when attacked on the Sabbath (the weekly day of rest) so as not to desecrate it.

The Seleucids robbed the Temple of its wealth and destroyed the walls of Jerusalem. They then attempted to paganise the country by brutal force. Those who observed the Jewish laws and customs were bitterly persecuted, pagan worship and practices were introduced into the Temple and they destroyed written records (scrolls) of the law whenever they could find them. The high priest Menelaus continued in office but served Jupiter.

Among the Jewish leadership were those who served the Seleucid rulers by offering greater annual taxes for the sake of obtaining personal power. They collected them from the people. At the same time they weakened and opposed the influence of the Jewish religion so as to weaken the people. It was of course the people who suffered and who became more and more discontented.

Rulers and Establishment ('state', government)   <8> {7}

Mattathias (a priest) rebelled against pagan worship. The people could stand no more and led first by Mattathias and then by his son Judah Maccabee they rebelled against the imposed vicious rule of the Seleucids.

To begin with all were united and struggled against the brutal oppression. They struggled for God (Pentateuch), freedom and the people. Against them were foreign invaders who believed in slavery and who were trying to impose their way of life through imposing their beliefs. {1}

The uprising had one central unifying purpose: to build a country in which Jewish people could live as Jews and practise their faith (in which they could apply the social laws and social system of the Pentateuch to their daily lives), and gained ground.

Mattathias, his five sons and his grandson John Hyrcanus led the uprising and supported one another. Single minded, the members of the Maccabean family were loyal to the brother who was in command at the time. What is known is that whenever the brother who was ruling at the time was either killed in battle or assassinated by the enemy, one of the other brothers simply stepped into his place, provided the required leadership and was in turn supported by the rest of the family.

Judah Maccabee was followed by Jonathan who in turn was followed by Simeon. The leadership of the three brothers covers a period of 30 years during which much of the country was freed. John Hyrcanus was able to build the country and complete the work the others had started.

Jonathan was appointed high priest about 8 years after taking over the leadership. Simeon was confirmed by the 'Great Assembly' as high priest, ethnarch (ruler) and commander of the Jewish people. Simeon's positions were to be hereditary.

Appointing Jonathan as high priest transferred religious authority and power to a secular leader. When the Great Assembly confirmed Simeon's position, a few years after he had assumed the leadership, they confirmed that religious and secular as well as military authority and power had been vested in one person and were to be hereditary.

What had happened was that able military and secular leadership absorbed religious authority and power. That this concentration of all authority and power in the hands of one person was to be permanent and later to be transferred to his descendants is an indication that the establishment of the day was already concerned with consolidating its own position.

Following the popular uprising for Judaism, for Jewish law and thus for freedom, the rulers formed a dynasty and a supporting establishment. They tasted power, meant to have it and meant to cling to it. Instead of serving God and people, the rulers battled for power with each other, allied themselves with foreign powers against each other. In so doing they divided the people and weakened all. The Jewish leadership, the Jewish establishment, disregarded the welfare of the people, disregarded Jewish law, disregarded the intent and purpose of Jewish law. <8> {7}

The religious hierarchy became subservient to the secular rulers, with the rulers presumably using the religious hierarchy to motivate and tranquillise their people. And two generations after the uprising we see increasing internal confrontation between believing (Pentateuch-observing) people on the one hand against oppressive rulers and their oppressing establishment on the other. {1}

I think that combining all power in the hands of a single ruler is against the spirit and intent of Jewish law as religious authority, which should serve God and the people, which should indicate direction and provide drive, may then too readily be misused to serve the establishment of the day instead of God and the people. {7}

The Jewish leadership, the Jewish establishment, supported centralised power, the oppressive ruling authority and its influence, since the ideas which were being imported helped them to oppress their own people. In so doing they disregarded the welfare of the people, disregarded Jewish law, disregarded the intent and purpose of Jewish law. {7}

The oppression of Jew by Jew, of the Jewish people by their own rulers and establishment, and the resulting struggle between them defeated both. It ended Maccabean rule, lost the land which had been gained, resulted in enormous hardship to the people. It resulted in the handing over of the country and its people to Herod and the subsequent introduction and popularisation by Herod of a foreign ideology based on slavery and supporting it. It was indeed this which the Maccabees had struggled against. {7}

177

Outstanding is that the people were unable to restrain their leaders. The result was total destruction of people and country, and the dispersion of the Jewish people. {7}

Belief and Practice ('church', religion)   {8-9}

During the five generations after that of Simeon, that is during the Maccabean dynasty, the secular rulers gained control of the religious hierarchy and of what was being taught. There was discontent and opposition, but what was taught became increasingly establishment-orientated, serving an oppressing and exploiting establishment. The social laws ceased to be applied as a comprehensive system, as a way of life.

After three generations we see very clearly increasing internal confrontation, a struggle between those wishing to apply the God-given benevolent egalitarian social laws and system on the one hand against oppressive rulers and their establishment-serving religious hierarchy on the other. What had been the people's leaders had become rulers who battled for power with each other, allied themselves with foreign powers against each other, betrayed their people to a foreign power for the sake of personal power and influence. In so doing they divided the people and weakened all. This was virtually the end of independence for the country. {7}

The Jewish establishment (secular and religious) had been and were changing the application of God's benevolent social laws so that 'the law was becoming like two laws'. They argued in religious terms about social and political policies. What are recorded are the arguments, misrepresentations and falsehoods (untruths) used by establishment-orientated religious 'scholars' <9> against applying the Pentateuch's benevolent legislation, in effect misleading the population into acquiescing to changes which served the ruling establishment, which enabled the establishment to oppress and exploit the population.

It was then decided to record what was happening so that future generations would become aware of what had happened and of who had been doing what to whom. They also wanted future generations to learn from the lessons of the past. Their record of what took place is called the Talmud which covers many subjects in many volumes. To compile the whole Talmud took about 400 years in Jerusalem and about 500 years in Babylon. The Talmud was then 'frozen' ('canonised'). {8-9}

You can see how the Talmud records the bitter feelings of ordinary people about what establishment-serving scholars were doing to Pentateuch and people. And when some scholars attempted to provide their own statements with an authority they did not have, the practice was scathingly condemned in the Talmud. {9}

The Talmud describes how the God-serving religious hierarchy was replaced by an establishment-serving religious hierarchy {8}, how the people felt about this {9} and the subsequent antisocial changes to belief and practice. This is conclusively recorded in two different and separate ways which confirm each other. But Rabbinical Judaism (today's Judaism) does not teach this and so propagates the establishment's revisionist version of Jewish belief and practice. {8} <10>

Rabbinical Judaism (today's Judaism) teaches, and Jewish belief and practice follows, the Jewish establishment's version of belief and practice. This version has the essential core benevolent social laws bypassed and edited out from observance, and is followed by Jews at the present time.

We saw that the religious scholars were serving the rulers ('state', government) instead of serving God and people ('church', religion).

And saw the history of the two main confrontations, of the struggle, between the Jewish rulers ('state', government, establishment) and the people, from the recording of the Pentateuch to the birth of Christianity.

This struggle was about position, influence and control over communities, about changing God-given benevolent rules of behaviour so that people could be oppressed and exploited.

It changed Judaism, determined the fate of the Jewish people and gave rise to Christianity.

And we saw that attempts to argue against the rulers and their establishment were by themselves unable to change the course of events.

Christianity   {1}

Jesus Taught

A remnant of Jews kept alive the knowledge of the social laws of the Pentateuch. They gained motivation, numbers and strength by rallying round and following the teachings of Jesus (Teacher of Righteousness) in spite of opposition from the religious establishment. Christian beliefs were spreading largely among Jews, and Christianity was a group within Judaism. These Jews came together to follow the word of God.

Early Christians were called Jewish Christians because their membership consisted largely of Jews who had joined them and followed their beliefs and teachings. They believed Jesus was a prophet who had tried to make people more aware of the intent of the Pentateuch and had tried to intensify the application of its laws. The Pentateuch was of great importance to them and they kept its laws, keeping the sabbath and performing circumcision.

As Jews had in any case to follow and live according to the Pentateuch's laws, what were Jews and Jewish Christians arguing about?

The laws of the Pentateuch have to be followed and applied by Jews as a matter of law in their daily lives. However, it was such laws of behaviour and such social system laws which the rich simply did not want to apply and we saw above that they, the rich and powerful, had had the application of these benevolent laws bypassed {6-9}. Jesus tried to reverse this situation and to have such laws applied by people in their everyday lives.

Jesus taught that if the rich wish to be rewarded by God they need to follow all the commandments and the social laws of the Pentateuch. {1}

Jesus said that 'good deeds' by themselves are not enough to gain eternal life. Whoever keeps the commandments enters eternal life. To be a 'good person' and enter eternal life one has to keep the commandments. {1}

Matthew's gospel records Jesus making a specific point which applies in general. Those who are rich and powerful and who are not observing the important social laws, suffer and will suffer the unavoidable consequences as a result. {1}

So Jewish Christians believed in the laws of the Pentateuch and struggled for the application of these laws in daily life, struggling against an oppressive establishment which argued against and did not want to follow the social laws.

Paul's Ideology

Paul was Jewish and persecuted the Christians who were renewing their knowledge of the laws and the application of the laws in their daily lives. So he was acting on the side of, that is for, the oppressive establishment.

He was unsuccessful in this as Jewish Christianity spread and continued to spread.

He then said that he had had a 'vision' and called himself a Christian but he preached not for but against the social laws and against the social system of the Pentateuch. He preached against material independence, against social security, against freedom from oppression and exploitation.

Look again at the social laws and system of the Pentateuch <11> and you will see how the laws of the Pentateuch ensure freedom and material independence and provide a good life of high quality here and now, backed by effective social security. No one may oppress or exploit another and all are equal, as a matter of law.

It is these laws of behaviour, it is these social laws and this social system which Paul opposed and he then attempted to stop people from keeping these laws.

Paul's letters (epistles) are the oldest part of the New Testament, probably written about 50 AD, some considerable time after the death of Jesus <12>. What stands out is that no one before Paul wrote such letters and that no one did so afterwards.

Paul wrote {2} that
> 'the law brings wrath, but where there is no law there is no transgression',

saying that the God-given laws of Moses (in the Pentateuch) result in punishment for those who break the law and that a law that does not exist cannot be broken. {1}

Laws protect people when those who break them are punished. So Paul is saying that there would be no punishment if the laws were abolished, implying that antisocial activities can be allowed to take place without restraint.

Astonishingly and without good reason he states that those in authority rule by 'divine right', that whatever they do is justified because in his opinion they act on God's behalf. Whatever those in authority do or want is called 'good' by Paul and those who resist or oppose them do 'evil' and will be punished. Paul wants all to obey those in authority and to be obedient, to pay taxes and revenues, to respect and honour those in authority. {1}

He is arguing that one must fear and obey those in authority and do for them and give them all they ask, without regard to how selfish, corrupt, inhuman, vicious, murdering or evil they may be. {1}

What Paul is saying and putting forward is neither God's word nor is it what Jesus taught. Under the disguise of a religious sermon Paul is spreading political propaganda. Paul is preaching the political ideology of an oppressive establishment which wanted to be able to oppress so as to exploit without hindrance. He is preaching against observance of laws which ensure freedom, independence and equality. And he gives his opinions an authority which they would not otherwise have had by means of a self-proclaimed vision. {1}

So Paul preached against material independence, against social security, against freedom from oppression and exploitation. What he preached was the political ideology of an oppressive establishment.

This brought him into conflict with Jewish Christians and with the mostly Jewish Christian communities and he was unsuccessful in changing their beliefs and practices. He then concentrated on gaining converts from gentiles (people who are not Jewish) who presumably knew nothing or little about the laws of the Pentateuch and who would thus be more likely to follow his teachings without arguing about its content.

Paul's teachings were accepted to a considerable extent. The Gentile Christians' stories about the beginning of Christianity differ from those of the Jewish Christians and it is the versions of the Gentile Christians which were included in the Christian Canon and became official doctrine.

Paul's letters (epistles) were written about 50 AD. The Gospels were written about 70-100 AD and as a whole relate to the life and death of Jesus. Matthew's was written first, then Mark's, then Luke's. Luke also wrote The Acts.

Matthew's Record (Gospels)

Matthew's gospel was the first to be written. It appears that Matthew wrote his Gospel to counter Paul's distortions, recording what Jesus had actually been preaching. It is closest to the events and so perhaps it is not surprising that it has always been the most popular and revered of the gospels.

Matthew struggled to put the record straight, struggled to record what Jesus actually taught. Throughout the ages, Christians of goodwill chose intuitively to interpret Paul's statements about those in authority as meaning that

'the authority of those in authority only comes from God to the extent to which they themselves live according to and apply the Ten Commandments, the social laws and the social system laws' and that only those can 'love one another' who comply with all these laws. {1}

Matthew's Gospel was later followed by Mark's and this in turn was followed by Luke's gospel. The later authors were apparently aware of and knew the earlier gospels which seems confirmed by the successive changes which were made which changed the record of what Jesus taught and of the meaning of the stories and of the arguments. {1} <13>

Matthew's record was subtly changed in later gospels. Successive changes, one by one, changed meaning and intent further and further away from what is recorded in Matthew's gospel. {1}

Further and further away from Matthew's clear record and statement about what Jesus taught. Obscuring and confusing that which Jesus taught, so as to weaken arguments against Paul's distortions. {1}

So what happened was:

Jesus taught that all the laws had to be kept, that belief and practice included and had to include the Ten Commandments, the social laws and the social system of the Pentateuch.

Paul, however, acted on behalf of the rich and powerful when he tried to convince people that those in authority were God's representatives on earth and that the social laws did not have to be kept.

Paul's letter to the 'Romans' was written before the gospels. Matthew's later gospel records what Jesus actually taught and clearly makes the point that Paul was trying to subvert and turn upside down that which Jesus taught. As Matthew records what Jesus taught, this outweighs and overrides what Paul said.

Those who later favoured Paul's pro-establishment ideology could not challenge Matthew's record. Hence Matthew's gospel was subtly changed in later gospels, in an attempt to distort and hide that which Jesus had taught so as to weaken arguments against Paul's ideology.

Here also we see the establishment engaged in abrogating, in effect in annulling <14>, the benevolent social laws of the Pentateuch.

The establishment's version became accepted as official Christian doctrine and apparently it is this which tends to be taught today.

Christian Canon

Outstanding is that the contemporaneously written <15>, agreed and finalised Christian Canon and Jewish Talmud were shaped by, and independently record, the same confrontations and struggle and sequence of events. The Talmud was written contemporaneously with the gospels, starting in the first century AD. And both the Talmud and the Christian Canon were completed and agreed, canonified and frozen, at about the same time, roughly four-hundred years later. The agreement between Christian and Jewish writings is so complete that we are now reasonably certain about the main course of events. {1}

The Christian Canon continued to be compiled till it was approved by the Christian establishments and so presumably biased towards what the establishment wanted included or excluded, wanted said or unsaid. What became the Christian Canon, meaning by this the 'agreed' version of events and teachings, took about four hundred years before it was 'agreed' {5}.

It apparently took about four hundred years for written material and for people's memories to be changed, edited and modified, to conform to the establishment point of view. If it had just been a matter of recording facts, of recording the truth, the whole truth and nothing but the truth (the truth, nothing left out and nothing added), it would not have taken so long. After ten or so generations people would be regarding as factual that which they were being told was factual.

A similar if not identical process took place within Judaism during roughly the same period of time and here also the relevant social laws were side-tracked and bypassed. It does seem more than a coincidence that it took roughly the same period of time for Christianity and Judaism to contemporaneously finalise the Christian Canon and the Jewish Talmud, respectively.

Both the Talmud and the Canon tell of an outsider, of an outside establishment orientated ideology, corrupting what was being taught and undermining what people believed, corrupting and undermining what Jesus had taught.

In both religions the establishment versions became accepted as official doctrine.

Liberation Theology's 'Two Types of Christianity'

We can now understand much more clearly what Liberation Theology's teachings have been saying. As said already:

> Liberation theologians maintain that Christian belief and practice ranges along a continuous scale between two forms, one at each end. At one end of this scale is the kind which in effect serves the establishment, that is those in authority such as a government, and this kind teaches that reward will be a better life in a life to come. Liberation theologians advocate the second kind of Christianity, at the other end of the scale. They emphasise compassion and leadership in the struggle against oppressors, in the struggle for a better life here and now in this life. {5}

They (liberation theologists) are arguing that there are two kinds of Christianity. They say that there is the kind of Christianity that serves the rulers and their establishment and thus those who oppress and exploit. They say that there is also another kind of Christianity which bases its belief and practice on compassion for the poor and according to Christian texts which side with the poor against the rich, with the poor against the oppressor. {5}

Manfred Davidmann concluded that Christianity is struggling forward towards its roots in response to the social and economic problems of global humanity at the present time. Towards what Jesus taught, towards the social laws and social system of the Pentateuch. {5, 1}

Islam

Arab Life at the Time of Mohammed   {15} <16>

Arabs were mainly nomads living in the central and northern Arabian peninsula. Some of them had settled around the oases. There was no written code of laws, life was harsh and brutal.

The only restraint on an individual was the fear of vengeance. All members of a community (family, clan or tribe) were held responsible for the acts of any one of them. There was no wrong in killing someone not a member of one's tribe, but it would be unwise to do so if the victim's tribe was strong. Survival depended on the strength of one's tribe.

But no such restraints applied to communal acts of violence. The tribes were constantly at war with each other, except for four months of truce every year, with loot (material and human) apparently the key objective of intertribal skirmishes and warfare. Women and children captured in tribal warfare who were not ransomed became tribal slaves and could be bought and sold.

Mohammed is born into this kind of society of illiterate desert Arabs and teaches them (reveals to them) what God has commanded him to recite to his fellow Arabs.

Mohammed Taught

The Prophet Mohammed struggled throughout his preaching life against the powerful Meccan family which dominated Mecca, against the Quraysh. They first opposed and then persecuted him and his followers for ten years, and then he fought them for another ten years till he won. Shortly after that he died. {15}

At first Mohammed preached the word of God in this environment for roughly ten years. A small number believed, mostly of the poorer classes. The followers he drew were the rejected, the disadvantaged, the weak and the oppressed - slaves, women and minority tribes. {13-15}

His message to the Meccans was that they should abandon all forms of idolatry and devote themselves to following the directions of the one all-seeing and almighty but compassionate God, that it was necessary for people to be humble and grateful towards God and to worship Him, and the obligation of generosity and respect for the rights of the poor and the defenceless. {12}

Mohammed teaches that God's benevolent social laws and system have to be applied by people in their daily life, that those who in the past erred from God's way are in grave error {20}. The quotations from the Koran which follow speak for themselves.

The book (al-kitab, the Pentateuch) came down (tanzil) from God, the mighty, the wise-one.
> The arabic phrase for the Holy Koran is 'al-Koran'. The Pentateuch (the Five Books of Moses) is 'al-kitab', a religious book is 'mushaf'. <17>

{40:002, 45:002, 46:002}

We gave Moses guidance (al-huda)
> huda: guidance or guide.

and gave the book (al-kitab, the Pentateuch) to the Children of Israel to inherit.
A guide (huda) and a reminder (warning) to people who understand.
> To those who understand its commandments (message),
> it is a guide (about what is 'good', about what to do) and
> a warning (about what is evil, about what not to do).

{40:053-54}

We gave the Book (al-kitab, Pentateuch) to Moses, but disputes arose about it. ...
They are in serious doubt (about the belief).
{41:045}

We gave the book (al-kitab, the Pentateuch) to the Children of Israel
and gave them the knowledge and prophethood.
We provided them with good things and preferred them above (all)
people;
{45:016}

We proved the commandments (bayyinat amr) to them beyond doubt:
> Literal: We gave them clear proofs (indisputable
> evidence) of commandments.

but after the knowledge had come to them,
greed caused them to disagree among themselves.
> Greed: intense and selfish desire for wealth or power.

{45:017}

> The social laws and the social system of the Pentateuch
> have to be followed and applied by Jews as a matter of
> law in their daily lives.
>
> However, it was these laws of behaviour and the social
> system laws {3} which the Jewish ruling elite simply did
> not want to apply and they, the rich and powerful, had
> the application of the laws changed to suit themselves
> {8-9}.

And when Jesus came with the clear proofs (the indisputable evidence)
(al-bayyinat), he said:
I have come to you with wisdom
to clarify some of what you are differing about.
Fear God and obey (God).
God is my Lord and your Lord: therefore serve (follow) Him. That is the
right way (sirat mustakim).
But the factions among them differed.
{43:063-65}

> The social laws and the social system laws of the
> Pentateuch had been bypassed or abrogated by the
> Jewish ruling elite, by the rich and powerful.
>
> Jesus tried to reverse this situation and to have these
> laws again applied by people in their everyday lives. {1}
>
> But the ruling elite, backed by the Christian
> establishment, later modified Jesus' teachings (Christian
> beliefs) from within. {1}

(To Mohammed:) Say (to them): "I am only a mortal like you;
It has come to me (yuhi) that there is only one God.

187

So take the right way to Him, and ask His forgiveness."

> Literal: So 'you go in the right way' and ... (istakimu)

And woe to those who serve associates (mushrekin) beside Him;

> Mushrekin (associates): Guides, masters, overlords or supreme beings with whom a person associates (to which a person attributes) a god-like knowledge or authority. That which or those whom you consider to be like God, that or those whose orders you obey as if they came from God.

{41:006}

And now We have set you on the right way of our commandment (sharia amr),
so follow it, and do not follow the desires of ignorant people (those who do not have that knowledge)
for they cannot shield you from God.
{45:018}

And so Mohammed taught {20} that:

> God gave the Pentateuch to Moses but disputes arose about it (among the Jews) because of greed.

> When Jesus came clearly stating the law and asked people to follow it, again factions differed.

> Mohammed then continues, saying: 'It is revealed to me there is only one God, so take the right way to Him.'

Preaching the obligation of generosity and respect for the rights of the poor and the defenceless, soon aroused the opposition of the Meccan elite and Mohammed's followers were persecuted. {15}

Mohammed was forming a movement which all who were deprived could join. The traditional Arab tribe, and loyalty, were based on family, on blood relationships, and thus limited in size. Opposition may well have developed also from the fear that in time Mohammed's movement might unseat the ruling family, their establishment, their tribe. {15}

So here also we see the two opposed sides. On the one hand Mohammed preaching the words of benevolent and caring God (Allah), on the other side a self-serving ruling elite.

Traditions tell that during and almost immediately after the death of Mohammed his teachings of revelations from benevolent Allah who cared deeply about peoples' welfare and well-being, were collected and recorded by Zaid bin Thabit. {17-18}

Traditions also tell that about fifteen years later Caliph Uthman had an official text prepared which included Zaid bin Thabit's, that he ordered the compilers to change Zaid bin Thabit's manuscripts into reflecting 'the voice of' (the opinions of) the ruling elite, that is to make sure that their compilation stated the ruling elite's point of view. The same tradition states that Caliph Uthman then distributed copies of this ruling elite's compilation (Uthman's Koran) and ordered all other versions to be destroyed. {17-18}.

This is how Maxime Rodinson {12} describes what happened after the death of Mohammed:

> At the head of the Arab empire was the family of Quraysh which had been the most determined in its opposition to the Prophet. It was as if Mohammed had worked and preached, all for the greater glory and profit of his enemies.

It took about 300 years after the death of Mohammed before the 'reading' of the Koran was finally fixed. {17}

Throughout almost the whole of Mohammed's life as Prophet he struggled against the powerful Meccan family which dominated Mecca, against the Quraysh {15}. And after Mohammed died, the ruling elite took over and here also appears to have edited out from observance God's (Allah's) benevolent social laws and system.

Since then there has been continuous confrontation and struggle between secular and religious figureheads and hierarchies, between state (rulers, government) and religious authorities (clerics, religious hierarchy, religion). {17}:

> About what should and should not be done, about what must and must not be done, about who should be making these and similar decisions.

> About the personal role, authority, pay, standard of living and quality of life of the decision-takers.

> With each attempting to make the other serve its own ends.

It is this which shaped Muslim belief and practice to this day and it underlies the conflicts and confrontations we see today between Muslim rulers and Muslim clerics, between 'secular government' and 'rule by religious clerics'.

To me it seems that it also underlies the impoverished condition in some Muslim countries of those parts of their populations which are deprived, exploited, oppressed. {15-21}.

Findings

This work brings together Manfred Davidmann's ground-breaking discoveries from previously published separate major investigations <18> into the history of Judaism, Christianity and Islam. The complete sequence of events covering the three religions is shown here for the first time, is clear and to the point.

We saw the history of the two main confrontations between the Jewish rulers ('state', government, establishment) and their people, from the recording of the Pentateuch to the birth of Christianity. This struggle was about position, influence and control over communities, about changing God-given benevolent rules of behaviour so that people could be oppressed and exploited. It changed Judaism, determined the fate of the Jewish people and gave rise to Christianity.

We also saw that Jesus taught that all the laws had to be kept, that belief and practice included and had to include the Ten Commandments, the social laws and the social system of the Pentateuch. Paul, however, acted on behalf of the rich and powerful when he tried to convince people that those in authority were God's representatives on earth and that the social laws did not have to be kept.

Paul's letter to the 'Romans' was written before the gospels. Matthew's later gospel records what Jesus actually taught and clearly makes the point that Paul was trying to subvert that which Jesus taught. As Matthew records what Jesus taught, this outweighs and overrides what Paul said. Those who later favoured Paul's pro-establishment ideology could not challenge Matthew's record. Hence Matthew's gospel was subtly changed in later gospels.

Here also we saw the establishment engaged in abrogating, in effect in annulling <14>, the benevolent social laws of the Pentateuch. The establishment's version became accepted as official Christian doctrine and apparently it is this which tends to be taught today.

According to Liberation theologists, there are two kinds of Christianity. There is the kind of Christianity that serves the rulers and their establishment and thus those who oppress and exploit. And they say that there is also another kind of Christianity which bases its belief and practice on compassion for the poor and according to Christian texts which side with the poor against the rich, with the poor against the oppressor. {5}

Manfred Davidmann concluded that Christianity is struggling forward towards its roots in response to the social and economic problems of global humanity at the present time. Towards what Jesus taught, towards the social laws and social system of the Pentateuch. {5, 1}

Considering Islam, we saw that throughout almost the whole of Mohammed's life as Prophet he struggled against the powerful Meccan family which dominated Mecca, against the Quraysh {15}. And after Mohammed died, the ruling elite took over. We saw that hadiths (traditions) recorded that on the one hand we have the word of benevolent Allah as taught by Mohammed that people (believers) should have a good life of high quality in this life, but that on the other hand is the ruling elite's opposing viewpoint that people should be obedient and serve willingly without questioning their condition {18}. Since then there has been continuous confrontation and struggle between secular and religious figureheads and hierarchies, between state (rulers, government) and religious authorities (clerics, religious hierarchy, religion) {17} with each attempting to make the other serve its own ends.

It is this which shaped Muslim belief and practice to this day and it underlies the conflicts and confrontations we see today between Muslim rulers and Muslim clerics, between 'secular government' and 'rule by religious clerics'.

To me it seems that it also underlies the impoverished condition in some Muslim countries of those parts of their populations which are deprived, exploited, oppressed. {15-21}.

Conclusions

Underlying the Pentateuch's benevolent and egalitarian legislation are its social laws and social system, including the Ten Commandments and laws protecting the people by limiting the behaviour of their rulers.

The Jewish people undertook to live accordingly, to apply all of these in their daily lives. But their own rulers (kings, state, government, establishment) negated the application of these rules of behaviour and the people were oppressed and exploited. Rabbinical Judaism (today's Judaism) propagates the establishment's revisionist version of Jewish belief and practice. {8}

Jesus taught that all the Pentateuch's laws had to be kept, that belief and practice had to include them. Here again we saw that the establishment in effect negated the application of these benevolent rules of behaviour, that the Christian establishment's version became accepted and that the people were once again exposed to oppression and exploitation.

Mohammed knew about the events of the past and said so, calling for a return to following the ancient benevolent God-given social legislation. This knowledge may have been lost and since then there has been continuous confrontation and struggle between secular and religious figureheads and hierarchies, between state (rulers, government) and religious authorities (clerics, religious hierarchy, religion) {17}.

Notes <..>

< 1>   Pentateuch, part of the Bible. Also called 'The Five Books of Moses' (namely Genesis, Exodus, Leviticus, Numbers and Deuteronomy). Also called 'Torah'.

< 2>   Freedom: The right and power to act, speak, or think freely.
Liberty: The state of being free from oppression or imprisonment.
Independence: Self governing and not depending on another for livelihood or subsistence.

< 3>   For a more comprehensive and more detailed listing of the social laws and social system of the Pentateuch, see {3}

< 4>   For a full listing of the Ten Commandments, in biblical and plain English, see Appendix 5 of {6}. For a good discussion of its provisions see {6}.

< 5>   A country's wealth includes productive assets and capital, including land, enterprise and corporation ownership, property, bank deposits and reserves.

< 6>   At the time the Pentateuch was written, the sharing out of assets was to be updated after every 49 years. At present, updating at regular intervals of between three and not more than five calendar years is more appropriate.

< 7>   'Net assets' is the amount of money which would be left for distributing among the owners if everything belonging to an enterprise were sold and all its debts paid.

< 8>   For a comprehensive detailed account of events, generation by generation, see {7}.

< 9>   Establishment-orientated scholars, the 'experts' of the day. See {22} for a contemporary example.

<10>   In {8} see 'The Five Pairs (Zugot)' which includes Figure 2 'Names of the Pairs' and Figure 3 'Laying-on of Hands'.

<11>   See section on 'Pentateuch' and {3}

<12>   In {1} see 'Paul'.

<13>   In {1} see 'Gospels'.

<14>   Abrogate: Doing away with (a law or agreement). Annul: Declaring (a law or other legal contract) invalid.

<15>   Contemporaneous: At the same time, of the same period, contemporary.

<16>   See {15} Section: 'Arab Life and Living at the Time of Mohammed' for sources (references) and more comprehensive information.

<17>   In {18} see particularly 'Hadith 2: How Caliph Uthman Ordered the Compilation of an Official Koran Text' which clearly shows the meaning of these terms. And see the other relevant Koranic verses in {20}.

<18>   See {1, 6-9, 15-21, 5}

References {..}

{ 1}   See chapter 3:
'Origin of Christianity and Judaism:
What Actually Happened,
What Jesus Actually Taught and Later Changes'
Manfred Davidmann

{ 2}   Romans 4, 15

{ 3} See chapter 4:
'The God-given Human Rights, Social Laws and
Social System'
Manfred Davidmann

{ 4} See chapter 5:
'Family, Community, Sex and the Individual'
Manfred Davidmann

{ 5} See chapter 2:
'Liberation Theology: Basis - Past - Present – Future'
Manfred Davidmann

{ 6} In 'Judaism: Basis - Past - Present - Future, Part 1'
Manfred Davidmann
ISBN 978-0-85192-060-3
see chapter 2.1: 'Struggle for Freedom:
The Social Cause-and-Effect Relationship'

{ 7} In 'Judaism: Basis - Past - Present - Future, Part 1'
Manfred Davidmann
ISBN 978-0-85192-060-3
see chapter 2.2: 'History Speaks: Monarchy,
Exile and Maccabees'

{ 8} In 'Judaism: Basis - Past - Present - Future, Part 1'
Manfred Davidmann
ISBN 978-0-85192-060-3
see chapter 2.3: 'At the Time of Jesus,
This is What Actually Happened in Israel:
The Truth about Hillel and his Times'

{ 9} In 'Judaism: Basis - Past - Present - Future, Part 1'
Manfred Davidmann
ISBN 978-0-85192-060-3
see chapter 2.4: 'One Law for All: Freedom Now,
Freedom for Ever'

{10} In 'Judaism: Basis - Past - Present - Future, Part 1'
Manfred Davidmann
ISBN 978-0-85192-060-3
see chapter 5: 'The Right to the Land of Israel'

{11} Pentateuch:
Deuteronomy **17**, 14-20.

{12} Muhammad
Maxime Rodinson
Tauris Parke Paperbacks
1971, 2002

{13} Introduction to the Qur'an
Richard Bell
Edinburgh University Press, 1958

{14} Tune into the "new conscience of Islam"
Sophie Boukhari interviewing Abdou Filali-Ansari
Unesco Courier, November 2001

{15} In 'Islam: Basis – Past – Present – Future'
Manfred Davidmann
ISBN 978-0-85192-053-5
see chapter 2: 'Prophet Mohammed's Struggle
for a Better Life for All'

{16} In 'Islam: Basis – Past – Present – Future'
Manfred Davidmann
ISBN 978-0-85192-053-5
see chapter 3: 'Text, Language, Dialect and
Interpretation of the Koran'

{17} In 'Islam: Basis – Past – Present – Future'
Manfred Davidmann
ISBN 978-0-85192-053-5
see chapter 4: 'The Divine Right to Rule'

{18} In 'Islam: Basis – Past – Present – Future'
Manfred Davidmann
ISBN 978-0-85192-053-5
see chapter 5: 'Compiling the Koran: Hadiths
(Traditions) State the Underlying Reality'

{19} In 'Islam: Basis – Past – Present – Future'
Manfred Davidmann
ISBN 978-0-85192-053-5
see chapter 6: 'Uthman's Rearrangement of the
Chronological (as revealed) Koran's Chapters'

{20} In 'Islam: Basis – Past – Present – Future'
Manfred Davidmann
ISBN 978-0-85192-053-5
see chapter 7: 'Prophet Mohammed's Word of
Allah and the Voice of the Ruling Elite'

{21} In 'Islam: Basis – Past – Present – Future'
Manfred Davidmann
ISBN 978-0-85192-053-5
see chapter 8: 'Muslims and Jews'
Manfred Davidmann

{22} In 'The Real World in Which We Live:
The Social Rules and Social System under
Which We Suffer, Struggle, Survive and Prosper'
Manfred Davidmann
ISBN 978-0-85192-058-0
see chapter 14: 'Corrupted Economics and
Misguided (Misleading) Experts'

Press Notice

'Judaism, Christianity and Islam (Church and State, Government and Religion)': A Report by Manfred Davidmann.   (Texas Cable News)

Manfred Davidmann has shown that underlying Judaism, Christianity and Islam are the Pentateuch's benevolent and egalitarian social laws and social system which include laws protecting the people by restraining the behaviour of their rulers. Those in positions of trust, responsibility or authority must not oppress people and the laws forbid personal gain from the misuse of wealth or position.

Belief and practice were later changed covertly, but there were always those who recorded what had been done. Manfred Davidmann discovered, deciphered and collated this information, proving how beliefs and practices had been distorted or modified. In doing so, he exposed secrets to the light of day which are now fundamentally changing the teachings of the three main religions.

Manfred Davidmann's groundbreaking discoveries about Judaism, Christianity and Islam, published in nine reports over twenty-five years, the last in 2003, are acknowledged as major advances.

And in Manfred Davidmann's report "Judaism, Christianity and Islam", we see for the first time the complete sequence of consecutive events.

In Judaism, under Maccabean rule, the religious hierarchy became subservient to the secular rulers. Here Manfred Davidmann discovered the records which prove how religious scholars introduced changes which in effect enabled the ruling establishment to oppress and exploit the population. These changes gave rise to Christianity.

Today's rabbinical Judaism teaches, and Jewish belief and practice follows, the ruling establishment's version which has the essential core benevolent social laws bypassed and edited out from observance.

Jesus taught that all the Pentateuch's laws had to be kept, that belief and practice had to include the Ten Commandments, the social laws and the social system of the Pentateuch.

Manfred Davidmann shows how the establishment of the day in effect annulled the application of the Pentateuch's benevolent social laws and social system. He discovered that Matthew struggled to put the record straight and struggled to record what Jesus actually taught. But the establishment's version became accepted as official Christian doctrine and it is this which tends to be taught today.

The Koran records Prophet Mohammed repeatedly confirming the Pentateuch, referring to it both as a guide and as a warning, calling for a return to following the ancient benevolent God-given social legislation.

Validated traditions (hadith) tell that Caliph Uthman had an official text prepared of the Koran and that he instructed the compilers about its editing - also, that he then had copies of this text distributed and that he ordered all other versions to be destroyed.

Manfred Davidmann says "Humanity is once again struggling intuitively to achieve the application of these social laws and system, in response to the social and economic problems of global humanity at the present time. But struggling 'intuitively' is not enough, amounts to blindly hitting out in the dark without aim, amounts to treating symptoms instead of curing causes."

And he continues: "If we do not now observe and put into effect the social rules and social system first described in the Pentateuch, then the planet is likely to become uninhabitable for human beings in the near future."

When a scientist of Manfred Davidmann's proven track record (of achievement and objectivity) and international standing, makes such a statement, this needs to be taken seriously.

Compiled and correlated analyses and guidance can be found in the works of Manfred Davidmann.

See chapter 7.1:
'Church and State, Government and Religion:
Judaism, Christianity and Islam'
Manfred Davidmann

Church and State, Government and Religion: Religion, Government and Education

Education or Indoctrination: Who is to Teach What to Whom

There are now Christian sects who stand up for morality and chastity against the socially corrupting promiscuity of the societies in which they live, to the extent of withdrawing their children from the state school system of their host societies, consequently suffering much stress and strain.

Another reason for withdrawing from the state educational system is to ensure that their children are taught the Bible's [1] record of how the planet and human beings were created, instead of how the planet was formed and how human beings evolved by natural selection.

The struggle is to educate, to educate our children to live good lives as human beings.

On the one hand state school systems may teach socially-corrupting politically-convenient biased information and principles {20-24} while on the other parents may believe that their religious beliefs about morality and behaviour provide a fundamentally better and more rewarding way of life and living {3, 7}.

Some countries allow children to be taught and educated while allowing for their parents' expressed humane beliefs. Other countries insist that children be educated in state schools according to the state's preferences about what has to be taught and about what must not be taught.

This brings us to the present position in Germany where some Christian groups <2> refuse to let their children be educated in state schools because of what is seen by them as socially corrupting promiscuity which is propagated under the guise of 'sex education' and because state schools teach the science of evolution by natural selection instead of the creation of the planet and human beings as told in the Bible (Pentateuch) <1>. In Germany these parents face fines and jail as a consequence of withdrawing their children from the state school system.

In the USA there is much pressure from influential, at times powerful, Christian fundamentalists insisting that state education (in some states) teach the Bible's (Pentateuch's) record of creation instead of the science of evolution by natural selection.

Religion, Government and Education

Expressed in everyday language, since about 1960 I have investigated the social organisation of life and living on this planet, the social laws and social system of the Pentateuch, and the meaning and intent of Genesis <3>, and made and published many original discoveries. Expressed in the language of religion, I revealed them.

Visiting Israel at intervals from about 1971 onwards attempting to make people aware of the key importance of applying the social laws and social system of the Pentateuch in their daily lives.

Many Christians and Jews now follow what I published <4> and some groups (cults, sects) <5> and churches in different countries have attempted to absorb some of these teachings into their beliefs {8}, selecting which of the God-given social laws and social system they feel like accepting in line with personal political ideologies.

Jewish orthodox and particularly ultra-orthodox sects, for example, still largely and blindly believe in and follow traditions which are often far-removed from the word of God as recorded in the Pentateuch. {10-13, 15}

Religious leaderships, of course, are not god-like in knowledge and understanding. That is, they are not capable of annulling or overriding God's fundamental rules and their intent, would be in error and misleading if they proclaimed themselves to be 'infallible', that is proclaimed themselves to be 'incapable of making mistakes or being wrong'. <6>

So religious leaderships do not have the right to decide which God-given fundamental rules and laws are to be believed and followed and which are not, nor may they assign their own meanings (interpretations or misinterpretations according to personal likes, dislikes or preferences) to fundamental Bible (Pentateuch) texts. In other words, religious leadership may not decide which of the social laws and social system of the Pentateuch <1> should or should not be taught, as all need to be observed and applied.

And now consider the following.

The Pentateuch is the basic constitution which safeguards the rights of the people and points the way ahead. It may not be changed in any way either by adding or by taking away. {12}

But authority for changing the application of a law comes from the Pentateuch. In matters of dispute or doubt which cannot be resolved with reference to the Pentateuch's laws, then the religious leadership and judges of the day can decide the matter. The law they will teach and the judgement which is made are binding and have to be followed. {16}

They are thus authorised to modify the application of a Pentateuch law so as to keep it effective in achieving its intent in the light of changing conditions. They may, for example, change penalties and punishments. They may not change the basic constitution, they may not change Pentateuch law. {12}

They may modify the application of a Pentateuch law and do so by man-made decisions which together form the body of common and case law.

This common law thus aims to resolve new problems (social, economic and moral) which find no answer in the Pentateuch or in existing common law, by amending existing common law or by new decisions in the spirit and intent of the Pentateuch.

We have seen that the Pentateuch is the basic constitution which safeguards the people and points the way ahead. It may not be changed in any way either by adding or by taking away. {12}

We have also seen that the Pentateuch authorises common law, that is man-made decisions modifying the application of a law so as to keep it effective in achieving its intent in the light of changing conditions.

Common law is subordinate legislation, is a collection of man-made decisions. It is these decisions which may be abrogated or amended by other man-made decisions.

What stands out is that there can be no conflict, or contradiction, between the words of a benevolent almighty all-knowing God and the reality of life and living, between God's words and the world in which we live, between God's words and science.

It is when the word of God and the reality of life and living, and of science, are seen to agree that we are close to understanding both.

And in the confrontations between religion and state concerning evolution <7> and concerning morality <8> we are closing in on the very core problems of life and living in our times, as follows.

Evolution

When the Pentateuch <1> was written, people had but little knowledge about science or evolution compared with what is known today. So concepts for which we now have precise terms were described rather than stated.

Instead of the term 'scientific law' being used, for example, we see the description that
> 'what is written applies to all people, present or absent, past or future, will happen regardless of how one feels about it, that the results of certain actions are reversed if the actions are reversed'. {10} <9>

In Genesis the then-beyond-comprehension beginning of life on earth and its evolutionary progress towards humankind is being described to people to whom terms such as 'natural selection' were completely unknown. In the Bible, evolutionary change, a new life form, is an act of creation and we are told in precise terms how mammals evolved, how homo erectus spread out, how homo sapiens spread out and replaced homo erectus, and much more. {2}

However, there were some who seemed to think that they knew all there is to be known, that they could decide what is and what is not, that what they were not aware of did not exist, that what they did not understand could not be meaningful. For example, Hebrew grammar distinguishes between proper names of persons and general nouns such as 'life form'. This distinction has been ignored by Bible translators <10>.

Manfred Davidmann's 'The Meaning of Genesis: Creation, Evolution and the Origin of Evil' {2} shows that the distinction is meaningful and needs to be made if the text is to be understood as it was intended to be understood.

We see that there is no conflict, no contradiction, no divergence, only astonishing awe-inspiring agreement, between what is stated in Genesis and what we now know about the evolution of human beings. {2}.

Genesis is about matters of enormous significance and importance to humankind at the present time. {2}

Morality {7, 3}

We know there is no conflict or confrontation between the word of benevolent God as recorded in the Pentateuch on the one hand and social science on the other hand. We know the destructive effects on the population of promiscuity, that is of state-condoned or legalised promiscuity. These effects are known and predictable. {7}

We saw that concerning evolution, the Church has misunderstood, misinterpreted, the Bible. The state, science, is right. What is being taught at the present time agrees with what is stated in the Bible.

But concerning morality, the Church is right. The state is misinterpreting, is misapplying, scientific knowledge.

And so concerning morality the position is very different. Here it is those who struggle against state-condoned promiscuity and for morality who are struggling on God's behalf for the benefit of the oppressed and exploited population. {7, 3}

The Pentateuch contains detailed statements about what constitutes abnormal, promiscuous, adulterous sexual relations and prostitution, with associated comments.

The Pentateuch legislates in detail, stating what needs to be done and what is prohibited, by positive and negative rules of behaviour. Positive rules point the way ahead towards greater strength and liberty, negative rules (prohibitions) protect people from the antisocial behaviour of others, safeguard the people's strength and liberty. {11} <11>

The consequences of immorality and promiscuity, that is consequent weakening and breaking up of family, society and quality of life {7}, cannot be avoided {10} <12>. The Pentateuch's warnings, punishments and penalties concerning immorality are in most cases to the male {7}. Morality has to be protected by punishing immorality, by protecting people and punishing those who behave immorally. By punishing those who do not restrain their sex urges. By punishing those who spread immorality and seduce others into immoral behaviour.

In democracies or when people are struggling for their liberty, totalitarians condone and promote promiscuity so as to weaken the family and weaken the population. People are subjected to this conditioning towards immorality so as to weaken the working population to make them easier to exploit, and to weaken the society to weaken democracy. <13>

After gaining control, totalitarians of left or right or religious hierarchies then reverse the process by moving back towards greater morality, in this way enabling their people to gain strength in order to fight for and work for, their manipulating rulers. <14>

We know the predictable effects of promiscuity on the population {7}. Hence the importance of morality, of Pentateuch morality and laws of behaviour, of protecting communities and people by restraining immoral behaviour, conditioning and propaganda, by appropriately punishing the perpetrators.

Hence the importance of the stand taken by those who struggle against state-condoned teaching of promiscuity, who struggle for the teaching of morality, on God's behalf for the benefit of the oppressed and exploited population.

Education for a Better Life

Throughout history, from the writing down of the Pentateuch about 3,500 years ago, right to the present time, we have seen continuous struggle against the God-given benevolent and egalitarian social laws and social system of the Pentateuch. That the revelations by Moses, Jesus and Mohammed were followed by world-wide struggles for a better life is well-documented. This knowledge and understanding of what took place has once again been published (revealed) by Manfred Davidmann <15>.

This knowledge has been spreading since these works were first published, is being accepted within Judaism and Christianity. The works on Islam were only published recently.

But publication was followed by attempts by miscellaneous groups and movements to negate the knowledge in my writings by taking over certain parts and neglecting or misrepresenting key components.

My works show how people are confronted, manipulated or opposed by antisocial, socially irresponsible, elements. Such antisocial elements are exposed and condemned in the Pentateuch as primitive and vicious remnants of our pre-human past.

Manfred Davidmann's works are and need to be seen as an interconnected and consistent whole, which combines both religious and secular (scientific, state, social) aspects without contradiction. And they state and describe the God-given social laws and social system of the Pentateuch, their intent and relevance to life and living in our time.

Findings and Conclusions

Basic Constitution; Religious Leaderships

The Pentateuch is the basic constitution which safeguards the rights of the people and points the way ahead. It may not be changed in any way either by adding or by taking away. {12}

> Religious leaderships, of course, are not god-like in knowledge and understanding. That is, they are not capable of annulling or overriding God's fundamental rules and their intent, would be in error and misleading if they proclaimed themselves to be 'infallible', that is proclaimed themselves to be 'incapable of making mistakes or being wrong'. <6>
>
> So religious leaderships do not have the right to decide which God-given fundamental rules and laws are to be believed and followed and which are not, nor may they assign their own meanings (interpretations or misinterpretations according to personal likes, dislikes or preferences) to fundamental Bible (Pentateuch) texts. In other words, religious leadership may not decide which of the social laws and social system of the Pentateuch <1> should or should not be taught, as all need to be observed and applied.

The Pentateuch legislates in detail, stating what needs to be done and what is prohibited, by positive and negative rules of behaviour. Positive rules point the way ahead towards greater strength and liberty, negative rules (prohibitions) protect people from the antisocial behaviour of others, safeguard the people's strength and liberty. {11} <11>

In matters of dispute or doubt which cannot be resolved with reference to the Pentateuch's laws, then the religious leadership and judges of the day can decide the matter. The law they will teach and the judgement which is made are binding and have to be followed {16}. They are in this way authorised to modify the application of a Pentateuch law so as to keep it effective in achieving its intent in the light of changing conditions.

> They may, for example, change penalties and punishments. They may not change the basic constitution, they may not change Pentateuch law. {12}

They may modify the application of a Pentateuch law and do so by man-made decisions which together form the body of common and case law.

Religious Leadership and Judges; Common and Case Law

Common law is subordinate legislation, is a collection of man-made decisions. It is these decisions which may be abrogated or amended by other man-made decisions.

Common law aims to resolve new problems (social, economic and moral) which find no answer in the Pentateuch or in existing common law, by amending existing common law or by new decisions in the spirit and intent of the Pentateuch.

Evolution and Creationism

In Genesis the then-beyond-comprehension beginning of life on earth and its evolutionary progress towards humankind is being described to people to whom terms such as 'natural selection' were completely unknown. In the Bible, evolutionary change, a new life form, is an act of creation and we are told in precise terms how mammals evolved, how homo erectus spread out, how homo sapiens spread out and replaced homo erectus, and much more. {2}

> However, there were some who seemed to think that they knew all there is to be known, that they could decide what is and what is not, that what they were not aware of did not exist, that what they did not understand could not be meaningful. For example, Hebrew grammar distinguishes between proper names of persons and general nouns such as 'life form'. This distinction has been ignored by Bible translators <10>.
>
> Manfred Davidmann's 'The Meaning of Genesis: Creation, Evolution and the Origin of Evil' {2} shows that the

distinction is meaningful and needs to be made if the text is to be understood as it was intended to be understood.

We see that there is no conflict, no contradiction, no divergence, only astonishing awe-inspiring agreement, between what is stated in Genesis and what we now know about the evolution of human beings. {2}.

Morality, Life and Living

The Pentateuch contains detailed statements about what constitutes abnormal, promiscuous, adulterous sexual relations and prostitution, with associated comments.

The consequences of immorality and promiscuity, that is consequent weakening and breaking up of family, society and quality of life {7}, cannot be avoided {10} <12>. The Pentateuch's warnings, punishments and penalties concerning immorality are in most cases to the male {7}. Morality has to be protected by punishing immorality, by protecting people and punishing those who behave immorally. By punishing those who do not restrain their sex urges. By punishing those who spread immorality and seduce others into immoral behaviour.

In democracies or when people are struggling for their liberty, totalitarians condone and promote promiscuity so as to weaken the family and weaken the population. People are subjected to this conditioning towards immorality to weaken the working population to make them easier to exploit, and to weaken the society to weaken democracy. <13>

After gaining control, totalitarians of left or right or religious hierarchies then reverse the process by moving back towards greater morality, in this way enabling their people to gain strength in order to fight for and work for, their manipulating rulers. <14>

We know the predictable effects of promiscuity on the population {7}. Hence the importance of morality, of Pentateuch morality and laws of behaviour, of protecting communities and people by restraining immoral behaviour, conditioning and propaganda, by appropriately punishing the perpetrators.

Hence also the importance of the stand taken by those who struggle against state-condoned teaching of promiscuity, who struggle for the teaching of morality, on God's behalf for the benefit of the oppressed and exploited population.

Religion and Science, Church and State

It is when the word of God and the reality of life and living, and of science, are seen to agree that we are close to understanding both.

> And in the confrontations between religion and state concerning evolution <7> and concerning morality <8> we are closing in on the very core problems of life and living in our times, as follows.

We saw that concerning evolution, the Church has misunderstood, misinterpreted, the Bible. The state, science, is right. What is being taught at the present time about evolution agrees with what is stated in the Bible.

But concerning morality, the Church is right. The state is misinterpreting, is misapplying, scientific knowledge about the effects of promiscuity on the life and welfare of the population.

And so concerning morality the position is very different. Here it is those who struggle against state-condoned promiscuity and for morality who are struggling on God's behalf for the benefit of the oppressed and exploited population. {7, 3}

Manfred Davidmann's works show how people are confronted, manipulated or opposed by antisocial, socially irresponsible, elements. Such antisocial elements are exposed and condemned in the Pentateuch as primitive and vicious remnants of our pre-human past.

Manfred Davidmann's works are and need to be seen as an interconnected and consistent whole, which combines both religious and secular (scientific, state, social) aspects without contradiction. And they state and describe the God-given social laws and social system of the Pentateuch, their intent and relevance to life and living in our time.

Notes <..>

<1> The Pentateuch (The Five Books of Moses), part of the Bible. Also called the Torah.

<2> Cults, sects, small groups separated from mainstream Christianity.

<3> First volume of the Pentateuch

< 4> See {1-6, 9-13, 15}.

< 5> Sectarian: Putting the beliefs or interests of one's sect before more general interests.

< 6> See {8} 'Social Concept (Policies) of the Russian Orthodox Church: Letter to the Russians'

< 7> As opposed to creationism, to the Bible's (Pentateuch's) record of how the planet was formed and human beings appeared.

< 8> As opposed to immorality, to promiscuity.

< 9> In {10} see Appendix 4: Cause-and-effect Relationship in the Torah <1>.

<10> In {2} see Appendix 3: 'Adam' and Hebrew Grammar. Or see {5}.

<11> The information in this section has largely been reproduced from {3}: 'The Pentateuch and the Problems of Our Times'.

<12> In {10} see 'Cause-and-Effect Relationship'

<13> See {7}

<14> See {6}

<15> See chapter 7.1:
'Church and State, Government and Religion: Judaism, Christianity and Islam', which summarises findings from {1-3, 6, 8-9, 11-14, 17-19}.

References {..}

{ 1} See chapter 3:
'Origin of Christianity and Judaism:
What Actually Happened,
What Jesus Actually Taught and Later Changes'
Manfred Davidmann

{ 2} In 'God and People:
      The Social Laws and Social System Underlying
      Judaism, Christianity, Islam and Democracy'
      Manfred Davidmann
      ISBN 978-0-85192-054-2
      see chapter 6.1: 'The Meaning of Genesis:
      Creation, Evolution and the Origin of Evil'

{ 3} In 'God and People:
      The Social Laws and Social System Underlying
      Judaism, Christianity, Islam and Democracy'
      Manfred Davidmann
      ISBN 978-0-85192-054-2
      see chapter 6.3: 'The Meaning of Genesis:
      Morality, Sexual Behaviour and Depravity'

{ 4} In 'God and People:
      The Social Laws and Social System Underlying
      Judaism, Christianity, Islam and Democracy'
      Manfred Davidmann
      ISBN 978-0-85192-054-2
      see chapter 6.6: 'The Meaning of Genesis:
      'Meaning and Significance of the Names
      of God in Genesis'

{ 5}   In 'God and People:
      The Social Laws and Social System Underlying
      Judaism, Christianity, Islam and Democracy'
      Manfred Davidmann
      ISBN 978-0-85192-054-2
      see chapter 6.7: 'Meaning and Intent of Genesis:
      Essential Notes on Hebrew Grammar'

{ 6} In 'God and People:
      The Social Laws and Social System Underlying
      Judaism, Christianity, Islam and Democracy'
      Manfred Davidmann
      ISBN 978-0-85192-054-2
      see chapter 6.4: 'The Meaning of Genesis:
      Nephilim, Dominance and Liberty'

{ 7} See chapter 5:
      'Family, Community, Sex and the Individual'
      Manfred Davidmann

{ 8} See chapter 7.3:
      'Social Concept (Policies) of the Russian
      Orthodox Church: Letter to the Russians'
      Manfred Davidmann

{ 9} See chapter 2:
      'Liberation Theology: Basis - Past - Present – Future'
      Manfred Davidmann

{10} In 'Judaism: Basis - Past - Present - Future, Part 1'
      Manfred Davidmann
      ISBN 978-0-85192-060-3
      see chapter 2.1: 'Struggle for Freedom:
      The Social Cause-and-Effect Relationship'

{11} In 'Judaism: Basis - Past - Present - Future, Part 1'
      Manfred Davidmann
      ISBN 978-0-85192-060-3
      see chapter 2.2: 'History Speaks: Monarchy,
      Exile and Maccabees'

{12} In 'Judaism: Basis - Past - Present - Future, Part 1'
      Manfred Davidmann
      ISBN 978-0-85192-060-3
      see chapter 2.3: 'At the Time of Jesus,
      This is What Actually Happened in Israel:
      The Truth about Hillel and his Times'

{13} In 'Judaism: Basis - Past - Present - Future, Part 1'
      Manfred Davidmann
      ISBN 978-0-85192-060-3
      see chapter 2.4: 'One Law for All: Freedom Now,
      Freedom for Ever'

{14} In 'Judaism: Basis - Past - Present - Future, Part 1'
      Manfred Davidmann
      ISBN 978-0-85192-060-3
      see chapter 3: 'Jewish Belief and Practice'

{15} In 'Judaism: Basis - Past - Present - Future, Part 1'
      Manfred Davidmann
      ISBN 978-0-85192-060-3
      see chapter 5: 'The Right to the Land of Israel'

{16} Pentateuch
      Deuteronomy **17**, 8-11.

{17} In 'Islam: Basis – Past – Present – Future'
Manfred Davidmann
ISBN 978-0-85192-053-5
see chapter 5: 'Compiling the Koran: Hadiths
(Traditions) State the Underlying Reality'

{18} In 'Islam: Basis – Past – Present – Future'
Manfred Davidmann
ISBN 978-0-85192-053-5
see chapter 6: 'Uthman's Rearrangement of the
Chronological (as revealed) Koran's Chapters'

{19} In 'Islam: Basis – Past – Present – Future'
Manfred Davidmann
ISBN 978-0-85192-053-5
see chapter 7: 'Prophet Mohammed's Word of
Allah and the Voice of the Ruling Elite'

{20} In 'Management and Leadership:
Local, National, Multinational (Global),
Principles and Practice'
Manfred Davidmann
ISBN 978-0-85192-057-3
see chapter 8: 'Work and Pay'

{21} In 'The Real World in Which We Live:
The Social Rules and Social System under
Which We Suffer, Struggle, Survive and Prosper'
Manfred Davidmann
ISBN 978-0-85192-058-0
see chapter 7: 'Exporting and Importing of
Employment and Unemployment'

{22} In 'The Real World in Which We Live:
The Social Rules and Social System under
Which We Suffer, Struggle, Survive and Prosper'
Manfred Davidmann
ISBN 978-0-85192-058-0
see chapter 10: 'What People are Struggling
Against: How Society is Organised for Controlling
and Exploiting People'

{23} In 'The Real World in Which We Live:
      The Social Rules and Social System under
      Which We Suffer, Struggle, Survive and Prosper'
      Manfred Davidmann
      ISBN 978-0-85192-058-0
      see chapter 14: 'Corrupted Economics and
      Misguided (Misleading) Experts'

{24} In 'The Real World in Which We Live:
      The Social Rules and Social System under
      Which We Suffer, Struggle, Survive and Prosper'
      Manfred Davidmann
      ISBN 978-0-85192-058-0
      see chapter 17: 'Quotable Quotes about
      Democracy in the Real World'

Chapter 7.3:

Social Concept (Policies) of the Russian Orthodox Church: Letter to the Russians

Introduction

The Russian Orthodox Church's policies on church-state relations and on social problems of our times are stated and summarised in an extensive document called 'Bases of the Social Concept of the Russian Orthodox Church' {1}.

The church's Sacred Bishop's Council has adopted this document which lays down guidelines which are to be followed and applied by its episcopate, clergy and laity. <1>

For background information and underlying knowledge and understanding, see 'Relevant Current and Associated Works'*.

Note that quotations from the Russian Orthodox Church's document are here set in as follows:

"... quotation from church's document ..."

214

Intellectual Knowledge and Understanding;
Intellectual Property

In section VII.3 on property, the church acknowledges the growing significance of intellectual property and deplores the violation of copyright, stating that it

> "cannot approve the alienation and re-distribution of property with violations of the rights of its legitimate owners."

And in section XVI.3 on globalisation in the field of culture and information, societies are said to be becoming multicultural, and that this process is accompanied

> "by attempts to establish the dominion of the rich elite over the rest of the people ... worldwide ...,
>
> which is especially intolerable in the religious field,
>
> There being a tendency to regard universal culture as being entirely without spirituality, unrestrained in anything by absolute values or measures of the truth.
>
> **The globalisation developing in this way is compared** by many ... **to the construction of the Tower of Babel.**"

This knowledge and understanding appears to have come from Manfred Davidmann's report on 'Genesis: Nephilim, Dominance and Liberty' {5}. This may be one of his more popular works on Genesis, but the source of the insight could have been stated by the compilers of the church document.

In the church's document, in section VI.3 on 'Labour and its fruits', we find

> "Among the most vivid biblical images of the failure of the fallen humanity 'to make a name for itself' is the construction of the Tower of Babel 'whose top may reach unto heaven'. The Babel is presented as a symbol of people's joining efforts to achieve an ungodly goal. The Lord punishes the arrogant men: by confusing their tongues He makes understanding among them impossible and scattered them throughout the earth."

We see that the church's document refers to a 'fallen humanity' constructing the Tower of Babel. This interpretation (suggested meaning) has been overtaken by current knowledge of God's intended meaning of Genesis. Manfred Davidmann showed in 'The Meaning of Genesis: Creation, Evolution and the Origin of Evil' {4} that Genesis states that it is the later descendants of Seth (Genesis, Chapter 5) who know of, can distinguish between and can choose between, good and evil, who spread across the planet.

It is the 'fallen' nephilim {5} who are selfish, corrupt, dominating, exploiting and oppressing. The driving force behind the building of the Tower of Babel is stated to be Nimrod who is referred to as the people's king. It is the ability of such nephilim to manipulate ordinary people into working for the nephil, which is pointed out and criticised. Ordinary people are being manipulated into serving nephilim, into working to increase a selfish and corrupt nephil's personal influence and power. <2>

Aiming to reach heaven and become god-like, to set themselves up in opposition to God. Which means that Nimrod is attempting to gain, to assign to himself, god-like (absolute) authority and power. <3>

The allegory states that if any become too powerful, a threat to that which is humane and good, then they need to be, and are to be, dispersed. In other words, their tower <4> (power, organisation, country, empire, corporation, monopoly, government, rulers, multinational, global corporation, hierarchy) needs to be dispersed.

Power corrupts, absolute power corrupts absolutely. Hence the great need, and the importance of the need, for scattering and dispersal, for multiplicity and variety. {5}

Power corrupts, absolute power corrupts absolutely. Humanity and human behaviour depend on opposition and balance, on democracy. <9>

Men and Women, Family and Children

There is a genetic difference between men and women. {3}

> "... Man and woman are two different modes of existence in one humanity. ... (X. 1)"

Primarily the family exists to protect and support its young, and this means supporting and looking after the female bearing the child within her body, through birth and while she is protecting and teaching the young how to behave. {3}

It is women who bear the child and who need protecting and looking after while bearing the child and after childbirth. There clearly are close emotional bonds between mother and child. {3}

It is usually the woman whose role it is to ensure the family provides the young with the humane, emotionally and mentally stimulating environment they need to enable them to mature into socially responsible adults. {3}

Women generally look after people, after the welfare and well-being of the members of the family. Care, concern, affection and love, feelings and emotions, are important and matter, and women developed, and have, much skill and expertise in such matters. {3}

Men generally struggle outside the family to secure survival and good living for the family. A struggle for survival in a seemingly hostile environment engineered by other humans. {3}

> "... A man and a woman who love each other, united in marriage ... . Children become fruits of their love and communion, and their birth and upbringing belong, according to the Orthodox teaching, to one of the most important goals of marriage. (X. 4)
>
> ... The negligence of children is the greatest of all sins as it leads to extreme impiety ... (X. 4)"

When women are persuaded to regard work outside of the family as more important than caring for the young or the family's members, they are in effect handing over the family's key role to outsiders such as day-care businesses and television programme makers. With disastrous results on the way the young perceive home life and adult behaviour, tending to condition the young into behaving like fictional and unreal role models, for example concerning sexual behaviour. Instead of gaining an adult understanding of the reality of living, of family values and relationships, instead of understanding and experiencing socially-responsible behaviour caring for and living with other people, instead of seeing adults (parents) behave in socially responsible way struggling in a hostile environment to do the best they can for the young and for each other. {3}

The number of young people who run away from home and family, often becoming homeless, placing themselves at a big disadvantage right at the beginning of their lives, speaks for itself. {3}

> "... The experience of family relations teaches a person to overcome sinful egoism and lays the foundations for his sense of civil duty. It is in the family as a school of devotion that the right attitude to one's neighbours and therefore to one's people and society as a whole is formed. ... This is why it is so dangerous to distort the traditional parents-child relationship, which, unfortunately, have been in many ways endangered by the contemporary way of life. (X. 4)
>
> The diminished social significance of motherhood and fatherhood compared to the progress made by men and women in the professional field leads to the treatment of children as an unnecessary burden, contributing also to the

217

development of alienation and antagonism between generations. The role of family in the formation of the personality is exceptional; no other social institution can replace it. The erosion of family relations inevitably entails the deformation of the normal development of children and leaves a long, and to a certain extent indelible trace in them for life. (X. 4)"

Human rights are based on controlling primitive dominant behaviour, on concern, care and affection for our young, our families, for people, for our communities, and express themselves in co-operation and teamwork between men and women to achieve a good life of high quality. Men and women are struggling together to achieve a better life, a humane way of living and government, and social security. {3}

When one member of a family dominates others, then competition, conflict and struggle replace co-operation and teamwork. Dominance weakens all the family's members, robbing them of emotional and economic support, and so makes it easier to exploit them through their needs. All the family's members suffer as a result. {3}

"... While appreciating the social role of women and welcoming their political, cultural and social equality with men, the Church opposes the tendency to diminish the role of woman as wife and mother. ... . (but) **the Church cannot misconstrue the words of St. Paul about** the special responsibility of **husband who is** called to be "**the head of the wife**" ... **and about** the calling of **the wife to obey the husband** as the Church obeys Christ. (X. 5)"

The often quoted phrase '..., **and he shall rule over you.**' from Genesis {15}, is quite mistakenly assumed to lay down male dominance over the female. Genesis Chapter 3 describes the evolution of early human beings, the role of the family in bringing up their children, and the respective roles of husband and wife within the family. What is described is the so-necessary division of work and teamwork between them, between husband and wife, between equals. <5>

And among the first laws of behaviour to be established by the Patriarchs were the sanctity of marriage and of chastity, and the condemnation and punishment of rape. <6>

Morality

Chastity

Human beings work primarily for their family and members of a family stand by, support and help each other in times of need. The family looks after the interests of all its members, as individuals as well as collectively. This gives great strength to each member of the family in the struggle for daily bread, security and happiness. {6, 3}

It is control of the sexual urge which distinguishes human beings from animals. Promiscuous unrestrained sexual behaviour indicates cold inhuman, often harsh, behaviour towards others, is characteristic of the cold unemotional behaviour of those who exploit others. Sexual self-control and restraint indicates human caring behaviour. {6, 3}

Those who understand its effects know that when sex is restrained and controlled, it performs the enormously important function of creating a special single deep emotional relationship between two people which gives them the strength to overcome life's problems, to form a strong family unit which serves and protects all its members. To be strong the relationship has to be unique and secure. It depends on the ability of the partners to commit themselves to each other. The depth of such a relationship between husband and wife can be appreciated as one sees them both battling on together successfully regardless of how tough the struggle may be. {6, 3}

The family is the basic unit of society. Its strength depends on the ability of the partners to commit themselves to each other, that is its strength depends on those who restrict sexual relations to within marriage. Men and women who do so practice a form of self-control which enables them to form a deep and lasting relationship, which in turn lays the basis for happy and contented family life for themselves and their children. The relationship between them is based on mutual trust and respect arising from the sure knowledge that they are in a vital exclusive relationship to each other, that they are working and co-operating with each other for the common good of themselves and their children. {6, 3}

What gives the family strength is restricting sex to within marriage. {6, 3}

> "The virtue of chastity preached by the Church is the basis of the inner unity of the human personality, which should always be in the state of harmony between its mental and bodily powers. (X. 6)

219

... the Church invariably denounces prostitution and the preaching of the so-called free love in which physical intimacy is completely divorced from personal and spiritual communion, selflessness and all-round responsibility for each other, which are possible only in the lifetime conjugal faithfulness. (X. 6)"

Casual Sex (Fornication; Sexual Relations)

People who behave promiscuously (permissively) have sexual relations before marriage, or after marriage with a person other than their spouse. Promiscuity turns men against women, and women against men, and robs both of the support of their family. {3}

Promiscuous behaviour and casual sexual relationships separate people and turn them against each other, turn men against women and women against men. Promiscuous behaviour and casual sexual relationships break up families, isolate people and rob people of the strength to resist exploitation and oppression. {3}

Those who sleep around (behave promiscuously) pay a heavy price, namely lose the ability to form a satisfying emotionally deeply binding lasting and shared relationship with one other person. They also lose the emotional strength and economic backup such a shared relationship brings. Promiscuity turns men against women, and women against men, and robs both of the support of their family. {3}

In such ways promiscuity breaks up families, weakens the strength of individuals and thus of the community to resist exploitation and oppression. Society corrupts itself when human care, affection and concern for one's own family, and for other people, is weakened, is bypassed by self-interest at the expense of others. Promiscuity conditions people into primitive selfish uncaring behaviour which uses other people for personal gain (pleasure), creating a non-caring society, putting people against each other, at times brutalising them. {3}

> "Fornication inevitably ruins the harmony and integrity of one's life, damaging heavily one's spiritual health. Libertinism dulls the spiritual vision and hardens the heart, making it incapable of true love. The happiness of full-blooded family life becomes unattainable for the fornicator. Sins against chastity also lead to negative social consequences. (X. 6)"

220

There is increasing wanton antisocial behaviour such as vandalism and mugging. There is a loss of internal security, by loss of property and by attack against the person. The quality of life is lowered even further by those who pursue personal gain regardless of its cost to other people. {3}

As permissiveness has increased so we have seen increasing the number of people using others for their own gratification and pleasure without care or concern for them, and also the number of parents behaving brutally towards each other and their children. A process driven by those who want sexual gratification, knowingly or unknowingly without regard to the costs their 'partners' have to pay. {3}

History shows that free societies which allow themselves to become 'permissive' (promiscuous) weaken themselves to the point where their civilisation destroys itself, or is destroyed by outsiders. Those who wish to weaken democracy condone or encourage 'permissiveness'. On the other hand, those who restrict sex to within marriage gain creativity and increase their strength. {3}

> "The propaganda of vice is especially harmful for the still infirm souls of children and youth. Through books, films and other video products, as well as the mass media and some educational curricula, teenagers are often taught an idea of sexual relations extremely humiliating for the human dignity, since it gives no room to such notions as chastity, marital faithfulness and selfless love. Intimate relations between man and woman are not only exposed for show, offending the natural feeling of prudence, but also presented as an act of purely corporal gratification without any association with inner communion or any moral obligations. The Church urges the faithful to struggle, in co-operation with all morally healthy forces, against the propagation of this diabolical temptation, which, by destroying the family, undermines the foundations of society. ... (X. 6)"

Mass Media, Sex Education and Pornography

The media seem to be concentrating on portraying superstition, violence and casual-sex behaviour as acceptable, so strengthening primitive uncaring and antisocial behaviour towards others. And images penetrate deeply into the human mind. {3}

Sexually explicit and pornographic material would seem to be taking this process even further. {3}

So media are at present persuading and conditioning people into thinking that antisocial behaviour such as promiscuity will not have unpleasant consequences. However, the cost to the individual and to the community of the kind of negative and antisocial behaviour outlined in the sections above, of the lowering of the quality of life, is enormous. {3, 12, 11}

> "In the situation of a spiritual crisis of the human society, the mass media and the products of the so-called mass culture sometimes become instruments of moral corruption by praising sexual laxity, all kinds of sexual perversion and other sinful passions. (X. 6)
>
> Pornography, which is the exploitation of the sexual drive for commercial, political or ideological purposes, contributes to the suppression of the spiritual and moral principles, thus reducing man to an animal motivated by instinct alone. (X. 6)"

What we see is an almost intentional-seeming conditioning towards antisocial behaviour which breaks up families and so weakens individuals, and which divides people against each other and so weakens them even further. {3}

It looks as if men are being conditioned into opting out of their responsibilities for family, wife and children. Women, on the other hand, are apparently being conditioned into giving away the real support and security they and their children could expect from husband and family, for no real gain. {3}

But there are ways of teaching social responsibility, of teaching the young how to take responsibility for others, how to care for, work with and look after other people. Social responsibility, the caring, giving and sharing with others, the taking on of responsibility for others including conflict management, can be and is being taught. {13}

> "The mass media play an ever-increasing role in the contemporary world. ... It is important to remember at the same time that the information of the spectator, listener and reader should be based not only on the firm commitment to the truth, but also concern for the moral state of the individual and society. This involves the interpretation of positive ideals as well as the struggle with the spreading of evil, sin and vice. The propaganda of violence, enmity and hatred and ethnic, social and religious discord and the sinful exploitation of human instincts, including for commercial purposes, are inadmissible. The mass media, which have an enormous influence on the audience, bear a great responsibility for the education of

people, especially the younger generation. Journalists and mass media executives should never forget about this responsibility. (XV. 1.)" "Aware of the need for the school, along with the family, to give children and adolescents the knowledge of sexuality and the physical human nature, the Church cannot support those programs of sexual education in which premarital intercourse and, all the more so, various perversions are recognised as the norm. It is absolutely unacceptable to impose such programs upon schoolchildren. School is called to oppose vice which erodes the integrity of the personality, to educate children for chastity and prepare them for creating solid families based on faithfulness and purity. (X. 6.)"

Church and State

At issue between 'church' and 'state' are the laws of behaviour and the social system {5, 10} which are laid down in the Pentateuch <7>:

The Pentateuch states that all are equal, that no person may oppress or exploit another, that all have the right to be free and be independent masters of their own fate.

Every person is entitled as a matter of right to social security. This means that people are entitled to be supported by the community not only when they fall on hard times but also to maintain their independence as independent breadwinners for their families.

For example, the community has to provide backup funds to those who need them and they have to be provided as and when required. To prevent people being exploited through their need these funds have to be provided without charging interest and such 'loans' are cancelled every seventh year if the borrower has been unable to repay them.

The country's wealth, and this applies particularly to productive capital, belongs to all equally and has to be shared out. This equal and fair distribution of the community's wealth has to be updated at regular intervals.

The role of those who are rich is seen to be that of administering their wealth and money on behalf of and for the community and not that of enriching themselves at the expense of the community.

But support and co-operation have to be two-way flows. The community supports the individual but only if the individual supports the community. Those supported by the community are under obligation to support others in need of support, when able to do so, to share with others who are in need.

It is only those who themselves keep and apply the social laws and social system of the Pentateuch in their daily lives who are entitled to rights and benefits. Otherwise, to give but one example, funds provided by the community free-of-interest to a non-member (stranger) might be used by the stranger to exploit people by lending funds to others and charging interest so as to enrich himself.

Jesus Christ taught that all the laws had to be kept, that belief and practice included and had to include the Ten Commandments, the social laws and the social system of the Pentateuch. {2}

Included in the social laws of the Pentateuch, for example, are the kingship laws (Pentateuch, Deut 17: 14-20) which state that those in authority must not oppress people so as to increase their own possessions and power, that they must not put themselves above the people and so enrich themselves. They are warned against oppressing people and against forming enforcing squads or organisations so as to multiply their own power, must not be promiscuous and must not amass wealth. They must know and observe the Pentateuch law and its intent and aim to see the Pentateuch laws applied.

Romans 13: Verses 1-10

What came to be known as Paul's letters were written about 50 AD and what stands out is that no one before Paul wrote such letters and that no one did so afterwards. They give his own point of view and personal ideology and he gives them an authority which they would not otherwise have had by means of a self-proclaimed vision. {2}

For no apparent reason, without justification and without stating a source {2}, Paul says in his letter to the 'Romans' (Romans 13: 1-10) that:

1. All authority comes from God,
    so that rulers (those who are in a position of authority) have
    been appointed by God.
    Hence let every person
    submit to those who rule.

2. It follows that whoever resists the rulers
    resists whom God has appointed
    and those who resist rulers will be punished,

3. for rulers do not terrorise those whose conduct is "good", but those whose conduct is "evil".

   If you want to live without fearing the person who is in authority, then do what is "good" and you will be praised,

4. for he rules over you in God's place for your own good.

   But if you do that which is "evil", be afraid,
   for his is not an empty threat;
   he will in God's place punish the doer of "evil".

5. Therefore one must be obedient,
   to avoid their anger (if you do not obey)
   and because to obey is the right thing to do.

6. For the same reason you also pay taxes,
   for those in authority collecting taxes
   are acting on God's behalf.

7. Pay all those in authority what they demand,
   taxes, revenues, respect, honour.

8. Your only obligation to others is to love one another;
   Because he who loves another has fulfilled "the law".

9. For this
        You shall not commit adultery,
        You shall not murder,
        You shall not steal,
        You shall not bear false witness,
        You shall not covet;
   and if there be any other commandment,
   it is summed up in this saying:
   You shall love your neighbour as yourself.

10. Love does not do harm to a neighbour;
    therefore love (is) the fulfilling of the law.

Verses 1-7   (Romans 13:)

Astonishingly and without good reason he (Paul) states in verses 1-7 that those in authority rule by 'divine right', that whatever they do is justified because in his opinion they act on God's behalf. Whatever those in authority do or want is called 'good' by Paul and those who resist or oppose them do 'evil' and will be punished. Paul wants all to obey those in authority and to be obedient, to pay taxes and revenues, to respect and honour those in authority.

He is arguing that one must fear and obey those in authority and do for them and give them all they ask, without regard to how selfish, rotten, corrupt, inhuman, vicious, murdering or evil they may be.

> The Russian church's document {1} records Paul's statements thus: St. Paul wrote: "Let every soul be subject unto the higher powers. For there is no power but of God: the powers that be are ordained of God. Whosoever therefore resisteth the power, resisteth the ordinance of God; and they that resist shall receive to themselves damnation. For rulers are not a terror to good works, but to the evil. Wilt thou them not be afraid of the power? do that which is good, and thou shalt have praise of the same: for he is the minister of God to thee for good. But if thou do that which is evil, be afraid; for he beareth not the sword in vain: for he is the minister of God, a revenger to execute wrath upon him that doeth evil. Wherefore ye must needs be subject, not only for wrath, but also for conscience sake. For this cause pay ye tribute also: for they are God's ministers, attending continually upon this very thing. Render therefore to all their dues: tribute to whom tribute is due; custom to whom custom; fear to whom fear; honour to whom honour" (Rom. 13:1-7). (III.1)

The Russian church's document introduces this statement by saying that Paul is:

> "Explaining the teaching of Christ on the right attitude to state power".

However, what Paul is saying and putting forward is neither God's word nor is it what Jesus Christ taught. {2}

Verses 8-10   (Romans 13:)

Look again at the social laws and system of the Pentateuch which were briefly referred to at the beginning of this section and which include the kingship laws. You will see how the laws of the Pentateuch ensure freedom and material independence and provide a good life of high quality here and now, backed by effective social security. No one may oppress or exploit another and all are equal, as a matter of God-given law.

It is these laws of behaviour, it is these social laws and this social system which Paul opposes and he next (Romans 13: 8-10) attempts to stop people from keeping such laws.

Take the Ten Commandments.

The first five commandments are those which directly relate to freedom and independence, which give the working population strength in their struggle for a better life for themselves and their children against those who oppress and exploit. {2}

These laws state <8> that:

> The only way to gain and keep freedom and independence and a good life free from oppression and exploitation is to follow all these laws.
>
> One must not respect or serve oppressing, exploiting or enslaving beliefs or ideologies.
>
> One must not use God's name to lend authority to a statement which it would not otherwise have or to a false or misleading statement.
>
> One must observe the sabbath day, the seventh day which is a day of rest from work for all, on which all are equal and rest, on which our servants rest just as we do, remembering that it was God who by a mighty hand and by an outstretched arm freed us from most brutal service.
>
> One must honour one's father and one's mother and willingly accept God's commands and the tradition, knowledge and life experience of one's parents so that one will progress and advance in understanding and in life and so that one will have long and secure lives of high quality in the land God gives one.

The other five of the Ten Commandments <8> protect people against anti-social behaviour of others by prohibiting the doing of that which would harm or injure other people, prohibiting adultery, murder, theft, false witness and coveting.

Paul himself leaves us in no doubt about his intentions.

He says "Your **only** obligation to others is to love one another", and that this "**fulfils the law**" (Romans 13: 8)

Pointedly listing only the last five of the commandments <8>, namely those which protect people only against anti-social behaviour of others, he says that **all other commandments** are included in the **saying** "love your neighbour as yourself". (Romans 13: 9)

The laws he does not wish people to have to observe include the first five commandments <8> he pointedly left out from his list, the kingship laws, and the social laws and the social system laws which together ensure freedom and material independence and social security as rights and as entitlements.

And so Paul's letter seems to be more a vehicle for pronouncements directed against obligatory laws which ensure freedom, independence and equality. {2}

But the Russian church's document excludes from its extract these three key verses (Romans 13: 8-10) in which Paul attempts to annul those laws which directly relate to freedom and independence, which give the working population strength in their struggle for a better life for themselves and their children against those who oppress and exploit. {2}

And to that extent the church is quoting out of context.

> So much has been written about Christianity and Judaism that it is fairly easy to select one sentence or two from one place, and a sentence or two from a completely different place, and more from another part unrelated to the others, and so on. These can then be added together or compared to arrive at conclusions which back the personal opinion of the individual doing the selecting.

> What is valid within the meaning of one record is not necessarily valid within the meaning of another. And the process of 'quoting out of context' often results in conclusions which are totally different from the contexts from which they were selected.

> So that the Oxford Dictionary defines 'Out of context' as meaning 'without the surrounding words and therefore giving a false impression of the meaning'.

When Moses brought the tables of the law he brought 'freedom upon the tables' {10}. It is the Ten Commandments as a whole which underlie freedom, independence, a good life and strength to oppose and resist oppression.

We saw that Jesus Christ taught that all the laws had to be kept, that belief and practice included and had to include the Ten Commandments, the social laws and the social system of the Pentateuch. {2}

Paul, however, acted on behalf of the rich and powerful when he tried to convince people that those in authority were God's representatives on earth and that the social laws did not have to be kept. {2}

Matthew struggled to put the record straight, struggled to record what Jesus Christ actually taught (See Manfred Davidmann's 'Origin of Christianity and Judaism' {2}). Throughout the ages, Christians of goodwill chose intuitively to interpret Paul's statements about those in authority as meaning that

> 'the authority of those in authority only comes from God to the extent to which they themselves live according to and apply the Ten Commandments, the social laws and the social system laws' and that only those can 'love one another' who comply with all these laws. {2}

Policies of the Russian Orthodox Church

The church's extensive document 'Basis of the Social Concept of the Russian Orthodox Church' {1}, records its social aims and policies. It amounts to a considerable achievement.

The Russian Orthodox Church concludes and states, among other things, that (III.5)

> "The Church infallibly preaches the Truth of Christ and teaches moral commandments which came from God Himself. Therefore, she has no power to change anything in her teaching.
>
> Nor has she the power to fall silent and to stop preaching the truth whatever other teachings may be prescribed or propagated by state bodies.
>
> In this respect, the Church is absolutely free from the state. For the sake of the unhindered and internally free preaching of the truth, the Church suffered persecution by the enemies of Christ more than once in history.
>
> But the persecuted Church is also called to endure the persecution with patience, without refusing to be loyal to the state persecuting her."

And that (III.7)

> "... the Church should give more attention not to the system of the outer organisation of state, but to the inner condition of her members' hearts.
>
> Therefore, the Church does not believe it possible for her to become an initiator of any change in the form of government. Along the same line, the 1994 Bishops' Council of the Russian Orthodox Church stressed the soundness of the attitude whereby 'the Church does not give preference to any social system or any of the existing political doctrines'."

Abstract words (see Appendix 1) like 'infallibly' and 'truth' can mean different things to different people and this applies also to phrases such as 'truth of Christ' and 'right attitude'. Such words and phrases need to be clearly defined in detail when they are used.

For example, the word 'infallibly' is generally taken to mean 'incapable of making mistakes or being wrong'.

Another example is the word 'truth'. In Appendix 1 this is defined as follows:

> Consider two media reports of a current event. Each reports the same event, each apparently telling the truth, each report giving its viewers different impressions of what actually happened.
>
> How come? Can there be more than one truth?
>
> Such reports may tell only part of what happened, may report only what seems relevant to the reporter, may then be selecting what seems to support the particular viewpoint of those who prepared the report.
>
> Compare these 'truths' with that demanded from a witness in a court of law: 'The truth, the whole truth and nothing but the truth.'
>
> Which means that what is required in a court of law is the truth with nothing taken away and nothing added.
>
> If we agree on this as a definition, then the word 'truth' has become more meaningful.

So if we agree that for us the word 'truth' means the truth with nothing taken away and nothing added, then the word 'truth' has indeed become more meaningful.

Findings

The church is shown to be quoting out of context from Paul's letter to the Romans, in relation to what seems to be a central core teaching on Christian church-state relationships.

Manfred Davidmann's reports 'Origin of Christianity and Judaism' {2} and 'Struggle for Freedom: The Social Cause-and-Effect Relationship' {10}, show that the consequences of not following the word of God, knowingly or unknowingly, are bitter and unavoidable.

A good deal of the church's social knowledge and understanding appears to follow selected insights from the published findings of Manfred

Davidmann which were new at the time of publication. Insights such as those about the Tower of Babel, and Genesis generally. This could have been acknowledged in the church's document even although many of his insights have become public knowledge, are in the public domain and well-known.

The church's document also comments on social problems of 'globalisation'. Here I would suggest that reference could have been made to relevant reports by Manfred Davidmann {16-18}, also quoting from the maxims he laid down in 'Multinational Summits and Agreements, Top-level Decision-taking and Democracy' {16}, maxims such as

> Representatives, governments or government officials do not have the authority or right to override, reduce or sign away the participative (democratic) rights of the electors, of the population.

> No elected representative, government or government employee has overriding right or authority

> 1. to hand over to corporations (that is to those who own and control them), to any other organisation or to anyone else, an overriding control over the present and future, economic and social, welfare of the people, or

> 2. to sign away democratic rights of their people for the self-determination of key fundamental aspects of their lives.

> Decision-taking by leaderships has to be replaced by decision-taking at the level of the people.

> The real struggle is not between political left and right, but is a struggle for participation (the right to take decisions).

Abstract words like 'infallibly' and 'truth' (see Appendix 1) can mean different things to different people and this applies also to phrases such as 'right attitude'. Such words and phrases need to be clearly defined in detail when they are used, and particularly so when they are used for laying down principles of faith (doctrines).

Notes

< 1> episcopate: the bishops of a church or region collectively.
      clergy: the body of people ordained for religious duties in the
      Christian Church.
      laity: lay people (not ordained into or belonging to the clergy.

< 2> See {5}, Genesis **11**:6

< 3> See {5}, Genesis **11**:4

< 4> See {5}

< 5> In {4} see 'Garden of Eden'.

< 6> In {6} see 'Sanctity of Marriage' and 'Chastity and Rape: The Story
      of Dinah'.

< 7> Also known as the 'Five Books of Moses' and as 'Torah'.

< 8> In {2} see Appendix 1, 'Ten Commandments'.

< 9> See {12, 14, 7, 8}

References

{ 1} Ministry of Foreign Affairs of the Russian Federation
      Information and Press Department
      17/09/2003

{ 2} See chapter 3:
      'Origin of Christianity and Judaism:
      What Actually Happened,
      What Jesus Actually Taught and Later Changes'
      Manfred Davidmann

{ 3} See chapter 5:
      'Family, Community, Sex and the Individual'
      Manfred Davidmann'

{ 4} In 'God and People:
      The Social Laws and Social System Underlying
      Judaism, Christianity, Islam and Democracy'
      Manfred Davidmann
      ISBN 978-0-85192-054-2
      see chapter 6.1: 'The Meaning of Genesis:
      Creation, Evolution and the Origin of Evil'

{ 5} In 'God and People:
      The Social Laws and Social System Underlying
      Judaism, Christianity, Islam and Democracy'
      Manfred Davidmann
      ISBN 978-0-85192-054-2
      see chapter 6.4: 'The Meaning of Genesis:
      Nephilim, Dominance and Liberty'

{ 6} In 'God and People:
      The Social Laws and Social System Underlying
      Judaism, Christianity, Islam and Democracy'
      Manfred Davidmann
      ISBN 978-0-85192-054-2
      see chapter 6.3: 'The Meaning of Genesis:
      Morality, Sexual Behaviour and Depravity'

{ 7} In 'Management and Leadership:
      Local, National, Multinational (Global),
      Principles and Practice'
      Manfred Davidmann
      ISBN 978-0-85192-057-3
      see chapter 2: 'Style of Management and
      Leadership'

{ 8} In 'Cooperatives and Cooperation:
      Causes of Failure, Guidelines for Success'
      Manfred Davidmann
      ISBN 978-0-85192-056-6
      see chapter 2: 'Cooperatives and Cooperation'
      and chapter 3: 'Causes of Failure, Guidelines
      for Success'

{ 9} See chapter 6:
      'Using Words to Communicate Effectively'
      Manfred Davidmann

{10} In 'Judaism: Basis - Past - Present - Future, Part 1'
      Manfred Davidmann
      ISBN 978-0-85192-060-3
      see chapter 2.1: 'Struggle for Freedom:
      The Social Cause-and-Effect Relationship'

{11} In 'Messianic Struggle:
      The Worldwide Struggle for a Good and
      Secure Life for All, Here and Now'
      Manfred Davidmann
      ISBN 978-0-85192-059-7
      see chapter 2: 'Social Responsibility, Profits and
      Social Accountability'

{12} In 'Messianic Struggle:
      The Worldwide Struggle for a Good and
      Secure Life for All, Here and Now'
      Manfred Davidmann
      ISBN 978-0-85192-059-7
      see chapter 7: 'Social Responsibility and
      Accountability: Summary'

{13} To Give or Not To Give
      'Everyman' TV documentary
      Editor: Jane Drabble; Producer: Angela Kaye
      Broadcast on 5/1/92 by BBC 1
      Based on book 'The Altruistic Person' by
      Professor Sam Oliner

{14} In 'The Real World in Which We Live:
      The Social Rules and Social System under
      Which We Suffer, Struggle, Survive and Prosper'
      Manfred Davidmann
      ISBN 978-0-85192-058-0
      see chapter 10: 'What People are Struggling
      Against: How Society is Organised for Controlling
      and Exploiting People'

{15} Genesis 3:16

{16}   In 'The Real World in Which We Live:
       The Social Rules and Social System under
       Which We Suffer, Struggle, Survive and Prosper'
       Manfred Davidmann
       ISBN 978-0-85192-058-0
       see chapter 6: 'Multinational Summits and
       Agreements, Top-level Decision-making and
       Democracy'

{17}   In 'The Real World in Which We Live:
       The Social Rules and Social System under
       Which We Suffer, Struggle, Survive and Prosper'
       Manfred Davidmann
       ISBN 978-0-85192-058-0
       see chapter 7: 'Exporting and Importing of
       Employment and Unemployment'

{18}   In 'The Real World in Which We Live:
       The Social Rules and Social System under
       Which We Suffer, Struggle, Survive and Prosper'
       Manfred Davidmann
       ISBN 978-0-85192-058-0
       see chapter 8: 'Transfer Pricing and Taxation'

Additions by the Editor:

*   In 'https://www.solhaam.org/articles/ruschur.html'
    see 'Relevant Current and Associated Works'

Appendix 1

Meaning and Use of Words   {9}

Words vary considerably as regards their value for communication. They differ in their level of abstraction. The greater the level of abstraction, the less meaning do they have, do they convey.

LEVELS OF ABSTRACTION

1. **Objects**

   Objects represent a relatively low level of abstraction as they can be seen and touched and their characteristics detailed accurately.

   Examples are: Table, chair.

2. **Events**

   In addition to objects, both action and time are implied, and so these are more complex.

   Examples are: Accident, sale, party.

3. **Generalisations**

   Words are also used as labels for groups and collections of objects or events. These generalisations are more abstract and less precise.

   Examples of such labels are: Furniture, machine tools, employees, parents.

   Employees, for example, can be full-time, part-time, shift working, office working, home working, male, female, young, old, single, married, unskilled, skilled, professional, and more.

4. **Value Judgements or Ideology**

   Value judgements and ideology are at the highest level of abstraction and words used as labels for them are quite useless for effective communication until the meaning of the word used is clearly defined in detail.

Examples of such labels are: Beautiful, valuable, necessary, luxury, lazy, free enterprise, truth, infallible, 'right attitude'.

Such words can be strung together and mixed with generalisations to provide good-sounding speeches and statements of the kind politicians like to use, to provide speeches and statements with no real meaning attached to the words used. Listeners or readers use their own idea of what the words mean and so their understanding of what is being said differs widely from person to person.

I listed the word 'truth' as an example of a label for a meaningless abstraction. Surely 'truth' ought to be more than a meaningless value judgement, so let us look at this in more detail.

Consider two media reports of a current event. Each reports the same event, each apparently telling the truth, each report giving its viewers different impressions of what actually happened.

How come? Can there be more than one truth?

Such reports may tell only part of what happened, may report only what seems relevant to the reporter, may then be selecting what seems to support the particular viewpoint of those who prepared the report.

Compare these 'truths' with that demanded from a witness in a court of law: 'The truth, the whole truth and nothing but the truth.'

Which means that what is required in a court of law is the truth with nothing taken away and nothing added.

If we agree on this as a definition, then the word 'truth' has become more meaningful.

Social Policies (Doctrine) of the Roman Catholic Church: An Evaluation

Introduction
Purpose of the Church's Social Doctrine
Intellectual Property Rights
God-given Social Laws and Social System
    Pentateuch
    Good Government and Management
    Trustful Co-operation (Ten Commandments)
    Social and Economic Security
    Community
Catholic Church's Social Policies and Church-State Relations
    Underlying Basis
    Romans 13: Verses 1-10
    Verses 1-7 (Romans 13): Church and State
    Verses 8-10 (Romans 13): Social Laws and Social System
Participation and Decision-making
Meaning and Use of Abstract Words and Phrases
Social Cause-and-Effect Relationship
    Unavoidable Consequences of Behaviour
    Predictions of the Prophets
    Hardships and Suffering
    Open Your Hand to Your Needy Brother
Genesis and Evolution
    Genesis
    Original Sin and Fallen Humanity
    Adam and Eve in Garden of Eden
Power Corrupts
    Nephilim and the Tower of Babel
    Globalisation
Planet-wide Danger
    The Flood
The Flaming Sword

Introduction

Before me lies the Catholic Church's volume called 'Compendium of the Social Doctrine of the Church' which was released on 25 October 2004 at a Press Conference at the Vatican {27}.

Social knowledge and policies are intermingled with religious pronouncements and beliefs and with guidelines about politics and church-state relations. It seems a more appropriate title would have been 'Statement by the Catholic Church of its Social Policies and about its Church-State Relations'.

This is the first time that the Vatican has published such a statement. Its text is over 300 pages long, and intended *"first of all for Bishops"*, then for *"priests"* and then for *"men and women religious"*.

We begin our evaluation by looking at church and state, government and religion, at their aims and purpose, at the conflicts and confrontations between them. Taking the information from {11}, what words such as state and religion mean and imply, is as follows:

    Government

        The group or organisation ruling a country or conducting its affairs. It can also refer to the government's style of management (authoritarian or participative, dictatorship or democracy).

Religion

A system of faith and worship, based on belief in the existence of a God (mostly benevolent), usually expressed by believers living according to its doctrine (principles, rules of behaviour, customs).

State

Somewhat vague term which refers to the combination of government and the community (country, population) being governed. Its use ignores important distinctions between people, government and the government's style of management, and their often conflicting interests. For example it does not distinguish between a government which serves its people and one which serves a country's rulers.

Church

Refers to the religion's clergy, or to its hierarchy. It can also refer to the religion's organisation, its decision-making processes, the doctrine it follows and the policies it applies.

But then there are different kinds of states and different kinds of churches {16}:

Some states consist of governments which serve the rulers by oppressing the people so that they can be exploited and such states stifle opposition and protest. Here those at the top and their experts tell people what they should do and have to do.

Other states consist of governments where those who govern serve the people and are accountable to them, where decisions are made at the lowest possible level by referendum with experts explaining the consequences both ways when a decision has to be made.

Similarly some churches serve rulers and in effect condition their people into gladly serving the rulers, into gladly allowing themselves to be exploited, the general approach then being 'gladly accept the tough life you are leading, the reward will come in a next life'.

And other churches preach that it is the will of God that all people are equal, that no person may exploit another, that it is the role of the establishment to serve the people.

For background information and underlying knowledge and understanding, see section 'Relevant Current and Associated Works'* which lists titles (as links) and short descriptions.

Purpose of the Church's Social Doctrine

Throughout, quotations from the Church's statement are set in as follows:

> *"Quotation from church's statement ... ..."*

The purpose of the Church's social concerns is clearly stated, as follows:

> *"... **the Church's social teaching is** itself a **valid instrument of evangelization.** ... In this light, **and only in this light,** does it concern itself with everything else: the human rights of the individual, and in particular of the 'working class', the family and education, the duties of the State, the ordering of national and international society, economic life, culture, war and peace, and respect for life from the moment of conception until death".* {40}

'Of evangelization' means 'Of preaching or of spreading the Gospel to, of winning over to Christianity' {26}.

'In the light of' means 'taking into consideration' so that 'only in the light of' means 'taking only this into consideration'.

> In other words:

> **The Church's social teaching is ... a valid instrument of** preaching and **converting** to Christianity. Taking only this into consideration **(For this purpose only)** ... **it concern itself with social teaching** ('doctrine') about everything else: the human rights of the individual, ...'

The lay faithful are to be formed on the basis of the Church's social teaching ('doctrine'), to serve the common good in their daily activities. And a political conscience should be formed

> *"in order to prepare lay Christians **to exercise political power.** 'Those with a talent for the difficult yet noble art of politics, or whose talents in this matter can be developed, should prepare themselves for it, and forgetting their*

241

*own convenience and material interests, they
should engage in political activity'."* {53}

So the purpose of the Church's 'Social Doctrine' is to convert others to
the Catholic Church's type of Christianity and to gain political influence.

Intellectual Property Rights

The Church's statement lists over 1200 references to sources from which
it quotes. The extracts it quotes are to a large extent selected
sentences. With the exception of some references to the Bible, the
extracts are largely drawn from what appear to be internal sources, that
is, Vatican announcements and pronouncements <17>.

Referring to internal documents as sources makes it difficult to change
and update earlier statements and publications, to correct past
mistakes, as people know each other and as the credibility of the
organisation and hierarchy could be affected. The same mistakes tend
to be made again and again, tend to be perpetuated.

Sentences from different internal (Vatican) sources tend to follow each
other in order to make a point. Successive sentences then tend to use
similar-seeming but different terms, and so the sentences could be out-
of-context.

We are told by the Church that

1. *"The Church's social doctrine finds its
   essential foundation in biblical revelation
   and in the tradition of the Church."* {30}

2. *"The Church's social doctrine avails itself of
   contributions from all branches of
   knowledge, whatever their source, ..."* {31}

3. *"The social doctrine belongs to the Church
   because the Church is the subject that
   formulates it, disseminates it and teaches
   it."* {32}

In this context, the word 'doctrine' means 'set of principles and beliefs
held by a religious group'. The word 'policy' means 'course or general
plan of action adopted by a church'. {26}

The word 'doctrine' is well applied to social policies based on biblical
revelation, as shown below. But no matter how well-intended and
plausible-seeming the points being made, the Church appears to be
pronouncing on social problems from a standpoint which differs

materially from that of the God-given religion on which it is based. And it appears to be struggling to find ways of linking its social policies to its religious foundation and teachings, as we shall see.

Here, however, we continue by looking at points (2) and (3) above, in which the Church states the source of its social doctrine and policies.

What is clearly missing from the Church's statement are references to the vast body of existing and new knowledge and understanding about the social, economic and political problems of our times, local and multinational (global), which have been and are being made world-wide. Perhaps now we know why.

The Church seems to state, in point (2) above, that it can include all knowledge regardless of its source. And in point (3), that when they include such knowledge in their teachings that this knowledge then belongs to the Church.

Which would appear to be a recipe for appropriating intellectual property belonging to others without acknowledging the source, and without paying for the use of that knowledge. Seemingly rephrasing and anonymising other people's achievements, apparently taking credit for, appropriating, the achievements of others.

To me it seems that the problem this Church is trying to overcome is simply that it cannot any more convincingly teach religion, the Bible (Pentateuch), Genesis and what this states (for example, about evolution, morality, or good and evil) without including (the simultaneously both revealed and proved) religious and social findings (discoveries) in my published works <18>. If they included the findings, they would need to acknowledge the source which is outside their Church's hierarchy or tradition.

This could be a reason for the Church appearing to claim that it can use (that is, include in its 'social doctrine')

> *'contributions from all branches of knowledge,*
> *whatever their source',*

which then belong to the Church

> *'because the Church is the subject that*
> *formulates it, disseminates it and teaches it.'*

As far as I can see, being a church does not allow a church to plagiarize <15>, or to appropriate another's intellectual property.

Intellectual property (advances in human knowledge and understanding, their source, ownership and copyright) have to be respected and acknowledged.

And in this case, the use of another's intellectual property has also to be paid for. After all, I had to pay a considerable sum of money for the Vatican-published copy of the Church's Social Doctrine which I am here evaluating.

God-given Social Laws and Social System   <1>

Pentateuch   {1}

What stands out is that human beings, guided by God, learned the difference between the brutal behaviour of their beastly ancestors, and the humane socially-responsible behaviour of human beings.

Their struggles and achievements were recorded in the Pentateuch <2> which has been handed down unaltered to this day. Also recorded were the social system and social rules of behaviour which underlie a good life of high quality combining freedom, independence and liberty <3>. Positive and constructive, rewarding what is good, punishing that which is inhuman, providing social security and a good life of high quality, limiting and restraining those in authority in government and management.

The beliefs of Christianity include the social laws and social system of the Pentateuch. Jesus taught that all the laws had to be kept, that belief and practice included and had to include the Ten Commandments, the social laws and the social system of the Pentateuch which include the Good Government (Kingship) laws. {2, 11}

Struggle between church and state, religion and government, is about the application in our everyday lives of the social provisions of the Pentateuch. So first we look at some key social laws of the Pentateuch, and describe its social system, to illustrate what the confrontation between religion and government, between 'church' and 'state', is about. <1>

Good Government and Management   {1}

The laws of the Pentateuch restrain the behaviour and limit the power of 'rulers', that is of government, of top executives and of the establishment, of those in positions of trust, responsibility or authority, no matter whether secular, religious or military, no matter what the hierarchy or organisation. {13, 14}. The Pentateuch {7} states clearly what they must not do.

They may not amass servants and may not oppress the people. They may not amass possessions and wealth, may not grasp power or behave promiscuously. In other words, they may not put themselves above others by grasping power, may not satisfy personal desires at the expense of others.

And a ruler (person in position of trust, responsibility or authority) has to follow these laws and abide by them every day if he wishes 'to prolong his days in his kingdom, he and his children'. For 'kingdom' read 'position' and include 'influence'.

These Pentateuch laws lay down that those in positions of trust, responsibility or authority must not oppress people so as to increase their own possessions and power. These laws forbid personal gain from the misuse of authority, wealth or position. Those in positions of trust, responsibility or authority may not grasp power, may not oppress the people, may not behave promiscuously, may not gain wives or wealth. {13}

Trustful Co-operation (Ten Commandments) {1}

The Ten Commandments <4> are so important and are so well known because behaviour in accordance with these rules is the basis for people trusting each other and so for people co-operating and working well with each other. The Ten Commandments underlie freedom, independence and strength to oppose and resist oppression. Wherever there is any independence of the mind and material freedom today it exists because people followed these rules of behaviour and it exists to the extent to which they do so. {13}

Take these two commandments (principles of behaviour):
You must not steal.
You must not desire anything which belongs to your neighbour.

Much trust and community friendliness is gained when people follow these principles.

But consider that these laws apply equally to the rich and powerful. It is also the rich and powerful who must not steal from the poor even the little which the poor have. It is the rich and powerful who must not cast longing glances at what little the rest of us possess, it is the rich and powerful who must not aim to gain at our expense.

Social and Economic Security {1}

All persons have the right to be free and independent masters of their own fate and no person may oppress or exploit another. Because people can be exploited through their needs there has to be a system of social and economic security which guarantees freedom from needs and so protects people from becoming dependent on others for essential income, protects against loss of material and spiritual independence.

This is what is laid down in the Pentateuch as a matter of law {13}:

1. The community has to provide ('lend') money to those who need it, free of interest.
2. All such loans, if outstanding, are to be cancelled every seventh year.

Community {1}

But only those are supported who themselves genuinely support the Pentateuch's benevolent ideals and principles and their application and who themselves live and act accordingly, who behave humanely. {13}

Catholic Church's Social Policies and Church-State Relations

Underlying Basis

The Church states that

> "The Church's social doctrine finds its essential foundation in biblical revelation and in the tradition of the Church." {30}

Bible revelation clearly refers to something which has been made known for the first time in the Bible.

A tradition is a belief, custom or procedure, often long-established and often handed down verbally.

The Church states that its social doctrine is based on Bible revelation and on the Church's tradition, and this confuses and ignores the important distinction between the sources, namely their relative authority.

We know that parts of the Bible have been compiled, edited and translated by man, at times with misleading results {3}, and throughout we need to distinguish between God-given revelation and rules of behaviour on the one hand, and man-made statements and assertions on the other. Man-made assertions and statements cannot override God-given revelation and rules of behaviour.

At issue between 'church' and 'state' are the God-given social laws and social system. These include the Good Government (Kingship) laws and the Ten Commandments.

The Good Government (Kingship) laws lay down that those in positions of trust, responsibility or authority must not oppress people so as to exploit them. These laws forbid personal gain from the misuse of authority or position.

The Ten Commandments underlie freedom, independence and strength to oppose and resist oppression.

Jesus taught that all these laws had to be kept, that belief and practice included and had to include the Ten Commandments, the social laws and the social system of the Pentateuch which include the Good Government (Kingship) laws. {2, 11}

So we would expect the Church's 'Social Doctrine' to be based on the God-given social laws and social system and the Church to be in the forefront of the struggle for a better life here on earth on behalf of God and people.

And what do we find in the published Social Doctrine of the Church? In other words, what are the Church's actual teachings, beliefs and practice?

The Catholic Church states {45} that

> *'Saint Paul defines the relationships and duties*
> *that a Christian is to have towards the*
> *authorities (Romans 13: 1-7).'*

Which means that the relationships and duties of a Christian towards the authorities are as stated by Paul in (Romans 13: 1-7) and that the Church is apparently teaching this.

Romans 13: Verses 1-10

Paul's letter is clear and to the point, as follows (Romans 13: 1-10):

1. All authority comes from God,
    so that rulers (those who are in a position of authority) have been appointed by God.
    Hence let every person
    submit to those who rule.

2. It follows that whoever resists the rulers
   resists whom God has appointed
   and those who resist rulers will be punished,

3. for rulers do not terrorize those whose conduct is "good", but
   those whose conduct is "evil".

   If you want to live without fearing the person who is in authority,
   then do what is "good" and you will be praised,

4. for he rules over you in God's place for your own good.

   But if you do that which is "evil", be afraid,
   for his is not an empty threat;
   he will in God's place punish the doer of "evil".

5. Therefore one must be obedient,
   to avoid their anger (if you do not obey)
   and because to obey is the right thing to do.

6. For the same reason you also pay taxes,
   for those in authority collecting taxes
   are acting on God's behalf.

7. Pay all those in authority what they demand,
   taxes, revenues, respect, honour.

8. Your only obligation to others is to love one another;
   Because he who loves another has fulfilled "the law".

9. For this
   You shall not commit adultery,
   You shall not murder,
   You shall not steal,
   You shall not bear false witness,
   You shall not covet;
   and if there be any other commandment,
   it is summed up in this saying:
   You shall love your neighbour as yourself.

10. Love does not do harm to a neighbour;
    therefore love (is) the fulfilling of the law.

Verses 1-7 (Romans 13): Church and State

According to the Catholic Church, Paul's verses 1-7 define "the relationships and duties that a Christian is to have towards the authorities".

Consider them for a moment.

They give his own point of view and personal ideology and he gave them an authority which they would not otherwise have had by means of a self-proclaimed vision. {2}

Astonishingly and without good reason he states that those in authority rule by 'divine right', that whatever they do is justified because in his opinion they act on God's behalf. Paul calls 'good' whatever those in authority do or want and those who resist or oppose them do 'evil' and will be punished. Paul wants all to obey those in authority and to be obedient, to pay taxes and revenues, to respect and honour those in authority. {2}

He is arguing that one must fear and obey those in authority and do for them and give them all they ask, without regard to how selfish, corrupt, inhuman or evil they may be. What Paul is saying and putting forward in (Romans 13) is neither God's word nor is it what Jesus taught. {2}

My findings, about the origin of Christianity, describe and prove how Paul changed what Jesus had taught, were first published in 1994 {2}. And in our more educated and enlightened age, what Paul is putting forward in verses 1-7 about the absolute power of those in authority, has become unacceptable to ordinary people, to many Christians.

So the Church appears now to be softening what it is preaching and teaching:

For example, the Church's paragraph {45} <16> also states that
> '... insofar as the authorities are at the service
> of God for the good of the person
> (Romans 13: 4)'.

Verse 4 (Romans 13: 4) on its own, that is out of context, away from what Paul is saying in verses 1-7, gives a misleading impression of what Paul said.

It is not Paul but the Church which is implying that one also needs to consider the extent to which an authority serves God for the good of the person.

The Church repeatedly attempts to soften Paul's political ideology, as follows:

> "Since God made men social by nature ... every
> civilized community must have a ruling
> authority, and this authority ... has ... God for
> its author." {46}

> "Political authority must always be exercised
> within the limits of morality and on behalf of
> the dynamically conceived common good,

according to some kind of legal framework.
When such is the case citizens are conscience-
bound to obey." {47}

"The mere consent of the people is not,
however, sufficient for considering 'just' the
ways in which political authority is exercised."
{48}

"Authority must be guided by the moral law.
{49}

The moral order ... has God for its first source
and final end."
The moral order precedes authority and is its
basis and ... 'has no existence except in God'."
{49}

The Church's next statement to look at {50}, is:
"Authority must ... respect ... essential human
and moral values.
These are innate ... .
... and must simply be ... respected ... as
elements of an objective moral law, ..."

Let us look at this statement {50} in more detail:
"Authority must ... respect ... essential human
and moral values.
Well-sounding but vague without clear meaning provided for the words
used. Readers use their own individual and widely-varying ideas of what
the words mean. Perhaps the Church ought to define in clear terms what
it considers to be 'essential', 'human' and 'moral' 'values'? <5>
These are innate ... .
The word 'innate' means 'born with it', and the Church appears to be
mistaken when it says that human beings are born with the 'essential
human and moral values'. To resolve this question the Church would
need to clearly define the 'essential human and moral values' they are
referring to.
... and must simply be ... respected ... as
elements of an objective moral law, ..."
At this point we do not know what the Church means by 'moral law', or
how an 'objective moral law' differs from this. <5>

Concerning what is innate, that is what people are born with, and
relevant essential human and moral values, see the following:

1. For comprehensive information on how the human mind evolved
   and works, see {9, 3, 6}.

2. For comprehensive information about the family and how it functions and the pressures which it faces from outside the family and from within, see {10, 3, 5}.

In the next paragraph of the Church's statement {51}, the Church cites Paul (Romans 13: 2), stating:

> "Authority must enact ... laws that correspond to what is required by right reason. ...
>
> Authority that governs according to reason places citizens in ... obedience to the moral order and, therefore,
> (in obedience) to God himself
> who is the ultimate source."
>
> "Whoever refuses to obey an authority that is acting in accordance with the moral order 'resists what God has appointed (Romans 13: 2)'."

The Church here appears to be stating that:

An authority which governs and enacts laws according to 'right reason' makes people obey the 'moral order' and thus God.

Such an authority rules by 'divine right' and has to be obeyed (Romans 13: 2).

Compare this with what Paul actually said {2} in his letter to the 'Romans' (Romans 13: 1-2), namely that:

1. All authority comes from God,
   so that rulers (those who are in a position of authority) have been appointed by God.
   Hence let every person
   submit to those who rule.

2. It follows that whoever resists the rulers (authorities)
   resists whom God has appointed
   and those who resist rulers (authorities) will be punished,

So Paul said that every person has to submit to those who rule, and that those who resist rulers are to be punished.

The Church, however, with reference to (Romans 13: 1-2), states that every person has to submit to those who rule as long as those who rule make people obey the 'moral order', and that those who resist such rulers are to be punished.

In each one of this sequence of paragraphs {46-51}, the Church moderates Paul's statements in such ways, for example referring to morality, to the common good, to human and moral values, to right reason, to moral law, and to moral order.

We now see clearly and understand what the Church is doing. The Church is softening the application of Paul's statement by saying it applies only to rulers who follow and apply such abstract undefined <5> value judgements and ideologies.

However, my published findings {2} were that, throughout the ages, Christians of goodwill chose intuitively to interpret Paul's statements about those in authority, and about Christian belief and practice, as meaning that
> 'the authority of those in authority only comes from God to the extent to which they themselves live according to and apply the Ten Commandments, the social laws and the social system laws including the Good Government (Kingship) laws'. Only those can 'love one another' who comply with all these laws. {2}

Verses 8-10 (Romans 13): Social Laws and Social System   {2}   <6>

Look again at the social laws and social system of the Pentateuch <14> which include the Good Government (Kingship) laws. You will see how the laws of the Pentateuch ensure freedom and material independence and provide a good life of high quality here and now, backed by effective social security. No one may oppress or exploit another and all are equal, as a matter of God-given law. {1}

It is these laws of behaviour, it is these social laws and this social system which Paul opposes. Having just declared that those in authority rule by 'divine right' (Romans 13: 1-7), he next (Romans 13: 8-10) tells people that they do not need to keep the core social laws and social system of the Pentateuch, as follows {2} <6>:

> Paul lists only the last five of the Ten Commandments <4>. These five commandments protect people against anti-social behaviour of others by prohibiting the doing of that which would harm or injure other people, prohibiting adultery, murder, theft, false witness and coveting.

> But one person's idea of 'love' could be another person's 'insult' or 'hurt'. And to say that 'You shall love your neighbour as yourself' contains all the other laws, is in effect abrogating, bypassing, annulling the core social laws of the Pentateuch by replacing them with a person's likes and dislikes, even by a pervert's feelings.

Paul himself leaves us in no doubt about his intentions when he says that "Your only obligation to others is to love one another". His intentions are to stop people from observing other essential laws of the Pentateuch.

The laws he does not wish people to observe include the first five commandments (of the Ten Commandments) which he pointedly left out from his list and thus include the social laws and the social system laws which together ensure freedom and material independence and social security.

Among the commandments <4> he does not want people to observe, are:

> One must not respect or serve oppressing, exploiting or enslaving beliefs or ideologies.

> One must not use God's name to lend authority to a statement which it would not otherwise have or to a false or misleading statement.

Among the social laws of the Pentateuch, for example, are the Good Government (Kingship) laws <14> which state that those in authority must not oppress people so as to increase their own possessions and power, that they must not put themselves above the people and so enrich themselves. They are warned against oppressing people and against forming enforcing squads or organisations so as to multiply their own power, must not be promiscuous and must not amass wealth. They must know and observe the law and its intent and aim to see the law applied.

Jesus taught that all the laws had to be kept, that belief and practice included and had to include the Ten Commandments, the Good Government (Kingship) laws, the social laws and the social system of the Pentateuch. {2}

And so {Romans 13: 1-10} is of fundamental importance to Christian belief and practice because it runs counter to what Jesus had been teaching {2}. Verses 1-7 and 8-10 are part of a whole, adding to and explaining each other. Their meaning is crystal-clear when, as intended by Paul, they are read together. Paul acted on behalf of the rich and powerful when he tried to convince people that those in authority were God's representatives on earth and that the social laws did not have to be kept. {2}

But the Catholic Church pointedly refers only to verses 1-7. In all the 331 pages of its 'Compendium of the Social Doctrine of the Church', it does not even once refer to verses 8-10. Verses 1-10 stand or fall together. And to the extent to which the Church considers only verses 1-7, to that extent the Church appears to be quoting out of context, apparently condoning and teaching what Paul says in verses 8-10.

So much has been written about Christianity and Judaism that it is fairly easy to select one sentence or two from one place, and a sentence or two from a completely different place, and more from another part unrelated to the others, and so on. These can then be added together or compared to arrive at conclusions which back the personal opinion of the individual doing the selecting.

What is valid within the meaning of one record is not necessarily valid within the meaning of another. And the process of 'quoting out of context' often results in conclusions which are totally different from the contexts from which they were selected.

So that the Oxford Dictionary {26} defines 'Out of context' as meaning 'without the surrounding words and therefore giving a false impression of the meaning'.

Paul made changes which have had the most severe consequences for those who follow Paul's ideology. But more about this later.

Participation and Decision-making

Consider the difference between authoritarian and participative {17} management and government:

The style of management or government in different countries can be anywhere on a scale from fully authoritarian (dictatorship) at one end of the scale to fully participative (policy decided by the people) at the other end. {17}

This is a fundamental scale which cuts across artificial political divides - dictatorship of the left is dictatorship just like that of the right. Dictatorship is dictatorship no matter whether the organisation, hierarchy or political party is on the left or on the right of the political spectrum. Under authoritarian government or dictatorship the government and its 'experts' tell the people what the government or rulers decide the people have to follow. {17}

Under participative government and democracy the government and leadership put into effect the wishes of the people, the policy decided by delegates directly appointed by and directly responsible and accountable to the people. {17}

So the real conflict and struggle is about decision-making in all community organisations and at all levels, and the extent to which an organisation is either participative or authoritarian "depends ... on the degree of participation in decision-making which is practised. {17} <7>

"One can determine the degree of participation in decision-making <7> of any system of running a company or organisation, or of governing a country, by considering for example whether and to what extent decisions are being made at the various levels or whether people merely follow orders, ... and to what extent authority is centred at the top, or where the balance of power lies between those who direct and those who work, on the balance of authority between ruler and ruled, between owner and worker, between the establishment and the population." These findings were published years ago {17} and are taught worldwide.

The Church's statement shows that the Church follows Paul's ideology that rulers rule by 'Divine Right' and have to be obeyed. Rulers make the decisions, there is no question of decision-making by others, there is no question of participating in decision-making, of democratic decision-making by the people. This the Church shows by defining the word 'participation' to mean 'participating (taking part) in activities with other people' {37}. Participating in work being done or in community groups is very different from participating in making the decisions.

One could say, for example, that the Hebrew slaves in Egypt had a 'right to work' and that they participated in 'activities', in 'carried-out functions'. What the slaves did not have was a say about what to do, for whom, at what rate of pay, about when to work and when to rest, and so on.

Examples from the Church's 'Social Doctrine' are:

> "... participation ... is ... a series of activities by means of which the citizen ... contributes to the ... life of the ... community." {37}
>
> "... it is clearly evident that every democracy must be participative. This means that the different subjects ... at every level must be informed, listened to and involved in the exercise of the carried-out functions." {38}
>
> "... in ... countries ruled by totalitarian or dictatorial regimes, ... the ... right to participate in public life is denied at its origin, since it is considered a threat to the state itself." {39}

This question of decision-making (who decides what) is closely linked to what is referred to as 'globalisation'. Consider the relevant reports by Manfred Davidmann {18, 19, 20} and the maxims he laid down in 'Multinational Summits and Agreements, Top-level Decision-taking and Democracy' {18}, maxims such as

> Representatives, governments or government officials do not have the authority or right to override, reduce or sign away the participative (democratic) rights of the electors, of the population.

Meaning and Use of Abstract Words and Phrases

The Church ought to define in clear terms the many vague abstract words, phrases and ideologies which make up a considerable part of its 'social doctrine'. Like those already mentioned earlier on ('essential', 'human' and 'moral' 'values'). <5>

For example, abstract words (see Appendix 1) like 'infallibly' and 'truth' can mean different things to different people and this applies also to phrases such as 'right attitude'. Such words and phrases need to be clearly defined in detail when they are used.

For example, the word 'infallibly' is generally taken to mean 'incapable of making mistakes or being wrong'.

Another example is the word 'truth'. In Appendix 1 this is defined as follows:

> Consider two media reports of a current event. Each reports the same event, each apparently telling the truth, each report giving its viewers different impressions of what actually happened.
>
> How come? Can there be more than one truth?
>
> Such reports may tell only part of what happened, may report only what seems relevant to the reporter, may then be selecting what seems to support the particular viewpoint of those who prepared the report.
>
> Compare these 'truths' with that demanded from a witness in a court of law: 'The truth, the whole truth and nothing but the truth.'
>
> Which means that what is required in a court of law is the truth with nothing taken away and nothing added.
>
> If we agree on this as a definition, then the word 'truth' has become more meaningful.

256

So if we agree that for us the word 'truth' means the truth with nothing taken away and nothing added, then the word 'truth' has indeed become more meaningful.

Clearly, abstract words like 'infallibly' and 'truth' (see Appendix 1) can mean different things to different people. Such words and phrases need to be clearly defined in detail when they are used, and particularly so when they are used for laying down principles of faith (doctrines).

Social Cause-and-Effect Relationship <8>

Unavoidable Consequences of Behaviour {1}

The Social Cause-and-Effect Relationship is recorded in the Pentateuch as a fundamental scientific law, in the language of religion.

> "This law states <8> that the consequences of keeping or not keeping the Pentateuch's laws are inescapable, that what happens to one is in the end the inevitable result of one's own behaviour. Also clearly stated is that this is a scientific law which was defined and stated using the language of religion so that people would benefit from knowing the effects (consequences) of their behaviour. The relationship is stated in precise terms {1}. History {14} and social science {22} confirm it."

> "We are told that the relationship applies to all without exception and at all times, wherever one may be, regardless of type of government, form of religion or social system or country. It applies whether you like it or not, agree or disagree. We are also told that the process is reversible: Increasingly disregarding the laws (rules of behaviour) results in greater suffering and oppression, increasingly behaving according to the laws results in greater freedom, liberty, independence and a better life." {1}

> "If we want freedom, independence, good life of high quality, then we have to follow these laws. If we do not, then we lose freedom, independence, good life and the country in which we live. The consequences of our behaviour cannot be avoided but we can change the course of events by changing our behaviour." {1}

Predictions of the Prophets

The prophets <9> foretold what would happen as a result of how people were behaving if people continued to behave as they did. To someone who has no knowledge or understanding of science and its laws, a scientist's prediction appears to be a 'prophesy', a foretelling of what will happen as if by divine inspiration. And so the predictions of the prophets were regarded as divinely inspired prophesies by those unaware of the knowledge which the prophets had. {13}

> "The prophets, motivated by a deeply seated sense of social responsibility and urgency, by love of God, Pentateuch and people, continued with increasing frequency and increasing urgency to warn of the inevitable consequences unless rulers and establishment changed their ways, pointing out that all the people would suffer horribly unless behaviour changed. They were bitterly opposed by the rulers and establishment of the day and struggled for God and people while alone and unsupported. They were not listened to, the rulers and their establishments continued to corrupt and oppress the people until both kingdoms were destroyed and the people most viciously dispersed." {14}

What the prophets foretold were predictions based on knowledge and understanding of the Social Cause-and-Effect Relationship in the Pentateuch, and thus of the inevitability of the events predicted by them, of the events which would follow from the way the rulers and their secular and religious establishments were behaving. {13}

The Cause-and-Effect Relationship is just as valid today as then, and it applies to all at all times, no matter where they live or what they believe in or their state of development. {13}

Hardships and Suffering

We saw that Paul attempted to stop Christians from observing the God-given social laws and social system of the Pentateuch, and the Christian establishment near that time apparently based beliefs and practice on his verses. So Paul's (establishment's) version became accepted as official Christian doctrine and apparently it is this which tends to be taught today. {2, 11}

We also saw that the Social Cause-and-Effect Relationship is a scientific law which applies to all without exception and at all times. Increasingly disregarding the laws (rules of behaviour) results in suffering and oppression, increasingly behaving according to the laws results in greater freedom, liberty, independence and a better life. The consequences of keeping or not keeping the Pentateuch's laws are inescapable. What happens to one is in the end the inevitable result of one's own behaviour. {1} <8>

Hence the Christian establishment condemned Christians to unavoidable inescapable consequences, to sufferings and severe hardships according to the extent to which they follow Paul's ideology, in accordance with the Social Cause-and-Effect Relationship. Which the prophets knew and understood, which we now know and understand.

And which any Church which continues to preach Paul's ideology, needs to know and understand.

Open Your Hand to Your Needy Brother

In the Church's Social Doctrine {28} we find this quotation from the Pentateuch:

> "If there is among you a poor man, one of your brethren, ... you shall not harden your heart or shut your hand against your poor brother, but you shall open your hand to him, and lend him sufficient for his need" (Deut 15: 7-8).

The verse is quoted by the Church without any comment or explanation, which gives the reader the mistaken impression that believers are asked to 'lend' charitably to those in need. Left out is the phrase
'... within any of your gates, in your land which the Lord your God gives you, ...'
and the end of the verse
'in that which he wants.'

This verse actually refers to the Pentateuch's social system which is to be instituted and followed and in this case provides community-backed social security as a matter of right. This is what is laid down as a matter of law {13}:
1. The community has to provide ('lend') money to those who need it, free of interest.
2. All such loans, if outstanding, are to be cancelled every seventh year.

But the Church replaces effective social security as a right, with charity:
> "the more fortunate ... should place their goods more generously at the service of others." {36}

Charity can be used to exploit the needs of the needy by making the receiver indebted to, and depending on, the giver for survival.

Which compares with the Pentateuch's right to social security to enable the receiver to remain an independent breadwinner, to enable one to remain the master of one's own fate.

Consider the abject poverty of the bulk of the population in traditionally 'catholic' countries where Catholics are the majority, where the 'Church' appears to be influential, well off and apparently powerful. For example, in Latin American countries, in the Philippines. On the whole, the populations of these countries are poor, destitute and oppressed.

In such countries, however, individual Christians of all ranks speak up for, and stand beside, the oppressed and impoverished people <10>.

Genesis and Evolution

Genesis

In the Church's Social Doctrine can be found the following to my mind irrelevant and misguided interpretation which refers to (Gen 2: 18-24):
> *"The Book of Genesis teaches that human dominion over the world consists in naming things."* {33}

To illustrate the point, in {3} see 'Evolution towards Good' where the note to verse 20 states
> 'Man' learns to communicate which enables co-operation and teamwork with another (others). And lays the basis for closer associations between two or more of his own kind.

And verses 21-22 record that God made a woman, and brought her to the man.

So I consider that the naming process enabled 'man' and 'woman' to communicate and cooperate with each other and live together as a family. (Gen 2: 23-24)

Taking the matter further, in {3} we also see that:

> The immense knowledge and understanding which underlies the Pentateuch (of which Genesis is a part) could not have been understood or comprehended by those then living. And what is there has been overlaid with the dust of millennia, with accumulated interpretations and comments limited by the then current knowledge, understanding and misconceptions. What is stated in Genesis is thus much more meaningful than is generally appreciated.

In Genesis the then-beyond-comprehension beginning of life on earth and its evolutionary progress towards humankind is being described.

And Genesis records 'God' to be that which caused and generated the beginning and development of life on this planet and of its development from the first bacteria to humankind. What we have at the beginning of Genesis is a description of how life, human beings, good and evil developed on this planet, in religious terms.

Original Sin and Fallen Humanity

The Church spends much of its time both defining and teaching the difference between good and evil as it sees it, to enable its adherents to choose good instead of evil. Indeed the whole volume about the Church's Social Doctrine appears to be aimed, at least in theory, at showing their adherents what the Church considers 'good' or desirable.

Surprisingly, the Church has some harsh things to say about what took place when Adam and Eve found out in the Garden of Eden about the difference between good and evil. As follows:

> "It is in the free action of God the Creator that we find the very meaning of creation, even if it has been distorted by the experience of sin. In fact, the narrative of the first sin (Gen 3: 1-24)" describes (how Adam and Eve found out about the difference between good and evil)." {29}

> "It is in this original estrangement that are to be sought the deepest roots of all the evils that afflict social relations between people, of all the situations in economic and political life that attack the dignity of the person, that assail justice and solidarity." {29}

> "By yielding to the tempter, Adam and Eve committed a personal sin, but this sin affected the human nature that they would then transmit in a fallen state. It is a sin which will be transmitted by propagation to all mankind, that is, by the transmission of a human nature deprived of original holiness and justice." {34}

It seems that what the Church is suggesting is out of proportion to what it considers to have happened in the Garden of Eden. The second of the

261

Ten Commandments, for example, states that future generations of the worst kind of sinners would be punished, in the following ways.

First, the relevant extract <4> from the second commandment:

> For I the Lord your God am a jealous God, visiting the iniquity of the fathers upon the children, and upon the third and **upon the fourth generation** of them that hate Me, but showing mercy to the thousandth generation of those who love Me and keep My commandments.

Then the whole of the second commandment, in plain English <4>:

> Those who love Me and keep My commandments are shown mercy to the thousandth generation.

> But those who respect and serve other gods, respect or serve oppressing, exploiting or enslaving beliefs or ideologies, they hate me and they and their children will suffer the consequences even in their fourth generations.

The Church, however, teaches:

> *"The doctrine of original sin ... encourages men and women ... not to ... continuously (be) seeking scapegoats in other people and justification in the environment, in heredity, in institutions, in structures and in relationships."* {35}

So teachings about 'original sin' or a 'fallen humanity' appear to be aimed at telling suffering humanity to blame themselves and not the system or others, for the sufferings and hardships of their lives.

In other words, it seems that what is implied, what we are being told, is: 'Do not blame the Church (its doctrine, its teachings, its hierarchy), the government, or the oppressor, blame yourself.'

That is, blame yourself for all the sufferings and hardships of life brought about by the Church teaching Paul's ruler-serving pronouncements instead of standing up for the God-based teachings of Jesus. Sufferings and hardships which are so clearly described in the God-given Social Cause-and-Effect Relationship as the inevitable consequences of behaviour, of not following 'good', of choosing 'evil' instead of 'good'.

To me it seems unreasonable for the Church to guide its believers into following the word of man (Paul) instead of following the word of God, while apparently telling believers to blame themselves for the inevitable harsh and bitter consequences of following the Church's teachings, of following the words of Paul instead of following the teachings of Jesus.

Adam and Eve in Garden of Eden

(Genesis 3: 1-24) tells the well-known story of Adam and Eve in the Garden of Eden, is about how Adam and Eve became aware of the difference between good and evil, and the resulting consequences. This story is an allegory, that is it is

> 'a story or description in which the characters or events symbolize some deeper underlying meaning' {26}.

What is recorded in (Genesis 3: 1-24), what it really means, is:

Mammals had evolved from reptiles, and developed feelings of care and affection towards others and developed some more advanced brain functions. If there is to be further development towards good then there has to be knowledge of and understanding of good and evil and of the difference between them so that people can choose between them. {3}

And the human brain evolved from the mammalian brain. Homo erectus was followed and replaced by Homo sapiens (Wise man, ourselves, with considerably larger brain size), commonly referred to as humans, human beings, humanity.

It is the appearance of Homo sapiens, that is the evolution of the neocortex {9}, which is recorded in Chapter 3 of Genesis. The neocortex consists of the grey matter, the bulk of the brain in two symmetrical hemispheres, separate but communicating. To a considerable extent it is our neocortex which enables us to behave like human beings {9}, to know the difference between good and evil and to choose between them. {3}

It is this which is told in (Genesis 3: 1-24) including, for example, that childbirth became more difficult as a result of the increased brain size, and stating the necessary division of work between the male and the female in protecting and bringing up their children. {3, 10}

Genesis (Chapter 3) describes the evolution of Homo sapiens in a way which could be understood at the time it was written, and which can now be understood as it was intended to be understood, following the publication of Manfred Davidmann's 'The Meaning of Genesis: Creation, Evolution and the Origin of Evil' {3}. This shows that there is no conflict, no contradiction, only agreement, between what is recorded in Genesis and what we know about the evolution of human beings. And Genesis defines good and evil, pointing to the root of evil.

Power Corrupts

Nephilim and the Tower of Babel {6}

The Church records that there were some who were turned against God but apparently fails to see the extremely important teachings {6} of the allegory of The Tower of Babel. The Church records:

> *In the divine plan, all peoples had "one language and the same words" (Gen 11: 1), but humanity became divided, turning its back on the Creator (Gen 11: 4).* {52}

Actually, the allegory <11> of The Tower of Babel describes key and focal events which determined the quality of life itself, and which enabled the development of humane behaviour, life and living. Of the greatest importance then, of utter and determining importance at the present time. {6}

It is essential that we understand the deeper underlying meaning and significance of these events and apply the knowledge we will have gained to the way in which we live and organise our lives, to communities, societies and social organisation. {6}

At the present time, the fate and future of humankind, of all human beings, is balanced on a razors edge between oppression, exploitation and enslavement on the one side, and liberty, equality and a good life for all on the other side. {6}

So what is the underlying meaning of the allegory? What follows has been taken from, or is based on, Manfred Davidmann's 'Genesis: Nephilim, Dominance and Liberty' {6}:

> We are told that 'Nephilim' are human beings with hereditary abilities which seem extraordinary. Their abilities and skills appear to be somewhat rare. These abilities apparently enable them to influence, organise, manipulate, control, dominate other human beings. {6}

> They are 'anshe ha-shem' (People of name, that is 'well-known people'). They are misusing their abilities for their own ends, their behaviour is 'evil'. Nephilim are corruptly and evilly misusing their extraordinary abilities. {6}

> And in Genesis we can see that an individual called Nimrod was one of the nephilim, that the beginning of his kingdom was Babel in the land of Shinar. In this way Nimrod is linked with the events

told in the allegory <11> of The Tower of Babel, that is with founding the city (Babel, Gate of God) and with building the tower 'with its top in heaven'. {6}

The driving force behind the building of the tower appears to be Nimrod. The 'fallen' nephilim are selfish, corrupt, dominating, exploiting and oppressing. It is the ability of such nephilim to manipulate ordinary people into working for the nephil, which is here being pointed out and criticized. Ordinary people are being manipulated into serving nephilim, into working to increase a selfish and corrupt nephil's personal influence and power. {6}

Aiming to reach heaven and become god-like, to set themselves up in opposition to God. Which means that Nimrod, who is referred to as their king, is attempting to gain, to assign to himself, god-like (absolute) authority and power. Assuming, taking to themselves, god-like power over people concerning good life or bad life, concerning life or death. Opposing God by what they were doing, they were scattered by God. {6}

So 'let us go down' ... 'and there confound their language': 'In this way we shall destroy the prerequisite that assures the success of their work' {8}. That is, destroy their organisation and their ability to organise on a large, overall dominating, scale by destroying their ability to communicate and cooperate, their teamwork. {6}

So they are apparently driven by Nimrod who, being one of the nephilim, is using his extraordinary abilities for setting himself up as all-powerful overlord in opposition to God, that is in opposition to humane behaviour, equality, independence, liberty, shared wealth and good life for all. {6}

We know that they are with us here and now just as before, within our communities at the present time. That they are referred to as 'fallen' indicates that their capabilities are being used for selfish ends. Their descendants are 'mighty' (powerful) and 'of renown' (well-known, prominent, in the public eye). {6}

In other words, there are among us people with extraordinary abilities which are hereditary and who are using them for their own selfish ends, and who are likely to be powerful or influential and well-known. {6}

And so the allegory states that if any become too powerful, a threat to that which is humane and good, then they need to be, and are to be, dispersed. In other words, their tower (power, organisation, country, empire, corporation, monopoly, government, rulers, multinational, global corporation, hierarchy) needs to be dispersed. {6}

'Power corrupts, absolute power corrupts absolutely'. Humanity and human behaviour depend on opposition and balance, on scattering and dispersal, on democracy, on limiting and taming the struggle for global power and dominance. {6} <12>

Globalisation

> What the Church advocates in its Social Doctrine concerning globalisation, can be seen from the *extracts* below which are set in like this example,

and which are followed by what may be clearer descriptions in plainer English of what they seem to be saying, set in like this.

> *Our modern era is marked by the complex phenomenon of economic and financial globalization, a process that progressively integrates national economies at the level of the exchange of goods and services and of financial transactions.* {41}

Economic and financial globalisation progressively integrates national economies (exchange of goods and services, financial transactions).

> *It is evident that, because of the great disparities between countries regarding access to technical and scientific knowledge and to the most recent products of technology, the process of globalization ends up increasing rather than decreasing the inequalities between countries in terms of economic and social development.* {42}

... the process of globalization ends up increasing rather than decreasing the inequalities between countries in terms of economic and social development.

> *The loss of centrality on the part of States must coincide with a greater commitment on the part of the international community to exercise a strong guiding role. In fact, an important consequence of the process of globalization consists in the gradual loss of effectiveness of nation-states in directing the dynamics of*

266

national economic-financial systems. The governments of individual countries find their actions in the economic and social spheres ever more strongly conditioned by the expectations of international capital markets and by the ever more pressing requests for credibility coming from the financial world. Because of the new bonds of interdependence among global operators, the traditional defensive measures of States appear to be destined to failure and, in the presence of new areas of competition, the very notion of a national market recedes into the background. {43}

International 'capital' is increasingly determining the economic, financial and social policies of individual countries who are increasingly losing their independence to interdependent global operators. Probably meaning that Capital (global corporations) are increasingly overpowering democratic national governments.

The sphere of politics too, just like that of the economy, must be in a position to extend its range of action beyond national boundaries, quickly taking on an operative worldwide dimension which alone will permit it to direct the processes now underway not only according to economic parameters but also according to moral criteria. The basic goal is to guide economic processes by ensuring that the dignity of man and his complete development as a person are respected, in the context of the common good. Taking on this task entails the responsibility of accelerating the consolidation of existing institutions and the creation of new entities responsible for this. Economic development, in fact, will be lasting only to the extent that it takes place within a clear and defined normative context and within a broad plan for the moral, civil and cultural growth of the entire human family. {44}

Politics must extend its beyond-national-boundaries actions worldwide to direct the processes now under way (globalisation) in economics and morality. Globalisation (planet-wide commercial operations?) can only last if it is combined with political control which has a broad plan for moral, civil and cultural growth (which are more warm and comforting abstractions which are meaningless till their meaning is defined).

It seems to me that the Church, supporting 'globalisation',

apparently fails to see or understand the important teachings {6} of the allegory of the Tower of Babel, and

seems to have forgotten that, within living memory, totally corrupted governments were defeated during the Second World War only by external forces, as were the Khmer Rouge.

Regarding the social problems of 'globalisation', I would suggest that reference could have been made to relevant reports by Manfred Davidmann {18, 19, 20}, also quoting from the maxims he laid down in 'Multinational Summits and Agreements, Top-level Decision-taking and Democracy' {18}, maxims such as

Representatives, governments or government officials do not have the authority or right to override, reduce or sign away the participative (democratic) rights of the electors, of the population.

No elected representative, government or government employee has overriding right or authority

1. to hand over to corporations (that is to those who own and control them), to any other organisation or to anyone else, an overriding control over the present and future, economic and social, welfare of the people, or

2. to sign away democratic rights of their people for the self-determination of key fundamental aspects of their lives.

Where 'Participative (democratic) rights', of course, includes decision-making by a well-informed population.

Decision-making by leaderships has to be replaced by decision-making at the level of the people.

The real struggle is not between political left and right, but is a struggle for participation (the right to take decisions).

But we are not allowed to follow a multitude to do evil.

Planet-wide Danger

The Flood (Genesis Chapters 6-8)

The material in this section has to a considerable extent been taken from "Genesis' Secrets: Pre-flood Evils and the Social Problems of Our Time" {4} which is comprehensive and detailed, published in year 2,000.

Life forms are evolving towards greater viciousness (evolution by the survival of the strongest, most vicious), human beings are misusing and exploiting each other for personal gain. So they were wiped out, Noah was the exception.

The history of life on this planet tells of a major planet-wide happening which corresponds to what is recorded in Genesis about the Flood, caused by a massive volcanic eruption in Sumatra, occurring at the right time in the history of human beings. As follows <13>:

Thousands (Thousands of years ago)	
75	About 75 thousand years ago there was a massive volcanic eruption in Sumatra which severely affected the climate causing a planet-wide (average) drop in temperature of something like 5 degrees C. It seems that at roughly the same time there was apparently an enormous reduction of world population. It has recently been estimated from a reduction in genetic diversity which occurred at about this time that only a few thousand (say 5 to 10 thousand) human beings could have survived. The two events appear to be connected.
70	Human beings in Africa.
50	Human beings in Australia
40	Human beings in Europe
30	From 30,000 years ago, to the present, all cultures and remains are those of human beings.

Pre-flood there was no objective knowledge of what constituted good, humane, behaviour. There were no rules of behaviour to enable people to resist and overcome the temptations of evil. Human beings as a whole were using their thinking and evaluating abilities towards evil, towards evil behaviour.

Genesis Chapters 6-8 record the events of the Flood, linking what happened to the inhuman ways in which human beings behaved.

Genesis from then on defines evil more closely and describes and lays down what humane behaviour is and how it can be achieved, stressing justice and retribution. Genesis describes what constitutes humane, good, behaviour, how to resist, counter, overcome beastly temptations, to compare good with evil so as to choose good. And Genesis makes the point that if human beings wish to survive and prosper they need to follow the rules of behaviour laid down by God.

The Flaming Sword

Following the flood, Genesis states (Gen 8: 22) that
> 'While the earth remains, seedtime and harvest, and cold and heat, and summer and winter, and day and night shall not cease.'

To me it seems that the list seedtime and harvest, and cold and heat, and summer and winter, and day and night, refers to essential environmental characteristics on which depends the continuation of human life on the planet. A warning to humanity.

Again, following the flood, Genesis (Gen 9: 9) records God saying
> 'As for Me, behold, I establish My covenant with you, and with your seed after you;'

A covenant is an agreement in which each of the parties undertakes duties and obligations towards the other. It is not a one-sided promise or obligation.

And so God is saying:
> 'As for Me, behold':
meaning 'On my part (as long as you do your part, as long as you behave like human beings), I ...'

Genesis (Gen 3: 1-24) describes, in the language of religion, the evolution of Homo sapiens, human beings, ourselves. We know the difference between good and evil and can choose between them.

But verse 24 (Gen 3: 24) states:
>   So He drove out the man;
>   and He placed at the east of the garden of Eden the cherubim,
>   and the flaming sword which turned every way,
>   to keep the way to the tree of life.

We have come a long way towards creating and modifying life forms, towards selecting different characteristics. Such work is proceeding in different directions in a haphazard way, uncontrolled, in often socially irresponsible seeming directions. Now threatening the survival of human beings on this planet as a species, because such knowledge and understanding is being misused for personal profit without concern for the survival of the species or the good of the community of human beings.

It is the rich and powerful, the nephilim of our times, who would be able to appropriate knowledge about extending lifespan, would consider modifying or replacing Homo sapiens (human beings, ourselves) for benefiting only themselves.

Brutal viciousness, oppression, exploitation, corruption, evil could dominate unbalanced if they gained the upper hand, and this cannot be allowed to happen under any circumstances.

Many fires are started by socially irresponsible behaviour, by carelessness or by accident, but are noticed in time and are put out before too much damage results. What frightens us is that the fire brigade can arrive too late to control the fire, that one socially irresponsible act may drastically and irreversibly condemn future as yet unborn generations, that one incident can start a sequence of events which could make this planet uninhabitable for human beings. {22}

The fate and future of humankind, of all human beings, is balanced on a razors edge between oppression, exploitation and enslavement on the one side, and liberty, equality and a good life for all on the other side. {6}

Choice and Decision-making

Here I find myself in the position of the medical specialist who is talking to a very good friend and notices certain symptoms. Unless treated the disease is fatal. So what can one do? I can ask him how he feels, and he says he feels well. I suggest he goes and sees a doctor and as he is feeling well that could be the end of a beautiful friendship. But I know and he doesn't know that he can be cured but only if he takes action fairly quickly. In the end all that I can do is to tell him something about my qualifications, describe one or two of the symptoms in a mild sort of way and suggest that investigation is required. What he does after that is up to him. {24}

Meaning that the Catholic Church has a conscious choice to make, has to decide. It can continue to follow Paul (Romans 13: 1-10, as a whole or in part) and so condemn its catholic believers to the unavoidable consequences, to sufferings and hardships, which followed in the past and will continue to follow. Or begin to understand, follow and teach the God-given social laws and social system of the Pentateuch including the laws of Good Government (Kingship).

But wherever there is extreme poverty and suffering and pain you are likely to find Christians who are struggling on the side of the oppressed. Christians, for example, such as priests who provide encouragement and guidance to oppressed and suffering people in their struggle for a better life against the ruling establishment, against the established ruling oppressors, doing so at much risk and without thought of personal gain. {12}

Conclusions

Purpose of the Church's 'Social Doctrine'

The purpose of the Church's 'Social Doctrine' is clearly stated, namely to convert others to the Catholic Church's kind of Christianity and to gain political influence.

Jesus Taught: The God-given Social Laws and Social System

The social laws and social system of the Pentateuch ensure freedom and material independence and provide a good life of high quality here and now, backed by effective social security. No one may oppress or exploit another and all are equal, as a matter of God-given law. {1}

Jesus taught that all the social laws and the social system of the Pentateuch had to be kept, that belief and practice included and had also to include the Ten Commandments and the Good Government (Kingship) laws. {2, 11}

The Ten Commandments underlie freedom, independence and strength to oppose and resist oppression. The Good Government (Kingship) laws lay down that those in positions of trust, responsibility or authority must not oppress people and also forbid personal gain from the misuse of authority or position. Those in authority must not be promiscuous and must not amass wealth.

The Church Preaches (Teaches)

Paul acted on behalf of the rich and powerful when he proclaimed that those in authority were God's representatives on earth and had to be obeyed, and that the social laws and social system did not have to be kept. What Paul said and put forward in (Romans 13: 1-10) apparently became official Christian doctrine and is still taught today. But it is neither God's word nor is it what Jesus taught. {2, 11}

We saw that the Social Cause-and-Effect Relationship is a scientific law which applies to all without exception and at all times. It clearly states that increasingly disregarding the laws (rules of behaviour) results in suffering and oppression, increasingly behaving according to the laws results in greater freedom, liberty, independence and a better life. The prophets knew and understood this relationship, and predicted accordingly, just as we now know and understand it. The consequences of keeping or not keeping the Pentateuch's laws are inescapable. What happens to one is in the end the inevitable result of one's own behaviour. And we can change the course of events by changing our behaviour. {1} <8>

Hence the Christian establishment condemned Christians to unavoidable inescapable consequences, to suffering and hardships, according to the extent to which they follow Paul's ideology.

When looking at Genesis Chapter 3 (Adam and Eve in Garden of Eden) we see that it is misunderstood as if it implied some kind of personal guilt. What we are being told by the Church in teachings about 'original sin' or a 'fallen humanity' appears to be: 'Do not blame the Church (its doctrine, its teachings, its hierarchy), the government, or the oppressor, for the sufferings and hardships of your lives, blame yourself.' It appears that the teachings of the religious hierarchy condemn their Christian believers to sufferings and hardships while the hierarchy seems to tell the believers to blame themselves and not the hierarchy!

The Church is apparently teaching that the relationships and duties of a Christian towards the authorities are as stated by Paul in (Romans 13: 1-7). The Church's statement shows that the Church follows Paul's ideology that rulers rule by 'Divine Right' and have to be obeyed.

My findings, about the origin of Christianity, describe and prove how Paul changed what Jesus had taught and were first published in 1994 {2}. And in our more educated and enlightened age, what Paul is putting forward in verses 1-7 about the absolute power of those in authority, has become unacceptable to ordinary people, that is, to many Christians.

So the Church appears now to be softening the application of Paul's statement by saying that one obeys those rulers who follow and apply some kind of vague abstract benevolent-sounding but undefined ideology <5>.

Verses 1-10 of (Romans 13:) stand or fall together. And to the extent to which the Church considers only verses 1-7, while ignoring the core social statements in verses 8-10, to that extent the Church is quoting out of context, apparently condoning, and allowing to stand, Paul's annulling of the God-given social laws and social system. And thus opening the door to, condemning their believers to, the inevitable sufferings and severe hardships which the Social Cause-and-Effect Relationship so clearly states.

The Pentateuch's right to social security, for example, enables the receiver to remain an independent breadwinner, to remain the master of his fate.

But the Church replaces the right to effective social security, with charity:

> "the more fortunate ... should place their goods
> more generously at the service of others." {36}

Charity can be used to exploit the needs of the needy by making the receiver indebted to, and depending on, the giver for survival.

In the context of management, government and church-state relations, participation means participating in decision-making.

But it seems that to the Church it is rulers who decide, that there is no question of participating in decision-making, of democratic decision-making by the people. This the Church shows by defining the word 'participation' to mean

'participating (taking part) in activities with other people' {37}.

Participating in work being done or in community groups is a very different matter from participating in making the decisions.

Vague Abstract Words and Phrases

One is left with the impression that the Church's volume consists of a large number of extracts from other Church documents, the Church using a wide range of abstract words with the reader left to imagine what the words could possibly mean. Wishful thinking on the reader's part makes him imagine that what he would like the meaning to be, is what is actually meant. Benevolent appearing, apparently well intended, warm sounding, comforting and vague and thus to that extent opinions and assertions. Which means the Church ought to define in clear terms these vague abstract words and phrases which make up such a considerable part of its 'Social Doctrine'.

Abstract words like 'essential', 'human', 'moral', 'infallibly' and 'truth' (see Appendix 1) can mean different things to different people <5>. Such words and phrases need to be clearly defined in detail when they are used, and particularly so when they are used for laying down principles of faith (doctrine).

Intellectual Property, Acknowledgement and Copyright

The Church seems to state that it can include all knowledge regardless of its source. And that when they include such knowledge in their teachings that this knowledge then belongs to the Church.

Which would appear to be a way of appropriating intellectual property belonging to others without acknowledging the source, and without paying for the use of that knowledge. Seemingly rephrasing and anonymising other people's achievements, apparently taking credit for, appropriating, the achievements of others.

To me it seems that the problem this Church is trying to overcome is simply that it cannot any more convincingly teach religion, the Bible (Pentateuch), Genesis and what this states (for example, about evolution, morality, or good and evil) without including (the simultaneously both revealed and proved) religious and social findings (discoveries) in my published works <18>. If they included the findings, they would need to acknowledge the source which is outside the Church's hierarchy or tradition.

This could be a reason for the Church appearing to claim that it can use (that is, include in its 'Social Doctrine')
> 'contributions from all branches of knowledge,
> whatever their source',

which then belong to the Church
> 'because the Church is the subject that
> formulates it, disseminates it and teaches it.'

As far as I can see, being a church does not allow a church to plagiarize <15>, or to appropriate another's intellectual property.

Intellectual property (advances in human knowledge and understanding, their source, ownership and copyright) have to be respected and acknowledged.

And in this case, the use of another's intellectual property has also to be paid for. After all, I had to pay a considerable sum of money for the Vatican-published copy of the Church's Social Doctrine which I am here evaluating.

Nephilim and Globalisation

There are among us people with extraordinary abilities which are hereditary and who are using them for selfish ends, and who are likely to be powerful or influential and well-known. {6}

The allegory of the Tower of Babel states that if any of them become too powerful, a threat to that which is humane and good, then they need to be, and are to be, dispersed. In other words, their tower (power, organisation, country, empire, corporation, monopoly, government, rulers, multinational, global corporation, hierarchy) needs to be dispersed. {6}

Power corrupts, absolute power corrupts absolutely. Humanity and human behaviour depend on opposition and balance, on democracy. Hence the great need, and the importance of the need, for scattering and dispersal, for limiting and taming the struggle for global power and dominance. {6} <12>

It seems to me that the Church, supporting 'globalisation',

> apparently fails to see or understand the important teachings {6} of the allegory of the Tower of Babel, and

> seem to have forgotten that, within living memory, totally corrupted governments were defeated during the Second World War only by external forces, as were the Khmer Rouge.

The question of decision-making (who decides what) is closely linked to what is referred to as 'globalisation'. Consider the relevant reports by Manfred Davidmann {18, 19, 20} and the maxims he laid down in 'Multinational Summits and Agreements, Top-level Decision-taking and Democracy' {18}, maxims such as

> Representatives, governments or government officials do not have the authority or right to override, reduce or sign away the participative (democratic) rights of the electors, of the population.

Where 'Participative (democratic) rights', of course, includes decision-making by a well-informed population.

Adam and Eve in Garden of Eden, 'Original Sin' and 'Fallen Humanity'

The Church's teachings about 'original sin' or a 'fallen humanity' seem to be based on a misinterpretation of Pentateuch texts and appear to be telling suffering humanity to blame themselves and not the system or others, for the sufferings and hardships of their lives.

In reality, Genesis Chapter 3 (Adam and Eve in Garden of Eden) actually describes the evolution of Homo sapiens in a way which could be understood at the time it was written, and which can now be understood as it was intended to be understood, following the publication of Manfred Davidmann's 'The Meaning of Genesis: Creation, Evolution and the Origin of Evil' {3}. For example, Genesis records that childbirth became more difficult as a result of the increased brain size, and states the necessary division of work between the male and the female, as equals in different roles, in protecting and bringing up their children.

Evolution and 'Flaming Sword'

Genesis (Gen 3: 1-24) describes, in the language of religion, the evolution of Homo sapiens, human beings, ourselves. We know the difference between good and evil and can choose between them. {3}

But verse 24 (Gen 3: 24) states:
>So He drove out the man;
>and He placed at the east of the garden of Eden the cherubim,
>and the flaming sword which turned every way,
>to keep the way to the tree of life.

We have come a long way towards creating and modifying life forms, towards selecting different human characteristics. Such work is proceeding in different directions in a haphazard way, uncontrolled, in often socially irresponsible seeming directions. Now threatening the survival of human beings on this planet as a species, because such knowledge and understanding is being misused for personal profit without concern for the survival of the species or the good of the community of human beings.

It is the rich and powerful, the nephilim of our times, who would be able to appropriate knowledge about extending lifespan, would consider modifying or replacing Homo sapiens (human beings, ourselves) for benefiting only themselves.

Planetary Danger

Following the flood, Genesis states (Gen 8: 22) that
> 'While the earth remains, seedtime and harvest, and cold and heat, and summer and winter, and day and night shall not cease.'

To me it seems that the list seedtime and harvest, and cold and heat, and summer and winter, and day and night, refers to essential environmental characteristics on which depends the continuation of human life on the planet. A warning to humanity.

Again, following the flood, Genesis (Gen 9: 9) records God saying
> 'As for Me, behold, I establish My covenant with you, and with your seed after you;

A covenant is an agreement in which each of the parties undertakes duties and obligations towards the other. It is not a one-sided promise or obligation.

And so God is saying:
> 'As for Me, behold':

meaning 'On my part (as long as you do your part, as long as you behave like human beings), I ...'

Genesis from then on defines evil more closely and describes and lays down what humane behaviour is and how it can be achieved, stressing justice and retribution. Genesis describes what constitutes humane, good, behaviour, how to resist, counter, overcome beastly temptations, to compare good with evil so as to choose good. And Genesis makes the point that if human beings wish to survive and prosper they need to follow the rules of behaviour laid down by God.

I warned a long time ago that if we did not observe and put into effect the social laws (rules) and social system of the Pentateuch and its code of behaviour, then the planet would become uninhabitable for human beings. This danger has since become common knowledge, people have become aware of the risks. {22}

The fate and future of humankind, of all human beings, is now balanced on a razors edge between oppression, exploitation and enslavement on the one side, and liberty, equality and a good life for all on the other side. {6}

278

Recommendations

Here I find myself in the position of the medical specialist who is talking to a very good friend and notices certain symptoms. Unless treated the disease is fatal. So what can one do? I can ask him how he feels, and he says he feels well. I suggest he goes and sees a doctor and as he is feeling well that could be the end of a beautiful friendship. But I know and he doesn't know that he can be cured but only if he takes action fairly quickly. In the end all that I can do is to tell him something about my qualifications, describe one or two of the symptoms in a mild sort of way and suggest that investigation is required. What he does after that is up to him. {24}

And now the Catholic Church has a conscious choice to make, has to decide. It can continue to follow Paul (Romans 13: 1-10, as a whole or in part) and so continue to condemn its catholic believers to the unavoidable consequences, suffering, hardships and evil which followed in the past. Or it can begin to understand, follow and teach the God-given social laws and social system of the Pentateuch including the laws of Good Government (Kingship).

It is only when people struggle for a better life, struggle for the God-given social laws and social system to be applied and followed, that a better quality of life can be achieved on this planet for all human beings, instead of just for a few at the expense of poverty and deprivation for many. {12}

My published findings {2} were that, throughout the ages, Christians of goodwill chose intuitively to interpret Paul's statements about those in authority and about Christian belief and practice, as meaning that

> 'the authority of those in authority only comes from God to the extent to which they themselves live according to and apply the Ten Commandments, the social laws and the social system laws including the Good Government (Kingship) laws'. Only those can 'love one another' who comply with all these laws. {2}

Wherever there is extreme poverty and suffering and pain you are likely to find Christians who are struggling on the side of the oppressed. Christians, for example, such as priests who provide encouragement and guidance to oppressed and suffering people in their struggle for a better life against the ruling establishment, against established ruling oppressors, doing so at much risk and without thought of personal gain. {12}

Notes

< 1> For a more comprehensive and more detailed listing of the social laws and social system of the Pentateuch, see {1}

< 2> Pentateuch. Also known as 'The Five Books of Moses' (namely Genesis, Exodus, Leviticus, Numbers and Deuteronomy). Also called 'Torah'. Part of Old Testament.

< 3> Freedom: The right and power to act, speak, or think freely.
Liberty: The state of being free from oppression or imprisonment.
Independence: Self governing and not depending on another for livelihood or subsistence.

< 4> For a full listing of the Ten Commandments, in biblical and plain English, see Appendix 1 of {2}. For a good discussion of its provisions see {13}.

< 5> See {25}

< 6> For comprehensive details, in {2} see 'Romans 13: 8-10'.

< 7> At some point in my writings I started to use the phrase 'decision-taking' as well as 'decision-making'. There is no implied difference. Both have the same meaning.

< 8> In {1} see section on 'Unavoidable Consequences of One's Behaviour'.

The Social Cause-and-Effect Relationship is also listed (in biblical language and in plain English) in Appendix 4 of {13}, with references to the Pentateuch text.

< 9> In {13} see 'Predictions of the Prophets'.
In {14} see 'Warnings of the Prophets'.
In {15} see 'Role of Prophets'.

<10> See {12}

<11> An allegory is 'a story or description in which the characters or events symbolize some deeper underlying meaning' {26}

<12>   See {22, 21, 17, 23}

<13>   In {3}, see Appendix 2: 'Creation of Planet and Life;
       Evolution of Human Beings'.

<14>   See section 'God-given Social Laws and Social System'

<15>   Plagiarize: To take and use (another person's ideas or
       writings or inventions) as one's own. {26}

<16>   In references to the Church's Social Doctrine, 'Para' stands
       for 'paragraph', 'p' stands for 'page'.

<17>   Largely consisting of

         Vatican Ecumenical Councils (Meetings of those
         Bishops who are entitled to take part, from world-
         wide, presumably discussing and advising on
         something, the reference apparently referring to their
         published conclusions or recommendations).

         Apostolic Letters (Letters issued by the Pope or in his
         name).

         Encyclical Letters (Circular letters from the Pope, to
         Archbishops and Bishops).

         Papal speeches and messages.

         Catechism (Summary of principles).

<18>   See section on 'Relevant Current and Associated Works'*.

References

{ 1}   See chapter 4:
       'The God-given Human Rights, Social Laws and
       Social System'
       Manfred Davidmann

{ 2}   See chapter 3:
       'Origin of Christianity and Judaism:
       What Actually Happened,
       What Jesus Actually Taught and Later Changes'
       Manfred Davidmann

{ 3} In 'God and People:
       The Social Laws and Social System Underlying
       Judaism, Christianity, Islam and Democracy'
       Manfred Davidmann
       ISBN 978-0-85192-054-2
       see chapter 6.1: 'The Meaning of Genesis:
       Creation, Evolution and the Origin of Evil'

{ 4} In 'God and People:
       The Social Laws and Social System Underlying
       Judaism, Christianity, Islam and Democracy'
       Manfred Davidmann
       ISBN 978-0-85192-054-2
       see chapter 6.2: 'The Meaning of Genesis:
       Pre-flood Evils and the Social Problems of Our Time'

{ 5} In 'God and People:
       The Social Laws and Social System Underlying
       Judaism, Christianity, Islam and Democracy'
       Manfred Davidmann
       ISBN 978-0-85192-054-2
       see chapter 6.3: 'The Meaning of Genesis:
       Morality, Sexual Behaviour and Depravity'

{ 6} In 'God and People:
       The Social Laws and Social System Underlying
       Judaism, Christianity, Islam and Democracy'
       Manfred Davidmann
       ISBN 978-0-85192-054-2
       see chapter 6.4: 'The Meaning of Genesis:
       Nephilim, Dominance and Liberty'

{ 7} Pentateuch: Deuteronomy 17, 14-20.

{ 8} A Commentary on the Book of Genesis.
       Part 1: From Adam to Noah;
       Part 2: From Noah to Abraham.
       By U. Cassuto (1944)
       Translated from the Hebrew by Israel Abrahams (1961)
       The Magnes Press, The Hebrew University, Jerusalem.

{ 9} In 'The Human Mind and How it Works:
      Group Minds in Action:
      How the Human Group Mind Shapes
      the Quality of Our Life and Living'
      Manfred Davidmann
      ISBN 978-0-85192-055-9
      see chapter 2: 'How the Human Brain
      Developed and How the Human Mind Works'

{10} See chapter 5:
      'Family, Community, Sex and the Individual'
      Manfred Davidmann'

{11} See chapter 7.1:
      'Church and State, Government and Religion:
      Judaism, Christianity and Islam'
      Manfred Davidmann

{12} See chapter 2:
      'Liberation Theology: Basis - Past - Present - Future'
      Manfred Davidmann

{13} In 'Judaism: Basis - Past - Present - Future, Part 1'
      Manfred Davidmann
      ISBN 978-0-85192-060-3
      see chapter 2.1: 'Struggle for Freedom:
      The Social Cause-and-Effect Relationship'

{14} In 'Judaism: Basis - Past - Present - Future, Part 1'
      Manfred Davidmann
      ISBN 978-0-85192-060-3
      see chapter 2.2: 'History Speaks: Monarchy,
      Exile and Maccabees'

{15} In 'Judaism: Basis - Past - Present - Future, Part 1'
      Manfred Davidmann
      ISBN 978-0-85192-060-3
      see chapter 2.4: 'One Law for All: Freedom Now,
      Freedom for Ever'

{16} In 'Judaism: Basis - Past - Present - Future, Part 1'
      Manfred Davidmann
      ISBN 978-0-85192-060-3
      see chapter 5: 'The Right to the Land of Israel'

{17}   In 'Management and Leadership:
       Local, National, Multinational (Global),
       Principles and Practice'
       Manfred Davidmann
       ISBN 978-0-85192-057-3
       see chapter 2: 'Style of Management and
       Leadership'

{18}   In 'The Real World in Which We Live:
       The Social Rules and Social System under
       Which We Suffer, Struggle, Survive and Prosper'
       Manfred Davidmann
       ISBN 978-0-85192-058-0
       see chapter 6: 'Multinational Summits and
       Agreements, Top-level Decision-making and
       Democracy'

{19}   In 'The Real World in Which We Live:
       The Social Rules and Social System under
       Which We Suffer, Struggle, Survive and Prosper'
       Manfred Davidmann
       ISBN 978-0-85192-058-0
       see chapter 7: 'Exporting and Importing of
       Employment and Unemployment'

{20}   In 'The Real World in Which We Live:
       The Social Rules and Social System under
       Which We Suffer, Struggle, Survive and Prosper'
       Manfred Davidmann
       ISBN 978-0-85192-058-0
       see chapter 8: 'Transfer Pricing and Taxation'

{21}   In 'The Real World in Which We Live:
       The Social Rules and Social System under
       Which We Suffer, Struggle, Survive and Prosper'
       Manfred Davidmann
       ISBN 978-0-85192-058-0
       see chapter 10: 'What People are Struggling
       Against: How Society is Organised for Controlling
       and Exploiting People'

{22} In 'Messianic Struggle:
The Worldwide Struggle for a Good and
Secure Life for All, Here and Now'
Manfred Davidmann
ISBN 978-0-85192-059-7
see chapter 2: 'Social Responsibility, Profits and
Social Accountability' (1979, 1982, 1995).
or the later
chapter 7: 'Social Responsibility and
Accountability: Summary' (2002).

{23} In 'Cooperatives and Cooperation:
Causes of Failure, Guidelines for Success'
Manfred Davidmann
ISBN 978-0-85192-056-6
see chapter 2: 'Cooperatives and Cooperation'
and chapter 3: 'Causes of Failure, Guidelines
for Success'

{24} 'If you want a future, read on ...'
Manfred Davidmann (David Baram)
Social Organisation Ltd, 1978
ISBN 0 85192 008 X

{25} See chapter 6:
'Using Words to Communicate Effectively'
Manfred Davidmann

{26} Oxford Concise Dictionary
Oxford University Press

{27} Compendium of the Social Doctrine of the Church
Libreria Editrice Vaticana, 2004
Released 25 October 2004 at a Press Conference at the
Vatican by
the Pontifical Council for Justice and Peace
ISBN 88-209-7651-X

'Para' stands for 'paragraph', 'p' stands for 'page'.

{28} Para 23, page 14, in {27}
{29} Para 27, p16 in {27}
{30} Para 74, p40 in {27}
{31} Para 76, p41 in {27}

{32}   Para 79, p43 in {27}

{33}   Para 113, p64 in {27}

{34}   Para 115, p66 in {27}

{35}   Para 120, p68 in {27}

{36}   Para 158, p89 in {27}

{37}   Para 189, p107 in {27}

{38}   Para 190, p108 in {27}

{39}   Para 191, p109 in {27}

{40}   Between Para 208 and Para 209, p121 in {27}

{41}   Para 361, p203 in {27}

{42}   Para 363, p204 in {27}

{43}   Para 370, p208 in {27}

{44}   Para 372, p209 in {27}

{45}   Para 380, p215 in {27}

{46}   Para 393, p222 in {27}

{47}   Para 394, p222 in {27}

{48}   Para 395, p223 in {27}

{49}   Para 396, p223 in {27}

{50}   Para 397, p224 in {27}

{51}   Para 398, p224 in {27}

{52}   Para 429, p241 in {27}

{53}   Para 531, p302 in {27}

Additions by the Editor:

*   In 'https://www.solhaam.org/teachings/relsta3.html'
     see 'Relevant Current and Associated Works'

Appendix 1

Meaning and Use of Words   {25}

Words vary considerably as regards their value for communication. They differ in their level of abstraction. The greater the level of abstraction, the less meaning do they have, do they convey.

LEVELS OF ABSTRACTION

1. **Objects**

   Objects represent a relatively low level of abstraction as they can be seen and touched and their characteristics detailed accurately.

   Examples are: Table, chair.

2. **Events**

   In addition to objects, both action and time are implied, and so these are more complex.

   Examples are: Accident, sale, party.

3. **Generalisations**

   Words are also used as labels for groups and collections of objects or events. These generalisations are more abstract and less precise.

   Examples of such labels are: Furniture, machine tools, employees, parents.

   Employees, for example, can be full-time, part-time, shift working, office working, home working, male, female, young, old, single, married, unskilled, skilled, professional, and more.

4. **Value Judgements or Ideology**

   Value judgements and ideology are at the highest level of abstraction and words used as labels for them are quite useless for effective communication until the meaning of the word used is clearly defined in detail.

Examples of such labels are: Beautiful, valuable, necessary, luxury, lazy, free enterprise, truth, infallible, 'right attitude'.

Such words can be strung together and mixed with generalisations to provide good-sounding speeches and statements of the kind politicians like to use, to provide speeches and statements with no real meaning attached to the words used. Listeners or readers use their own idea of what the words mean and so their understanding of what is being said differs widely from person to person.

I listed the word 'truth' as an example of a label for a meaningless abstraction. Surely 'truth' ought to be more than a meaningless value judgement, so let us look at this in more detail.

Consider two media reports of a current event. Each reports the same event, each apparently telling the truth, each report giving its viewers different impressions of what actually happened.

How come? Can there be more than one truth?

Such reports may tell only part of what happened, may report only what seems relevant to the reporter, may then be selecting what seems to support the particular viewpoint of those who prepared the report.

Compare these 'truths' with that demanded from a witness in a court of law: 'The truth, the whole truth and nothing but the truth.'

Which means that what is required in a court of law is the truth with nothing taken away and nothing added.

If we agree on this as a definition, then the word 'truth' has become more meaningful.

The Global (Worldwide) Struggle for a Better Life and
The Root of all Evil, the Source of All Good, and the Messianic Struggle

Hidden Causes of Struggle; What People are Struggling Against

**The Global (Worldwide) Struggle for Social Decision-making.
In all Organisations and Communities, at all Levels**

Antisocial Telepathic Manipulations

Church and State; Religion, Government and People

Judaism, Christianity and Islam: The Messianic Struggle for a Better Life

**Freedom, Liberty, Independence, Good Secure Life.
Now and for Ever**

The Messianic Struggle in Our Time: Extracts from my Diary and Press Notices.

Introduction
Human and Inhuman Behaviour
The Human Mind, Mental Health and Mental Illness
Conflict Within the Mind
Conflict between Church and State
Government, Management and Leadership
    Organisation
    Authoritarian Organisation
    Participative Organisation
    Style of Government, Management and Leadership
The Struggle for Social Decision-making
    The Meaning of 'Democracy' (Participative Organisation)
    Personal Power and Control (Authoritarian Organisation)
    Top-level Leaderships (Global Operations and Agreements)
Global (Worldwide) Struggle
    Worldwide Struggle
    The Hidden Factor

Introduction

In this report, Manfred Davidmann exposes humanity's innermost secrets to the light of day.

As you read the report, you are brought ever closer to humanity's hidden core confrontations and the reality of the struggle for a better life. That is, you will see what humankind is struggling against; you will see the fundamental cause. You will see the core and source of evil, corruption, brutality, perversion, oppression and enslavement.

This report is about past and present struggles, achievements and defeats, about whole communities betrayed and misled, about religious teachings distorted and even turned upside down. And it is about how to achieve our own well-being, about our ensuring that we as individuals have good and satisfying lives.

And you will see how that which is good arises from the selfless and unstinting efforts of human beings cooperating for the common good.

And if the facts are unexpected or if you do not like the facts then don't blame me. I am merely recording them.

Human and Inhuman Behaviour {16}

The human brain evolved in three main stages. Its ancient and primitive part is the innermost core reptilian brain. Next evolved the mammalian brain by adding new functions and new ways of controlling the body. Then evolved the third part of the brain, the neocortex, the grey matter, the bulk of the brain in two symmetrical hemispheres, separate but communicating. To a considerable extent, it is our neocortex which enables us to behave like human beings. {1} <1>

So the human brain consists of these three different but interconnected brains and the way in which these three brains interact with each other underlies human behaviour. {1} <1>

Our primitive animal ancestors behaved instinctively. Hunt for food, kill or be killed, fight or flee, copulate, care for own young for a very short and limited period. Self before others, regardless of needs of others, marking out and defending territory.

Later mammals tend to have feelings, care and affection for their young.

Human beings think as well as feel, and care for and look after their young for many years.

So conditioning to fight, injure and kill amounts to a throwback to primitive animal behaviour, to behaviour which puts self before others. A throwback to beast-like behaviour for those who attack, and also a throwback to beast-like behaviour for those who have to defend themselves.

Similarly, society corrupts itself when human care, affection and concern for one's own family, and for other people, are weakened by self-interest, by selfishness, by personal gain at expense of others. {16}

In such circumstances the instinctive behaviour of the non-feeling primitive animal is asserting itself, is attempting to override human feelings of care, affection, concern for members of one's own family and for other people in human societies.

And there is increasing antisocial behaviour such as vandalism and mugging. There is a loss of internal security, by loss of property and by attack against the person. The quality of life is lowered even further by those who pursue personal gain regardless of its cost to other people.

But only some people behave in such corrupted ways. There are those many who put people first, who know the difference between human and inhuman (instinctive beast-like) behaviour, who believe in cooperative behaviour and in democratic government.

And there are ways of teaching social responsibility, of teaching the young how to take responsibility for others, how to care for, work with and look after other people. Social responsibility, the caring, giving and sharing with others, the taking on of responsibility for others including conflict management, can be and is being taught. {6}

The Human Mind, Mental Health and Mental Illness   {22}

Here we see how conflict arises within the mind, look at mental health and illness, look at dominance. We are here looking at what motivates and drives human beings, seeing how the human mind shapes the way in which we live, suffer, struggle and achieve.

But when it comes to how the human mind functions and operates, or to what happens within the mind under stress or at times of conflict, we talk about an 'unconscious' part of the mind, accepting that there is much which is taking place without our being aware of it. {1}

Psychology has been defined as 'the scientific study of the human mind and its functions, especially those affecting behaviour in a given context'. And Stevens considers that
> '... all psychological phenomena, from slips of the tongue to the most elaborate psychiatric symptoms (are) determined by events proceeding beneath the threshold of consciousness ... ' {5}

That is, we are not aware of where they come from and how they originate.

Psychologists and psychiatrists have for some time looked at how people behave and why, at how internal stress originates, at what causes mental breakdown. Mental tension is said to result from unresolved conflict and they have been attempting to identify the opposing forces which are in conflict.

Sigmund Freud (Psychoanalysis) saw the conflict in his patients, explained it as a conflict between love and hate, concluding that sexuality was all-important.

The unconscious is a part of the mind which is said to be inaccessible to the conscious mind but which affects behaviour and emotions. Mental disorders can be caused by conflict between the unconscious and conscious parts of the mind and Freud considered that such conflicts can be resolved by bringing repressed fears and conflicts into the conscious mind.

I think that by bringing hidden conflict into the open he came close to seeing that a key problem was that of controlling sexuality, of controlling primitive urges and behaviour.

Carl Jung (Analytical Psychology) called the unconscious part of the human mind the 'Personal Unconscious' and, like Freud, considered it to be the cause of complexes. Jung apparently concluded that
        'the personal unconscious is composed of complexes {5} and these' he considered to be independently capable of influencing consciousness without our being aware of them. <2>

What Jung called 'personal unconscious' appears to consist of component entities with independent feelings or thoughts which behave as if they were personalities.

Jung also suggested that there existed something else which he called 'Collective Unconscious' which he supposed to be made up of what he called 'archetypes'. He considered archetypes to be some kind of primitive mental images inherited from our earliest ancestors, examples being predator, sexual and enemy archetypes. Later he had to elaborate this model by including also archetypes of archetypes.

When Jung refers to a 'collective unconscious', he is referring to what could be primitive urges and behaviour which human beings subdue and control, and which human beings need to subdue and control.

Conflict Within the Mind   {22}

Psychotherapy considers that the conscious mind reasons and evaluates and the unconscious mind is said to underlie action based on intuition and emotion. When there is conflict between the conscious and the unconscious minds, between reason and emotion, then this conflict can produce mental tension.

The question which has remained unresolved so far is just what the 'opposing forces' are which produce the tension.

Manfred Davidmann considers that there is no conflict when reason and emotions both aim to achieve humane behaviour and existence (human, normal).

Similarly, there is no conflict when reason and emotions both aim at inhumane behaviour and existence (inhuman, abnormal).

So conflict arises when feelings and emotions which insist on humane behaviour are opposed by verbal skills and reasoning insisting on behaviour contrary to human rights and welfare.

And conflict also arises if a person's feelings and emotions insist on behaviour contrary to human rights and welfare, but are opposed by reason, knowledge and understanding which insist on humane behaviour.

Hence conflict within the mind can arise when people are being misinformed or misled into inhumane behaviour, and also when they are being manipulated through their emotions into behaving inhumanly without knowing why they are doing so (such as blindly doing as told or as directed by the top).

And thus conflict can be seen as arising from the clash between opposing social ideologies. These conflicts arise within the human mind and shape our minds, mental well-being and also behaviour. As can be seen below, they are similar to the conflicts which arise between church and state.

Conflict between Church and State   {27, 34-35}

Here Manfred Davidmann was the first to define and explain in clear meaningful language the meaning of what was simply being referred to as 'church' and 'state', defining also 'government' and 'religion' to lay bare the real causes of conflict and confrontation between them.

So before we consider their aims and purpose, and the conflicts and confrontations between them, we begin by looking at what people mean and imply when they use words such as 'church' and 'state' {27}, as follows:

Church
> Refers to the religion's clergy, or to its hierarchy. It can also refer to the religion's organisation, its decision-making processes, the doctrine it follows and the policies it applies.

State
> Somewhat vague term which refers to the combination of government and the community (country, population) being governed. Its use ignores important distinctions between people, government and the government's style of management, and their often conflicting interests. For example it does not distinguish between a government which serves its people and one which serves a country's rulers.

So 'church' and 'state' are vague terms which mean and imply different things to different people. They are vague because their meanings are imprecise and roundabout.

Such terms are often used to avoid bluntly stating harsh realities, or used instead of a term one considers improper. And they are often used dishonestly when they are used to conceal and deceive. <18>

More precise and useful are the words {35}:

Government
> The group or organisation ruling a country or conducting its affairs. It can also refer to the government's style of management (authoritarian or participative, that is dictatorial or democratic).

Religion
> A system of faith and worship, based on belief in the existence of a God (mostly benevolent), usually expressed by believers living according to its doctrine (principles, rules of behaviour, customs).

So that there are different kinds of states and different kinds of churches {34}:

> Some states consist of governments which serve the rulers by oppressing the people so that they can be exploited and such states stifle opposition and protest. Here those at the top and their experts tell people what they should do and have to do.

> Other states consist of governments where those who govern serve the people and are accountable to them, where decisions are made at the lowest possible level by referendum with experts

explaining the consequences both ways when a decision has to be made.

Similarly some churches teach a version of religion which serves the rulers and so in effect condition their people into gladly serving the rulers, into gladly allowing themselves to be exploited, the general approach then being 'gladly accept the tough life you are leading, the reward will come in a next life'.

And other churches preach that it is the will of God that all people are equal, that no person may exploit another, that it is the role of the government, of the establishment, to serve the people.

So we see that there is no conflict when both the government and the church believe in authoritarian rule, that is when

states consist of governments which serve the rulers by oppressing the people so that they can be exploited, stifling opposition and protest, those at the top and their experts telling people what they should do and have to do.

And when churches serve rulers by in effect conditioning their people into gladly serving the rulers, into gladly allowing themselves to be exploited, their general approach then being 'gladly accept the tough life you are leading, your reward will come in a next life'.

And similarly there is no conflict when both the government and the church believe in participative government, that is

When states consist of governments where those who govern serve the people and are accountable to them, where decisions are made at the lowest possible level by referendum with experts explaining to the people the consequences both ways when a decision has to be made.

And when churches preach that it is the will of God that all people are equal, that no person may exploit another, that it is the role of those who rule, of the government, of the establishment, to serve the people.

But there is conflict and confrontation

when 'religion' and 'government' ('church' and 'state') preach, teach and practice opposing 'ideologies' (authoritarian rule opposing participative government), or when their hierarchies compete with each other for power.

So Manfred Davidmann concludes {27, 34-35} that

> What is clear is that differences of opinion, conflicts and confrontations between a 'church' and a 'state' arise only when church and state believe in and practice opposing ideologies, and to the extent to which they do so.

What matters regarding agreement, conflict or confrontation between a 'state' and a 'church' is the social ideology which each of them believes in, teaches and practices. Conflict and confrontation are about the right to social decision-making, and social decision-making depends on the kind of social ideology those in power believe in, teach and practice. <3>

Government, Management and Leadership   {15}

Participation, meaning by this 'participation in decision-making', was first coined, and defined, by Manfred Davidmann when he published his analysis and recommendations about the style of management, in 1981. He defined, described and illustrated his scale of 'style of management and government' from 'fully participative' at one end of the scale, to 'fully authoritarian' at the other end.

Manfred Davidmann's concept of participative government and management, of participation in decision-making, has become a household word, in daily use when referring to government and management styles, worldwide. His concepts are applied all the way from village government and community projects to national policies and elections, are applied by cooperatives, companies and global corporations alike.

What Manfred Davidmann has done in his work on the general management of enterprises and communities is to lay the foundation for, and develop, what is now called 'management science'.

His works on style of management and on participation in decision-making in management, leadership and government, are widely known, studied and applied, sprouted a whole literature ranging from the scientific on the one hand to, on the other hand, misleading politically motivated misrepresentations.

Organisation   {15}

The whole pattern of different ways of organising is a sequence from one extreme to the other, is a kind of scale. At one end of the scale is the completely authoritarian organisation, at the other end the fully participative organisation. Governments, corporations (companies) and other organisations fall somewhere along the scale.

Authoritarian Organisation   {15}

Kings ruled by 'divine' right and they enforced obedience through, in the end, the death penalty. Under private ownership, authority is derived from ownership of the means of production and the penalty for disobedience is dismissal. In each case authority is centred at the top. It is the owners who delegate authority to the chief executive, and it is immaterial whether the owners are shareholders as in some countries, or the state in countries such as Russia.

In authoritarian organisations, it is orders which are passed down from above and the manager's role is to pass orders down the 'chain of command'. He is usually not expected to make decisions and so carries little responsibility. He does order and may compel the worker to carry out the tasks demanded from him, to produce.

Those who run society on such lines find that the working population does not willingly work for the benefit of only its rulers and then they attempt to compel the working population to work. The stick is unemployment and the compelling force is the fear of the economic consequences of unemployment, is the threat of need.

Hence it is those who believe in an authoritarian kind of organisation who advocate that the level of unemployment should be kept above a certain minimum level or that it should be increased, and who want to reduce social security spending.

Or they attempt to persuade and condition the working population into willingly serving and working for the rulers and their establishment regardless of the working population's hardships, suffering and need.

Which applies to community organisation and government in the same way.

Participative Organisation   {15}

Employees participate when they agree to allow themselves to be organised by an employer, and organisation which is based on consent of those being organised is participative. In a participative organisation people accept responsibility for work to be done, accept that it is their job to carry out a part of the organisation's activities and that they will be held accountable for the quality of their work. The manager's job is to back his subordinate by removing obstacles from the subordinate's path, the subordinate asking for such assistance as the need arises. The manager coordinates the work of the group which he manages with that of the higher group in which he is a subordinate.

The shop steward is elected so that his authority stems from those who elected him and who work in factory and office. The source of his authority is the consent of the managed to be managed. The method of power is the withdrawal of that consent which is in effect the withdrawal of one's labour, for example by going on strike.

And similarly a representative or delegate is elected so that his authority stems from those who elected him and who are members of the community, who are citizens. The source of his authority is the consent of the governed to be governed. The method of power is the withdrawal of that consent which is in effect the withdrawal of one's cooperation, of delegated authority, for example by demonstrating.

An organisation built on this basis is participative, and this means that participation through decision-making, including setting of targets, takes place at all levels of the organisation {15}, and this applies equally well to government, management and leadership.

Style of Government, Management and Leadership {15}

We have described here in outline the two systems of organisation which can be regarded as forming either end of the scale. The position of any organisation on this scale depends in each case on the balance between the two kinds of authority, that is depends on the degree of participation in decision-making which is practised.

One can place on this scale any system of running a company or of governing a country, by considering, for example,

> whether and to what extent decisions are being made at the various levels or whether people merely follow orders, or whether and to what extent people are free to withdraw their labour, are free to strike.

In other words, by considering to what extent authority is centred at the top, or where the balance of power lies between management and worker, or between government and citizen.

The position where an organisation is placed thus depends on the balance of authority between ruler and ruled, between owner and worker, between the establishment and the population.

The way in which countries are managed, that is their style of management, of government, of course varies from country to country and changes as time passes {15}. Authoritarian attitudes result in confrontation, leadership and cooperation result in economic success.

And we now know that the real struggle is not between political left and right but is a struggle for democracy against dictatorship (authoritarian style of management) in all community organisations and at all levels, is for participating in social decision-making in all organisations and at all levels.

The Struggle for Social Decision-making <4> {19}

The Meaning of 'Democracy' (Participative Organisation) <5> {20}

Manfred Davidmann outlined and defined the role of representatives and the decision-making process:

> Participative (democratic) organisation rests on the population electing representatives, on the basis of each person having one vote. Representatives are responsible to, and accountable to, the population for putting into effect policies decided by the population. What underlies participative organisation (democracy) is decision-making by the people at the level of the people. And representatives, governments or government officials do not have the authority or right to reduce or sign away the participative (democratic) rights of the electors, of the population.

> What needs to be stressed is that in a participative (democratic) organisation policies are decided by a well-informed population at the level of the population and that policies then become binding on management or government. <6>

In an authoritarian organisation, the policy decisions are taken at the top or near the top by the hierarchy (establishment) and are binding on the organisation's members. Decision-making at the top is sometimes referred to as 'deciding centrally'. Authoritarian organisation is the opposite of democracy and underlies dictatorship.

And what we see is conflict between authoritarian minds wishing to dominate, control and exploit on the one hand and, on the other hand, citizens wishing to maintain and improve the standard of living and quality of life for the population as a whole by democratic (grass-roots level) decision-making. {20}

So the real struggle is not between political left and right, but is a struggle for participation (the right to make decisions).

And there is the fundamental problem that ill-informed or misguided voters may be persuaded or conditioned into taking harmful or socially destructive decisions.

Personal Power and Control (Authoritarian Organisation) {19}

Authoritarian minds attempt to take over and place democratically controlled organisations under authoritarian control. They do so by struggling to take over the decision-making in the management and control of companies, enterprises and all types of community organisations.

The confrontation between on the one hand elected policy-making bodies, and on the other hand those who are supposed to put their policies into effect, can be seen in many areas.

We can see the struggle in all organisations and at all levels. It is a struggle against authoritarian management or government for the right to make decisions. And in all democratic organisations it is a struggle against the authoritarian mind taking over the decision-making.

A continuous battle is taking place between on the one hand policy-deciding by the many through elected assemblies, and on the other hand policy-deciding at the top, by a few. This is clearly shown by the way in which full-time officials and executives attempt to take power away from their policy-setting assemblies, after which they attempt to impose their will on the membership or population.

These attempts to take over and control decision-making processes are far more one-sided than would be the case if we were looking at unrelated chance events, at unrelated local struggles. At times the pattern seems progressive as if it were planned.

Top-level Leaderships (Global Operations and Agreements) {19}

Recently negotiated top-level trading agreements (GATT and the proposed MAI) appear to be taking away the control over key aspects of the internal affairs of participating countries. Taking control away from their elected governments, giving the control to multinational corporations. {19}

MAI stands for 'Multilateral Agreement on Investment'. But its name does not reflect those aspects which are of deep concern.

Disturbing are not only the provisions of this proposed treaty but also that the provisions were debated in complete secrecy till a leaked copy became available on the Internet in 1997. Apparently it was adverse publicity relating to its restrictive provisions which delayed completion as concerned groups of citizens publicised their concerns. And some governments have now withdrawn their support.

It appears that under MAI the national governments would have handed over control, that is authority to act, over much of the economic and social welfare of their citizens to multinational corporations (that is to those who own and direct these corporations), if they had agreed to this treaty.

In other words, multinationals would have been given overriding authority over democratically elected governments.

Global (Worldwide) Struggle

Worldwide Struggle

In 'The Will to Work: What People Struggle to Achieve' {3}, Manfred Davidmann clearly defines and describes motivation, its basis, and 'motivating'. Starting by considering motivation from the point of view of the employer (productivity, remuneration, job satisfaction), this leads to considering what people want and what they struggle to achieve. A key part of the report is community orientated, including a detailed step-by-step listing of what people are struggling to achieve, their needs and wants, their achievements and objectives. This progression shows underdeveloped and developed people as they are, human beings at different stages of an identical struggle for a better life against those who wish to profit from their condition. <7>

We see a worldwide struggle to achieve a humane way of life. Each person, family or community is struggling to advance at their own level of development, struggling against those who wish to dominate, exploit, oppress. {16, 3}

The struggle is against those who wish to dominate other people. Against those who wish to exploit, against those who may brutally and without feeling oppress human beings so as to exploit them. {2, 3}

And 'to exploit' includes the whole range of antisocial decisions and activities of those who put profit before people and community. {4, 19}

In 'Liberation Theology' {26}, Manfred Davidmann explores why life is a struggle, why life is so tough for so many human beings on this planet. Exploring why thousands of years of struggle, why the enormous technological powers we command, why the vast human manpower, abilities and skills which are now at our disposal, are not providing us with secure lives of high quality.

And so 'Liberation Theology' starts by finding answers to some basic questions, such as:
Why do we have to struggle?
What are we struggling against?
What are we struggling for?
Why do we not have good lives of high quality?

Quoting from the report:

> Where there is struggle there must be resistance, there is opposition. We have to struggle because our attempts to achieve good lives for ourselves and our children are being resisted, are opposed.

> We have to struggle to protect earlier gains as well as to improve our lives. Hence we are struggling to defend our present standard of living and we are struggling to better it. Which means that the opposition is attacking us to lower our standard of living and to prevent us from improving it.

> We as thinking feeling human beings ought to be able to do very much better. So now more questions present themselves:

>> Who or what is doing all this to us, is attacking us? Who or what is attempting to reduce the quality of our lives, is attempting to prevent us from improving it? Who or what is attempting to increase the toughness of life itself, is attempting to increase our need?

>> Why this intense, brutal and hidden struggle when there is enough for all of us, when all can have good secure lives of high quality.

>> Why is it done in such a hidden way, why the secrecy?

In secular terms, what is it that would wish to prevent us from increasing our standard of living, that would wish to reduce our standard of living and our social security?

Here also the answer appears to be that we are struggling against those who wish to exploit others, who wish to oppress so as to exploit, who see their wealth and power increasing whenever they lower our pay relative to their own so as to increase their own profits and wealth and power over us.

It is they who wish to reduce, and so struggle to reduce, our social security since higher unemployment, greater personal need, and physical as well as emotional weakness, reduce our bargaining strength

303

and make us more dependent on them for survival. They are enabled in this way to exploit us through our need and to push down our pay even further when compared with their own much greater gains. And this is why they are operating so furtively behind their masks.

And so we see a worldwide (global) struggle to achieve a humane way of life and living.

We know that dominating does not work in normal circumstances. Authoritarian organisations are much less effective than participative ones. In authoritarian organisations morale is low, people cease to care and tend to work against each other instead of cooperating with each other for the benefit of the organisation. {15}

It is in democracies that a high standard of living has been achieved. In democracies people can struggle openly for a better life but we see that what has been gained has to be defended and extended. {16, 15}

So why does this struggle take place in all organisations, at all levels, in all communities and countries? Why do we have to struggle? Why are all of our communities and countries being managed more or less on behalf of their rulers or ruling level? Why are not at least half of our communities and countries being managed completely by, on behalf of, and for, their people?

There is simply no way in which
    this lack of balance between the authoritarian and the participative,
    this authoritarian rule and government in so many countries worldwide,
    this widespread struggle in democratic countries for a better life,
can be due to chance alone.

Quite clearly an additional unknown factor is operating and determining how people live together, causing people to have to struggle at all levels, organisations, communities and countries, for a better life.

The Hidden Factor

We have already covered much ground, reviewed the results of decades of published research by Manfred Davidmann. And what we have seen can be summarised as follows:

> We saw that society corrupts itself when human care, affection and concern for one's own family, and for other people, are weakened by self-interest, by selfishness, by personal gain at expense of others.

In such circumstances the instinctive behaviour of the non-feeling primitive animal is asserting itself, is attempting to override human feelings of care, affection and concern for members of one's own family and for other people in human societies.

When society allows itself to be corrupted, there is increasing antisocial behaviour such as vandalism and mugging. There is a loss of internal security, by loss of property and by attack against the person. The quality of life is lowered even further by those who pursue personal gain regardless of its cost to other people.

So in our societies there is conflict between human care, affection and social responsibility on the one hand and primitive animal urges towards selfish gain regardless of the cost to others.

And the conflict was seen to arise from the clash between opposing social ideologies which advocate affection and concern for people, family and community on the one hand, and on the other hand selfishness and the urge for personal gain at expense of others.

These conflicts which arise within the human mind and shape our minds, mental well-being and also behaviour, are similar, and indeed appear identical, to those which arise between church and state.

We saw that there is conflict and confrontation between church and state
> when 'religion' and 'government' ('church' and 'state') preach, teach and practice opposing 'ideologies' (authoritarian rule opposing participative government), or when their hierarchies compete with each other for power.

So what matters regarding agreement, conflict or confrontation between a 'state' and a 'church' is the social ideology which each of them believes in, teaches and practices.

So conflict and confrontation are about the right to social decision-making, and social decision-making depends on the kind of social ideology those in power believe in, teach and practice.

We saw that how any country or organisation is ruled or managed depends on, and can be seen from, the balance between the two kinds of authority (authoritarian or participative), thus depends on the balance of authority between ruler and ruled, between owner and worker, between the establishment and the population. And so it can be observed from, can be seen by, the degree of participation in decision-making which is practised.

Authoritarian organisation is the opposite of democracy and underlies dictatorship. Authoritarian attitudes result in confrontation. Democratic leadership and cooperation result in economic success.

And we now know that the real struggle is not between political left and right but is a struggle for democracy against dictatorship (authoritarian style of management) in all community organisations and at all levels, is for participating in social decision-making in all organisations and at all levels, is a struggle for participation (the right to make decisions).

And what we see is conflict between authoritarian minds wishing to dominate, control and exploit on the one hand and, on the other hand, citizens wishing to maintain and improve the standard of living and quality of life for the population as a whole by democratic (grass-roots level) decision-making.

A continuous struggle is taking place between on the one hand policy-deciding by the many through elected assemblies, and on the other hand policy-deciding at the top, by a few. We can see the struggle in all organisations and at all levels. It is a struggle against authoritarian management or government for the right to make decisions. And in all democratic organisations it is a struggle against the authoritarian mind taking over the decision-making.

These attempts to take over and control decision-making processes are far more one-sided than would be the case if we were looking at unrelated chance events, at unrelated local struggles. At times the pattern seems progressive as if it were planned.

Recently negotiated top-level trading agreements (GATT and the proposed MAI) appear to be taking away the control over key aspects of the internal affairs of participating countries. Taking control away from their elected governments, giving the control to multinational corporations. In other words, multinationals appear to be aiming at getting overriding authority over democratically elected governments.

We saw underdeveloped and developed people as they are, human beings at different stages of an identical struggle for a better life against those who wish to profit from their condition, we saw a worldwide struggle to achieve a humane way of life. Each person, family or community is struggling to advance at their own level of development, struggling against those who wish to dominate, exploit, oppress.

The struggle is against those who wish to dominate other people. Against those who wish to exploit, against those who may brutally and without feeling oppress human beings so as to exploit them.

It is in democracies that a high standard of living has been achieved. In democracies people can struggle openly for a better life but we saw that what has been gained has to be defended and extended.

So why does this struggle take place in all organisations, at all levels, in all communities and countries? Why do we have to struggle? Why are all of our communities and countries being managed more or less on behalf of their rulers or ruling level? Why are not at least half of our communities and countries being managed completely by, on behalf of, and for, their people?

There is simply no way in which
> this lack of balance between the authoritarian and the participative,
>
> this authoritarian rule and government in so many countries worldwide,
>
> this widespread struggle in democratic countries for a better life,

can be due to chance alone.

Hence quite clearly an additional unknown factor is operating and determining how people live together, causing people to have to struggle at all levels, organisations, communities and countries, for a better life.

So now we go on to explore some of the darker, more hidden, parts of the human mind, so as to locate and describe what people have to struggle against, what has been so continuously attacking people, to locate and describe this hidden unknown factor.

Human Group Minds {21}

When Manfred Davidmann first announced his Group Mind Theory in 1973, this theory and his concepts and terms such as 'group minds', were completely new and unheard of. The second edition was published in 1998 and made available on the internet in 1999.

Manfred Davidmann's Group Mind Science is objective, demonstrating enormous beneficial and healing powers. Following the work of Freud and Jung, it is regarded as scientifically proved, as meaningful, objective and practical, as applying worldwide to all human beings in all societies and cultures and at all stages of development.

His human group minds and how they function, that is the Group Mind Science he originated, are now widely quoted and discussed, have sprouted a whole literature about group minds ranging from publications of scientific institutions and in reference books, to unscientific misleading look-alikes about human minds.

Manfred Davidmann's report 'The Human Mind' {21} on how human minds work and operate, on human group minds, reviews the mind theories of Freud and of Jung and outlines Manfred Davidmann's Group Mind Theory. Included in the report are comprehensive but concise reviews of mental health and mental illness, of why people are struggling and what they are struggling against, how conflict arises within the mind, of the way in which society is organised, of dominance, conflict and cooperation.

The subconscious existence and workings of group minds become apparent by the extraordinary way in which they affect and determine what individuals and communities do. The sections of this report which deal with how we live and struggle, describe how our minds shape our lives, communities and society.

The workings of group minds is shown to explain how human communities and society are organised and the consequent confrontations and struggles from dictatorship to democracy. The Group Mind Theory was proved by the way in which it explains and predicts human activities and organisation as well as mental problems of individuals and society's social problems. The insights of Manfred Davidmann's Group Mind Science enable us to solve such problems effectively.

It is a mind science which allows for telepathic contacts between people and the available evidence has been detailed on the basis that if there are telepaths using their abilities then such activities can be observed by their effects. Previously reported work by others shows that telepathic activity is well known and documented. A considerable amount of telepathic activity is taking place and known to be taking place.

Here also we see a hidden struggle between opposite factions which, for example, accounts for the feeling of resistance and mental struggle so strongly felt by those who are creating, for the compulsions experienced by authors and artists, and for the mental problems of voice hearers. <8, 25>

Manfred Davidmann concluded that it is this which is causing people to have to struggle for a better life, which is opposing them and holding them down, that the observed unknown factor consists of hidden antisocial telepathic manipulations. <25> {21}

Nephilim and Globalisation   {10}

Nephilim   {10}

The immense knowledge and understanding which underlies the Pentateuch (of which Genesis is a part) could not have been understood or comprehended by those living when the Pentateuch <17> {17} was recorded. And what is there has been overlaid with the dust of millennia, with accumulated interpretations and comments limited by the then current knowledge, understanding and misconceptions. It was Manfred Davidmann who proved that what is stated in Genesis <16> is thus much more meaningful than is generally appreciated. {7} <10>

And people have always wondered just who the nephilim were (or are) who are stated in Genesis to be well-known and powerful.

The Pentateuch states {10} that there are among us people with extraordinary abilities who are likely to be powerful or influential and well known. They are called 'nephilim' and their abilities apparently enable them to influence, organise, manipulate, control and dominate other human beings.

We are told that these 'nephilim' are without distinguishing physical characteristics, that they intermarry with other human beings and that their extraordinary abilities and skills are hereditary <11>.

Genesis is associating nephilim with evil, possibly as a hidden cause. They are misusing their abilities for personal gain, are corrupting, are dominating, are the 'fallen' ones.

We are told that Nimrod was one of the nephilim, and that the beginning of his kingdom was Babel in the land of Shinar. In this way is Nimrod linked with the events told in the allegory <12> of The Tower of Babel.

'Tower of Babel'   {10}

Here Manfred Davidmann showed that this allegory consists of two intertwined, interwoven and interconnected, stories. The first is about building the tower, the second is about the scattering of people and their developing different languages.

We are told that their aim was to reach heaven and become god-like, to set themselves up in opposition to God. Which means that Nimrod who is referred to as their king is attempting to gain, to assign to himself, god-like authority and power. <13>

So they are apparently driven by Nimrod who, being one of the nephilim, is using his extraordinary abilities for setting himself up as all-powerful supremo in opposition to God, that is in opposition to humane behaviour, equality, independence, liberty, shared wealth and good life for all. <13>

The people were scattered because they were building the tower. We are told that they then stopped building the city but pointedly are not told that they stopped building the tower.

Common explanation for it not being stated that they stopped building the tower is that it follows that they had to stop building the tower when they were dispersed. But 'building the tower' is the primary cause of the scattering and so it seems that there is another reason why it is not mentioned.

The most likely reason is that they kept on building 'towers' wherever they lived, that they kept on doing what 'building towers' stands for wherever they built their smaller settlements and communities. And that 'tower' stands for organisation, command structure, chain of command of kings, of rulers, of those with authority, of leaderships.

So it appears that they stopped building this city and consequently the tower they had been building. And, having been dispersed, they continued to build cities, smaller cities, elsewhere, each presumably with its own smaller 'tower'.

Thus the allegory states that if any become too powerful, a threat to that which is humane and good, then they need to be, and are to be, dispersed. In other words, their tower (power, organisation, country, empire, corporation, monopoly, government, rulers, multinational, global corporation) needs to be dispersed.

What follows in Genesis is the direct line of descendants {10} to Abram, that is to Abraham the Patriarch. So the point is being made that 'Good' developed, prospered and gained strength following the scattering of the power-seekers and the development of separate and distinct languages, customs and traditions. {11}

Globalisation {10}

And here, so far, we have seen:

> Human beings are capable of distinguishing between good and evil and of choosing good while rejecting evil. But the nephilim among them are corruptly and evilly misusing their extraordinary and hereditary abilities to dominate, corrupt, control and manipulate other human beings.

> They are with us here and now just as before, within our communities at the present time. That they are referred to as 'fallen' indicates that their abilities are being used for selfish ends, that their behaviour is 'evil'. Their descendants are 'mighty' (powerful) and 'of renown' (well-known, prominent, in the public eye).

> In other words, there are among us people with extraordinary abilities which are hereditary and who are using these abilities for their own selfish corrupt ends, and who are likely to be powerful or influential and well known.

> Nimrod, for example, being one of the nephilim, is using his extraordinary abilities for setting himself up as all-powerful supremo in opposition to God, that is in opposition to humane behaviour, equality, independence, liberty, shared wealth and good life for all. <13>

> And the allegory of the Tower of Babel states that if any become too powerful, a threat to that which is humane and good, then they need to be, and are to be, dispersed. In other words, their tower (power, organisation, country, empire, corporation, monopoly, government, rulers, multinational, global corporation) needs to be dispersed.

> Power corrupts, absolute power corrupts absolutely. Hence the great need, and the importance of the need, for scattering and dispersal, for multiplicity and variety.

> Power corrupts, absolute power corrupts absolutely. Humanity and human behaviour depend on diversity, on opposition and balance, on democracy. <14>

The Root of all Evil (Nephilim)

Following Manfred Davidmann's report 'The Meaning of Genesis: Creation, Evolution and the Origin of Evil', we now know Genesis to be an accurate description in religious language of the way the planet was created (formed), of the evolution and of the behaviour of early man and of human beings as they evolved {7}. When Genesis was recorded, people had no knowledge of concepts such as evolution or life form, telepathy or telepaths. Concepts like these had simply not been formulated or defined. Instead of being stated using well-defined words, such concepts were described in language people could understand at that time.

Instead of the term 'scientific law' being used, for example, we see described that 'what is written applies to all people, present or absent, past or future, will happen regardless of how one feels about it, that the results of certain actions are reversed if the actions are reversed'. {7}

And Genesis' description of the abilities of the nephilim, and of the behaviour of those among them who are misusing their abilities for exploiting and oppressing ordinary people {10}, namely that

> there are among us people with extraordinary abilities which are hereditary and who are using these abilities for their own selfish corrupt ends, and who are likely to be powerful or influential and well known,

corresponds to and parallels what has been said here about telepathic organisation, manipulation and exploitation of ordinary people.

So we may take it that 'nephilim' means 'telepaths' and that Genesis refers to those who are using their extraordinary abilities for selfish and corrupt ends.

In this way Genesis confirms what Manfred Davidmann proved about telepaths and about telepathic organisation, manipulation and exploitation of ordinary people. We now know that Nephilim (telepaths) are among us and are competing with each other in a race for local and global power over people and resources, for god-like power, authority, riches and a life of luxury. And Genesis states that if any nephil <15> becomes too powerful, a threat to that which is humane and good, then the nephil's organisation needs to be, and has to be, dispersed. {10}

In other words, there are among us individuals with extraordinary abilities for influencing, organising, manipulating, controlling and dominating other human beings. Their abilities being hereditary, they are with us here and now just as before, within our communities at the present time. Some of these individuals are likely to be using their abilities for selfish corrupt ends, and they are likely to be powerful or influential and well known. Power corrupts, absolute power corrupts absolutely, and Genesis states that their power and influence needs to be split into many small parts and scattered (dispersed).

In other words, the 'Unknown Factor' which is the cause of our having to struggle all our lives wherever we may be, is the telepathic manipulation and exploitation of ordinary people.

This can now be taken as fully proved, as established fact.

Conflict between Church and State, between Religion, Government and People

The opposing forces which are in conflict between church and state have been identified {27} as opposing social ideologies, as follows:

There is no conflict when both the government and the church believe in authoritarian rule, that is when

> states consist of governments which serve the rulers by oppressing the people so that they can be exploited, stifling opposition and protest, those at the top and their experts telling people what they should do and have to do.

> And when churches serve rulers by in effect conditioning their people into gladly serving the rulers, into gladly allowing themselves to be exploited, their general approach then being 'gladly accept the tough life you are leading, your reward will come in a next life'.

And similarly there is no conflict when both the government and the church believe in participative government, that is

> When states consist of governments where those who govern serve the people and are accountable to them, where decisions are made at the lowest possible level by referendum with experts explaining to the people the consequences both ways when a decision has to be made.

> And when churches preach that it is the will of God that all people are equal, that no person may exploit another, that it is the role of those who rule, of the establishment, to serve the people.

But there is conflict and confrontation

> when 'religion' and 'government' ('church' and 'state') preach, teach and practice opposing 'ideologies' (authoritarian rule opposing participative government), or when their hierarchies compete with each other for power.

What is clear is that differences of opinion, conflicts and confrontations between a 'church' and a 'state' arise only when church and state believe in and practice opposing ideologies, and to the extent to which they do so.

So what matters regarding agreement, conflict or confrontation between a 'state' and a 'church' is the social ideology which each of them believes in, teaches and practices. Conflict and confrontation are about the right to social decision-making, and social decision-making depends on the kind of social ideology those in power believe in, teach and practice. <3>

Social Laws and Social System of the Pentateuch in Judaism, Christianity and Islam

Underlying the three main religions of Judaism, Christianity and Islam is the Pentateuch <17>. Its benevolent social laws and social system underlie all human rights, freedom, independence and liberty, underlie a good life of high quality for all {17} <9>.

For example, the laws of the Pentateuch restrain the behaviour and limit the power of 'rulers', that is of government, of top executives and of the establishment, of those in positions of trust, responsibility or authority, no matter whether secular, religious or military, no matter what the hierarchy or organisation. {29, 30}. The Pentateuch {37} states clearly what they must not do.

They may not amass servants and may not oppress the people. They may not amass possessions and wealth, may not grasp power or behave promiscuously. In other words, they may not put themselves above others by grasping power, may not satisfy personal desires at the expense of others. And a ruler (person in position of trust, responsibility or authority) has to follow these laws and abide by them every day if he wishes 'to prolong his days in his kingdom, he and his children'. For 'kingdom' read 'position' and include 'influence'.

So these Pentateuch laws lay down that those in positions of trust, responsibility or authority must not oppress people so as to increase their own possessions and power. These laws forbid personal gain from the misuse of authority, wealth or position. Those in positions of trust, responsibility or authority may not grasp power, may not oppress the people, may not behave promiscuously, may not gain wives or wealth. {17}

And now we see that struggle between church and state, religion and government, is about the application in our everyday lives of the social provisions of the Pentateuch. Its benevolent and egalitarian legislation, its social laws and social system, include the Ten Commandments and laws protecting the people by limiting the behaviour of their rulers. The struggle is between those who wish to oppress so as to exploit and those who wish to live good lives of high quality which would be theirs if the social laws and social system of the Pentateuch were followed. <4>

The history of the struggle is a fascinating story in which those in authority struggled in the past and are struggling in our time to delete the social and 'good government' laws of the Pentateuch from observance, that is to prevent them being observed, applied and enforced, to prevent people from even finding out about the existence of these benevolent revelations, to change religious belief and practice so that believers would gladly serve oppressive rulers and slave drivers instead of serving benevolent God and people. A horrendous story of human suffering imposed and being imposed in the name of private profit for the benefit those in authority.

So the Pentateuch underlies the three main religions of Judaism, Christianity and Islam. Its benevolent social laws and social system underlie all human rights, freedom, independence and liberty, underlie a good life of high quality for all. And we now see and understand

> the basic struggle and confrontation all over the planet in all aspects and levels of life and living

> between those who wish to oppress so as to exploit and

> those who wish to live good lives of high quality which would be theirs if the social laws and social system of the Pentateuch were followed. {27}

THE MESSIANIC STRUGGLE FOR A BETTER LIFE

History of the Messianic Struggle

What has been uncovered by Manfred Davidmann during the last twenty years by biblical archaeology tells us what took place. In outline, what actually happened was as follows:

Moses

Following Moses, the Jewish people undertook to live according to the Pentateuch's provisions, to apply all of them in their daily lives. But

Judaism was then corrupted from within, by its rulers and by its ruler-serving religious establishment who edited out from observance the 'Good Government' (Kingship) laws and the benevolent social laws and social system laws, and who obscured the 'Social Cause-and-Effect Relationship' as this stated that the punishing consequences of ignoring the Pentateuch's laws were inevitable. And the people were oppressed and exploited. {29-32, 27}

From the recording of the Pentateuch to the birth of Christianity, there were two main confrontations between the Jewish rulers ('state', government, establishment) and their people. This struggle was about position, influence and control over communities, about changing God-given benevolent rules of behaviour so that people could be oppressed and exploited. It changed Judaism, determined the fate of the Jewish people and gave rise to Christianity. {30, 27}

Jesus

The rulers had corrupted Judaism. Jesus then taught that all the laws had to be kept, that belief and practice included and had to include the Ten Commandments, the social laws and the social system of the Pentateuch which include the Good Government (Kingship) laws. The beliefs of Christianity thus include the social laws and social system of the Pentateuch. {33, 17, 27}

Paul, however, acted on behalf of the rich and powerful when he tried to convince people that those in authority were God's representatives on earth and had to be obeyed, and that the social laws did not have to be kept. Paul's letter to the 'Romans' was written before the gospels. Matthew's later gospel records what Jesus actually taught and clearly makes the point that Paul was trying to subvert that which Jesus taught. As Matthew records what Jesus taught, this outweighs and overrides what Paul said. Those who later favoured Paul's pro-establishment ideology could not challenge Matthew's record. Hence Matthew's gospel was subtly changed in later gospels. {33, 27}

Jesus taught that all the Pentateuch's laws had to be kept, that belief and practice had to include them. The Christian establishment later abrogated, in effect annulled <5>, the benevolent social laws of the Pentateuch and in this way corrupted Christianity from within. The Christian establishment's version became accepted as official Christian doctrine and the people were once again exposed to oppression and exploitation. {33, 27, 35, 36}

Mohammed

About two-hundred years later, Mohammed pointed out what had happened to Jews and Christians and to the inevitable outcome of not following the Pentateuch's teachings, and that all the laws of the Pentateuch had to be kept. {44}

Throughout almost the whole of Mohammed's life as Prophet he struggled against the powerful Meccan family which dominated Mecca {39}. And after Mohammed died, the ruling elite took over {41}. Hadiths (traditions) record that on the one hand we have the word of benevolent Allah as taught by Mohammed that people (believers) should have a good life of high quality in this life {42, 44}, but that on the other hand is the ruling elite's opposing viewpoint that people should be obedient and serve willingly without questioning their condition {43, 44}.

Mohammed knew about the events of the past and said so, calling for a return to following the ancient benevolent God-given social legislation. This is not taught and also not taught as such are Mohammed's teachings that the consequences of not following the benevolent social laws and social system of the Pentateuch in this life are grim and inevitable, that to follow them results in believers having good and secure lives of high quality {44}.

After Mohammed's death, Caliph Uthman had an official manuscript of the Koran compiled, edited and distributed. We are told that he ordered the compilers always to prefer the ruling-elite's version of Islam and that he then ordered all other Koranic materials to be destroyed. {42-44}

Since then there has been continuous confrontation and struggle between secular and religious figureheads and hierarchies, between state (rulers, government) and religious authorities (clerics, religious hierarchy, religion) {41} with each attempting to make the other serve its own ends. {27}

To this Point of Time

What these religions have in common is that in each case a ruling elite succeeded in bypassing or overturning humanity's essential God-given benevolent Pentateuch-recorded social provisions and human rights, in this way exposing their communities and whole populations to oppression and exploitation. {17}

And among the consequences we see around us at the present time are that

> Rabbinical Judaism (today's Judaism) propagates the establishment's revisionist version of Jewish belief and practice. {31}

> Many Christians are now taught a tranquillising ruler-serving ideology and to blame themselves for the punishing inevitable consequences of following their church's teachings {35, 36}.

>> But Manfred Davidmann concluded that with Liberation Theology we see Christianity struggling forward towards its roots in response to the social and economic problems of global humanity at the present time. Towards what Jesus taught, towards the social laws and social system of the Pentateuch. {27}

> Within Islam we see confrontation and struggle between secular and religious figureheads and hierarchies, between state (rulers, government) and religious authorities (clerics, religious hierarchy, religion) {41} with each attempting to make the other serve its own ends. The poverty-stricken and uneducated condition of so many Muslims in Islamic countries speaks for itself. {39-45, 27}.

And there are religions which teach, as a matter of policy:
That the poor are poor and evermore shall be so!
That reward for obedient suffering in the service of the rich and powerful comes in some other life!
Or after death in some imaginary other existence!

The Messianic Struggle

Religion and Reality

So far I have defined religion as

> A system of faith and worship, based on belief in the existence of a God (mostly benevolent), usually expressed by believers living according to its doctrine (principles, rules of behaviour, customs).

And shown that

> what matters regarding agreement, conflict or confrontation between a 'state' and a 'church' is the social ideology which each of them believes in, teaches and practices. Conflict and confrontation are about the right to social decision-making, and

social decision-making depends on the kind of social ideology those in power believe in, teach and practice. <3>

We saw that

some churches (religions) serve rulers by in effect conditioning their people into gladly serving the rulers, conditioning their people into gladly allowing themselves to be exploited, the church's general approach then being 'gladly accept the tough life you are leading, your reward will come in some kind of other life'.

and that

struggle between church and state, religion and government, is about the application in our everyday lives of the social provisions of the Pentateuch.

Its benevolent and egalitarian legislation, its social laws and social system, include the Ten Commandments and laws protecting the people by limiting the behavior of their rulers.

The struggle is between those who wish to oppress so as to exploit and those who wish to live good lives of high quality which would be theirs if the social laws and social system of the Pentateuch were followed. <19>

So the word 'religion' is also used as a euphemism <18> for a movement (organisation, hierarchy) which serves the rich and powerful by brainwashing (conditioning, indoctrinating) the population, particularly their young when impressionable, into willingly and gladly serving the rulers, conditioning its believers into gladly allowing themselves to be exploited. Into gladly accepting the tough life they are leading, their reward given to them in some kind of other life. Conditioning them into willingly accepting that the rich and powerful live in heaven on earth in this life while they, the people, suffer and live harsh lives being merely promised fantastic rewards in some other life after death.

Faith and belief are part of 'religion'. The individual believer can be convinced, can be made to feel certain, that his religious beliefs are true, that they correspond to reality. Regardless of evidence, regardless of proofs to the contrary.

But following Manfred Davidmann's publications, we now know that, one after the other, the Jewish, Christian and Muslim ruling establishments modified the religious beliefs of their people so as to bypass, abrogate, in effect annul, the 'God-given' social laws and social system of the Pentateuch, so as to tranquillise their people into obedience. {17}

I have already said

> The Pentateuch underlies the three main religions of Judaism, Christianity and Islam.

> Its benevolent and egalitarian social laws and social system include the Ten Commandments and laws protecting the people by limiting the behaviour of their rulers. Those in positions of trust, responsibility or authority may not grasp power, may not oppress the people, may not behave promiscuously, may not gain wives or wealth.

> The Pentateuch's social laws and social system underlie all human rights, freedom, independence and liberty, underlie a good life of high quality for all.

> And struggle between church and state, religion and government, is about the application in our everyday lives of the social provisions of the Pentateuch. {17}

Why the Pentateuch is so Special

The Pentateuch was collated and written down about 3400 years ago, has been handed down and preserved unaltered to this day as a consonantal text without vowels.

When the Pentateuch was written, people had but little knowledge about science or evolution compared with what is known today. So concepts for which we now have precise terms were described rather than stated. Instead of 'this is a scientific law', for example, we see 'what is written applies to all people, present or absent, past or future, will happen regardless of how one feels about it, that the results of certain actions are reversed if the actions are reversed'. <7> {10}

Genesis can now be understood as it was intended to be understood, following the publication of "The Meaning of Genesis: Creation, Evolution and the Origin of Evil" by Manfred Davidmann. {7}

There is no conflict or contradiction between evolution by natural selection and what is written in Genesis. Conflicts have arisen because parts of Genesis were misunderstood and misinterpreted as the necessary scientific knowledge was not known at time of translation, and parts were consequently mistranslated in spite of best intentions.

The later chapters and verses in Genesis describe the formation of the earth and early plant life, the survival of the fittest, the evolution from reptilian to mammalian instincts and behaviour, and the evolution of human beings from humanoid to Homo erectus to Homo sapiens and their corresponding changes of behaviour, feeling and thinking. It defines human behaviour by stating what is good and what is evil. {7, 17}

The Pentateuch records how human beings learned to distinguish and overcome the brutal inhuman behaviour of their primitive past and learned the behaviour of human beings. It does so by clearly defining what is known as good and evil, the difference between them and the root cause of evil.

Trustful Cooperation (Ten Commandments) {17}

The Ten Commandments <22> are so important and are so well known because behaviour in accordance with these rules is the basis for people trusting each other and so for people cooperating and working well with each other. The Ten Commandments underlie freedom, independence and strength to oppose and resist oppression. Wherever there is any independence of the mind and material freedom today it exists because people followed these rules of behaviour and it exists to the extent to which they do so. {29}

The Pentateuch's laws are just and it warns against preferring the rich or favouring the poor {38} and much trust and community friendliness is gained when people follow these principles.

But consider that these laws apply equally to the rich and powerful. It is also the rich and powerful who must not steal from the poor even the little which the poor have. It is the rich and powerful who must not cast longing glances at what little the rest of us possess, it is the rich and powerful who must not aim to gain at our expense.

The Social Cause-and-Effect Relationship

We saw <23> how determining and far-seeing the Pentateuch's rules are by the way in which rulers (those in authority) are restrained in a few sentences which protect the people from being oppressed and exploited by their rulers.

And Manfred Davidmann revealed that the Pentateuch also states {29, 17} the Social Cause-and-Effect Relationship as a scientific law which applies to all without exception and at all times, and that the law is listed in detail so that people would benefit from knowing the effects (consequences) of their behaviour.

This law states that the consequences of keeping or not keeping the Pentateuch's laws are inescapable, that what happens to one is in the end the inevitable result of one's own behaviour.

We are told that the process is reversible: Increasingly disregarding the laws (rules of behaviour) results in greater suffering and oppression, increasingly behaving according to the laws results in greater freedom, liberty, independence and a better life. {29}

We are also told that the relationship applies wherever one may be, regardless of type of government, form of religion or social system or country. It applies whether you like it or not, agree or disagree. {29}

The relationship is stated in precise terms, stated both in religious terms and described in plain language {29}. History and social science confirm it. {17} <21>

So what happens to one is in the end the inevitable result of one's own behaviour. And we can change the course of events by changing our behaviour, but only to the point of no-return.

The prophets knew and understood this relationship, and predicted accordingly, just as we now know and understand it.

The Pentateuch not only outlines that those in responsible positions need to practice restraint or be restrained but also states in clear language the scientific law that the consequences of not restraining the powerful and the opinion-formers are unavoidable, detailing the consequences both ways. The pattern of events confirms the Pentateuch's statements, both in history and in our time.

If we want freedom, independence, good life of high quality, then we have to follow these laws. If we do not, then we lose freedom, independence, good life and the country in which we live. The consequences of our behaviour cannot be avoided but we can change the course of events by changing our behaviour, but only to the point of no-return. {29}

The Messianic Struggle in Our Time <24>

> For Freedom, Independence and Liberty,
> For a Secure and Good Life of High Quality,
> **My Knowledge Must be Taught to the People,**
> **By Me and In My Name**

Extracts from my Diary and from Press Notices   {52} <24>

1977
The people have to know, have to learn, understand and follow the word of God if God's anger is to be turned away.

Jerusalem 1980
The knowledge which I have must be taught by me and in my name to the people.

April 1990
I have to lead the people to freedom. The knowledge which I have must be taught by me and in my name to the people, must reach the people and spread among them.

To 1992 Apr
I have worked hard to spread God's word but the people and their establishment do not wish to listen, have left me almost completely isolated, without the support and means required for getting the kind of publicity which is so necessary. I have been prevented from making my voice heard, worldwide.

To 1994 Jul
It also seems that the planet will destroy itself, meaning by this that it would become uninhabitable for human beings of any shape or kind.

To 2000 Dec
But for me these have been years of hard work and achievement. I have written and published much which had to be told.

2001 {35}
At the present time, the fate and future of humankind, of all human beings, is balanced on a razors edge between oppression, exploitation and enslavement on the one side, and liberty, equality and a good life for all on the other side.

2003 {17}
So now we do not have a choice. If we do not now observe and put into effect the social laws (rules) and social system of the Pentateuch and its code of behaviour then the planet will become uninhabitable for human beings.

To 2004 Sep
The quality of life has continued to deteriorate from bad to worse for the human beings on this planet.

To 2006 Apr
The quality of life has continued to deteriorate.
But I have published more of what I know.

To 2007 Apr

I feel strongly that time has almost run out for humanity and its look-alikes, that the planet may soon become uninhabitable for them all.

2007 Apr

He (Manfred Davidmann) states "A new factor has entered the equation. It is now possible for the first time in the history of human beings on this planet for just one or only a few socially irresponsible persons to do something or to introduce changes which could destroy us all or else make this planet uninhabitable for human beings."

> (Los Angeles Times)
> About 'The God-given Human Rights, Social Laws and Social System' {17}

2007 May

Manfred Davidmann says "Humanity is once again struggling intuitively to achieve the application of these social laws and system, in response to the social and economic problems of global humanity at the present time. But struggling 'intuitively' is not enough, amounts to blindly hitting out in the dark without aim, amounts to treating symptoms instead of curing causes."

And he continues: "If we do not now observe and put into effect the social rules and social system first described in the Pentateuch, then the planet is likely to become uninhabitable for human beings in the near future."

When a scientist of Manfred Davidmann's proven track record (of achievement and objectivity) and international standing, makes such a statement, this needs to be taken seriously.

Compiled and correlated analyses and guidance can be found in the works of Manfred Davidmann.

> (Texas Cable News)
> About 'Judaism, Christianity and Islam   (Church and State, Government and Religion)' {27}

In My Name

My published works are fundamental and original. Together they make up a single comprehensive and self-contained body of knowledge consisting of all the publications at present available on the solhaam website*.

These works not only clearly describe and outline what human beings are thinking and doing, and how they treat each other, but also what has to be done, and how human beings need to behave, if human beings are to survive. The future of humankind depends on these works and on the knowledge they contain.

My teachings and my knowledge are spreading, being used worldwide to an ever increasing extent and are changing what people think and believe and how they live.

However, my works have sprouted whole literatures based on their contents and about their subject areas, ranging from publications of scientific institutions and in reference books, to unscientific and misleading look-alikes.

Much has been used only partially or used out of context, selected to suit the personal likes, dislikes, preferences or purposes of those apparently using my published works for their own personal or hidden political ends or for self-glorification. Much has been rephrased, misinterpreted and misrepresented, has been quoted or used without giving credit to the author.

These seem to attempt to obscure, negate or bypass the key core fundamental content of my works, of my teachings.

So my works have to be taught, and need to spread, as a whole and as they are, without change. Which means that they have to be taught and spread in my name, with nothing added and nothing taken away.

If this were not done, then my core teachings about what humane behaviour is, about the benevolent social laws and the social system of the Pentateuch, and about the behaviour which needs to be followed if human beings are to survive, would have been negated by the root of all evil.

And thus the source and intellectual ownership of my teachings, their knowledge, discoveries, achievements, insights, revelations and advances in human knowledge and understanding, need to be clearly attributed, that is stated, giving credit to me as the author, without exception.

The benevolent social laws and the social system of the Pentateuch were negated and turned upside down, three times in the history of human beings. If this were allowed to happen a fourth time, the result would be the end of humanity on this planet.

And so we have come to the final parting of the ways, to the final moment of decision. The future and survival of human beings and of their look-alikes is now balanced on a razor's edge, depends on my teachings as a whole being acknowledged and taught in my name and accepted and followed worldwide.

Stand Up and Be Counted   (Diary Extract <24>)

"If we fail again this time, then the Covenant would be broken completely and irredeemably. If I were to fail then mankind would rapidly destroy itself. Hence we cannot and will not fail. This is a battle we simply have to and therefore will win.

If we do not succeed then this planet will be rendered uninhabitable for human beings of any shape or kind including manipulating beasts in human form.

But always there is the race against time which is either used to achieve our aims or else is irretrievably lost.

When people do not act for God and people, then God withdraws his protection from them. The consequences cannot be avoided.

But he rewards manifold those who act for him.

God helps and protects those who act for God and people.

Stand up and be counted.

This is a matter of survival, of hard work, of strain and effort, to succeed in our endeavour. And to this end we work together, all of us, human beings, proud and erect, hand in hand, irrespective of our creed or religion, the colour of our skin, the shape of our eyes, or where we happen to live, for freedom and humanity."

Notes <..>

<1> {1} quoting 'A Triune Concept of the Brain and Behaviour'; P D MacLean; University of Toronto Press, 1973.

For comprehensive information on how the human mind evolved and works, see {1}.

<2> {5} quoting from 'The Collected Works of C J Jung, CW8, paras. 200-203'

< 3> For background information and underlying knowledge and understanding, see section 'Relevant Current and Associated Works'** which lists titles (as links) as well as short descriptions.

< 4> The information in this section comes from the comprehensive report 'What People are Struggling Against: How Society is Organised for Controlling and Exploiting People'. See {19}.

< 5> Extracted from {20} which discusses the meaning of democracy, and its necessary requirements, in more detail.

< 6> See also {18} for a more comprehensive discussion of the electing, appointing and appraisal of managers, directors and elected representatives, the right to know, the right to be heard, and of work, pay and differentials.

< 7> Using {3} you can assess how far the country/community you are living in has advanced in the struggle for independence and a good life for all, or where you yourself are on this scale.

< 8> In {22} see 'Creativity' and 'Hearing Voices'.

< 9> Where to be free means to be independent, which means not being dependent on, and not being controlled by, another person, group, organisation, or thing.

And where liberty means freedom from captivity, slavery, imprisonment or despotic control by others, means freedom from social, economic, political, mental or physical control by others, that is freedom from antisocial control or manipulation by others.

And antisocial is understood as being contrary to the benevolent rules of behaviour and organisation brought together in Part 4 {25}.

<10> The information in reports {7-11, also 12-14} enables us to understand Genesis to a much greater extent, gives us a better understanding of the Pentateuch's contents.

<11> 'Heredity' is the inheritance of mental or physical characteristics from parents or ancestors. So 'hereditary' does not imply 'to all sons' nor does it imply 'in every generation'.

<12> An allegory is a story or description in which the characters and events symbolise some deeper underlying meaning {28}

<13> For detailed analysis, references, proofs and derivations, see {10}.

<14> See {4, 19, 15, 18}

<15> nephil: One of the nephilim.
nephilim: The plural form of 'nephil'; More than one nephil

<16> Genesis. First volume of the Pentateuch. See <17>.

<17> Pentateuch. Also known as 'The Five Books of Moses' (namely Genesis, Exodus, Leviticus, Numbers and Deuteronomy). Also called 'Torah'. Part of 'Old Testament'.

<18> A vague, mild or inoffensive word or phrase used instead of one considered improper or too harsh or blunt, is called a 'euphemism'. Euphemisms are dishonest when they are used to avoid facing unpleasant activities or to conceal and deceive. Dishonest uses are frequent in political and military language. {28}

EXAMPLES

Meaning	Term(s) Used (Euphemism)	Source
Toilet room	Washroom, bathroom, restroom, men's room or women's room	{49}
Mass firing of employees	Layoffs, downsizing, rightsizing	{49}
Death	'Passed away' or 'departed'	{50}
Obscene language	Adult language	{50}
Strikes	Industrial action	{51}
Manfred Davidmann's terms 'Exporting employment' and 'Importing unemployment'	Outsourcing	{47}
Multinational corporation	Global corporation	{48}
'Multinational operations' or 'Corporate multinational operations'	Globalisation	{46, 48}
Oppressive absolute rule	Rule by 'divine right'	{15}

<19> For a more comprehensive and more detailed listing of the social laws and social system of the Pentateuch, see {17}

<20> Abrogate: Doing away with (a law or agreement).
Annul: Declaring (a law or other legal contract)
invalid.

<21> In {17} see section on 'Unavoidable Consequences
of One's Behaviour'.

The Social Cause-and-Effect Relationship is also
listed (in biblical language and in plain English) in
Appendix 4 of {29}, with references to the
Pentateuch text.

<22> For a full listing of the Ten Commandments, in
biblical and plain English, see Appendix 1 of {33}.
For a good discussion of its provisions see {29}.

<23> In this report, see the first four paragraphs in
'Social Laws and Social System of the Pentateuch in
Judaism, Christianity and Islam'

<24> Copyright © Manfred Davidmann 1977, 1980,
1990, 1992, 1994, 1996, 2000, 2004, 2006, 2007
All rights reserved

<25> When individuals, communities and populations are
manipulated, then behaviour is all-important. This
report (Part 4) {25} shows how we can overcome
corrupt manipulations, how behaviour determines
our standard of living and the quality of our lives,
and describes the kind of behaviour and social
organisation on which depend liberty, freedom and
a good and secure life for all. <9>

References {..}

{ 1} In 'The Human Mind and How it Works:
Group Minds in Action:
How the Human Group Mind Shapes
the Quality of Our Life and Living'
Manfred Davidmann
ISBN 978-0-85192-055-9
see chapter 2: 'How the Human Brain
Developed and How the Human Mind Works'

{ 2} In 'The Human Mind and How it Works:
      Group Minds in Action:
      How the Human Group Mind Shapes
      the Quality of Our Life and Living'
      Manfred Davidmann
      ISBN 978-0-85192-055-9
      see chapter 7: 'Motivation Summary'

{ 3} In 'The Human Mind and How it Works:
      Group Minds in Action:
      How the Human Group Mind Shapes
      the Quality of Our Life and Living'
      Manfred Davidmann
      ISBN 978-0-85192-055-9
      see chapter 9: 'The Will to Work:
      What People Struggle to Achieve'

{ 4} In 'Messianic Struggle:
      The Worldwide Struggle for a Good and
      Secure Life for All, Here and Now'
      Manfred Davidmann
      ISBN 978-0-85192-059-7
      see chapter 7: 'Social Responsibility and
      Accountability: Summary'

{ 5} Private Myths: Dreams and Dreaming
      Anthony Stevens
      Penguin Books, 1996

{ 6} To Give or Not To Give
      'Everyman' TV documentary
      Editor: Jane Drabble; Producer: Angela Kaye
      Broadcast on 5/1/92 by BBC 1
      Based on book 'The Altruistic Person' by
      Professor Sam Oliner

{ 7} In 'God and People:
      The Social Laws and Social System Underlying
      Judaism, Christianity, Islam and Democracy'
      Manfred Davidmann
      ISBN 978-0-85192-054-2
      see chapter 6.1: 'The Meaning of Genesis:
      Creation, Evolution and the Origin of Evil'

{ 8} In 'God and People:
        The Social Laws and Social System Underlying
        Judaism, Christianity, Islam and Democracy'
        Manfred Davidmann
        ISBN 978-0-85192-054-2
        see chapter 6.2: 'The Meaning of Genesis:
        Pre-flood Evils and the Social Problems of Our Time'

{ 9} In 'God and People:
        The Social Laws and Social System Underlying
        Judaism, Christianity, Islam and Democracy'
        Manfred Davidmann
        ISBN 978-0-85192-054-2
        see chapter 6.3: 'The Meaning of Genesis:
        Morality, Sexual Behaviour and Depravity'

{10} In 'God and People:
        The Social Laws and Social System Underlying
        Judaism, Christianity, Islam and Democracy'
        Manfred Davidmann
        ISBN 978-0-85192-054-2
        see chapter 6.4: 'The Meaning of Genesis:
        Nephilim, Dominance and Liberty'

{11} In 'God and People:
        The Social Laws and Social System Underlying
        Judaism, Christianity, Islam and Democracy'
        Manfred Davidmann
        ISBN 978-0-85192-054-2
        see chapter 6.5: 'The Meaning of Genesis:
        Differentiating Between Good and Evil'

{12} In 'God and People:
        The Social Laws and Social System Underlying
        Judaism, Christianity, Islam and Democracy'
        Manfred Davidmann
        ISBN 978-0-85192-054-2
        see chapter 6.6: 'The Meaning of Genesis:
        Meaning and Significance of the Names
        of God in Genesis'

{13} In 'God and People:
The Social Laws and Social System Underlying
Judaism, Christianity, Islam and Democracy'
Manfred Davidmann
ISBN 978-0-85192-054-2
see chapter 6.7: 'Meaning and Intent of Genesis:
Essential Notes on Hebrew Grammar'

{14} In 'God and People:
The Social Laws and Social System Underlying
Judaism, Christianity, Islam and Democracy'
Manfred Davidmann
ISBN 978-0-85192-054-2
see chapter 6.8: 'The Meaning of Genesis:
Bible Translations, Versions, Codes and
Hidden Information in Bible and Talmud'

{15} In 'Management and Leadership:
Local, National, Multinational (Global),
Principles and Practice'
Manfred Davidmann
ISBN 978-0-85192-057-3
see chapter 2: 'Style of Management and
Leadership'

{16} See chapter 5:
'Family, Community, Sex and the Individual'
Manfred Davidmann

{17} See chapter 4:
'The God-given Human Rights, Social Laws and
Social System'
Manfred Davidmann

{18} In 'Cooperatives and Cooperation:
Causes of Failure, Guidelines for Success'
Manfred Davidmann
ISBN 978-0-85192-056-6
see chapter 2: 'Cooperatives and Cooperation'
and chapter 3: 'Causes of Failure, Guidelines for
Success'

{19} In 'The Real World in Which We Live:
The Social Rules and Social System under
Which We Suffer, Struggle, Survive and Prosper'
Manfred Davidmann
ISBN 978-0-85192-058-0
see chapter 10: 'What People are Struggling
Against: How Society is Organised for Controlling
and Exploiting People'

{20} In 'The Real World in Which We Live:
The Social Rules and Social System under
Which We Suffer, Struggle, Survive and Prosper'
Manfred Davidmann
ISBN 978-0-85192-058-0
see chapter 11: 'Democracy Under Attack:
Top-level Leadership and Decision-making'

{21} In 'The Human Mind and How it Works:
Group Minds in Action:
How the Human Group Mind Shapes
the Quality of Our Life and Living'
Manfred Davidmann
ISBN 978-0-85192-055-9
see chapter 3: 'The Human Group Mind and
How It Works'

see chapter 4: 'Manipulated Communities and
Populations'

see chapter 5: 'Manipulated Individuals'

see chapter 6: 'Freedom, Liberty and Good Life:
Overcoming Corrupt Manipulations'

{22} In 'The Human Mind and How it Works:
Group Minds in Action:
How the Human Group Mind Shapes
the Quality of Our Life and Living'
Manfred Davidmann
ISBN 978-0-85192-055-9
see chapter 3: 'The Human Group Mind and
How It Works'

{23} In 'The Human Mind and How it Works:
Group Minds in Action:
How the Human Group Mind Shapes
the Quality of Our Life and Living'
Manfred Davidmann
ISBN 978-0-85192-055-9
see chapter 4: 'Manipulated Communities and
Populations'

{24} In 'The Human Mind and How it Works:
Group Minds in Action:
How the Human Group Mind Shapes
the Quality of Our Life and Living'
Manfred Davidmann
ISBN 978-0-85192-055-9
see chapter 5: 'Manipulated Individuals'

{25} In 'The Human Mind and How it Works:
Group Minds in Action:
How the Human Group Mind Shapes
the Quality of Our Life and Living'
Manfred Davidmann
ISBN 978-0-85192-055-9
see chapter 6: 'Freedom, Liberty and Good Life:
Overcoming Corrupt Manipulations'

{26} See chapter 2:
'Liberation Theology: Basis - Past - Present – Future'
Manfred Davidmann

{27} See chapter 7.1:
'Church and State, Government and Religion:
Judaism, Christianity and Islam'
Manfred Davidmann

{28} Oxford Dictionary

{29} In 'Judaism: Basis - Past - Present - Future, Part 1'
Manfred Davidmann
ISBN 978-0-85192-060-3
see chapter 2.1: 'Struggle for Freedom:
The Social Cause-and-Effect Relationship'

{30} In 'Judaism: Basis - Past - Present - Future, Part 1'
Manfred Davidmann
ISBN 978-0-85192-060-3
see chapter 2.2: 'History Speaks: Monarchy,
Exile and Maccabees'

{31} In 'Judaism: Basis - Past - Present - Future, Part 1'
Manfred Davidmann
ISBN 978-0-85192-060-3
see chapter 2.3: 'At the Time of Jesus,
This is What Actually Happened in Israel:
The Truth about Hillel and his Times'

{32} In 'Judaism: Basis - Past - Present - Future, Part 1'
Manfred Davidmann
ISBN 978-0-85192-060-3
see chapter 2.4: 'One Law for All: Freedom Now,
Freedom for Ever'

{33} See chapter 3:
'Origin of Christianity and Judaism:
What Actually Happened,
What Jesus Actually Taught and Later Changes'
Manfred Davidmann

{34} In 'Judaism: Basis - Past - Present - Future, Part 1'
Manfred Davidmann
ISBN 978-0-85192-060-3
see chapter 5: 'The Right to the Land of Israel'

{35} See chapter 7.4:
'Social Policies (Doctrine) of the Roman Catholic
Church: An Evaluation'
Manfred Davidmann

{36} See chapter 7.3:
'Social Concept (Policies) of the Russian
Orthodox Church: Letter to the Russians'
Manfred Davidmann

{37} Pentateuch: Deuteronomy **17**, 14-20

{38} Pentateuch: Leviticus **19**: 15

{39} In 'Islam: Basis – Past – Present – Future'
Manfred Davidmann
ISBN 978-0-85192-053-5
see chapter 2: 'Prophet Mohammed's
Struggle for a Better Life for All'

{40} In 'Islam: Basis – Past – Present – Future'
Manfred Davidmann
ISBN 978-0-85192-053-5
see chapter 3: 'Text, Language, Dialect
and Interpretation of the Koran'

{41} In 'Islam: Basis – Past – Present – Future'
Manfred Davidmann
ISBN 978-0-85192-053-5
see chapter 4: 'The Divine Right to Rule'

{42} In 'Islam: Basis – Past – Present – Future'
Manfred Davidmann
ISBN 978-0-85192-053-5
see chapter 5: 'Compiling the Koran: Hadiths
(Traditions) State the Underlying Reality'

{43} In 'Islam: Basis – Past – Present – Future'
Manfred Davidmann
ISBN 978-0-85192-053-5
see chapter 6: 'Uthman's Rearrangement of the
Chronological (as revealed) Koran's Chapters'

{44} In 'Islam: Basis – Past – Present – Future'
Manfred Davidmann
ISBN 978-0-85192-053-5
see chapter 7: 'Prophet Mohammed's Word of
Allah and the Voice of the Ruling Elite'

{45} In 'Islam: Basis – Past – Present – Future'
Manfred Davidmann
ISBN 978-0-85192-053-5
see chapter 8: 'Muslims and Jews'

{46} In 'The Real World in Which We Live:
The Social Rules and Social System under
Which We Suffer, Struggle, Survive and Prosper'
Manfred Davidmann
ISBN 978-0-85192-058-0
see chapter 8: 'Transfer Pricing and Taxation'

{47} In 'The Real World in Which We Live:
       The Social Rules and Social System under
       Which We Suffer, Struggle, Survive and Prosper'
       Manfred Davidmann
       ISBN 978-0-85192-058-0
       see chapter 7: 'Exporting and Importing of
       Employment and Unemployment'

{48} In 'The Real World in Which We Live:
       The Social Rules and Social System under
       Which We Suffer, Struggle, Survive and Prosper'
       Manfred Davidmann
       ISBN 978-0-85192-058-0
       see chapter 6: 'Multinational Summits and
       Agreements, Top-level Decision-making and
       Democracy'

{49} Euphemism
       http://euphemism.biography.ms/

{50} Euphemisms
       http://info-pollution.com/euphemisms.htm

{51} Guide to English Usage

{52} 'Press Notices about the Works of
       Manfred Davidmann'
       https://www.solhaam.org/indexes/press.html

Additions by the Editor:

*   Manfred Davidmann's website 'https://www.solhaam.org'

** In 'https://www.solhaam.org/teachings/relsta5.html'
     see 'Relevant Current and Associated Works'

Creationism and Intelligent Design, Evolution, Education or Indoctrination

Introduction

Manfred Davidmann has written a number of scientific books and reports that have had considerable impact. His work usually breaks new ground, opening up new areas of understanding. Outstanding is that his work and reports are generally accepted as objective, factual, proved, unbiased and independent.

When the Pentateuch <1> was written {1}, people had only little knowledge about science or evolution compared with what is known today. Hence concepts for which we now have precise terms were described rather than stated. Instead of the term 'scientific law' being used, for example, we see described that 'what is written applies to all people, present or absent, past or future, will happen regardless of how one feels about it, that the results of certain actions are reversed if the actions are reversed' <2>.

So the first step towards understanding the content of the Bible is to gain knowledge about its language, that is to understand how recorded letters and symbols were used to state the meaning of words. Such knowledge and understanding is particularly important when considering what scholars and clerics have done and are doing when they are 'interpreting' the text of the Bible.

Reading, Interpreting, Translating of Consonantal Texts

Just why there has been so much confusion about reading, interpreting and translating of consonantal texts can be seen from the following definitions {13}:

'Consonant'	A letter of the alphabet other than a vowel
'Reading'	Choosing between likely words which fit the written groups of consonants while allowing for the likely meaning of the sentence or verse in which they appear.
'Interpreting'	Somehow deciding between, or choosing from, alternative meanings for the selected words or sentences.
	Interpretation attempts to suggest or provide meaning where the text itself is unclear, ambiguous, seems to have none.

'Reading' and 'interpreting' are closely interconnected since choice of words determines the meaning of the sentence, of the text.

Translating scholars, working from a consonantal text (no vowels), had to 'read' the text. That is, they had to decide between, or choose from, alternative meanings for given groups of letters (words), considering and selecting the most likely meaning of the sentence (interpretation).

Of course, they could only 'read' and 'interpret' the text, could only select a 'most likely' meaning, within their own knowledge and understanding. That is, within the knowledge and understanding available to them at that time, in those days. {12}

When the Hebrew word "ereb" was taken to mean "evening", and the Hebrew word "boker" was taken to mean "morning", then the phrase at the end of each stage of creation in Genesis could be interpreted to mean "there was evening and there was morning, one day." A reading and interpretation which corresponded to the knowledge and understanding of those doing the translating in those times. The knowledge needed for understanding Genesis was simply not available at time of translation. <3>

340

But the Hebrew 'word' ereb, said Manfred Davidmann {5}, can mean "evening," or else "to mingle," or "not to distinguish between them." Likewise, the Hebrew 'word' boker can mean "morning," or "to search," "to examine," and possibly "to check carefully." The statement about evening and morning, then, can just as easily be translated as

> "there was a mingling and a uniformity and a searching for differences and an examination of differences"

- a clear statement of the process of evolutionary advance which, said Manfred Davidmann, is both valid and relevant considering our understanding of Genesis and our present scientific knowledge.

Knowledge for Understanding not Available at Time of Translation

Adam   {See 5, 11, 12}

Hebrew grammar distinguishes between proper names of persons and general nouns such as 'life form'. This distinction <4> has been ignored by Bible translators when reading and interpreting 'adam'. However, the distinction is meaningful and needs to be made if Genesis is to be understood as it was intended to be understood {5, 11}. <5>

The Bible translators were apparently not aware of knowledge such as this, and so parts of Genesis were misread, misinterpreted or mistranslated.

Manfred Davidmann clearly states and illustrates the simple, relevant and basic rules of Hebrew grammar which distinguish between individuals and life forms. These distinctions need to be made if Genesis is to be read and understood as intended, and were first made by Manfred Davidmann in 'The Meaning of Genesis: Creation, Evolution and the Origin of Evil' {5, 11}.

Politically Motivated Changes and Misinterpretations

But there are other reasons for making changes and for insisting on them!

Names of God   {See 5, 10, 12}

Some 150 years ago, there were those who wondered why God was being referred to by different names in Genesis. At that time a likely explanation appeared to be that Genesis had been written by a number of people pretending it had all been written by one person but that each author naively referred to God by a different designation. This multi-author hypothesis has undertones of propaganda aimed at discrediting the Pentateuch and its benevolent social teachings, by discrediting its single-author-based religious authority.

The multi-author hypothesis was disproved some time ago {2, 3}. However, Manfred Davidmann was the first who clearly stated and explained the meaning of the different names (designations) of God in Genesis, and who illustrated their importance. {5, 10}

You can see in 'The Meaning of Genesis: Creation, Evolution and the Origin of Evil' {5} that the different designations for God are not only meaningful but also extremely important. <6>

Adam and Eve   {See 5, 14, 15}

It was Manfred Davidmann who proved {5} that the allegory about Adam and Eve in the Garden of Eden describes the evolution of Homo sapiens (human beings, ourselves) from Homo erectus.

He showed, for example, that Genesis records that childbirth became more difficult as a result of the increased brain size (evolution of neocortex) which enabled Homo sapiens to know the difference between good and evil and to choose between them.

And that Genesis states the necessary division of work between the male and the female, as equals in different roles, in protecting and bringing up their children.

And much else.

Obscuring Meaning by Making Changes   (Bible Versions)

There were also those who seemed to think that they knew all there is to be known, that they could decide what is and what is not, that what they were not aware of did not exist, that what they did not understand could not be meaningful.

In Genesis Chapter 5, for example, the Septuagint and the Samaritan Pentateuchs smoothed out the Masoretic chronology's listed life spans

{12}, each in a different way, and so smoothed out, obscured, clues needed for understanding the meaning of the text.

Creationism and Intelligent Design

The terms "evolution" and "natural selection" did not exist and the author of Genesis instead described the progress of evolution.

The translations (readings and interpretations) of the early translators are based on the limited knowledge and understanding available to them at the time of translation. Current translations of Genesis are in turn based on their work and we saw that conflicts have arisen because parts of Genesis have been mistranslated or misinterpreted.

Creationism apparently assumes that the resulting erroneous text correctly states God's deeds.

Following the publication of Manfred Davidmann's Genesis reports {5, 6-12}, and of the publicity they generated, the 'Creationism' hypothesis was largely abandoned in USA as untenable. But a similar hypothesis was then put forward called 'Intelligent Design'.

And it seems that 'Intelligent Design' assumes that the same erroneous text could correctly state the deeds of some other supernatural being.

Evolution, Education or Indoctrination

Manfred Davidmann shows and proves that the record of creation in the original text of Genesis corresponds in the major steps to the order in which the earth and life are known to have been formed and developed. {5}

Described is the formation of the earth and early plant life, and evolution by 'the survival of the fittest'. The evolution from reptilian to mammalian instincts, feelings and behaviour is clearly stated, as is the evolution and corresponding behaviour, feeling and thinking of human beings from humanoids (animals resembling humans) through Homo erectus (early man) to Homo sapiens (human beings, ourselves).

There is no conflict or contradiction between what is recorded in Genesis and our scientific knowledge about evolution of human beings and of our planet.

Findings and Conclusions

Conflicts have arisen because parts of Genesis have been mistranslated or misinterpreted.

The 'Creationism' hypothesis apparently assumes that the resulting erroneous text correctly states God's deeds.

And it seems that the 'Intelligent Design' hypothesis assumes that the same erroneous text could correctly state the deeds of some other supernatural being.

The source text of Genesis does not contradict the modern science of evolution.

Manfred Davidmann's research and discoveries showed and proved that the source text of Genesis, written several thousand years ago, corresponds in the major steps to the order in which the earth and life are known to have been formed and developed. {5}

Described is the formation of the earth and early plant life, and evolution by 'the survival of the fittest'. The evolution from reptilian to mammalian instincts, feelings and behaviour is clearly stated, as is the evolution and corresponding behaviour, feeling and thinking of human beings from humanoids (animals resembling humans) through Homo erectus (early man) to Homo sapiens (human beings, ourselves). {5}

There is no conflict or contradiction between what is recorded in the source text of Genesis and our scientific knowledge about evolution of human beings and of our planet.

Notes <..>

<1>   Pentateuch, part of the Bible. Also called 'The Five Books of Moses' (namely Genesis, Exodus, Leviticus, Numbers and Deuteronomy). Also called 'Torah'.

<2>   In {4} see section on 'The Social Cause-and-Effect Relationship'.
The Social Cause-and-Effect Relationship is also listed (in biblical language and in plain English) in Appendix 4 of {4}, with references to the Pentateuch text.

<3>   See {5} and {12}

<4>   In {5}, see Appendix 3: 'Adam' and Hebrew Grammar

<5>   I gratefully acknowledge the assistance I received
       from Esther Shouby without whose professional
       knowledge of Hebrew I might not have been able to
       explain the meaning of the ancient Hebrew texts.

<6>   In {5}, see Appendix 1: Names of God

References {..}

{ 1} See chapter 4:
      'The God-given Human Rights, Social Laws and
      Social System'
      Manfred Davidmann

{ 2} Genesis, Wellhausen and the Computer
      Y. T. Radday, H. Shore, M. A. Pollatschek and
      D. Wickmann
      Zeitschrift fuer die Alttestamentliche Wissenschaft
      94. Band, Heft 4, 1982
      Walter de Gruyter, Berlin, New York

{ 3} A Commentary on the Book of Genesis.
      Part 1: From Adam to Noah;
      Part 2: From Noah to Abraham.
      By U. Cassuto (1944)
      Translated from the Hebrew by
      Israel Abrahams (1961)
      The Magnes Press, The Hebrew University,
      Jerusalem.

{ 4} In 'Judaism: Basis - Past - Present - Future, Part 1'
      Manfred Davidmann
      ISBN 978-0-85192-060-3
      see chapter 2.1: 'Struggle for Freedom:
      The Social Cause-and-Effect Relationship'

{ 5} In 'God and People:
      The Social Laws and Social System Underlying
      Judaism, Christianity, Islam and Democracy'
      Manfred Davidmann
      ISBN 978-0-85192-054-2
      see chapter 6.1: 'The Meaning of Genesis:
      Creation, Evolution and the Origin of Evil'

{ 6} In 'God and People:
      The Social Laws and Social System Underlying
      Judaism, Christianity, Islam and Democracy'
      Manfred Davidmann
      ISBN 978-0-85192-054-2
      see chapter 6.2: 'The Meaning of Genesis:
      Pre-flood Evils and the Social Problems of Our Time'

{ 7} In 'God and People:
      The Social Laws and Social System Underlying
      Judaism, Christianity, Islam and Democracy'
      Manfred Davidmann
      ISBN 978-0-85192-054-2
      see chapter 6.5: 'The Meaning of Genesis:
      Differentiating Between Good and Evil'

{ 8} In 'God and People:
      The Social Laws and Social System Underlying
      Judaism, Christianity, Islam and Democracy'
      Manfred Davidmann
      ISBN 978-0-85192-054-2
      see chapter 6.3: 'The Meaning of Genesis:
      Morality, Sexual Behaviour and Depravity'

{ 9} In 'God and People:
      The Social Laws and Social System Underlying
      Judaism, Christianity, Islam and Democracy'
      Manfred Davidmann
      ISBN 978-0-85192-054-2
      see chapter 6.4: 'The Meaning of Genesis:
      Nephilim, Dominance and Liberty'

{10} In 'God and People:
The Social Laws and Social System Underlying
Judaism, Christianity, Islam and Democracy'
Manfred Davidmann
ISBN 978-0-85192-054-2
see chapter 6.6: 'The Meaning of Genesis:
'Meaning and Significance of the Names of
God in Genesis'

{11} In 'God and People:
The Social Laws and Social System Underlying
Judaism, Christianity, Islam and Democracy'
Manfred Davidmann
ISBN 978-0-85192-054-2
see chapter 6.7: 'Meaning and Intent of Genesis:
Essential Notes on Hebrew Grammar'

{12} In 'God and People:
The Social Laws and Social System Underlying
Judaism, Christianity, Islam and Democracy'
Manfred Davidmann
ISBN 978-0-85192-054-2
see chapter 6.8: 'The Meaning of Genesis:
'Bible Translations, Versions, Codes and Hidden
Information in Bible and Talmud'

{13} In 'Islam: Basis - Past - Present - Future'
Manfred Davidmann
ISBN 978-0-85192-053-5
see chapter 3: 'Text, Language, Dialect and
Interpretation of the Koran'

{14} See chapter 7.4:
'Social Policies (Doctrine) of the Roman Catholic
Church: An Evaluation'
Manfred Davidmann

{15} See chapter 7.3:
'Social Concept (Policies) of the Russian
Orthodox Church: Letter to the Russians'
Manfred Davidmann

Chapter 8

Press Notices about Genesis and Evolution

The report

"The Meaning of Genesis: Creation, Evolution and the Origin of Evil" {1}*

was published in year 2000, and publicised in 2002 by the following press release:

Report Proves There is No Conflict between the Bible (Genesis) and Evolution. (02/04/2002, Press Release)

A report entitled "The Meaning of Genesis: Creation, Evolution and the Origin of Evil" {1}*, by Manfred Davidmann, renowned author in the fields of General Management, Christianity and Judaism, proves that there is no conflict between Genesis and the theory of evolution. The report shows that instead of conflict there is in fact agreement between what is recorded in Genesis and the scientific theory of the evolution.

The report examines and analyzes Genesis and the Bible in sections at a time including The Days of Creation; Evolution and Evil; Meaning of the Names of God; Garden of Eden; Evolution of Human Beings; Cain and Abel; and The Descendants of Seth. This report is one of a series that together describe and illustrate the meaning and intent of Genesis. Each is self-contained but together they provide the knowledge needed for understanding Genesis, its allegories and their significance. These allegories illustrate and define the difference between good and evil, and the importance of behaviour on social strength, well-being and good life under modern conditions.

Further relevant knowledge and information necessary for understanding the meaning of Genesis can be found in the following reports: "Meaning and Significance of the Names of God in Genesis" {2}*, "Meaning and Intent of Genesis: Essential Notes on Hebrew Grammar" {3}* and "Bible Translations, Versions, Codes and Hidden Information in Bible and Talmud" {4}*.

About the Author:
Manfred Davidmann has written a number of books and reports that have had considerable impact. His work usually breaks new ground, opening up new areas of understanding. Outstanding is that his work and reports are generally accepted as objective, factual, unbiased and independent.

A complete listing of his reports can be viewed by visiting the website https://www.solhaam.org** where users can download his reports and view them online.

> Following the publication of Manfred Davidmann's report {1}*, and of the publicity it generated, the 'Creationism' hypothesis was abandoned as untenable. But a similar hypothesis was then put forward called 'Intelligent Design'.

> However, later publicity over a period of about seven months, resulted in increased interest in the original and scientific discoveries of Manfred Davidmann:

Manfred Davidmann on Evolution and 'Intelligent Design' (Creationism)
Debate in U.S. Court. (04/10/2005, KGW NewsChannel 8)

There is no conflict or contradiction between Darwin's theory of evolution by natural selection and what is written in Genesis. Conflicts have arisen because some parts of Genesis have been mistranslated or misinterpreted.

Creationism apparently assumes that the resulting erroneous text correctly states God's deeds.

And it seems that 'Intelligent Design' assumes that the same erroneous text could correctly state the deeds of some other supernatural being.

Genesis can now be understood as it was intended to be understood, following the publication of "The Meaning of Genesis: Creation, Evolution and the Origin of Evil" {1}* by Manfred Davidmann.

There is no conflict or contradiction between what is recorded in Genesis and what we know about evolution of human beings. Genesis states clearly how Hominoids, then Homo erectus, then Homo sapiens evolved, and their corresponding changes of behaviour, feeling and thinking.

For example, the allegory telling about Adam and Eve in the Garden of Eden describes the evolution of Homo sapiens (human beings, ourselves) from Homo erectus in a way which could be understood at the time it was written. Genesis records that childbirth became more difficult as a result of the increased brain size (evolution of neocortex) which enabled Homo sapiens to know the difference between good and evil and to choose between them. Also stated is the necessary division of work between the male and the female, as equals in different roles, in protecting and bringing up their children, and much more.

Genesis' main concern is religious, is to define good and evil and point to the root of evil.

Researcher Manfred Davidmann: No Contradiction between Genesis, Evolution. (10/01/2006, The Seattle Times)

The Book of Genesis, when read in the original Hebrew, does not contradict the modern science of evolution, Solhaam.org (https://www.solhaam.org)** announced today. In fact, said Solhaam founder and researcher Manfred Davidmann, it actually proves Genesis accurately described evolution in language commonly understood several thousand years ago.

Of course, around 1400 B.C., the terms "evolution" and "natural selection" didn't exist. So the author of Genesis instead described the process of evolution. Adding to the confusion were the early translators of the Bible from Hebrew: Current translations of Genesis are based on their limited knowledge and understanding at the time of translation. Contradictions arose between Genesis and the science of evolution, said Davidmann, when readers assumed the translations correctly stated God's deeds and words.

"There is no contradiction between the God-given original text and the science of evolution as we know it," Davidmann explained. "When we closely examine Genesis in its original Hebrew, we find evolution accurately described in broad terms the general population could understand at the time it was written."

In subsequent translations, however, those descriptions became murky at best. At the end of each stage of creation in Genesis, for example, is a statement like "there was evening and there was morning, one day." But the Hebrew word "ereb," said Davidmann, can mean "evening," or else "to mingle," or "not to distinguish between them." Likewise, the Hebrew word "boker" can mean "morning," or "to search," "to examine," and possibly "to check carefully." The statement about evening and morning, then, could just as easily be translated as "there was a mingling and a uniformity and a searching for differences and an examination of differences" - a likelier conclusion, said Davidmann, when considering the entire text of Genesis.

"In light of more plausible translations of Genesis, which describe what is now known to be the basis of evolution by natural selection, it appears that 'one day' refers to a stage of evolutionary advance as well as to a stage of creation," Davidmann stated. "What stands out in any translation is that the record of creation in Genesis corresponds in the major steps to the order in which the earth and life are known to have been formed and developed."

The later chapters and verses in Genesis describe the formation of the earth and early plant life, the survival of the fittest, the evolution from reptilian to mammalian instincts and behaviour, and the evolution of human beings from humanoid to Homo erectus to Homo sapiens.

Details about Manfred Davidmann's work on the Book of Genesis in relation to evolution can be found in {1}*. Other works by Manfred Davidmann, on a variety of topics from social responsibility to the origins of Judaism and Christianity, are available on the website https://www.solhaam.org**.

Manfred Davidmann on Genesis and Evolution - Major Scientific Breakthrough. (03/05/2006, Texas Cable News)

Manfred Davidmann's research and discoveries prove that there is no conflict or contradiction between Darwin's theory of evolution and what is written in Genesis.

He proves that Genesis describes our present scientific knowledge about evolution, in religious terms. The evolution from reptilian to mammalian instincts, feelings and behaviour is clearly stated, as is the evolution and behaviour of human beings from humanoids (animals resembling humans) through Homo erectus (early man) to Homo sapiens (human beings, ourselves).

Major breakthroughs are:

>   -- that he states and illustrates the simple relevant and basic rules of Hebrew grammar which distinguish between individuals and life forms, and

>   -- that he describes and explains the meaning of the different names (designations) of God in Genesis.

These distinctions need to be made if Genesis is to be read and understood as intended.

Original Bible translators were not aware of this knowledge, and so some parts of Genesis were misinterpreted or mistranslated.

As a result of Manfred Davidmann's work, Genesis can now be understood as it was intended to be understood, following the publication of his "The Meaning of Genesis: Creation, Evolution and the Origin of Evil." {1}*

He proves, for example, that the allegory about Adam and Eve in the Garden of Eden describes the evolution of Homo sapiens (human beings, ourselves) from Homo erectus. Just two of his points are that Genesis records that childbirth became more difficult as a result of the increased brain size (evolution of neocortex) which enabled Homo sapiens to know the difference between good and evil and to choose between them. And that Genesis states the necessary division of work between the male and the female, as equals in different roles, in protecting and bringing up their children.

See the report:
"The Meaning of Genesis: Creation, Evolution and the Origin of Evil" {1}*

Additions by the Editor:

{1}* In 'God and People:
The Social Laws and Social System Underlying
Judaism, Christianity, Islam and Democracy'
Manfred Davidmann
ISBN 978-0-85192-054-2
see chapter 6.1: 'The Meaning of Genesis:
Creation, Evolution and the Origin of Evil'

{2}* In 'God and People:
The Social Laws and Social System Underlying
Judaism, Christianity, Islam and Democracy'
Manfred Davidmann
ISBN 978-0-85192-054-2
see chapter 6.6: 'The Meaning of Genesis:
'Meaning and Significance of the Names of
God in Genesis'

{3}* In 'God and People:
The Social Laws and Social System Underlying
Judaism, Christianity, Islam and Democracy'
Manfred Davidmann
ISBN 978-0-85192-054-2
see chapter 6.7: 'Meaning and Intent of Genesis:
Essential Notes on Hebrew Grammar'

{4}* In 'God and People:
The Social Laws and Social System Underlying
Judaism, Christianity, Islam and Democracy'
Manfred Davidmann
ISBN 978-0-85192-054-2
see chapter 6.8: 'The Meaning of Genesis:
'Bible Translations, Versions, Codes and Hidden
Information in Bible and Talmud'

The Book

'God and People:
The Social Laws and Social System Underlying
Judaism, Christianity, Islam and Democracy'
by Manfred Davidmann
ISBN 978-0-85192-054-2

also contains:

Chapter 6.2: 'The Meaning of Genesis:
'Pre-flood Evils and the Social Problems of Our Time'

Chapter 6.3: 'The Meaning of Genesis:
'Morality, Sexual Behaviour and Depravity'

Chapter 6.4: 'The Meaning of Genesis:
'Nephilim, Dominance and Liberty'

Chapter 6.5: 'The Meaning of Genesis:
'Differentiating Between Good and Evil'

** Manfred Davidmann's Website 'https://www.solhaam.org'

Chapter 9

Creationism and Intelligent Design, Evolution, Education or Indoctrination.
And
Reading, Interpreting, Translating of Ancient Consonantal Texts like the Bible or the Koran.

Reading, Interpreting, Translating of Ancient Consonantal Texts like the Bible or the Koran.

The first step towards understanding the content of the Bible is to understand how recorded letters and symbols were used to state the meaning of words. Such knowledge and understanding is particularly important when considering what scholars and clerics have done and are doing when they are 'interpreting' the text of the Bible.

Just why there has been so much confusion about reading, interpreting and translating of consonantal texts (like the Bible) can be seen from the following definitions:

'Consonant'	A letter of the alphabet other than a vowel
'Reading'	Choosing between likely words which fit the written groups of consonants while allowing for the likely meaning of the sentence or verse in which they appear.
'Interpreting'	Somehow deciding between, or choosing from, alternative meanings for the selected words or sentences.
	Interpretation attempts to suggest or provide meaning where the text itself is unclear, ambiguous, seems to have none.

'Reading' and 'interpreting' are closely interconnected since choice of words determines the meaning of the sentence, of the text.

Translating scholars, working from a consonantal text (no vowels), had to 'read' the text. That is, they had to decide between, or choose from, alternative meanings for given groups of letters (words), considering and selecting the most likely meaning of the sentence (interpretation).

Of course, they could only 'read' and 'interpret' the text, could only select a 'most likely' meaning, within their own knowledge and understanding. That is, within the knowledge and understanding available to them at that time, at the time of translation.

For much else, including notes and sources, see the report
'Text, Language, Dialect and Interpretation of the Koran' {1}*
by Manfred Davidmann

Creationism and Intelligent Design, Evolution, Education or Indoctrination.

When the word "ereb" was taken to mean "evening", and the word "boker" was taken to mean "morning", then the phrase at the end of each stage of creation in Genesis could be interpreted to mean "there was evening and there was morning, one day." A reading and interpretation which corresponded to the knowledge and understanding of those doing the translating in those times. The knowledge needed for understanding Genesis was simply not available at time of translation.

But the 'word' ereb, said Manfred Davidmann, can mean "evening," or else "to mingle," or "not to distinguish between them." Likewise, the 'word' boker can mean "morning," or "to search," "to examine," and possibly "to check carefully." The statement about evening and morning, then, can just as easily be translated as

> "there was a mingling and a uniformity and a searching for differences and an examination of differences"

- a clear statement of the process of evolutionary advance which, said Manfred Davidmann, is both valid and relevant considering our understanding of Genesis and our present scientific knowledge.

For much else, including notes and sources, see the report
'Creationism and Intelligent Design, Evolution, Education or Indoctrination' {2}*
by Manfred Davidmann

Sources:

{1}*   In 'Islam: Basis – Past – Present – Future'
       Manfred Davidmann
       ISBN 978-0-85192-053-5
       see chapter 3: 'Text, Language, Dialect and
       Interpretation of the Koran'

{2}*   See chapter 7.6:
       'Creationism and Intelligent Design, Evolution,
       Education or Indoctrination'
       Manfred Davidmann

Additions by the Editor:

In the original text of this chapter on the https://www.solhaam.org website Manfred Davidmann referred to other reports in form of links.

Here these reports are marked { }* and the sources are stated.

Chapter 10

Faith and Trust in God, No Matter by What Name called

Faith and Trust in God, No Matter by What Name called
Stand Up and Be Counted
Notes <...>

Faith and Trust in God, No Matter by What Name called

Continuously there is the race against the enemy within <1> who would separate, engulf and destroy some or all of us the human beings on this our planet and thus we listen at all times to the ticking of the clock denoting the passage of time which is either used to further our purpose or else is irretrievably lost.

This is a matter of survival, of hard work, of strain and effort, to succeed in our endeavour. And to this end we work together, all of us, human beings, proud and erect, hand in hand, irrespective of our creed or religion, the colour of our skin, the shape of our eyes, or where we happen to live, for freedom and humanity.

We climb together through mists of uncertainty, guided by our Elders <2>.

Our Elders impress upon their people the need to act, having been charged by all our people with doing this effectively.

In the history of any or all of our people:
> Whenever the guidance of the Elders has been ignored, the most terrible consequences have always followed.

We place our faith and trust in God, no matter by what name called, and in all our people all over the planet.

We are guided ably and powerfully and for this we are truly grateful.

God helps and protects those who act for God and people.

God acts when people act for God and people.

When people do not act for God and people, then God withdraws his protection from them.

Ideas, inspirations and voices are intended to guide or lead astray, to help or betray.

Beast eats beast. You cannot trust manipulating slave owners or slave drivers and cannot trust that which originates from them.

When in doubt one must do that which is right (humane, good, caring, putting people first).

God,

Beasts have continued to disown you, and they have continued to disown me,

but I have the sure knowledge that they will be weak and fall by the wayside,
while we will be strong, survive and succeed.

Their idols of wood, stone and plastic, of concrete and steel, of flesh and bones,
their golden calves,
cannot guide them or save them.

Every time they open their mouths they condemn themselves.

Whenever life has been so tough in the past then I have been very close to, almost immediately before, a major breakthrough or success.

And God has always turned tough situations into gains and advances in unexpected directions.

God

See my loneliness
See my isolation
See how my time has been wasted instead of teaching your laws in your name.

Stand by me and guide me.

Those who argue against me argue against God,
those who are against me are against God
and will suffer the inevitable consequences,
will not be listened to, will lose what influence they have, will not learn nor teach what little they will know or remember.

God

In you we trust.
Guide us in our hours of need,
show us the way to freedom.

We struggle to re-establish your law
so that all people can be freed
and gain strength and good life.

If we fail again this time, then the Covenant would be broken
completely and irredeemably.
If I were to fail then mankind would rapidly destroy itself.
Hence I cannot and will not fail.
This is a battle we simply have to and therefore will win.

If I do not succeed then this planet will be rendered uninhabitable for
human beings of any shape or kind including manipulating beasts in
human form.

But always there is the race against time which is either used to achieve
our aims or else is irretrievably lost.

Stand Up and Be Counted

When people do not act for God and people,
then God withdraws his protection from them.
The consequences cannot be avoided.

But God helps, protects and rewards manifold those who act for God and
people.

This is a matter of survival, of hard work, of strain and effort, to
succeed in our endeavour. And to this end we work together, all of us,
human beings, proud and erect, hand in hand, irrespective of our creed
or religion, the colour of our skin, the shape of our eyes, or where we
happen to live, for freedom and humanity.

Notes <..>

<1> The enemy within, that is a manipulating ruling class
or slave-driving manipulators.

<2> Our Elders are known only by God and serve God and
people, remain unknown to human beings.

Chapter 11

Christianity at the Crossroads, at the Final Parting of the Ways

Jesus Taught: The God-given Social Laws and Social System
The Catholic Church Preaches (Teaches)
Sources

Jesus Taught: The God-given Social Laws and Social System

The social laws and social system of the Pentateuch ensure freedom and material independence and provide a good life of high quality here and now, backed by effective social security. No one may oppress or exploit another and all are equal, as a matter of God-given law.

See 'The God-given Human Rights, Social Laws and
Social System' {1}*

Jesus taught that all the social laws and the social system of the Pentateuch had to be kept, that belief and practice included and had also to include the Ten Commandments and the Good Government (Kingship) laws.

The Ten Commandments underlie freedom, independence and strength to oppose and resist oppression.

The Good Government (Kingship) laws lay down that those in positions of trust, responsibility or authority must not oppress people and also forbid personal gain from the misuse of authority or position. Those in authority must not be promiscuous and must not amass wealth.

See 'Origin of Christianity and Judaism' {2}*
about What Jesus Actually Taught

The Pentateuch's Social Cause-and-Effect Relationship is a scientific law which applies to all without exception and at all times. It clearly states that increasingly disregarding the laws (rules of behaviour) results in greater suffering and oppression, increasingly behaving according to the laws results in greater freedom, liberty, independence and a better life. The prophets knew and understood this relationship, and predicted accordingly, just as we now know and understand it. The consequences of keeping or not keeping the Pentateuch's laws are inescapable. What happens to one is in the end the inevitable result of one's own behaviour.

In 'The God-given Human Rights, Social Laws and Social System' {1}* see section on 'Unavoidable Consequences of One's Behaviour'.

The Social Cause-and-Effect Relationship is also listed (in biblical language and in plain English) in Appendix 4 of 'Struggle for Freedom: The Social Cause-and-Effect Relationship' {3}*, with detailed references to the Pentateuch text.

The Catholic Church Preaches (Teaches)

Paul acted on behalf of the rich and powerful when he proclaimed that those in authority were God's representatives on earth and had to be obeyed, and that some of the Pentateuch's social laws and social system did not have to be kept. What Paul said and put forward apparently became official Christian doctrine and is still taught today. But it is neither God's word nor is it according to what Jesus taught.

> See 'Origin of Christianity and Judaism' {2}*
> about What Actually Happened and Later Changes

Hence, according to the Social Cause-and-Effect Relationship, the Christian establishment condemns Christians to unavoidable harsh and inescapable consequences, to suffering and hardships, in measure with the extent to which they follow the ideology of Paul which the Catholic Church teaches and preaches.

And, when looking at Genesis Chapter 3 (Adam and Eve in Garden of Eden) we see that this is apparently interpreted by the Catholic Church as if it implied some kind of personal guilt. What we are being told in teachings about 'original sin' or a 'fallen humanity' appears to be: 'Do not blame the Church (its doctrine, its teachings, its hierarchy), the government, or the oppressor, for the sufferings and hardships of your lives, blame yourself.'

> See 'Social Policies (Doctrine) of the Roman Catholic
> Church: An Evaluation' {4}*

So it appears that the teachings of the religious hierarchy condemn their Christian believers to sufferings and hardships. At the same time the hierarchy seems to expect believers to blame themselves for the consequences of following the hierarchy's teachings.

Here are just a few isolated examples from the Church's social teachings:

> The Pentateuch's right to social security enables the recipient to remain an independent breadwinner, to remain the master of his fate. The Church replaces the 'right' to effective social security, with 'charity', stating
>> the more fortunate ... should place their goods more generously at the service of others.
> Charity can be used to exploit the needs of the needy by making the recipient indebted to, and depending on, the giver for survival.

> In the context of management, government and church-state relations, participation means participating in decision-making.

> But it seems that to the Church it is rulers who decide, that there is no question of participating in decision-making, of democratic decision-making by the people. This the Church shows by defining the word 'participation' to mean
>> participating (taking part) in activities with other people.
> Participating in work being done or in community groups is a very different matter from participating in making the decisions.

> As said already, Paul acted on behalf of the rich and powerful when he proclaimed that those in authority were God's representatives on earth and had to be obeyed, and that some of the Pentateuch's social laws and social system did not have to be kept. What Paul said and put forward apparently became official Christian doctrine and is still taught today. But it is neither God's word nor is it according to what Jesus taught.

> See 'Social Policies (Doctrine) of the Roman Catholic Church: An Evaluation' {4}*

> and see 'Church and State, Government and Religion: Judaism, Christianity and Islam {5}*

Sources:

{1}* See chapter 4:
     'The God-given Human Rights, Social Laws and
     Social System'
     Manfred Davidmann

{2}* See chapter 3:
      'Origin of Christianity and Judaism:
      What Actually Happened,
      What Jesus Actually Taught and Later Changes'
      Manfred Davidmann

{3}* In 'Judaism: Basis - Past - Present - Future, Part 1'
      Manfred Davidmann
      ISBN 978-0-85192-060-3
      see chapter 2.1: 'Struggle for Freedom:
      The Social Cause-and-Effect Relationship'

{4}* See chapter 7.4:
      'Social Policies (Doctrine) of the Roman Catholic
      Church: An Evaluation'
      Manfred Davidmann

{5}* See chapter 7.1:
      'Church and State, Government and Religion:
      Judaism, Christianity and Islam'
      Manfred Davidmann

Additions by the Editor:

In the original text of this chapter on the https://www.solhaam.org
website Manfred Davidmann referred to other reports in form of links.

Here these reports are marked { }* and the sources are stated.

Chapter 12

The choice is yours:
Unemployment, Charitable Social Security and Today's Religious Teachings
or
High Standard of Living, Satisfying Work and a Good Life, as God-given rights.

Social and Economic Security
Government and Management
Equality and Ownership
Role of the Biblical Prophets, and their Warnings
And Now
Sources

A covenant is an agreement in which each of the parties undertakes duties and obligations towards the other. And the Pentateuch records God's promise that human beings will have a good life of high quality as long as human beings fulfil their obligations under the covenant, as long as human beings follow God's laws, that is as long as they behave like human beings.

This is also recorded in the Pentateuch as a fundamental scientific law, the Social Cause-and-Effect Relationship. This states that the consequences of keeping or not keeping the Pentateuch's laws are inescapable, that what happens to one is in the end the inevitable result of one's own behaviour. Also clearly stated is that this is a scientific law which was defined and stated using the language of religion so that people would benefit from knowing the effects (consequences) of their behaviour.

See 'The God-given Human Rights, Social Laws and
Social System' {1}*, which lists detailed sources and
relevant notes.

We are told that the relationship applies to all without exception and at all times, wherever one may be, regardless of type of government, form of religion or social system or country. It applies whether you like it or not, agree or disagree.

The consequences of one's behaviour are detailed both ways, clearly and powerfully illustrating intermediate stages between the two ends of the scale, and we are told that the process is reversible: Increasingly disregarding the laws (rules of behaviour) results in greater suffering and oppression, increasingly behaving according to the laws results in greater freedom, liberty, independence and a better life.

The relationship applies to all. Ignorance is no excuse, not knowing the law does not prevent consequences of one's behaviour, and the relationship is stated in a way which enables people to benefit from knowing the effects of their behaviour, even if they do not understand the underlying relationship.

The relationship is clearly stated in the Pentateuch in precise terms. History and social science confirm it, and it is confirmed by Jesus Christ and by the Prophet Mohammed. The Koran records Mohammed repeatedly confirming the Pentateuch, referring to it both as a guide and as a warning, and Arab and Muslim history illustrates the working of the cause-and-effect relationship.

> See
> (1) 'History Speaks: Monarchy, Exile and Maccabees' {2}*
> (2) 'Social Responsibility, Profits and Social Accountability' {3}*
> (3) 'Origin of Christianity and Judaism' {4}*
> (4) 'Prophet Mohammed's Word of Allah and the Voice of the Ruling Elite' {5}*

And what we have in the Pentateuch are rules of behaviour which point to the essence of humane behaviour. We know that ignoring them results in social corruption, oppression and exploitation of the many by the few. And we know that following these rules ensures social strength and a good life for all.

If we want freedom, independence, good life of high quality, then we have to follow these laws. If we do not, then we lose freedom, independence, good life and the country in which we live. The consequences of our behaviour cannot be avoided but we can change the course of events by changing our behaviour.

Social and Economic Security

All persons have the right to be free and independent masters of their own fate and no person may oppress or exploit another. Because people can be exploited through their needs there has to be a system of social and economic security which guarantees freedom from needs and so protects people from becoming dependent on others for essential income, which protects against loss of material independence and which protects people from losing their spiritual independence.

Every community member is entitled as a matter of right to full social security. This means that community members are entitled to be supported by the community not only when they fall on hard times but also to maintain their independence as independent breadwinners for their families. For example, the community has to provide backup funds to those who need them and they have to be provided as and when required.

To prevent people being exploited through their need these funds have to be provided without charging interest. They are called 'loans' because the recipient is under moral obligation to repay them to the community if he can do so. However, such 'loans' are cancelled every seventh calendar year if the borrower has been unable to repay them.

These essential social provisions of the Pentateuch are clear and to the point. This is what is laid down as a matter of law:

The community has to provide ('lend') money to those who need it, free of interest. All such loans, if outstanding, are to be cancelled every seventh year.

And what we have in the Pentateuch are rules of behaviour which point to the essence of humane behaviour. We know that ignoring them results in social corruption, oppression and exploitation of the many by the few. And we know that following these rules ensures social strength and a good life for all.

Government and Management

The Pentateuch's laws of government relate to 'rulers', apply to all in positions of trust, responsibility or authority, no matter whether secular, religious or military, no matter what the hierarchy or organisation.

These laws control the behaviour and limit the power of government, of top executives and of the establishment, of those in positions of trust, responsibility or authority. The Pentateuch leaves little doubt about what they must not do.

Such people may not amass servants and may not oppress the people for their own benefit. They may not amass possessions and wealth, may not grasp power or behave promiscuously. In other words, they may not put themselves above others by grasping power, may not satisfy personal desires at the expense of others.

So these Pentateuch laws quoted here protect people and safeguard their strength and freedom by laying down that those in positions of trust, responsibility or authority may not grasp power, may not oppress the people, may not behave promiscuously, may not enrich themselves. Those in authority must not oppress people so as to increase their own possessions and power, must not form enforcing squads or organisations so as to multiply their own power.

Equality and Ownership

Ownership is the right to possess something and to decide what is to be done with it. If I own something it belongs to me and I decide what is to be done with it. An example would be owning a house.

Possession is having something in one's custody as distinct from owning it. If I possess something it belongs to another but I can decide how to use it. An example would be renting a house.

Another example would be deciding what to do with my money (ownership) or deciding and controlling the use of money belonging to someone else (possession).

And considering the right to ownership, two questions need to be considered. Namely where does the right come from and how is it exercised.

The right to own property varies among societies. Ownership laws which assign ownership 'rights' to owners have been devised by the owners themselves or by those who serve them.

Ownership of land and means of production, of funds and wealth, has always been accumulated at someone else's expense. All belonged to the community, belonged to all alike. And this is what Chapter 5 of Genesis appears to be saying.

A human right is a something one may legally or morally claim, is the state of being entitled to a privilege or immunity or authority to act. Human rights are those held to be claimable by any living person, apply to all living people. Every living person is entitled to them.

So ownership of land and means of production, of funds and wealth, rightfully belongs to the community, belongs to all alike, is a human right. Those who have accumulated them have only possession, which means they can use and apply them but may do so only on behalf of, and for the benefit of, the community and that they are accountable to the community for the way in which they do so.

Hence we have the use of possessions as long as we use them to provide a good living for our family, and beyond that for the benefit of the community. For the benefit of others less able or fortunate, for the benefit of the community around us and then for the benefit of communities abroad.

Role of the Biblical Prophets, and their Warnings

The sayings of the prophets show clearly that the prophets were very much aware of the consequences of what was taking place. They pointed out what was bound to happen if the rulers, their secular and religious establishments, and perhaps also the people, continued to behave as they were doing, and events proved them right.

The prophets appear to have had a clear understanding of the inevitability with which the law acts, with which events follow the Social Cause-and-Effect Relationship. And they accuse the rulers and the ruling level for what they do and hold them responsible for what their establishment does and thus for the behaviour of the people.

The prophets were not listened to, the rulers and their establishments continued to corrupt and oppress the people until both kingdoms were destroyed and the people most viciously dispersed.

The Cause-and-Effect Relationship tells us that disaster and destruction were inevitably caused by the behaviour of the rulers and their establishment, and by the resulting behaviour of the people.

So now let us look at the kind of behaviour the prophets warned against as it was that kind of behaviour which was weakening the people and thus the country.

We see that the prophets warned about the consequences of delinquency, crime, sexual permissiveness and corruption. They warned about land being concentrated in the hands of a few, of Jew exploiting and oppressing Jew, of people being oppressed and enslaved through debt and through need.

Outstanding is that the warnings of the prophets were ignored, that the establishment of the day ignored the writing on the wall. They did not act then, they did not act at other times. In so doing they did not just oppress their people, what they were doing was to destroy their people and to destroy themselves as well.

See 'History Speaks: Monarchy, Exile and Maccabees' {2}*
and see 'One Law for All: Freedom Now, Freedom for Ever' {7}*

And Now

I showed years ago, in 'Social Responsibility, Profits and Social Accountability', that we were experiencing a sequence of accidents and catastrophes which were occurring more and more frequently and were affecting more and more people.

Since then most people have become aware of this. But I also showed what could and should be done about this trend of events. However, a new factor has entered the equation. It is now possible for the first time in the history of human beings on this planet for just one or only a few socially irresponsible persons to do something or to introduce changes which could destroy us all or else make this planet uninhabitable for human beings.

So now we do not have a choice. If we do not now observe and put into effect the social laws (rules) and social system of the Pentateuch and its code of behaviour, then the planet is likely to become uninhabitable for human beings and their look-alikes.

Sources:

{1}* See chapter 4:
      'The God-given Human Rights, Social Laws and
      Social System'
      Manfred Davidmann

{2}* In 'Judaism: Basis - Past - Present - Future, Part 1'
      Manfred Davidmann
      ISBN 978-0-85192-060-3
      see chapter 2.2: 'History Speaks: Monarchy,
      Exile and Maccabees'

{3}* In 'Messianic Struggle:
      The Worldwide Struggle for a Good and
      Secure Life for All, Here and Now'
      Manfred Davidmann
      ISBN 978-0-85192-059-7
      see chapter 2: 'Social Responsibility, Profits and
      Social Accountability'

{4}*   See chapter 3:
       'Origin of Christianity and Judaism:
       What Actually Happened,
       What Jesus Actually Taught and Later Changes'
       Manfred Davidmann

{5}*   In 'Islam: Basis – Past – Present – Future'
       Manfred Davidmann
       ISBN 978-0-85192-053-5
       see chapter: 7: 'Prophet Mohammed's Word of
       Allah and the Voice of the Ruling Elite'

{6}*   In 'Judaism: Basis - Past - Present - Future, Part 1'
       Manfred Davidmann
       ISBN 978-0-85192-060-3
       see chapter 2.1: 'Struggle for Freedom:
       The Social Cause-and-Effect Relationship'

{7}*   In 'Judaism: Basis - Past - Present - Future, Part 1'
       Manfred Davidmann
       ISBN 978-0-85192-060-3
       see chapter 2.4: 'One Law for All: Freedom Now,
       Freedom for Ever'

Additions by the Editor:

In the original text of this chapter on the https://www.solhaam.org website Manfred Davidmann referred to other reports in form of links.

Here these reports are marked { }* and the sources are stated.

Chapter 13

Quotable Quotes about Christianity

What Jesus Taught

The social laws and social system of the Pentateuch (Five Books of Moses) ensure freedom and material independence and provide a good life of high quality here and now, backed by effective social security. No one may oppress or exploit another and all are equal, as a matter of God-given law.

Jesus taught that all the social laws and the social system of the Pentateuch had to be kept, that belief and practice included and had also to include the Ten Commandments and the Good Government (Kingship) laws.

The Ten Commandments underlie freedom, independence and strength to oppose and resist oppression. The Good Government (Kingship) laws lay down that those in positions of trust, responsibility or authority must not oppress people and also forbid personal gain from the misuse of authority or position. Those in authority must not be promiscuous and must not amass wealth.

> From 'Social Policies (Doctrine) of the Roman
> Catholic Church: An Evaluation' (2005) {1}*

At issue are the laws of behaviour and the social system which are laid down in the Pentateuch:

> The Pentateuch states that all are equal, that no person may oppress or exploit another, that all have the right to be free and be independent masters of their own fate.

371

Every person is entitled as a matter of right to social security. This means that people are entitled to be supported by the community not only when they fall on hard times but also to maintain their independence as independent breadwinners for their families.

For example, the community has to provide backup funds to those who need them and they have to be provided as and when required. To prevent people being exploited through their need these funds have to be provided without charging interest and such 'loans' are cancelled every seventh year if the borrower has been unable to repay them.

From 'Origin of Christianity and Judaism' (1994) {2}*

So the Pentateuch laws quoted here protect people and safeguard their strength and freedom by laying down that those in positions of trust, responsibility or authority may not grasp power, may not oppress the people, may not behave promiscuously, may not enrich themselves.

Those in authority must not oppress people so as to increase their own possessions and power, must not form enforcing squads or organisations so as to multiply their own power, must not behave promiscuously, must not gain wives or wealth (Pentateuch, Deut 17: 14-20).

They must know and observe the Pentateuch law and its intent and aim to see the Pentateuch laws applied.

From 'The God-given Human Rights, Social Laws and Social System' (2003) {3}*

Jesus taught that if the rich wish to be rewarded by God they will need to follow that which Jesus teaches by keeping all the commandments and the social laws of the Pentateuch. Jesus said that 'good deeds' by themselves are not enough to gain eternal life. Whoever keeps the commandments enters eternal life. To be a 'good person' and enter eternal life one has to keep the commandments.

From 'Origin of Christianity and Judaism' (1994) {2}*

The laws of the Pentateuch restrain the behaviour and limit the power of 'rulers', that is of government, of top executives and of the establishment, of those in positions of trust, responsibility or authority, no matter whether secular, religious or military, no matter what the hierarchy or organisation. The Pentateuch states clearly what they must not do.

They may not amass servants and may not oppress the people. They may not amass possessions and wealth, may not grasp power or behave promiscuously. In other words, they may not put themselves above others by grasping power, may not satisfy personal desires at the expense of others.

And a ruler (person in position of trust, responsibility or authority) has to follow these laws and abide by them every day if he wishes 'to prolong his days in his kingdom, he and his children'. For 'kingdom' read 'position' and include 'influence'.

From 'Social Policies (Doctrine) of the Roman Catholic Church: An Evaluation' (2005) {1}*

Christianity is struggling forward towards its roots in response to the social and economic problems of global humanity at the present time. Towards what Jesus taught, towards the social laws and social system of the Pentateuch which were being argued about and discussed by Paul and the writers of the Gospels (see the later 'Origin of Christianity').

From 'Liberation Theology: Basis - Past - Present – Future' (1991, 1994) {4}*

We will see how writers of the gospels struggled to put the record straight, struggled to record what Jesus actually taught. Throughout the ages, Christians of goodwill chose intuitively to interpret Paul's statements about those in authority as meaning that 'the authority of those in authority only comes from God to the extent to which they themselves live according to and apply the Ten Commandments, the social laws and the social system laws', and that only those can 'love one another' who comply with all these laws.

From 'Origin of Christianity and Judaism' (1994) {2}*

And wherever there is extreme poverty and suffering and pain you are likely to find Christians who are struggling on the side of the oppressed. Christians such as priests and nuns who provide encouragement and guidance to oppressed and suffering people in their struggle for a better life against the ruling establishment, against established ruling oppressors, doing so at much risk and without thought of personal gain.

From 'Liberation Theology: Basis - Past - Present – Future' (1991, 1994) {4}*

Genesis and Evolution

Genesis begins by describing how the planet was created, in other words how it was formed, the changes which occurred as the planet aged, how plants and animals were formed, evolved and populated the planet. It describes how human beings evolved and also how the behaviour of life forms changed as human beings evolved.

When the Pentateuch (Five Books of Moses) was written about 3,400 years ago, people had but little knowledge about science or evolution compared with what is known today. So concepts for which we now have precise terms were described rather than stated and expressed in religious terms so that they could be appreciated and followed by the population.

Understanding this we see that there is no conflict, no contradiction, no divergence, only awe-inspiring agreement, between what is stated in Genesis and what we now know about the evolution of human beings by natural selection.

> From 'The Meaning of Genesis: Creation, Evolution
> and the Origin of Evil' (2000, 2001) {5}*

And some 150 years ago there were those who wondered why God was being referred to by different names in Genesis. At that time a likely explanation appeared to be that Genesis had been written by a number of people pretending it had all been written by one person but that each author naively referred to God by a different designation. This multiauthor hypothesis has undertones of propaganda aimed at discrediting the Pentateuch (Torah, Five Books of Moses) and its benevolent social teachings, by discrediting its single-author-based religious authority. The multi-author hypothesis was disproved some time ago. And what you will see here is that the different designations for God are not only meaningful but extremely important.

> From 'The Meaning of Genesis: Creation, Evolution
> and the Origin of Evil' (2000, 2001) {5}*

In reality, Genesis Chapter 3 (Adam and Eve in Garden of Eden) actually describes the evolution of Homo sapiens in a way which could be understood at the time it was written, and which can now be understood as it was intended to be understood, following the publication of Manfred Davidmann's 'The Meaning of Genesis: Creation, Evolution and the Origin of Evil'. For example, Genesis records that childbirth became more difficult as a result of the increased brain size, and states the necessary division of work between the male and the female, as equals in different roles, in protecting and bringing up their children.

From 'Social Policies (Doctrine) of the Roman
Catholic Church: An Evaluation' (2005) {1}*

Life as we know it today appears to have developed very, very slowly by a process of trial and error. Each change was evaluated by the extent to which it enabled a life form to survive and multiply in a largely hostile environment in competition with other life forms.

Remarkable is the enormous timescale during which this slow process has enabled ourselves to be created. We are the most complicated and advanced life form and there are many gaps in our knowledge and appreciation of the way in which we exist, function, live and behave.

Alarming is the infinitesimally small period of time in which our technological progress has so vastly exceeded our social organisation and behaviour that now the survival of our species is in doubt.

Evil must not gain the upper hand under any circumstances.

From 'The Meaning of Genesis: Creation, Evolution
and the Origin of Evil' (2000, 2001) {5}*

Each person can now have access to vast knowledge undreamt of only a few years ago.

But this needs to be supplemented with the ability to think clearly, to assess and evaluate reliability and applicability, on the basis of knowledge of good and evil and of the essential need for behaving humanely, for following (doing) good instead of evil.

It is here that the relevance and importance of the Pentateuch's social laws and teachings become apparent. The Pentateuch adds to mere mechanistic and chance processes the knowledge that human beings need to behave humanely if they wish to prosper and succeed. Stating clearly what is, and is not, humane behaviour, clearly defining the difference between good (including human rights and justice) and evil, adding that human beings stand or fall by the way they behave.

From 'The Meaning of Genesis: Creation, Evolution
and the Origin of Evil' (2000, 2001) {5}*

Origins

Outstanding is that the contemporaneously written, agreed and finalised Christian Canon and Jewish Talmud were shaped by and independently record the same confrontations and struggle and sequence of events we have here seen unfold.

The agreement between Christian and Jewish writings is so complete that we are now reasonably certain about the main course of events.

For the first time we can now see the whole pattern.

From 'Origin of Christianity and Judaism' (1994) {2}*

Paul wrote (Romans) that
> 'the law brings wrath, but where there is no law there is no transgression',

saying that the God-given laws in the Pentateuch result in punishment for those who break the law and that a law that does not exist cannot be broken.

Laws protect people when those who break them are punished. So Paul is saying that there would be no punishment if the laws were abolished, implying that antisocial activities can be allowed to take place without restraint.

From 'Origin of Christianity and Judaism' (1994) {2}*

So what happened was:

> Jesus taught that all the laws had to be kept, that belief and practice included and had to include the Ten Commandments, the Good Government (Kingship) laws, the social laws and the social system of the Pentateuch.

> Paul, however, acted on behalf of the rich and powerful when he tried to convince people that those in authority were God's representatives on earth and that the social laws did not have to be kept.

> The writers of the gospels struggled to put the record straight, struggled to record what Jesus Christ actually taught (See Manfred Davidmann's 'Origin of Christianity and Judaism'). Throughout the ages, Christians of goodwill chose intuitively to interpret Paul's statements about those in authority as meaning that 'the authority of those in authority only comes from God to the extent to which they themselves live according to and apply the Ten Commandments, the social laws and the social system laws', and that only those can 'love one another' who comply with all these laws.

From 'Origin of Christianity and Judaism' (1994) {2}*

The social laws and social system of the Pentateuch ensure freedom and material independence and provide a good life of high quality here and now, backed by effective social security. No one may oppress or exploit another and all are equal, as a matter of God-given law.

> From 'The God-given Human Rights, Social Laws and
> Social System' (2003) {3}*

Paul acted on behalf of the rich and powerful when he proclaimed that those in authority were God's representatives on earth and had to be obeyed, and that the social laws and social system did not have to be kept. What Paul said and put forward in (Romans 13: 1-10) apparently became official Christian doctrine and is still taught today. But it is neither God's word nor is it what Jesus taught.

> Among the commandments Paul does not want people to observe, are:

>> One must not respect or serve oppressing, exploiting or enslaving beliefs or ideologies.

>> One must not use God's name to lend authority to a statement which it would not otherwise have or to a false or misleading statement.

> From 'Social Policies (Doctrine) of the Roman
> Catholic Church: An Evaluation' (2005) {1}*

The Catholic Church's statement on its social doctrine, for example, shows that the Church follows Paul's ideology that rulers rule by 'Divine Right' and have to be obeyed, that the Church is apparently teaching that the relationships and duties of a Christian towards the authorities are as stated by Paul in (Romans 13: 1-7).

For example, in the context of management, government and church-state relations, participation means participating in decision-making. But it seems that to the Church it is rulers who decide, that there is no question of participating in decision-making, of democratic decision-making by the people. This the Church shows by defining the word 'participation' to mean
'participating (taking part) in activities with other people'.
Participating in work being done or in community groups is a very different matter from participating in making the decisions.

And the Pentateuch's God-given right to social security enables those who benefit to remain independent breadwinners, enables each to remain the master of his fate. But the Church replaces the right to effective social security, with charity, and charity can be used to exploit the needs of the needy by making the receiver indebted to, and depending on, the giver for survival.

Hence the Christian establishment condemned and condemns Christians to unavoidable inescapable consequences, to sufferings and severe hardships according to the extent to which they follow Paul's ideology, in accordance with the Social Cause-and-Effect Relationship. Which the prophets knew and understood, which we now know and understand.

> From 'Social Policies (Doctrine) of the Roman
> Catholic Church: An Evaluation' (2005) {1}*

Family

The often quoted phrase '..., *and he shall rule over you.*' from Genesis, is quite mistakenly assumed to lay down male dominance over the female. Genesis Chapter 3 describes the evolution of early human beings, the role of the family in bringing up their children, and the respective roles of husband and wife within the family. What is described is the so-necessary division of work and teamwork between them, between husband and wife, between equals.

> From 'Social Concept (Policies) of the Russian
> Orthodox Church: Letter to the Russians' (2004) {6}*

Each member of the family gets strength from the others. Two heads are better than one, and work divided between two people in such a way that each can become expert in his or her own area is done much better than one person trying to do it all. The family gives people enormous emotional and economic strength to overcome life's problems. Husband and wife battle on together back-to-back and they do so successfully regardless of how tough the struggle may be. You cannot win all the battles but what cements the relationship is not just battles won but battles fought together. The depth of such a relationship between husband and wife and the wealth of strength it gives regardless of the opposition, this you know as well as I do. The children follow the example of their parents, gain the same strength and pass it on. It all depends on deep and secure emotional involvement between two people, between husband and wife.

> From 'Family, Community, Sex and the Individual'
> (1998) {7}*

The relationship between the two spouses is a functional relationship and functional relationships are often misunderstood and misrepresented.

The spouses share out between themselves what needs to be done, each specialising, concentrating on, areas of work in accordance with their abilities, knowledge, understanding, (and the) likes and dislikes of each.

Equal as people, each takes the decisions falling within their own area of competence and responsibility. ... But each discusses matters with the other family members before deciding from the point of view of what is best for the family as a whole. ...

Such a functional division of work and responsibilities, of co-operation and teamwork between experts, enables us to survive and do well in the dangerous environment in which we find ourselves.

> From 'Family, Community, Sex and the Individual'
> (1998) {7}*

All this was clear (way back) in the seventies:

> In all countries where sex education has been introduced the same corruptive pattern of social change has been observed {Louise W. Eickoff, Consultant Psychiatrist}: sexual experimentation starts and promiscuity increases. Promiscuity leads to increasing sexual dissatisfaction, to the weakening of family life and marriage bonds and to sexual excesses. The substitute satisfactions of smoking, drinking, and drug-taking increase and there is a lowering of the age of those involved. There is an upsurge in wanton destructive aggression in the community and a rise in aggressive juvenile delinquency. There is increasing concern over the harm done on young children by the practices and by the lack of concern and commitment of their parents, and concern has already been expressed over increasing male impotence. These effects are now obvious to any intelligent reader of the informed press.
>
> ... Increasing divorce rates, the resultant delinquency of children, the casual and inhuman ways some parents treat each other and their children, are almost the direct outcome of pre-marital and adulterous, that is promiscuous, sexual relations.

Destructive aggression, viciousness and brutality of people towards each other, disregard of the value of the individual and of life itself, are not normal behaviour. People who behave in such ways become isolated and divided against each other.

> From 'Family, Community, Sex and the Individual'
> (1998) {7}*

Truth

Consider two media reports of a current event. Each reports the same event, each apparently telling the truth, each report giving its viewers different impressions of what actually happened.

How come? Can there be more than one truth?

Such reports may tell only part of what happened, may report only what seems relevant to the reporter, may then be selecting what seems to support the particular viewpoint of those who prepared the report.

Compare these 'truths' with that demanded from a witness in a court of law: 'The truth, the whole truth and nothing but the truth.'

Which means that what is required in a court of law is the truth with nothing taken away and nothing added.

If we agree on this as a definition, then the word 'truth' has become more meaningful.

From 'Using Words to Communicate Effectively' (1998) {8}*

Planetary Danger

Following the flood, Genesis states (Gen 8: 22) that
'While the earth remains, seedtime and harvest, and cold and heat, and summer and winter, and day and night shall not cease.'

To me it seems that the list seedtime and harvest, and cold and heat, and summer and winter, and day and night, refers to essential environmental characteristics on which depends the continuation of human life on the planet. A warning to humanity.

From 'Social Policies (Doctrine) of the Roman Catholic Church: An Evaluation' (2005) {1}*

Again, following the flood, Genesis (Gen 9: 9) records God saying
'As for Me, behold, I establish My covenant with you, and with your seed after you;

A covenant is an agreement in which each of the parties undertakes duties and obligations towards the other. It is not a one-sided promise or obligation.

And so God is saying:

'As for Me, behold':

meaning 'On my part (as long as you do your part, as long as you behave like human beings), I ...'

Genesis from then on defines evil more closely and describes and lays down what humane behaviour is and how it can be achieved, stressing justice and retribution. Genesis describes what constitutes humane, good, behaviour, how to resist, counter, overcome beastly temptations, to compare good with evil so as to choose good. And Genesis makes the point that if human beings wish to survive and prosper they need to follow the rules of behaviour laid down by God.

I warned a long time ago that if we did not observe and put into effect the social laws (rules) and social system of the Pentateuch and its code of behaviour, then the planet would become uninhabitable for human beings. This danger has since become common knowledge, people have become aware of the risks.

From 'Social Policies (Doctrine) of the Roman
Catholic Church: An Evaluation' (2005) {1}*

Roman Catholic Church

Here I find myself in the position of the medical specialist who is talking to a very good friend and notices certain symptoms. Unless treated the disease is fatal. So what can one do? I can ask him how he feels, and he says he feels well. I suggest he goes and sees a doctor and as he is feeling well that could be the end of a beautiful friendship. But I know and he doesn't know that he can be cured but only if he takes action fairly quickly. In the end all that I can do is to tell him something about my qualifications, describe one or two of the symptoms in a mild sort of way and suggest that investigation is required. What he does after that is up to him.

And now the Catholic Church has a conscious choice to make, has to decide. It can continue to follow Paul (Romans 13: 1-10, as a whole or in part) and so continue to condemn its catholic believers to the unavoidable consequences, suffering, hardships and evil which followed in the past. Or it can begin to understand, follow and teach the God-given social laws and social system of the Pentateuch including the laws of Good Government (Kingship).

It is only when people struggle for a better life, struggle for the God-given social laws and social system to be applied and followed, that a better quality of life can be achieved on this planet for all human beings, instead of just for a few at the expense of poverty and deprivation for many.

From 'Social Policies (Doctrine) of the Roman
Catholic Church: An Evaluation' (2005) {1}*

So it appears that the teachings of the religious hierarchy condemn their Christian believers to sufferings and hardships while the hierarchy seems to tell the believers to blame themselves and not the religious hierarchy!

To me it seems unreasonable for the Church to guide its believers into following the word of man (Paul) instead of following the word of God, apparently telling believers to blame themselves for the inevitable harsh and bitter consequences of following the Church's teachings, of following the words of Paul instead of following the teachings of Jesus.

From 'Social Policies (Doctrine) of the Roman
Catholic Church: An Evaluation' (2005) {1}*

Sources:

{1}* See chapter 7.4:
      'Social Policies (Doctrine) of the Roman Catholic
      Church: An Evaluation'
      Manfred Davidmann

{2}* See chapter 3:
      'Origin of Christianity and Judaism:
      What Actually Happened,
      What Jesus Actually Taught and Later Changes'
      Manfred Davidmann

{3}* See chapter 4:
      'The God-given Human Rights, Social Laws and
      Social System'
      Manfred Davidmann

{4}* See chapter 2:
      'Liberation Theology: Basis – Past – Present – Future'
      Manfred Davidmann

{5}*   In 'God and People:
      The Social Laws and Social System Underlying
      Judaism, Christianity, Islam and Democracy'
      Manfred Davidmann
      ISBN 978-0-85192-054-2
      see chapter 6.1: 'The Meaning of Genesis:
      Creation, Evolution and the Origin of Evil'

{6}*   See chapter 7.3:
      'Social Concept (Policies) of the Russian
      Orthodox Church: Letter to the Russians'
      Manfred Davidmann

{7}*   See chapter 5:
      'Family, Community, Sex and the Individual'
      Manfred Davidmann

{8}*   See chapter 6:
      'Using Words to Communicate Effectively'
      Manfred Davidmann

Additions by the Editor:

In the original text of this chapter on the https://www.solhaam.org website Manfred Davidmann referred to other reports in form of links.

Here these reports are marked { }* and the sources are stated.

The Social Laws and Social System of the Pentateuch:
(Ha Mim) The Word of Allah as Taught by Mohammed

The right to the land in which one lives, that is the strength and success of a people, depends on how people behave towards each other. The Pentateuch <1> states which kind of behaviour gives strength, which provides a good life of high quality, which ensures independence and freedom from oppression and exploitation.

These behaviour guidelines apply to all.

In the language of religion, the land does not belong to anyone other than God. Those who live in it may use, and benefit from, the land but only as long as they follow God's laws. If they do not, then in due course the land is repossessed and transferred to someone else. Ignorance is no excuse. Those who stop following the law lose their entitlement to use it and are in due course driven out and persecuted.

In everyday language and in the language of science we know that people are affected and changed by their own behaviour and that communities stand or fall according to their actions, as a result of the behaviour of the community as a whole. Oppress and exploit and your community will get weaker and weaker and fail in the end. Follow a pattern of social behaviour and establish a social system which are based on social fairness and justice and you will gain strength and prosper and this will continue while you are doing so. People have to be told about the relevance of the social laws under present conditions.

(Ha Mim) The Word of Allah as Taught by Mohammed

Mohammed's social teachings are here stated from Koran chapters (suras) singled out by 'Abbreviated Letters', statements of revelation from compassionate and caring Allah.

The quotations from the Koran are within their context. Those recording the word of Allah as taught by Mohammed are drawn from all the suras (chapters) beginning with the abbreviated letters 'ha mim' (suras 40-41, 43-46), but not from the one sura (sura 42) which begins with the abbreviated letters 'ha mim: ain sin qaf'.

Umm al-Kitab - The Mother of the Book (Its Source)

Mohammed teaches that God's benevolent social laws and system have to be applied by people in their daily life, that those who in the past erred from God's way are in grave error.

The content of the corresponding compassionate and benevolent teachings are described as are the Koran's stated rewards for following them and the consequences of ignoring or opposing them. (See 'Prophet Mohammed's Word of Allah and the Voice of the Ruling Elite' {1}*)

The quotations from the Koran which follow speak for themselves.

The book (al-kitab, the Pentateuch) came down (tanzil) from God, the mighty, the wise-one.
> The arabic phrase for the Holy Koran is 'al-Koran'. The Pentateuch (the Five Books of Moses) is 'al-kitab', a religious book is 'mushaf'.
> <2>
{40:002, 45:002, 46:002}

We gave Moses guidance (al-huda)
> huda: guidance or guide.
and gave the book (al-kitab, the Pentateuch) to the Children of Israel to inherit.
A guide (huda) and a reminder (warning) to people who understand.
> To those who understand its commandments (message), it is a guide (about what is 'good', about what to do) and a warning (about what is evil, about what not to do).
{40:053-54}

In the name of God, the Compassionate, the Merciful,
by the book (al-kitab, the Pentateuch) that explains clearly,
We made it an arabic teaching (qur'an, koran) so that you become wiser.

The word 'koran' (Arabic: qur'an) came from the Syro-Aramaic
'qeryan' (current at the time of Mohammed) meaning teachings or
lectures.
It (the teaching) is from the mother text which we have,
    'umm al-kitab': the Pentateuch referred to as mother text, as
    source text.
sublime and full of wisdom.
{43:001-4}

Before (the teaching) the Book of Moses (kitab Musa)
was a standard for judging (imam) and a (source of) compassion
and this book (kitab) is confirmed in the Arabic language
to warn those who are unjust (wrongdoers) and to give good news to the
righteous.
{46:012}

We made this easy (to understand) in your own language
so that they may take heed.
    Take heed: to pay (or take) careful attention; In modern Arabic:
    'to remember'.
{44:058}

And now We have set you on the right way of our commandment (sharia
amr),
so follow it, and do not follow the desires of ignorant people (those who
do not have that knowledge)
for they cannot shield you from God.
{45:018}

The wrongdoers (zalamin) are supporters (awliya) of each others (help
and support, protect, each other);
    Zalamin (wrongdoers): Those who transgress, wrong other people,
    treat others badly, are unjust, are unfair, oppress, exploit.
but the protector (wali) of those who guard against evil (resist
temptation) is God.
{45:019}

Guide and Warning: Be Guided (do well and prosper) or
Ignore (fail, want and suffer)

Here Mohammed reveals the word of almighty God, stating the
Pentateuch's Cause-and-Effect Relationship in religious terms so that his
listeners can understand and be guided, can follow and prosper, are
warned about the dire consequences of not following what he is
teaching.

What happens to an individual and a community depends on present and past behaviour and not just on good intentions. The wrongdoer (unbeliever) does not understand he is drawing serious consequences (punishment) upon himself as the inevitable inescapable consequence of his own behaviour. If people reject or oppose God, if God's laws are not followed, God withdraws his protection from them. Misfortune (evil) strikes until they change their ways and return to God, that is, until they apply God's social laws and social system in their daily lives.

One has to talk to people in language they can understand and here we see how, at God's request, Mohammed revealed the Social Cause-and-Effect Relationship, referring to it in religious terms both as guide and warning.

Say (to them): "I am only a mortal like you;
It has come to me (yuhi) that there is only one God.
So take the right way to Him, and ask His forgiveness."
     Literal: So 'you go in the right way' and ... (istakimu)
And woe to those who serve associates (mushrekin) beside Him;
     Mushrekin (associates): Guides, masters, overlords or supreme
     beings with whom a person associates (to which a person
     attributes) a god-like knowledge or authority. That which or those
     whom you consider to be like God, that or those whose orders you
     obey as if they came from God.
{41:006}

(To) those who reject the warning when it is preached to them:
It is an unassailable scripture (kitab aziz).
Falsehood cannot come from it or from that which follows it,
sent down (tanzil) from one full of wisdom, worthy of praise.
{41:041-42}

Nothing is said to you that has not been said to the other messengers before you.
Your Lord is forgiving, but also punishes severely.
Say: To those who believe, it is guidance and healing;
But those who do not believe are deaf and blind.
They are like men called to from a far-off place.
{41:043-44}

He that does what is right does it for his own good;
and he that commits evil does so at his own peril.
Your Lord is never unjust to human beings (abid).
{41:046}

When We bestow favours on a human being,
and he then turns aside and withdraws himself,
evil befalls him (till) his prayer is broad.

> 'Till his prayer is broad': Till he returns to the right way by following God's commandments. Till he prays (follows God's way) on a wide front.

{41:051}

> A clear statement of the Pentateuch's 'Social Cause-and-Effect Relationship'. See description at beginning of this section.

> And continuing the statement of the 'Social Cause-and-Effect Relationship', showing how it operates, as described at the beginning of this section.

Those who say, God is our Master, and then continue on the right way,
shall have no fear nor shall they grieve.

> The right way is to live by following God's commandments (ayaat, directives, divine rules) in everyday life.

{46:013}

But those who dispute God's directives (ayaat) do not have (God's) authority to do so.
They are driven by
the ambition to become great

> To achieve power over, to dominate, to control, others; to become powerful

which they will never achieve.
Therefore seek refuge in God; God hears all and observes all.

> Literal: seek protection (from or in) God.

{40:056}

Those that reject Our directives (ayaat) when they know little of them
shall have humiliating sorrow.
{45:009}

Behind them is hell,

> Hell follows them, they cannot escape.

They will not profit from their labours (earnings),

> Literal: What they earned will not make them richer.

nor will those whom they have chosen to protect them (awliya) beside Allah.

> awliya: rulers, masters, protectors in authority

Grievous sorrow awaits them.
{45:010}

Sources

{1}* In 'Islam: Basis – Past – Present – Future'
      Manfred Davidmann
      ISBN 978-0-85192-053-5
      see chapter 7: 'Prophet Mohammed's Word of
      Allah and the Voice of the Ruling Elite'
from which this theme's information was extracted.

Also see
      In 'Judaism: Basis - Past - Present - Future, Part 1'
      Manfred Davidmann
      ISBN 978-0-85192-060-3
      see chapter 5: 'The Right to the Land of Israel'*

and in this book:
      see chapter 4:
      'The God-given Human Rights, Social Laws and
      Social System'*
      Manfred Davidmann

and
      see chapter 7.1:
      'Church and State, Government and Religion:
      Judaism, Christianity and Islam'*
      Manfred Davidmann

Notes <..>

<1> The Pentateuch, that is the five books of Moses
    (Also called Torah; Part of Old Testament).

<2> In 'Islam: Basis – Past – Present – Future'
    Manfred Davidmann
    ISBN 978-0-85192-053-5
    see chapter 5: 'Compiling the Koran:
    Hadiths (Traditions) State the Underlying Reality'*
    see particularly 'Hadith 2: How Caliph Uthman
    Ordered the Compilation of an Official Koran Text'
    which clearly shows the meaning of these terms.
    And see the other relevant Koranic verses below
    in this report.

Additions by the Editor:

In the original text of this chapter on the https://www.solhaam.org website Manfred Davidmann referred to other reports in form of links.

Here these reports are marked * and the sources are stated.

Chapter 15

Israel and The Social Laws and Social System of the Pentateuch

The right to the land in which one lives, that is the strength and success of a people, depends on how people behave towards each other. The Pentateuch <1> states which kind of behaviour gives strength, which provides a good life of high quality, which ensures independence and freedom from oppression and exploitation.

These behavioural guidelines apply to all, and Jewish history proves the matter.

Israel

To the Jewish people, Israel is the promised land, the land which was promised to Jews by God and that it is thus their land.

It is perhaps because this property, this land in which milk and honey flows, has been singled out in such a special way by God, that so many try to benefit from the good life surely granted to all its inhabitants, that so many have struggled and are struggling to own and control this most desirable of all properties.

Persians, Babylonians, Seleucids and Egyptians all had a go as did Macedonians, Romans, Ottomans and Arabs. Christianity and Islam struggled to possess it for many years. Last but not least the Hebrews, the Jews of today, twice gained the country God had promised them only to be driven out later. Returning each time, they have now returned once again and re-established for the third time their rule over the country.

One can understand that such a wonderful gift from God should be in such demand - but how come the land changed hands so frequently, how come the bailiffs came so often and so regularly?

Perhaps it is simplistic to consider that God would enter into a one-sided and unconditional commitment, saying "There it is. It is yours to do with as you please" and then turn his back on subsequent proceedings.

There is the matter of the 'Covenant'. It is this which makes Jews the 'chosen' people. At Mount Sinai, Jews in effect agreed the Covenant, that contract between God and the Jewish people by which Jews agreed to accept and observe the Pentateuch's rules of behaviour and to be held accountable for the extent to which they did so. If they observed these rules of behaviour, then they and their descendants would live secure lives of high quality in the promised land.

So Jews are entitled to stay and use the land but only to the extent to which the Pentateuch's rules of behaviour are followed and observed. The bailiffs have come in so often in the past to expel the land's occupants because these did not observe these essential rules of behavior.

In the language of religion, the land of Israel does not belong to anyone other than God. Those who live in it may use and benefit from the land but only as long as they follow God's laws. If they do not, then in due course the land is repossessed and transferred to someone else. Ignorance is no excuse. Those who stop following the law lose their entitlement to use it and are in due course driven out and persecuted. (See 'The Right to the Land of Israel' {1}*)

The Social Laws and Social System of the Pentateuch

The contract document, namely the Pentateuch, was written down at the time, has not been changed, is public knowledge.

It lays down in precise terms a comprehensive social system and rules of behaviour which form the basis of, and ensure, a quality of life and a standard of living which have still not been achieved. It also states clearly the rewards for observing and the dire consequences of ignoring or breaking its rules of behaviour.

We are told that the consequences of one's behaviour are inevitable since they are determined by a scientific and inescapable Cause-and-Effect Relationship (See 'The Right to the Land of Israel' {1}*). Hence the right to the land of Israel and the future prosperity of its inhabitants depend on following the social laws and the social system of the Pentateuch. Ignorance is no excuse. What is outstandingly important is that the Cause-and-Effect Relationship applies to all people and at all times, and history clearly and convincingly illustrates the working of the relationship.

The Pentateuch teaches that all are equal and that one may neither exploit nor be exploited, and sets out a social system for ensuring that these laws are applied, for ensuring that rulers and establishments serve their people.

The social system guarantees everyone's personal and material independence with the community supporting those who are in need, supporting those whose independence is threatened or those who wish to establish their own material independence, say by setting up their own enterprise.

The role of the establishment (your leadership, rulers, managers, bureaucracy) is to lead you in the struggle for a better and more secure life of better quality, struggling by your side and for you, living as you do and at your standard of living.

The laws of government in the Pentateuch in effect lay down that it is the establishment which should serve the people and not the other way about.

The establishment may not enrich themselves, may not form enforcing organisations or systems, may not have a better quality of life than that of the community.

However, it is much easier to tell the rich to share their wealth than actually convince them to do so. But history has proved beyond doubt that the consequences of one's behaviour are as stated. The reason some of our lives resemble hell rather than heaven is because we have been unable to ensure that all are equal, because we have allowed some of us to oppress and exploit the others.

In everyday language and in the language of science we know that people are affected and changed by their own behaviour and that communities stand or fall according to their actions, as a result of the behaviour of the community as a whole. Oppress and exploit and your community will get weaker and weaker and fail in the end. Follow a pattern of social behaviour and establish a social system which are based on social fairness and justice and you will gain strength and prosper and this will continue while you are doing so. The people have to be told about the relevance of the social laws and under present conditions.

Sources

{1}*   In 'Judaism: Basis – Past – Present – Future, Part 1'
        Manfred Davidmann
        ISBN 978-0-85192-060-3
        see chapter 5: 'The Right to the Land of Israel'
from which this theme's information was extracted.

Also in this book:
        see chapter 4:
        'The God-given Human Rights, Social Laws and
        Social System'*
        Manfred Davidmann
and
        see chapter 7.1:
        'Church and State, Government and Religion:
        Judaism, Christianity and Islam'*
        Manfred Davidmann

Notes <..>

> <1> The Pentateuch, that is the five books of Moses
> (Also called Torah; Part of Old Testament).

Additions by the Editor:

In the original text of this chapter on the https://www.solhaam.org website Manfred Davidmann referred to other reports in form of links.

Here these reports are marked * and the sources are stated.

Chapter 16

About the Author

Manfred Davidmann is an internationally well-known and respected scientist and consultant, and author of a number of books and reports which have had considerable impact. His work usually breaks new ground and opens up new understanding and is written in meaningful and easily understood language. Outstanding is that his work is generally accepted as factual, objective and unbiased.

His works have made known and publicised the human rights, the social laws and social system, and the intense worldwide struggle to achieve them, to achieve freedom, liberty, independence and a good and secure life, here and now in this life.

Here some of his works are described under the following headings

> General Management (Middle, Senior and Top Level)
>
> Community Conflicts and Confrontations
>
> The Worldwide Struggle for a Better Life
>
> Brain, Mind and Group Minds. Mental Health and Corresponding Social Organisations, of Individuals, People and Communities
>
> Government and Religion, Church and State
>
> Cooperatives and Cooperation

General Management (Middle, Senior and Top Level)

As said already, Manfred Davidmann is an internationally well-known and respected scientist and consultant, and author of a number of books and reports which have had considerable impact. His work usually breaks new ground and opens up new understanding and is written in meaningful and easily understood language. Outstanding is that his work is generally accepted as factual, objective and unbiased.

He brings to his tasks a rare combination of practical experience, knowledge and understanding backed by years spent training middle and top-level managers. Expert knowledge is expressed in clear and meaningful language.

What Manfred Davidmann has done in his work on the general management of enterprises and communities is to lay the foundation for, and develop, 'management science'. He developed and defined the scope and content of General Management, in these reports:

Directing and Managing Change

Organising

Motivation

Style of Management and Leadership

Role of Managers under Different Styles of Management

Work and Pay, Incomes and Differentials: Employer, Employee and Community

Using Words to Communicate Effectively

'Directing and Managing Change' (1979, 2006) {1}**
includes
adapting to change, deciding what needs to be done;
planning ahead, getting results, evaluating progress
and performance;
and appraisal interviews and target-setting meetings.

'Using Words to Communicate Effectively' (1998, 2006) (see chapter 6)*
shows how to communicate more effectively, covering aspects of thinking, writing, speaking and listening as well as formal and informal communications. Consists of guidelines found useful by practising middle and senior managers and by university students.

'Organising' (1981, 2006) {1}**
is a comprehensive review showing how to arrange matters so that people can work together successfully and well. It is about achieving effective co-operation and teamwork, particularly in large organisations where many experts have to work together in teams to enable aims and objectives to be achieved.

The most confused and intractable organisational problems tend to be about functional relationships and coordinating. Concerning these, the report's descriptions, definitions, specifications and examples, are outstanding.

'Motivation Summary' (1982, 1998) {4}**
In **'Motivation Summary'**, Manfred Davidmann summarises different motivation theories, draws on his earlier work including evidence from his U.K. study, and utilises material used by him for lecturing to degree-level students and for training experienced middle and senior managers.

'Style of Management and Leadership' (1981, 2006) {1}**
Manfred Davidmann's work **'Style of Management and Leadership'** is a landmark in management and community science and methodology. Over 770,000 copies have been downloaded from his website, worldwide, so far (April 2011).

'Role of Managers under Different Styles of Management' (1982, 1998)
{1}**

is a short summary of the role of managers under authoritarian and participative styles of management. It also covers decision making and the basic characteristics of each style.

The term 'Participation', meaning by this 'participation in decision-making', was first coined, and defined, by Manfred Davidmann when he published his analysis and recommendations about the style of management, in 1981. His works on style of management and on participation in decision-making in management, leadership and government, are widely known, studied and applied, and sprouted a whole literature ranging from the scientific to misleading politically-motivated misrepresentations.

It was Manfred Davidmann who in 1981 formulated, clearly stated and then published ('Style of Management and Leadership', 1981) his principle that the real political struggle was not between political 'left' and 'right', but was for participation in decision-making, for the right to make the decisions.

Manfred Davidmann's concept of participative government and management, of participation in decision-making, has become a household word, in daily use when referring to government and management styles, worldwide. His concepts are applied all the way from village government and community projects to national policies and elections, are applied by cooperatives, companies and global corporations alike.

Clearly defined and described in 'Style of Management and Leadership' is the whole scale of style of management and organising, from fully authoritarian to fully participative. It applies to community organisations, commercial enterprises, political parties, whole countries. The social assumptions underlying each of the styles are given, as are problems they create, the symptoms by which they can be recognised, and the ways people work together or against each other within them.

The extent to which authority is balanced between top and bottom, and the corresponding style of management, are also discussed. This work pulls the diverse world-wide events in labour relations and in government/people confrontation into a meaningful, clear and highly significant picture of interrelated events fitting into a consistent pattern.

Community Conflicts and Confrontations

How local and national governments are managing our affairs is of crucial importance to every citizen. Government has to make ends meet, has to bring about a rising standard of secure living, social security and an increasing quality of life for its citizens.

"There can be ups and downs but", says Manfred Davidmann, "failure to make ends meet is just as directly and surely the result of bad leadership and management as it is in any commercial enterprise." This is a severe criticism also of the kind of experts and consultants used, and of the way they are used. "The quality of one's experts and whether and how their expertise is used, and applied, are of decisive importance."

Manfred Davidmann's report 'Work and Pay, Incomes and Differentials: Employer, Employee and Community' (1981, 2007) {2}** is a concise all-embracing review and analysis of the whole subject, in clear and easily understood language. What makes this report so special is that it covers incomes and differentials from the point of view of the owner or employer, from that of the individual and his family and from that of the community, discussing their interests and requirements.

When talking about pay, incomes and differentials we are dealing with matters which are at the centre of confrontation and conflict and around which rage controversy and strife. We are dealing with matters which determine how one man stands in relation to another, with something which depends on negotiation and bargaining between those who employ and those who are employed. The result is that almost all one sees about pay and differentials is biased towards one side or the other and both points of view are then equally misleading.

But Manfred Davidmann here provides the underlying knowledge and understanding for scientific determination and prediction of rates of pay, remuneration and differentials, of remuneration scales and of national patterns of pay and differentials.

These correlations and methods represent a major breakthrough and rates of pay, incomes and differentials can be assessed with a high degree of reliability. Now pay bargaining can include agreeing basic guide-lines of the kind described here as governing pay increases.

Illustrated are National Remuneration Scales which record the remuneration pattern for a group or profession and the position of every individual in it, showing also how income depends on age and degree of success. Illustrated also is the National Remuneration Pattern which is a precise pictorial record of the differentials within a country, from top to bottom, from young to old. Both are used to assess changes in pay, remuneration and differentials for individuals, groups and professions.

However, it is easier to tell the rich to share their wealth with the poor than to persuade them to actually do so. And companies, corporations and governments, owners, managers, experts and politicians, too often work for personal gain instead of serving employees, customers or citizens, exploiting instead of serving their community.

Just consider the following examples of corporate and individual antisocial practices.

One of the most controversial operations of multinationals, transfer pricing, has been clearly described and defined by Manfred Davidmann in his report 'Multinational Operations: Transfer Pricing and Taxation' (1991, 2006) {3}**.

The report showed that multinational companies were minimising their liability for corporation tax by transfer pricing, that is by making book entries which transfer profits to the country with the lowest corporation tax.

Say a multinational has increased its profits in such ways. As the government's expenses have not changed it must make up this shortfall elsewhere. From its other tax payers, say from its citizens. So its citizens pay more tax, the government can now spend the same amount as before, the multinational's profits have increased.

This tax avoidance is legal and governments have not legislated to prevent this practice.

The multinational, and this means the owners and directors of the multinational, are thus in effect taxing the country's citizens, its population, in this way increasing the multinational's profits and thus their own incomes and wealth.

A matter far removed from earning reasonable profits from providing needed quality goods and services at reasonable prices in open competition with other corporations.

Fifteen years ago, Manfred Davidmann coined the phrase 'Exporting Employment and Importing Unemployment', and pointed to, and warned about, the social and economic consequences of what is now often euphemistically called 'outsourcing' or 'globalisation'.

In his report 'Exporting and Importing of Employment and Unemployment' (1996, 2002) {3}** he pointed out that imports were being priced at what the market will bear, or just under, and that if the enormous profit margins were left uncontrolled, these would then cause production to move from high-wage to low-wage countries. The consequence is a lowering of the standard of living in high-wage countries to that in low-wage countries, instead of a raising of the standard of living in low-wage countries to that in high wage countries.

"Unemployment has reached an unacceptable level" says Manfred Davidmann. It is a principle of economics that social costs have to be paid by those causing them. But manufacturers and suppliers tend to increase their profits by passing on to the community the social costs of their operations, costs such as disposal of packaging and waste, or of polluting.

"The social costs of unemployment have to be paid by the enterprise which caused the unemployment in the first place" says Manfred Davidmann. "Social costs need to be allowed for when making decisions, need to be charged to the enterprise or organisation which is causing them. And this applies equally well to the social costs of redundancy and unemployment when transferring operations to countries with lower wages or fewer environmental safeguards."

It was Manfred Davidmann who twenty years ago demolished the then-current economic myths about 'Price Inflation' and 'Wage Inflation', and about inflation and unemployment.

In **'Inflation, Balance of Payments and Currency Exchange Rates'** (1981, 2006) {1}**, Manfred Davidmann explores how national and international accounts and accounting reflect the quality of management in national and local government, reflect multinational operations such as devaluation pricing, profits maximisation, transfer pricing, importing from low-wage countries, transferring work to low-wage countries. And he reviews different ways of balancing income and expenditure, causes of inflation, and tax avoidance.

In this report Manfred Davidmann reviews a country's ways out of a payments crisis and details the consequences of increasing interest rates, greater borrowing, selling assets or printing more money.

To give just a few examples, he:

> Shows how rising interest rates follow from balance of payments deficits.

> Shows how interest rates determine share prices and thus the extent to which pension funds are in surplus or underfunded.

> Shows how inflation affects currency exchange rates, trade and competing abroad.

Clear and meaningful language is backed by easily understood illustrations. And easy-to-follow diagrams illustrate the relationships.

The two coefficients of inequality between different countries, which Manfred Davidmann put forward in 1981 in this inflation report, are objective and effective measures of inequality and differentials.

The first he called 'Inequality between Countries'. The second, namely 'Relative Inequality between Countries', is numerically the same as the ratio between the GNP/person of the countries being compared. These measures of inequality are now in general use.

The Worldwide Struggle for a Better Life

In 'Motivation Summary' (1982, 1998) {4}**, Manfred Davidmann summarises different motivation theories, draws on his earlier work including evidence from the U.K. study, and utilises material used by him for lecturing to degree-level students and for training experienced middle and senior managers.

This chapter provides an objective, comprehensive and clear definition of 'motivation', of the factors which motivate and of what people are striving to achieve.

"Motivated behaviour is purposeful, directed towards some end" says Manfred Davidmann. "The driving force is need. The direction is towards perceived reward and away from perceived punishment."

And in the workplace one aims to achieve either job satisfaction or money rewards or both. "Motivation towards better performance depends on the satisfaction of needs for responsibility, achievement, recognition and growth."

One works to achieve that which one needs and which one does not have. "Attaining goals leads to feelings of self-respect, strength and confidence", and "persistent lack of rewards leads to a view of society as being hostile and unrewarding".

Manfred Davidmann's fundamental work on motivation, 'The Will to Work: What People Struggle to Achieve' (1981, 2006) {4}**, includes a detailed step-by-step listing of what people are struggling to achieve, their needs and wants, their achievements and objectives. It is a unique analysis of the worldwide struggle for a better life at all levels of life and development, in all countries.

What we see in the working environment is each person, family or community struggling to advance at their own level of development.

Manfred Davidmann here clearly defines and describes motivation, its basis and 'motivating'.

Starting by considering motivation from the point of view of the employer (productivity, remuneration, job satisfaction), this leads to considering what people want and what they struggle to achieve.

A key part of this chapter is community orientated, including a detailed step-by-step listing of what people are struggling to achieve, their needs and wants, their achievements and objectives.

It is a unique analysis of the worldwide struggle for a better life at all levels of life and development, in all countries. What we see in the working environment is each person, family or community struggling to advance at their own level of development.

This progression shows underdeveloped and developed people as they are, human beings at different stages of an identical struggle for a better life against those who wish to profit from their condition.

And you can assess how far the country/community you are living in has advanced in this struggle for independence and a good life for all, or where you are yourself on this scale.

Highlights are Figure 1 (Motivation of Directors) and Figure 3 (People's Needs and Wants, Achievements and Objectives: The Struggle for Independence and a Good Life).

In '**Family, Community, Sex and the Individual'** (1998, 2011) (see chapter 5)*, Manfred Davidmann exposes the causes of what seems to be a progressive breaking down of family life and of social strength.

Clearly described and defined is the role of the family under modern conditions, and the differences between the behaviour of human beings and that of the primitive animals from which human beings evolved. He illustrated the underlying basis of teamwork within the family, stating the various roles and responsibilities and functional relationships of its members for effective teamwork within the family.

He was the first to clearly describe and show, thirteen years ago, the effects of increasing life spans on the family, on its members and on their responsibilities.

We now live much longer and the time spent full-time at home looking after the family places women at a disadvantage when returning to work outside the family after the children have been brought up. So women need to be supported when returning to work.

And Manfred Davidmann showed that the family compensates women for the life-long effects of their contribution towards the upbringing of the children. It is the role of the spouse, of the husband, to continue to provide for the family. A life-long contribution from him which means she does not lose out for the rest of her life because she stayed at home to look after the children, the husband's input into the family balancing her input of bringing up the children and looking after the family's members.

This work also investigates the impact of casual sexual relations and its effects on individuals, family and community, on the social strength of individuals and communities.

And it examines and relates dominance and confrontation within the family to that in the working environment and considers oppression and exploitation within and outside the family.

Human rights are based on controlling primitive dominating behaviour, on concern, care and affection for our young and our families, for people and for our communities. Human rights express themselves in co-operation and teamwork between men and women to achieve a good life of high quality.

It is in democracies that a high standard of living has been achieved. In democracies people can struggle openly for a better life but we see that what has been gained has to be defended and extended.

This work is an unprecedented and comprehensive overview, states new insights, proves basic underlying causes.

The main report **'What People are Struggling Against: How Society is Organised for Controlling and Exploiting People'** (1998, 2002) {3}**, brings together key conclusions from four studies undertaken by Manfred Davidmann to obtain a better understanding of why people have to struggle throughout their adult lives, in all countries and organisations, at all levels, to maintain and improve their standard of living and quality of life. We know what people are struggling to achieve and so this study was undertaken to explore why people have to struggle by looking at what they are struggling against.

This work looks at the way 'Economics' is being used to misinform and mislead the general public, and looks at the role and vested interests of experts. It describes how companies (corporations) accumulate their capital and reserves from moneys taken from customers and how people's massive savings are placed under the control of others. And shows how taxpayers' moneys are used in different ways to enlarge the profits of companies.

It discusses and illustrates the internal struggles taking place in political parties and all other organisations, for achieving greater democracy and against those wishing to overpower democratic processes of decision-making.

In 'Democracy, Socialism and Communism: The Worldwide Struggle for a Better Life' (2008) {4}** Manfred Davidmann outlined the battlefield in these terms:

Participative (democratic) organisation rests on the population electing representatives, on the basis of each person having one vote. Representatives are responsible to, and accountable to, the population for putting into effect policies decided by the population.

What underlies participative organisation (democracy) is decision-making by the people at the level of the people.

What needs to be stressed is that in a participative (democratic) organisation policies are decided by a well-informed population at the level of the population and that policies then become binding on management or government. It was Manfred Davidmann who formulated, clearly stated and then published ('Style of Management and Leadership', 1981) his principle that the real political struggle was not between political 'left' and 'right', but was for participation in decision-making, for the right to make the decisions.

Representatives, governments or government officials do not have the authority or right to reduce or sign away the participative (democratic) rights of the electors, of the population.

The real struggle is not between political left and right, but is a struggle for participation, that is for the right of the population to be well-informed and to make the decisions which then become binding on management or government, as outlined by Manfred Davidmann in 'Multinational Summits and Agreements, Top-level Decision-making and Democracy' (2002) {3}**.

Brain, Mind and Group Minds. Mental Health and Corresponding Social Organisations, of Individuals, People and Communities.

In 'How the Human Brain Developed and How the Human Mind Works' (1998, 2006) {4}**, Manfred Davidmann explains how the human brain evolved and functions, how the human mind works, and how brain and mind interact. This fundamental work provides fascinating insights clearly expressed in meaningful language, including a much clearer appreciation of the different functions of the two halves of the brain, and of the different kinds of sleep and memory.

The work showed how brain and mind determine what people do and how they do it, what people aim to achieve and how in the struggle for a better life we adapt to the world in which we live.

It proved that images penetrate deeply into the ancient and primitive parts of the human brain and how certain images can be "brutalising society, seemingly legalising, making acceptable, inconsiderate and unfeeling behaviour towards other people."

Relating the functioning of the brain to behavior, this report showed how human behavior is affected by the primitive instincts of our reptilian ancestors. It seems that instinctive behavior has to be controlled, and is modified according to the environment in which we find ourselves, in every generation, and that the mammalian and human parts of the brain play a major part in this.

Manfred Davidmann considers that humane behavior is based on feelings of care and affection for the young and for the family, and then for other people and the community. From this emerges a sense of social responsibility: People matter and are important, and need to be treated well.

A key finding of Manfred Davidmann's report is that the right hemisphere of the human brain is able to communicate by using images with the brain's older and more primitive component organs which have no verbal skills. And this enables us to communicate intentionally (that is "consciously") with our autonomic nervous system and by visualizing control of body functions and to affect our body's immune system. Clinical trials have shown remarkable success in areas such as the treatment of cancer and heart disease.

The day-night-day sleep pattern, the "DEEP sleep"/"REM sleep" sequence, and how the different halves of the brain communicate by means of images with the older parts of the brain, are correlated and illustrated. Manfred Davidmann makes the point that the brain paralyzes the body to enable dreaming to take place, that dreaming performs an essential function, and he explains the role and meaning of dreams and dreaming.

Manfred Davidmann considers that humane behavior is based on feelings of care and affection for the young and for the family, and then for other people and the community. From this emerges a sense of social responsibility: People matter and are important, and need to be treated well.

As a result of the work in this report, there emerged a much clearer appreciation of what happens during the course of a night's sleep, and clear explanations of the role of dreaming and the meaning of dreams.

The report explores the functioning and role of the two halves of the human brain and the relationship between them. It is the right half which usually communicates with the primitive parts of the human brain and this is related to the functioning of the autonomic nervous system and the immune system.

When Manfred Davidmann first announced his Group Mind Theory in 1973, this theory and his concepts and terms such as 'group minds', were completely new and unheard of. The second edition was published in 1998 and made available on the internet in 1999.

His "human group minds and how they function", that is the Group Mind Science he originated, are now widely quoted and discussed, have sprouted a whole literature about group minds ranging from publications of scientific institutions and in reference books, to unscientific misleading look-alikes about human minds.

In 'The Human Group Mind and How It Works' (1973, 1978) {4}**, Manfred Davidmann outlines, describes, uncovers and proves the subconscious existence and workings of group minds by the extraordinary way in which they affect and determine what individuals and communities do. This is shown to explain how human communities and society are organised and function, countrywide and worldwide, and consequent confrontations and struggles from dictatorship to democracy. We are here looking at what motivates and drives human beings, seeing how the mind shapes the way in which we live, suffer, struggle and achieve.

Included are comprehensive but concise reviews of mental health and mental illness. There are sections which discuss how conflict arises within the mind, and the mind theories of Freud and of Jung are reviewed.

Manfred Davidmann's Group Mind Science is proved by the way in which it explains and predicts not only the mental problems of individuals but also society's social problems.

It predicts and explains the way in which society is organised as well as human activities and organisation, explains dominance, co-operation, non-conformity and conflict as well as why people are struggling and what they are struggling against.

The subconscious existence and workings of group minds become apparent by the extraordinary way in which they affect and determine what individuals and communities do. The chapters of this book which deal with how we live and struggle, with the way our communities and societies are organised and function, describe how our minds shape our lives, communities and society, and uncover the workings of group minds.

Manfred Davidmann's Group Mind Science represents substantial beneficial healing powers. Following the work of Freud and Jung, it is regarded as scientifically proved, as meaningful, objective and practical, as applying worldwide to all human beings in all societies and cultures and at all stages of development.

Manfred Davidmann's Group Mind Science is based on deep knowledge and understanding of the real world, and proved by the way in which it explains and predicts human activities and organisation as well as the mental problems of individuals and society's social problems. Its insights enable us to solve such problems effectively.

The work about 'The Human Group Mind', on how human minds work and operate, on human group minds, consists of four consecutive parts, as follows:

'The Human Group Mind and How It Works' (1973, 1998) {4}**

The 'Group Mind' science is outlined and described. There are sections which discuss how conflict arises within the mind, mental health and illness, dominance, creativity and hearing voices.

Shows how our minds shape our lives, communities and society.

'Manipulated Communities and Populations' (1973, 1998) {4}**

The workings of group minds is shown to explain how human communities and society are organised and the consequent confrontations and struggles from dictatorship to democracy.

Discusses how mass media are forming and manipulating public opinions and illustrates how writers and artists have been sensing and expressing the underlying subconscious reality.

'Manipulated Individuals' (1973, 1998) {4}**

Shows how emotional unreasoning behaviour is being reinforced to make it easier to mislead and exploit.

Reviews available information on incidence and causes of psychosomatic illnesses.

'Freedom, Liberty and Good Life: Overcoming Corrupt Manipulations' (1973, 2001) {4}**

The Group Mind science of the way in which human minds work is proved by the way in which it explains and predicts human activities and organisation as well as mental problems of individuals and society's social problems. Its insights enable us to solve such problems effectively.

When individuals, communities and populations are manipulated, then behaviour is all-important. This report shows how we can overcome corrupt manipulations, how behaviour determines our standard of living and the quality of our lives, and describes the kind of behaviour and social organisation on which depend liberty, freedom and a good and secure life for all.

Government and Religion, Church and State

Manfred Davidmann's **'The God-given Human Rights, Social Laws and Social System'** (2003) (see chapter 4)* is a comprehensive statement of the God-given human rights and obligations which underlie freedom, liberty, independence and well-being. They underlie and determine a good life of high quality. People at all stages of development are struggling to achieve these rights and benefits, all over the planet.

Directly relevant to today's social and economic problems, these rights and obligations determine the quality of life in areas such as social and economic security, social responsibility and accountability, ownership and decision-making, government and management, humane behaviour, teamwork and trustful cooperation.

> These human rights, these social rules and this social system, are the very foundation of the three main religions of Judaism, Christianity and Islam.
>
> Manfred Davidmann discovered that what these religions have in common is that in each case a ruling elite succeeded in bypassing or overturning the religion's essential God-given benevolent social provisions and human rights, in this way exposing their communities and whole populations to oppression and exploitation.

What Manfred Davidmann has done with his works on the Pentateuch and the Bible, on religion and church-state relations, is to expose and correct the misinterpretations and mistranslations of the past. His works are major breakthroughs, constituting essential information for understanding the meaning and significance of the Pentateuch and the Bible.

The Pentateuch records and details the Social Cause-and-Effect Relationship, a fundamental scientific law which is stated as such and which was discovered by Manfred Davidmann. In his **'Struggle for Freedom: The Social Cause-and-Effect Relationship'** (1978, 2002) {5}** he shows that this law states that the consequences of keeping or not keeping the social laws are inescapable, that what happens to one is in the end the inevitable result of one's own behavior. It is stated to enable people to benefit from knowing the effects of their behaviour.

Ignorance of these rules of behavior is no excuse and the relationship applies to all. History and social science confirm it, the prophets knew and understood it and predicted accordingly. Jesus confirmed it; the Koran records Prophet Mohammed repeatedly confirming the Pentateuch, referring to it both as a guide and as a warning.

Whole communities prosper or suffer as a consequence of their collective behavior. Manfred Davidmann says, "The consequences of our behavior cannot be avoided but we can change the course of events by changing our behavior."

He states "A new factor has entered the equation. It is now possible for the first time in the history of human beings on this planet for just one or only a few socially irresponsible persons to do something or to introduce changes which could destroy us all or else make this planet uninhabitable for human beings."

The Ten Commandments are so important and are so well known because it is behaviour in accordance with these laws which is the basis for people trusting each other and so for people co-operating and working well with each other. They are listed in '**Struggle for Freedom: The Social Cause-and-Effect Relationship**' (1978, 2002) {5}** both in biblical language and in plain English.

It is the Ten Commandments as a whole which underlie freedom, independence and strength to oppose and resist oppression. Wherever there is any spiritual and material freedom today it exists because people followed these laws (rules) of behaviour and it exists to the extent to which they do so. In other words, following the provisions of the law results in freedom and ensures it, ensures strength and security.

History shows that in the past the people have been betrayed again and again, by non-observant leaderships no matter whether right or left and by so-called orthodox or fundamentalist leaderships who weakened the application of the law so as to be able to oppress the people in order to exploit them. It was those who did not follow the law who in the past grasped power and then weakened and defeated the hope for achieving freedom and a good life for the people and thus in due course for all humanity.

It is equally certain that the same battle is being fought today and it is just as certain that on the one hand is the opportunity to gain freedom while on the other hand our defeat can only result in mankind rapidly destroying itself.

To free ourselves from mental conditioning and brainwashing we have to follow the Ten Commandments and apply the social laws and the social system of the Pentateuch.

In **'Democracy, Socialism and Communism: The Worldwide Struggle for a Better Life'** (2008) {4}**, Manfred Davidmann exposes what people are struggling against, the secretive manipulations of bureaucracy, oppressors and exploiters.

He shows that underlying Judaism, Christianity and Islam are the same fundamental benevolent and egalitarian social laws and social system which also underlie Democracy, Socialism and Communism (See **'The God-given Human Rights, Social Laws and Social System'** (2003) above). He traces them to their origin and proves from contemporary written records that in each case the ruling and religious hierarchies (bureaucracies) soon bypassed or annulled the 'God-given' social laws and social system, replacing them with 'man-made', ruler- and hierarchy-serving obedience-demanding protest-silencing indoctrination.

It is these revisionist versions which are being taught and believed today and here we see clearly the causes of present controversies and conflicts between church and state, between beliefs and practice, in these religions.

This work also covers dominance and confrontation within the family and in the working environment, how men and women relate to each other, and the role of the family. The family is decisive in determining the quality of life; it is a source of strength and support in a time of need.

It shows how the media are being used for 'social engineering', a kind of brainwashing aimed at turning the struggle of the working population into 'self-defeating' directions, into 'scoring own goals'.

Manfred Davidmann's groundbreaking discoveries about Judaism, Christianity and Islam, published over twenty-five years, are acknowledged as major advances. And in his report **'Judaism, Christianity and Islam'** (2004) (see chapter 7.1)*, we see for the first time the complete sequence of consecutive events.

Manfred Davidmann has shown that underlying Judaism, Christianity and Islam are the Pentateuch's benevolent and egalitarian social laws and social system which include laws protecting the people by restraining the behaviour of their rulers. Those in positions of trust, responsibility or authority must not oppress people and the laws forbid personal gain from the misuse of wealth or position.

He not only proves the meaning and intent of Genesis, the first volume of the Pentateuch, but also exposes the mistranslations and political misrepresentations of the past. For example he established the meaning of the names of God which had been 'lost'.

Manfred Davidmann's work **'The Meaning of Genesis: Creation, Evolution and the Origin of Evil'** (2000) {6}** proves that there is no conflict or contradiction between Darwin's theory of evolution by natural selection and what is written in Genesis. Conflicts have arisen because some parts of Genesis have been mistranslated or misinterpreted.

The 'Creationism' hypothesis apparently assumes that the resulting erroneous text correctly states God's deeds. Following the publication of Manfred Davidmann's work, and of the publicity it generated, the 'Creationism' hypothesis was abandoned as untenable. But a similar hypothesis was then put forward called 'Intelligent Design' which apparently assumes that the same erroneous text could correctly state the deeds of some other supernatural being.

What Manfred Davidmann proves in **'The Meaning of Genesis: Creation, Evolution and the Origin of Evil'** (2000) {6}** is that Genesis clearly states the evolution from reptilian to mammalian instincts, feelings and behaviour and the evolution and behaviour of human beings from humanoids (animals resembling humans) through Homo erectus (early man) to Homo sapiens (human beings, ourselves).

For example, the allegory telling about Adam and Eve in the Garden of Eden describes the evolution of Homo sapiens (human beings, ourselves) from Homo erectus. Genesis records that childbirth became more difficult as a result of the increased brain size (evolution of neocortex) which enabled Homo sapiens to know the difference between good and evil and to choose between them. Also stated is the necessary division of work between the male and the female, as equals in different roles, in protecting and bringing up their children, and much more.

What Manfred Davidmann has done with his works on the Pentateuch and the Bible, on religion and church-state relations, is to expose and correct the misinterpretations and mistranslations of the past. His works are major breakthroughs, constituting essential information for understanding the meaning and significance of the Pentateuch and the Bible.

For example, in "**Meaning and Significance of the Names of God in Genesis**" (2000) {6}**, Manfred Davidmann proved the meaning and significance of the different names of God which had been lost.

In "**Meaning and Intent of Genesis: Essential Notes on Hebrew Grammar,**" (2000) {6}** he stated the fundamental rules which were ignored at time of translation because required background knowledge was not available, with consequent mistranslations.

And in "**Bible Translations, Versions, Codes and Hidden Information in Bible and Talmud**" (2001) {6}**, he showed how changes made in the past obscured the intended meaning.

In his book '**ISLAM: Basis – Past – Present – Future**', (2003, 2010) {7}** Manfred Davidmann assembles, evaluates and objectively records the events of the formative years which shaped Islam. He enables one to understand how Islam came to be and its present beliefs and practices, conflicts and confrontations.

Knowing about Prophet Mohammed's struggle for recognition of his mission and message, is of vital importance if one wishes to understand what Mohammed taught and the Koran. Just what upset the elite so thoroughly and persistently that it caused him and his followers to be harshly opposed and actively persecuted?

The events and struggles which took place after Mohammed's death, and how the Koran and Islam came to be, shaped Muslim belief and practice, formed Sunnism and Shiism, underlie today's conflicts and confrontations within Islam.

Cooperatives and Cooperation

When people are exploited and oppressed they co-operate with each other to escape from poverty, to overcome exploitation and oppression. As do people wishing to improve working conditions and the quality of their lives. They get together and form co-operatives.

Manfred Davidmann's book '**Cooperatives and Cooperation: Causes of Failure, Guidelines for Success**' (1973-2006, 2011) {8}** is based on and includes a series of eight studies of co-operatives and mutual societies which were undertaken to determine causes of failure and reasons for success, to see how these enterprises were controlled and managed, to learn from their mistakes, to understand why members of established co-ops are dissatisfied with what they are getting from their co-ops.

As a matter of principle, all profits (surplus) made by a co-operative or mutual society belongs to its members as individuals. Any profit which is retained and added to reserves is the total of amounts which in effect were deducted from the profit share of each individual member.

Manfred Davidmann showed with these case studies that, for example, co-ops and mutual societies retain much of the profits and that their members then cease to be entitled to them.

Component Case Studies

> Mutual Societies
>> Trustee Savings Bank
>> Credit Unions
>> Building Societies

> Consumer Co-ops
>> Co-operative Retail Services Ltd
>> Co-operative Wholesale Society Ltd
>> The Co-operative Bank PLC
>> Co-operative Insurance Society Ltd

> Producer (Worker) Co-ops
>> John Lewis Partnership plc
>> Mondragon Co-operatives
>> Kibbutzim (Plural of 'kibbutz')

Additions by the Editor:

* Published in this book

** Published in the following books:

{1}** 'Management and Leadership:
Local, National, Multinational (Global),
Principles and Practice'
Manfred Davidmann
ISBN 978-0-85192-057-3

{2}** 'Messianic Struggle:
The Worldwide Struggle for a Good and
Secure Life for All, Here and Now'
Manfred Davidmann
ISBN 978-0-85192-059-7

{3}** 'The Real World in Which We Live:
The Social Rules and Social System under
Which We Suffer, Struggle, Survive and Prosper'
Manfred Davidmann
ISBN 978-0-85192-058-0

{4}**   'The Human Mind and How it Works:
Group Minds in Action:
How the Human Group Mind Shapes
the Quality of Our Life and Living'
Manfred Davidmann
ISBN 978-0-85192-055-9

{5}**   'Judaism: Basis - Past - Present - Future, Part 1'
Manfred Davidmann
ISBN 978-0-85192-060-3

{6}**   'God and People:
The Social Laws and Social System Underlying
Judaism, Christianity, Islam and Democracy'
Manfred Davidmann
ISBN 978-0-85192-054-2

{7}**   'Islam: Basis – Past – Present – Future'
Manfred Davidmann
ISBN 978-0-85192-053-5

{8}**   'Cooperatives and Cooperation:
Causes of Failure, Guidelines for Success'
Manfred Davidmann
ISBN 978-0-85192-056-6

Manfred Davidmann

ISLAM: Basis - Past - Present- Future

Knowing about Prophet Mohammed's struggle for recognition of his mission and message, is of vital importance if one wishes to understand what Mohammed taught and the Koran. Just what upset the elite so thoroughly and persistently that it caused him and his followers to be harshly opposed and actively persecuted?

The events and struggles which took place after Mohammed's death, and how the Koran and Islam came to be, shaped Muslim belief and practice, formed Sunnism and Shiism, underlie today's conflicts and confrontations within Islam.

In this book Manfred Davidmann assembles, evaluates and objectively records the events of the formative years which shaped Islam. He enables one to understand how Islam came to be and its present beliefs and practices, conflicts and confrontations. Comprehensiveness of information, and depth of analysis, can be judged by the book's chapter headings:

Prophet Mohammed's Struggle for a Better Life for All

Text, Language, Dialect and Interpretation of the Koran

The Divine Right to Rule

Compiling the Koran: Hadiths (Traditions) State the Underlying Reality

Caliph Uthman's Rearrangement of the 'as revealed' Koran's Chapters

Prophet Mohammed's Word of Allah and the Voice of the Ruling Elite

Muslims and Jews

Church and State, Government and Religion

Judaism, Christianity and Islam

Religion, Government and Education

The book, and the earlier individual research reports which are included in it, contains not only Manfred Davidmann's clear and factual compilations about what actually happened after Mohammed's death, but also his comprehensive and detailed findings, definitions and conclusions about the '**Text, Language, Dialect and Interpretation of the Koran**' (2003), about how the Koran was compiled and about its contents. Published 2003, guided to some extent by some of the Koran's 'abbreviated letters'.

Manfred Davidmann

God and People:
The Social Laws and Social System Underlying Judaism, Christianity, Islam and Democracy

This book is a collection of works by Manfred Davidmann about the God-given human rights, social laws and social system, and about the worldwide struggle to achieve them, to achieve freedom, liberty, independence and a good and secure life, here and now in this life.

Manfred Davidmann not only proves the meaning and intent of Genesis, the first volume of the Pentateuch, but also exposes the mistranslations and political misrepresentations of the past. For example he establishes the meaning of the names of God which 'had been lost'.

Clearly described and defined is the role of the family under modern conditions, and the differences between the behaviour of human beings and that of the primitive animals from which human beings evolved.

The main chapter headings are:

> The Real World in which We Live
>
> The God-given Human Rights, Social Laws and Social System
>
> Struggle for Freedom, Liberty and Independence: The Social Cause-and-Effect Relationship
>
> Family and Community: Family, Sex and the Individual
>
> The Meaning of Genesis

Manfred Davidmann is an internationally well-known and respected scientist and consultant, and author of a number of books and reports which have had considerable impact. His work usually breaks new ground and opens up new understanding and is written in meaningful and easily understood language. Outstanding is that his work is generally accepted as factual, objective and unbiased.

Manfred Davidmann

THE HUMAN MIND AND HOW IT WORKS:
Group Minds in Action: How the Human Group Mind Shapes the Quality of Our Life and Living

Manfred Davidmann shows how the human brain evolved and functions, how the human mind works, and how brain and mind interact. This fundamental work provides fascinating insights clearly expressed in meaningful language, shows how brain and mind determine what people do and how they do it, what people aim to achieve and how in the struggle for a better life we adapt to the world in which we live.

The chapters of this book which deal with how our communities and societies are organised and function, describe how our group minds shape our lives, communities and society, explain the consequent confrontations and struggles from dictatorship to democracy.

Relating the functioning of the brain to behaviour, this work shows how human behavior is affected by the primitive instincts of our reptilian ancestors. There are sections which discuss how conflict arises within the mind, mental health and illness, dominance, creativity and hearing voices.

Comprehensiveness of information, and depth of analysis, can be judged by the book's chapter headings:

> The Human Brain and the Human Mind
>> How the Human Brain Developed and How the Human Mind Works
>
> The Human Group Mind
>> The Human Group Mind and How It Works
>> Manipulated Communities and Populations
>> Manipulated Individuals
>> Freedom, Liberty and Good Life: Overcoming Corrupt Manipulations
>
> What People Struggle to Achieve
>> Motivation Summary
>> What People are Struggling Against: How Society is Organised for Controlling and Exploiting People
>> The Will to Work: What People Struggle to Achieve
>
> Worldwide Struggle
>> Democracy, Socialism and Communism: The Worldwide Struggle for a Better Life

Manfred Davidmann

Cooperatives and Cooperation:
Causes of Failure, Guidelines for Success

When people are exploited and oppressed they cooperate with each other to escape from poverty, to overcome exploitation and oppression. As do people wishing to improve working conditions and the quality of their lives. They get together and form cooperatives.

Different forms of cooperatives tackle different kinds of problems. What they have in common is that they serve their members and the community, aiming to improve the quality of life for their members.

As a matter of principle, all profit (surplus) made by a cooperative or mutual society belongs to its members as individuals. Any profit which is retained and added to reserves is the total of amounts which in effect were deducted from the profit share of each individual member.

This book is based on a series of eight studies of cooperatives and mutual societies which were undertaken to determine causes of failure and reasons for success, to see how these enterprises were controlled and managed, to learn from their mistakes.

Its conclusions and recommendations are relevant and cover fundamental and practical problems of coops and mutual societies, of members, of direction, management and control.

Manfred Davidmann showed with these case studies that, for example, coops and mutual societies retain much of the profits and that their members then cease to be entitled to them.

Component Case Studies

Mutual Societies
Trustee Savings Bank
Credit Unions
Building Societies

Consumer Coops
Cooperative Retail Services Ltd
Cooperative Wholesale Society Ltd
The Cooperative Bank PLC
Cooperative Insurance Society Ltd

Producer (Worker) Coops
John Lewis Partnership plc
Mondragon Cooperatives
Kibbutzim (Plural of 'kibbutz')

Manfred Davidmann

Management and Leadership:
Local, National, Multinational (Global),
Principles and Practice

The term 'Participation', meaning by this 'participation in decision-making', was first coined, and defined, by Manfred Davidmann when he published his analysis and recommendations about the style of management. His works on style of management and on participation in decision-making in management, leadership and government, are widely known, studied and applied.

Manfred Davidmann brings to his tasks a rare combination of practical experience, knowledge and understanding backed by years spent training middle and top-level managers. Expert knowledge is expressed in clear and meaningful language and easy-to-follow diagrams illustrate the relationships.

The main chapter headings are:

Style of Management and Leadership

Motivation

Directing and Managing Change

Organising

Work and Pay

Inflation, Balance of Payments and Currency Exchange Rates

Using Words to Communicate Effectively

How local and national governments are managing our affairs is of crucial importance to every citizen. Government has to make ends meet, has to bring about a rising standard of secure living, social security and an increasing quality of life for its citizens.

"There can be ups and downs but", says Manfred Davidmann, "failure to make ends meet is just as directly and surely the result of bad leadership and management as it is in any commercial enterprise."

Manfred Davidmann reviews ways of balancing income and expenditure, causes of inflation, and tax avoidance, reviews ways out of a payments crisis and details the consequences of increasing interest rates, greater borrowing, selling assets or printing more money.

One works to achieve that which one needs and which one does not have. "Attaining goals leads to feelings of self-respect, strength and confidence", and "persistent lack of rewards leads to a view of society as being hostile and unrewarding".

419

Manfred Davidmann

The Real World in Which We Live:
The Social Rules and Social System under Which We Suffer, Struggle, Survive and Prosper

This community orientated book brings together studies undertaken by Manfred Davidmann to obtain a better understanding of why people have to struggle throughout their adult lives, in all countries and organisations, at all levels, to maintain and improve their standard of living and quality of life. Manfred Davidmann says: "We know what people are struggling to achieve and so these studies explore why people have to struggle by looking at what they are struggling against".

He discusses and illustrates the internal struggles taking place in political parties and all other organisations for achieving greater democracy and against those wishing to overpower democratic processes of decision-making.

And Manfred Davidmann here clearly defines and describes motivation, its basis and 'motivating'. He includes a detailed step-by-step listing of what people are struggling to achieve, their needs and wants, their achievements and objectives.

The depth of his analysis can be judged by the main chapter headings:

Ownership and Limited Liability

Community and Public Ownership

Ownership and Deciding Policy: Companies, Shareholders, Directors and Community

Multinational Summits and Agreements, Top-level Decision-making and Democracy

Exporting and Importing of Employment and Unemployment

Transfer Pricing and Taxation

Creating, Patenting and Marketing of New Forms of Life

What People are Struggling Against: How Society is Organised for Controlling and Exploiting People

Democracy Under Attack: Top-level Leadership and Decision-making

Taxing the Population for Private Profit

Corrupted Economics and Misguided (Misleading) Experts

Using Words to Communicate Effectively

The Will to Work: What People Struggle to Achieve

Manfred Davidmann says: "Decision-taking by leaderships has to be replaced by decision-making at the level of the people. The real struggle is not between political left and right, but is a struggle for participation (the right to make decisions)".

Manfred Davidmann

Messianic Struggle:
The Worldwide Struggle for a Good and Secure Life for All, Here and Now

Manfred Davidmann's fundamental works about management principles and leadership, community economics and needs, profit motivation and social costs, and participation in decision-making at all levels are major advances in human knowledge and key findings.

The author exposes humanity's hidden core confrontations, the source of oppression and enslavement, the role of biblical prophets and their warnings, how religious teachings were distorted, and he states the scientific benevolent social laws of behaviour and community organisation.

Following Manfred Davidmann's publications and recommendations, people are struggling now worldwide for a better life, for the right to make the decisions, for social security, for equality, freedom and independence, for socially responsible and humane behaviour, and the survival of humanity on this planet.

Comprehensiveness of information, and depth of analysis, can be judged by the book's chapter headings:

Social Responsibility, Profits and Social Accountability. Incidents, Disasters and Catastrophes. The Worldwide Struggle for Social Accountability. Community Aims and Community Leadership.

Work and Pay, Incomes and Differentials: Employer, Employee and Community

The Right to Strike

Reorganising the National Health Service: An Evaluation of the Griffiths Report

Community Economics: Principles

Social Responsibility and Accountability: Summary

The World at War! Multinational (Global) Operations, and Government Of, By, and For the People: Democracy Under Attack: The Struggle for the Right to take the Decisions, and for Social Accountability

The choice is yours: Unemployment, Charitable Social Security and Today's Religious Teachings or High Standard of Living, Satisfying Work and a Good Life, as God-given rights

Creationism and Intelligent Design, Evolution, Education or Indoctrination

The Way Ahead: Policies for a Better Future

The Global (Worldwide) Struggle for a Better Life and The Root of all Evil, the Source of All Good, and the Messianic Struggle

Faith and Trust in God, No Matter by What Name called

Manfred Davidmann

Judaism: Basis - Past - Present - Future
Part 1

A major review and analysis by Manfred Davidmann of the essential but little-known social laws and social system of the Pentateuch (Torah) and of the fundamental scientific Social Cause-and-Effect Relationship which applies to all people everywhere at all times, and of Jewish history, finding the causes of subsequent defeat of the people and loss of country. The author provides a fully documented record of previously undiscovered material in the Talmud about Hillel. And he describes the struggles within Judaism which accompanied the birth of Rabbinical Judaism and how the Talmud recorded events.

Manfred Davidmann provides the required background knowledge of the essential core of Jewish belief and practice for drawing the only possible conclusion that the procedure called 'Prosbul' is contrary to the laws and intent of the Torah. He then annuls the Prosbul.

He shows that there are two separate root causes of antisemitism which one would normally not consider.

And he proves that the right to the land in which one lives, that is the strength and success of a people, depends on how people behave towards each other.

Comprehensiveness of information, and depth of analysis, can be judged by the book's chapter headings:

> Struggle for Freedom: The Social Cause-and-Effect Relationship
>
> History Speaks: Monarchy, Exile and Maccabees
>
> At the Time of Jesus, This is What Actually Happened in Israel: The Truth about Hillel and his Times
>
> One Law for All: Freedom Now, Freedom for Ever
>
> Jewish Belief and Practice
>
> Causes of Antisemitism
>
> The Right to the Land of Israel

Manfred Davidmann

Judaism: Basis - Past - Present - Future
Part 2

Manfred Davidmann shows that the Pentateuch's God-given social rules and social system are the very foundation of Judaism, Christianity and Islam and underlie freedom, liberty, independence and well-being. He proves that what these main religions have in common is that in each case a ruling elite succeeded in bypassing or overturning the religion's essential God-given benevolent social provisions and human rights, in this way exposing their communities and whole populations to oppression and exploitation.

The author reveals for each religion the controversies and conflicts between church and state, between beliefs and practice. He examines the root causes of major social problems and shows how to resolve the problems by dealing with their basic causes.

And Manfred Davidmann shows how to apply and put into practice the essential benevolent and egalitarian social provisions and human rights of the Pentateuch under modern conditions.

Comprehensiveness of information, and depth of analysis, can be judged by the book's chapter headings:

Church and State, Government and Religion:

The God-given Human Rights, Social Laws and Social System

Judaism, Christianity and Islam

Religion, Government and Education

Creationism and Intelligent Design, Evolution, Education or Indoctrination

Family, Community, Sex and the Individual

Kibbutzim

Quotable Quotes about Judaism

The Way Ahead: Policies for a Better Future

Faith and Trust in God, No Matter by What Name called

The choice is yours: Unemployment, Charitable Social Security and Today's Religious Teachings or High Standard of Living, Satisfying Work and a Good Life, as God-given rights.

The Meaning of Genesis

Meaning and Significance of the Names of God in Genesis

Meaning and Intent of Genesis: Essential Notes on Hebrew Grammar

Bible Translations, Versions, Codes and Hidden Information in Bible and Talmud

The Social Laws and Social System of the Pentateuch: (Ha Mim)
The Word of Allah as Taught by Mohammed

Judaism at the Crossroads, at the Final Parting of the Ways

Israel and The Social Laws and Social System of the Pentateuch

Muslims and Jews

The Global (Worldwide) Struggle for a Better Life and The Root of all Evil, the Source of All Good, and the Messianic Struggle